PRAISE FOR *THE STRATEGY-DRIVEN SUPPLY CHAIN*

"Another masterpiece and must-read for business executives and supply chain professionals. The integrated value planning and execution model has the potential to become the main business management process for companies in future."

Frank Vorrath, Vice President Service Delivery EMEA & APAC at Gartner Inc.

"One supply chain doesn't fit all. Supply chains differ per company, but also often internally per product market combination. In this great book Bram DeSmet describes how companies should balance service, cost and cash to let their different supply chains create the best value for their varying customers. This book is a must-read for every decision maker in manufacturing, wholesale and retail."

Martijn Lofvers, CEO and Chief Trendwatcher Supply Chain Media

"Despite all volatility and uncertainty getting the fundamentals of your supply strategy right is more important than ever before. The latest book from Dr Desmet connects the 'magic triangle' with consumer and customer, business and supply chain strategy in a unique and consistent way. Great read!"

Dirk Holbach, CSCO, Henkel Laundry & Homecare

"Supply chains are becoming incredibly more strategic for most of the companies and their roles have transformed to be crucial in value generation by providing customers with the right service, quality and experience. In his book Bram captures the essence of how strategy, finance and supply chain should interconnect to drive more value through strategy-driven supply chains. A warmly recommended read!"

Mourad Tamoud, Chief Supply Chain Officer, Schneider Electric

"This book goes to the essence of high-performance supply chains. That is, launching strategies to meet customer expectations, and then through operational excellence and innovation, freeing cash for reinvestment in projects to further improve performance. It's a virtuous circle."
John Gattorna, Global SC 'thought leader' and Author

"Supply Chain and Supply Chain Planning are key to value generation at Hero Group, as elegantly captured by the Supply Chain Triangle prominent in Bram's books. A highly recommended read for any finance or supply chain professional."
Witte van Capellen, CSCO, Hero

"An excellent book in which prof. Bram DeSmet illustrates how supply chain should be an integral and vital part in building and executing a business strategy. The clear concepts underpinned with good case studies trigger a lot of reflection and are very instrumental to help you in both the strategy exercise and the design of an effective supply chain"
Frank Vromant, Former CFO and Exec VP Bekaert (retired)

"In our increasingly volatile, complex and uncertain world, supply chain as the strategic balancing act between service, cost and cash cannot be underestimated. Mastering a strategy-driven supply chain implies the understanding that in a successful business strategy the value proposition and the corresponding supply chain are inseparable."
Patrick Reekmans, CEO Poppies Bakery Group

"This is a must read. Bram showed me the importance of making choices in order to come to a clear cut strategy which survives changing market conditions.

Exercises & cases helped me to see the connection between the supply chain triangle, financial metrics, the different strategic options and how these could lead to streamlined KPIs and organizational models. It offers an ideal framework for management teams."
Tom Hautekiet, CEO, Port Zeebrugge

"A fascinating book. It is a must-read for anyone who wants to use their supply chain to gain a financial edge"
Dr Harpal Singh, CEO, Arkieva

"The author, Bram Desmet has a strong appetite for seeing and revealing connections and pushing back boundaries. This is more than a supply chain and operations book but a business book that should be read by any CFO or CEO. This book helps provide a comprehensive methodology to connect business improvements and decisions with business performance and supply chain success."
Eric Wilson CPF, Director Thought Leadership Institute of Business Forecasting

"The strategic potential of supply chains has been poorly understood and woefully neglected for far too long, something that has come back to haunt many businesses during these disruptive times. Bram Desmet's first book was therefore a breath of fresh air, providing clear, understandable guidance to business leaders on how to strategically design their supply chains. 'The Strategy Driven Supply Chain' expands on those concepts, providing further indispensable insights into the art and science of designing supply chains that operate as strategic weapons of value generation. A timely and essential book. Bravo."
Sean Culey (SCOR-P, FCILT). Visiting Fellow – Supply Chain at Cranfield School of Management, business transformation adviser, author and award-winning keynote speaker.

" The times when supply chain management could be considered as merely an operational activity focused on cost-reduction are long gone. By introducing the supply chain triangle, thought-leader Bram DeSmet provided supply chain professionals a highly relevant framework to (re)think their contribution. In this inspiring and highly practical book he takes it one step further by addressing the indispensable next question: how can we make our supply chain a true strategic asset?"
Prof.dr. Jack AA van der Veen, Nyenrode Business Universiteit

"Bram Desmet has again proven to write a book that matters. Living in volatile times, overcoming our pandemic, digitalization and sustainability solutions in supply chain networks have become more than ever a must. Companies are now more connected than ever, new business models and ecosystems arise, whilst others disappear fast. Supply chain transformation is at the forefront now. Channel management, stock level management, all performance indicators need to be at the business management fingertips. In this book Bram Desmet describes in his unique practical style how cash, cost and service correlate, their influence on working capital and return on capital employed. All of this to be able to act swift and savvy in these connected times we live in. To be able to navigate in an optimal way in times now where also many new opportunities are at the horizon. Understanding and implementing his book can be the differentiator to be the successful business partner in the value chains you operate. It is a privilege to work with his insights and deep understanding, also for our customers and at our Brightlands Institute for Supply Chain Innovation."

Ton Geurts, Business Director

"The supply chain triangle has changed the way we translate the strategy of the company into targets for our different organizations. It makes the discussions less emotional, more fact based and increases the understanding of each other's goals."

Johan Heyman, Vice President Organizational Excellence, Barco

"In clear language, Bram proposes criteria and models that together form a guide for defining a supply chain strategy in line with the business strategy. It is no surprise that markets are in full evolution, accelerated lately by COVID. The right choices need to be made if you want your strategy to be successful. Bram's book also contains the good news that choosing is not losing, but on the contrary, the key to success."

André Céron, Logistics Director Retail Partners Colruyt Group

The Strategy-Driven Supply Chain

Integrating strategy, finance and supply chain for a competitive edge

Bram DeSmet

KoganPage

First published in Great Britain and the United States in 2021 by Kogan Page Limited

2nd Floor, 45 Gee Street
London
EC1V 3RS
United Kingdom

122 W 27th St, 10th Floor
New York, NY 10001
USA

4737/23 Ansari Road
Daryaganj
New Delhi 110002
India

www.koganpage.com

ISBNs

Hardback 9781398600485
Paperback 9781398600454
Ebook 9781398600478

British Library Cataloguing-in-Publication Data

A CIP record for this book is available from the British Library.

Library of Congress Control Number

2021933204

Typeset by Integra Software Services, Pondicherry
Print production managed by Jellyfish
Printed and bound by CPI Group (UK) Ltd, Croydon CR0 4YY

To my beloved parents,
for their dedication to my brothers and me

CONTENTS

LIST OF FIGURES

LIST OF TABLES

ABOUT THE AUTHOR

Dr Bram DeSmet is Adjunct Professor at the Vlerick Business School, where he is part of the Competence Centre of Supply Chain and Operations, and a visiting professor for the Beijing MBA Program at Peking University, where he teaches statistics and business analytics. Bram is also the CEO of Solventure, a company that helps companies to turn their supply chains into a competitive edge. Prior to that, Bram was a Partner in Strategy, Supply Chain and Operations at Möbius Research and Consulting.

Bram's research interests are in the domain of strategy, supply chain and advanced analytics. He combines academic research with practical applications. He obtained his PhD in the topic of multi-echelon inventory optimization and applied it at companies including Agfa-Gevaert and Daikin Europe. Within Solventure he is developing a new forecasting solution based on the use of leading macro-economic indicators.

With this book Bram hopes to contribute to the field of supply chain strategy, by combining the fields of strategy, supply chain and finance. Bram appreciates your thoughts and feedback. He can easily be reached via his contact page on LinkedIn.

FOREWORD

Several global megatrends are driving business disruptions, challenges and opportunities for companies. Changing demographics encompassing a move towards urbanization with a surging middle class concentrated in urban areas and ageing populations, energy and natural resources availability, sustainability and regulations, acceleration of digitalization and the recent COVID-19 pandemic – these all create challenges and opportunities for companies to create breakthroughs through new business models with the objective to add value to people, shareholders and their communities based on a new set of principles of sustainable business performance and results. We live in a new world of engagement and collaboration linked to a smart, connected, economic ecosystem-driven economy where everything around us is changing exponentially. In the future, a company won't just compete against other companies. Every company is and will be part of an economic ecosystem, and success will depend on how they can create or be part of a strong and sustainable economic ecosystem that is able to compete and win in the marketplace.

Sustainability, new digital business models accelerating future growth, strong business performance and results based on a strong set of foundations of liquidity and profitability are top priorities for companies, their leadership and employees to create long-lasting shareholder value.

Customer expectations have changed over the last years and will further change in future. Customers now want to buy products or services that are more personalized and in different ways tailor-made to their needs and linked to their personal preferences and values. Sustainability, reliability and responsiveness, and agility are more important than ever before and focusing just on scale, efficiency and cost management will not deliver the desired outcome. Many companies are stuck in their old thinking, mindset and behaviour but expecting to accelerate on change without a deeper understanding of what enables the change to be successful and sustainable. For many years strategic supply chain management has not been understood well enough, and supply chain professionals are battling to earn their seat at the C- Suite table as a business partner of choice. We have entered a 'perfect storm' in the lifecycle of supply chain management and the recent COVID-19 pandemic will accelerate the fundamental shift in thinking, mindset and behaviour which is required to transform companies to be ready to compete and to win in the new world of the smart, connected economic ecosystem.

Many companies have realized the importance of supply chain transformation in order to generate sustainable business performance and results. Some companies have successfully transformed their supply chain capabilities and some other companies have failed to transform them because of their missing strategic approach and appropriate planning prior to starting their transformation programmes.

Companies are trying to understand the most important and critical levers to drive successful and sustainable supply chain transformations to generate tangible and measurable business results and shareholder value as measured by the return on capital employed, which is the ultimate outcome. To uncover these levers, it will help companies to position themselves for the future while managing the current market dynamics and financial expectations of their shareholders.

Business and supply chain transformations are a means to an end, with the end being improved business performance and results leading to improved shareholder value as measured by return on capital. Great companies out-think, out-perform and out-compete the market by investing in building better supply chain capabilities than their competitors in a consistent way.

The Strategy-Driven Supply Chain by Bram DeSmet provides a practical framework for how to connect the value proposition, supply chain strategy and business strategy with different customers in the marketplace. The reader will understand through Dr DeSmet's framework that any value proposition, supply chain or business strategy is a deliberate choice and route to generate customer value and shareholder value as measured by the return on capital employed. This framework provides an overview of the three elements of service, cost and cash in the supply chain triangle, analyses the different customer buying behaviours in the marketplace and thereafter connects them with the right value proposition, supply chain strategy, business strategy, performance measurement and management.

Dr DeSmet's explains why companies struggle to balance the triangle of service, cost and cash in their old traditional thinking, mindset and behaviour. Different value propositions lead to different strategies to generate value, but require deliberate choices, trade-offs and a new level of discipline to execute. The book refers to the well-known Treacy and Wiersema framework of three defined strategic archetypes: operational excellence, customer intimacy and product leadership. A practical solution set is provided for benchmarking and target setting, which are important elements of any chosen supply chain and business strategy. This book provides valuable information and great insights into strategic supply chain management, and covers all necessary components, including understanding the different customer buying behaviours in the marketplace, aligning them with the right value proposition, setting the right supply chain strategy and connecting them to the right performance target levels within the process and financial metrics with the overall objective to make it to the chosen business strategy to generate value for customers and shareholders. The author provides the foundation and a framework for the business C-suite and any supply chain professionals as a solution to keep up with ever-changing threats and business disruptions. In this new age of global interconnectivity, collaboration and smart connected economic ecosystem, it is necessary to provide business executives and supply chain practitioners, both professionals and students, with valuable insights and state-of-the art knowledge on the frontier of supply chain management. Is strategic supply chain management part of your business, or is strategic supply chain management your business? We have been waiting to answer this question for a very long time. I hope you enjoy reading and learning as much as I did.

Frank Vorrath
Vice President, Service Delivery Team, EMEA & APAC, Gartner Inc
(former Vice President, Global Supply Chain, Johnson Controls)
November 2020

FOREWORD

Supply chain management as an idea is still relatively new and it is only in recent years that companies have started to give it the attention that it deserves. However, because organizations have traditionally been structured and managed on a vertical and functional basis they have often been unable to embrace the essentially cross-functional and integrative focus that effective supply chain management demands. As a result, opportunities for profit improvement have been missed and customer satisfaction and hence retention has not been maximized.

Now, however, many businesses are recognizing the strategic impact of supply chain decisions. In particular, they understand that the supply chain and the way in which it is managed are directly connected to their performance in the marketplace. The ability to serve customers to ever higher levels but at less cost has become a critical source of competitive advantage in most industries. At the same time, the effect of supply chain strategy on the profit and loss account and the balance sheet is much more clearly understood.

There is growing evidence that companies who are able to adopt an integrative approach to supply chain management out-perform those of their competitors with lesser capabilities in this respect. Hence the importance of the central message of this book: the need to take a holistic approach to formulating supply chain strategy. Bram DeSmet's powerful framework – the supply chain triangle – underpins this wider view of how a business should be run. Simple though the idea may be, few companies have found a way to manage service, cost and cash as three inter-related elements, all of which are impacted by supply chain strategy and performance.

In this new book, Bram DeSmet builds on the ground-breaking ideas introduced in his first book, *Supply Chain Strategy and Financial Metrics*. The linkage between success in the marketplace and the way in which the supply chain is designed and managed is highlighted and supported by detailed case examples.

This new book, like the first, will certainly have a place on my bookshelf and will definitely be one that I recommend to others who seek to improve supply chain performance.

Martin Christopher, Emeritus Professor of Marketing and Logistics, Cranfield University

PREFACE

When young people passionately ask me 'How can I become a supply chain expert?', I often tell the following story. You start by taking courses in supply chain. Once you have completed the supply chain courses, you'll need to start reading supply chain books. Once you have read all the supply chain books, it is time to write your own book.

Writing a book forces you to structure your mind. That is an intense but rewarding process. Rewarding, as it allows you to expose your thoughts to other people – people who have more experience, have a different background, are better in getting to the essence, are completely new to the topic. These people will start asking questions, good questions. They will make suggestions, excellent suggestions. So, they will make you smarter, a lot smarter. It will help you to deepen your insight, in the topic you were already so passionate about.

So around five years ago, I started working on my first book, *Supply Chain Strategy and Financial Metrics*. I forced my brain to bring structure to what I had learned on supply chain in the previous 15 years. When the last word was written some two years later I had no idea what to expect, or maybe I did, but I didn't want to take it for granted.

The book brought me so many good things. Intense discussions with people in writing the book. Many training courses, presentations, webinars and blogs, which triggered so many smart questions, remarks and suggestions. I used the concepts when discussing supply chain with companies, when working with clients. Many of them felt inspired, got energized and started their sometimes long and winding supply chain journey.

Receiving that much knowledge comes with an obligation. The obligation to return what you've learned. Which is exactly what I hope this second book will do. So, I forced my brain to structure what I have learned from the many interactions since the first book was published. This second book builds on the fundaments of the first, most notably the supply chain triangle, how it links to finance and what is the impact of strategy. In this book I have strengthened those fundaments and built a bigger house on them. The house of the strategy-driven supply chain. I literally can't wait to hear what you think of it, to hear your questions and your remarks.

I feel lucky that supply chain crossed my path some 20 years ago. I still feel like a novice, and, as we discuss in this book, it feels as if we're still defining what supply chain management is. But, oh boy, if this is only the start, I'm so curious for what is still to come. So, let's explore that together. Let's start with this book and your thoughts, and let's all push the boundaries of the supply chain profession together.

ACKNOWLEDGEMENTS

A first and special word of thanks goes to Frank Vorrath. Some four years ago, when Frank was still with Johnson Controls as the VP of Global Supply Chain, he was one of the first senior executives who saw the potential of this work. Ever since, Frank has been a big supporter and a great person to work with on so many interactions. In his current role at Gartner as the Vice President for Supply Chain Service Delivery for EMEA and APAC, Frank is developing supply chain thinking among senior supply chain leaders at leading manufacturing and retail companies. Frank, thank you for sharing your knowledge and your passion. Your belief has made me believe we can make a difference!

I want to thank the many people who have contributed to this new book. They are the ones who are doing it in real life. I'm grateful we have been able to work on some of it together and we could share some stories in this book: Annick Van Driessen, Director Supply Chain Operations, Indaver; Dr Dirk Holbach, Chief Supply Chain Officer, Laundry & Homecare at Henkel; Ruediger Fuchs, Head of Corporate Supply Chain, Bahlsen and former Senior Director Operating Model Innovation, Lego®; André Céron, Logistics Director, Colruyt Group; Johan Heyman, VP Organizational Excellence, Barco.

I also want to thank Martijn Lofvers, owner of Supply Chain Media and editor of *Supply Chain Movement*. Martijn has been a big supporter of the supply chain triangle. Thank you Martijn for the sparring and the out-of-the-box ideas. Some of them, like linking the book to a book website, came from your brain. Thank you for moving the boundaries of supply chain as a profession. You are a lighthouse in the world of supply chain.

I want to thank Prof Martin Christopher. When I entered the field of supply chain some 20 years ago, I learned by reading your books and articles. *Logistics and Supply Chain Management* has become a classic and an icon in the meantime. It's an honour to learn from the best and have this book introduced by you as a leading author in the supply chain field!

A special thanks to André Céron, Martine Pauwels, Erik Pappaerts, Jurgen Belsack, Peter Lanoizele and Dirk Leemans from Colruyt Group. Some eight years ago we started a journey called 'the supply chain academy'.

As logistics directors from the different retail brands in the Colruyt Group, you had the vision to invest in building supply chain knowledge and capabilities. Colruyt Group has applied many of the concepts developed in the book through the training. It has changed Colruyt as a company, how the executive teams think and work. It has been a true privilege to contribute to that and see that change happening from the front row. As the retail world keeps changing at a fast pace, the job is not finished but just starting. However, I believe Colruyt Group is much better equipped to tackle the strategic supply chain challenges going forward.

I also want to thank some supporters in the Netherlands. Prof Dr Jack Van Der Veen from Nyenrode Business University, who with Michel Van Buren runs an excellent supply chain club called the Supply Chain Executive Leadership Platform. I was lucky to present to that group when working on my first book and to maintain ad hoc interactions afterwards. This club is also moving the boundaries of supply chain thinking.

Let me thank my colleagues at the Vlerick Business School, especially Prof Dr Ann Vereecke, for the sparring, and for the opportunity to teach these topics in the supply chain courses at Vlerick.

Let me thank all my colleagues at Solventure. Working with a group of talented and passionate people is a privilege. Many of you dream in triangles. We make jokes about triangles. I learn from all of you daily. Thanks for staying with me if I'm too conceptual, impatient or overly ambitious. We are all in this together!

Let me finally thank my wife Leen, my kids Matties, Julie and Emiel. I've been writing at home, but equally been absent. Dads should have fun with their kids instead of having a serious expression and be writing books. Husbands should help with practical stuff in the house instead of being conceptual. I promise I'll do the dishes for the coming two weeks!

I hope that all those who have contributed share some of my pride in being able to present this result. It is our shared result. It may have passed through my brain, but it is based on the triggers, the questions, the thoughts, the examples and the support of each one of you.

Thank you all so much.

LIST OF ABBREVIATIONS

AI	artificial intelligence
AP	accounts payable
AR	accounts receivable
ATO	assemble to order
BOM	bill of material
CA	current assets
CAPEX	capital expenditure
CCC	cash conversion cycle
CL	current liabilities
CMSO	chief marketing and sales officer
COGS	cost of goods sold
COO	chief operating officer
CSCO	chief supply chain officer
CTO	configure to order
DCs	distribution centres
D/E	debt over equity
DIOH	days of inventory on hand
dlh	direct labour hour
DPO	days of payables outstanding
DSO	days of sales outstanding
EBIT	earnings before interest and taxes
EBITDA	earnings before interest, taxes, depreciation and amortization
EOL	end of life
EOQ	economic order quantity
EPS	earnings per share
ETO	engineer to order
FA	fixed assets
FCF	free cash flow
FMCG	fast-moving consumer goods
FP&A	financial planning and analysis
FPY	first pass yield
IBP	integrated business planning
IoT	Internet of Things

IVP&E	integrated value planning and execution
KPI	key performance indicator
LP	linear programming
M&A	mergers and acquisitions
MOQ	minimum order quantity
MPS	master production schedule
MRO	maintenance, repair and overhaul
MRP	material requirements planning
MTO	make to order
MTS	make to stock
MVV	mission, vision and values
net PPE	net property, plant and equipment
NOPAT	net operating profit after tax
NPI	new product introductions
OEE	original equipment efficiency
opex	operational excellence (in the context of strategy)
OPEX	operational expense (in the context of financial planning and analysis)
OTIF	on-time, in-full
P&L	profit and loss
PESTEL	political, economic, social, technological, environmental and legal
R&D	research and development
RCCP	rough cut capacity plan
ROA	return on assets
ROCE	return on capital employed
ROE	return on equity
S&OE	sales and operations execution
S&OP	sales and operations planning
SCOR	supply chain operations reference model
SG&A	selling, general and administrative
SKU	stock keeping unit
SWOT	strengths, weaknesses, opportunities and threats
VMI	vendor-managed inventory
WACC	weighted average cost of capital
WIP	work in progress

Introduction

This book builds on our first, *Supply Chain Strategy and Financial Metrics*. In Chapters 1 to 4 we deepen the fundaments laid out in the first book in Chapters 1 and 2. In Chapter 5 to 8 we build our world of the strategy-driven supply chain on top of these fundaments.

In Chapter 1 we introduce our supply chain triangle of *service*, *cost* and *cash*. We have included exercises you can perform to reveal the balance in your supply chain triangle. There are also practical examples that can act as a reference. In Chapter 2 we link the triangle to finance through the return on capital employed (ROCE). We show how ROCE can be used to perform a financial benchmark and how to set targets for key financial metrics such as inventory turns. We do that based on practical examples, using reports that are available to you, to play around with, on this book's website: www.strategydrivensupplychain.com. Still in Chapter 2, we expand on commonly used alternatives to ROCE including return on assets (ROA), return on equity (ROE), and earnings per share (EPS). We expand on how ROCE links to other important financial metrics like the free cash flow (FCF). If we want to connect to finance, we need to understand what is driving finance and we need to learn to speak its language.

In Chapter 3 we link the supply chain triangle to strategy. Using the strategy model of Treacy and Wiersema, we explain how different strategies lead to a different balance in the triangle. Different strategies are in fact just different routes to generate the same ROCE, in a different combination of earnings before interest and taxes (EBIT) and capital employed. In Chapter 4 we start with common strategy fails. Over the last years we have learnt that if strategy is about making choices, companies are bad at strategy. We hate making choices, as we think choosing is losing. Strategy literature says the opposite. If you don't make choices, you will be stuck in the middle. We continue Chapter 4 with multiple example cases. We discuss companies that have changed (or tried to change) strategy and how that impacts the balance in their triangle. We discuss the multi-year transformation of Johnson Controls, how it affected their strategy and financial metrics. We show a benchmark in food retail and how different strategies lead to different balances there.

In Chapters 5 to 8 we build our world of the strategy-driven supply chain on top of these fundaments. Chapters 5 and 6 discuss how to design your strategy-driven supply chain. We refine the modelling of strategy through introducing and refining the strategy model of Crawford and Mathews. We illustrate that it all starts with defining a strategic value proposition. Strategic means that you must make a choice on what driver to dominate and on which driver to differentiate, knowing that for the others you'll play at par. In Chapter 6 we refine how to translate this into a supply chain design. We do so by showing how your chosen market and strategic positioning translate into a given level of complexity and variability. As you define your desired level of responsiveness, that translates into a given level of cost and capital employed. We could design our supply chain to be more efficient or to be more responsive, but above all it needs to be effective. It needs to deliver our chosen strategic value proposition to the market.

In Chapter 7 we introduce the need to better integrate strategic, financial and operational planning. If we really want to balance the triangle and drive more value, we'll need to make better trade-offs in each of those planning processes and these processes need to be more closely integrated. We call this strategy-driven integrated value planning and execution (IVP&E). IVP&E is a next step beyond sales and operations planning (S&OP) and integrated business planning (IBP). The core of the integration is a solid financial modelling capability. We believe that S&OP tools can do that. There is no reason why they would not show a projected profit and loss (P&L), balance sheet and cash flow 12 to 18 months out. Start by integrating operational and financial planning. That should be the basis for stronger and more financially driven strategic planning and modelling.

In Chapter 8 we help you in defining your strategy-driven roadmap. If you are the CEO or chair of your company this can be done top-down. Start by defining your DNA, your strategic value proposition, your operating model and your value model. Identify your gaps, your improvement roadmap, gather the right people and get started on the improvements. If you are the VP supply chain you may have difficulties in selling this. In that case, you can start from the bottom up, from operational planning or from the existing sales and operations planning process. We show you how to integrate with finance and from there how to integrate with strategy. We also discuss our seven-step approach. We've learnt the hard way how to combine people, processes, tools and analytics in driving sustainable and value-adding change. You can use it as a checklist on where to start and how to move it forward. We conclude Chapter 8 and our book by discussing the new role of supply chain. If we really want to balance the triangle, we believe we need to reshuffle the power balance in the executive team. Balance doesn't happen automatically. We have proven that to ourselves over the last 30 years. Our proposal is to put supply chain at the centre of the triangle, with ROCE as a balancing metric, and with strategy-driven IVP&E, as introduced in Chapter 7, as the primary tool. We need to shift from the old conflict model of organizing, to a new strategy-driven or value-driven way of organizing. We know that is a sensitive topic, but we believe it is needed and long overdue.

I hope you will enjoy reading this book as much as I have enjoyed writing it and all the discussion that fed into it. I'm most curious to hear your thoughts and comments, so please reach out to me on LinkedIn and let's have a great conversation!

01

The supply chain triangle of service, cost and cash

In this chapter, we will introduce the supply chain triangle of service, cost and cash. The supply chain triangle captures the struggle we see in many companies, in balancing service, cost and cash. We believe this balancing act is the essence of supply chain management. We show how the triangle can be used in your company to create a common understanding among different departments on where are your most pressing challenges.

What is supply chain management?

There is a great deal of confusion about what exactly supply chain management means. A commonly used definition is the management of a flow of goods and an inverse flow of information and cash, as shown in Figure 1.1. As consumers buy more from the store, the information about increased sales will travel upstream in the supply chain and trigger extra production. The extra production will flow downstream to the shops. Cash is exchanged for the goods.

This 'process' type of definition is at the heart of the supply chain operations reference model (SCOR). SCOR is a process reference model developed and endorsed by the Supply Chain Council. SCOR v10 has defined the following key processes: plan, source, make, deliver and return. As shown in Figure 1.2, it focuses on the so-called 'extended' supply chain, where we manage the flow of goods, information and cash from the customers' customer to the suppliers' supplier. SCOR has also developed a set of complementary key performance indicators (KPIs) as the basis for cross-industry benchmarks. SCOR was launched in 2017, and the most recent version is v12.0.

FIGURE 1.1 Managing a flow of goods and an inverse flow of information and cash

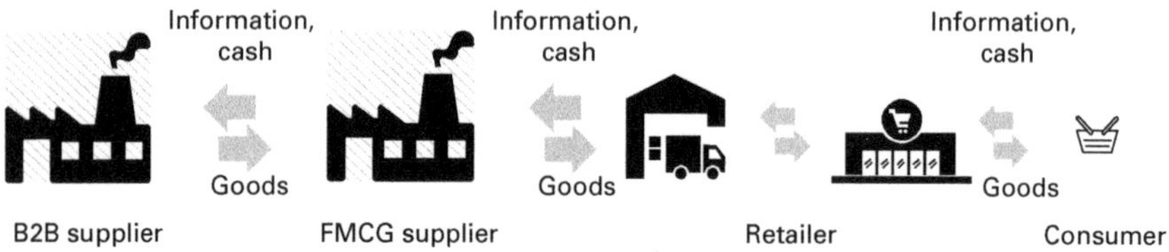

FIGURE 1.2 Key processes of the SCOR model in the extended supply chain

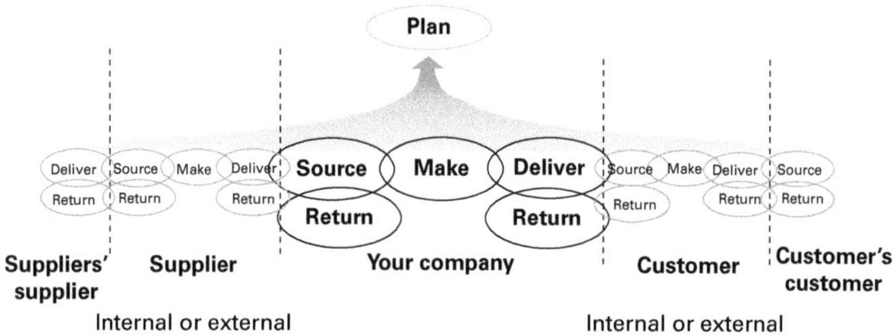

Next to the above, 'process' type of definition, many companies have defined supply chain as a function in the organization. The literature abounds with books where supply chain is claimed as an extension of purchasing, or as the new name for logistics. This has added to the confusion about what supply chain management is. In many companies the supply chain manager is responsible for: tactical planning across production sites (this is typically called sales and operations planning); managing inventory of the finished product; and logistics. In some companies, that is extended to customer service, purchasing, or the operational planning within the production sites. If you added 'production', the VP of supply chain could be the new name for the chief operating officer (COO).

A third type of definition, next to the 'process' and 'functional' definitions, is more strategic. Martin Christopher, Emeritus Professor of Marketing and Logistics at Cranfield School of Management, coined in 1998 the idea that 'one of the most significant paradigm shifts of modern business management is that individual businesses no longer compete as solely autonomous entities, but rather with supply chains'.[1] It is his intimate belief that, given the emerging global competitive environment, the ultimate success of a single business will depend on its management's ability to integrate the company's intricate network of business relationships. It is no longer companies competing against companies, it is supply chains competing against supply chains.

People such as Peter Drucker, the late management guru, combined the process view and the strategic view in stating that 'successful supply chain management requires cross-functional integration of key business processes within the firm and across the network of firms that comprise the supply chain'.[2] The Supply Chain Management Institute has tried to capture that idea in a long list of 'end-to-end' processes, all claimed to be part of supply chain management: customer relationship management, demand management, order fulfilment, manufacturing flow management, supplier relationship management, product development and commercialization, and finally returns management.[3] While it is true that managing end-to-end processes is key to improving the management of the supply chain, it is probably too far a stretch to claim each of these processes to be part of a supply chain function.

Reviewing the above confirms the confusion about what supply chain management means. Throughout this book we will give our answer. A first pillar, also laid out in our previous book, *Supply Chain Strategy and Financial Metrics*,[4] is explained in the next section.

The supply chain triangle of service, cost and cash

Figure 1.3 shows what we will call the supply chain triangle of service, cost and cash. The triangle captures how, as organizations, we deliver different types of 'service' to our customers, which comes at a certain 'cost', and requires a given amount of 'inventory', or more generically 'cash'. Step-by-step, we will argue that the essence of supply chain management is about balancing this triangle. Let us first explore each of the corners in more detail.

Service

The 'service' corner captures the services we, as a supply chain, deliver to our customers. A dominant service metric in the supply chain is the 'service level'. It measures the percentage of cases in which we deliver according to an agreed target. There is a myriad of definitions in use. Many companies talk about 'on-time, in-full' (OTIF), which describes the target for the delivery of goods. That seems straightforward, but it is not.

FIGURE 1.3 The supply chain triangle of service, cost and cash

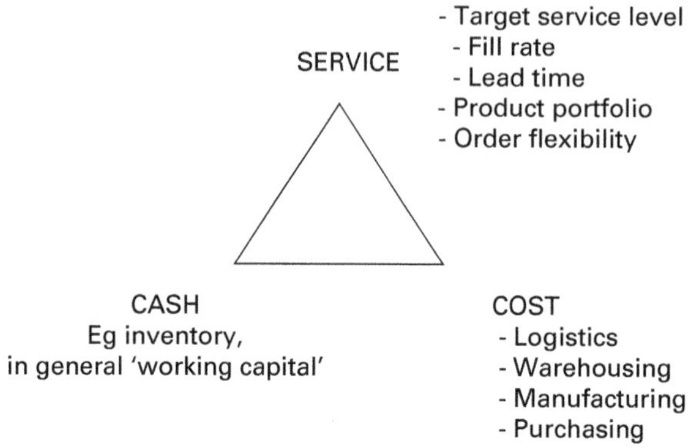

Do we measure 'on time' against the date of shipment, or against the date of delivery? Are we actually able to measure the date of delivery? Do we measure against the requested delivery date, or against the confirmed delivery date? How do we promise dates to customers? Do we have standard lead times depending on the customers and the products? Do we promise dates based on the availability of product and/or production?

Do we say 'in full' if the order is delivered in full, with all of its order lines? It is more common for companies to measure the percentage of order lines or the percentage of volume delivered OTIF. These are called order line or volume fill rates.

Service goes way beyond service level. Service level is so dominant in supply chain that there is a tendency to ignore the rest. However, to give two examples, service extends into the 'product portfolio' and the 'order flexibility' offered. Customers will value a broader product portfolio as an improved service. It allows them to choose the product that is best fit for purpose. A wider choice allows them to work with fewer suppliers, which lowers their transaction costs. Order flexibility relates to how flexible I am with regards to the timing of ordering, the order quantity, any minimum order quantity (MOQ), any changes to orders already placed. Customers value more order flexibility as it allows them to be more responsive and avoid any unnecessary inventory because of any type of restrictions on the ordering.

Cost

To deliver service, we have costs. Figure 1.3 lists the typical costs associated with the source, make and deliver from SCOR. We purchase components or raw materials, we manufacture products in house or at partners, we have the cost of the warehousing for the finished product and we have the logistics cost of shipping our finished product to our customers.

Cash

Where service and cost are easy to grasp, cash is more difficult and requires basic accounting knowledge. We use cash as a synonym for working capital. For working capital we will use the simplified definition in which it equals the inventory plus the accounts receivable, minus the accounts payable. We have included a section on accounting basics in the appendix at the end of this chapter (page 30). We will assume that basic knowledge as we dig into more detail below.

Inventory is probably the most difficult of the working capital components. There are multiple reasons why companies need to hold inventory. Getting a grip on inventory requires a grip on the different underlying drivers. Figure 1.4 summarizes five key reasons why we hold inventory. We discuss each of them in more detail below.

Cycle stock results from the need to produce or order in batches. The lean philosophy works towards a one-piece flow. However, as long as we are confronted with significant changeover or ordering costs, the well-known economic order quantity (EOQ) principle[5] teaches us it is more economical

FIGURE 1.4 Five key reasons why we hold inventory

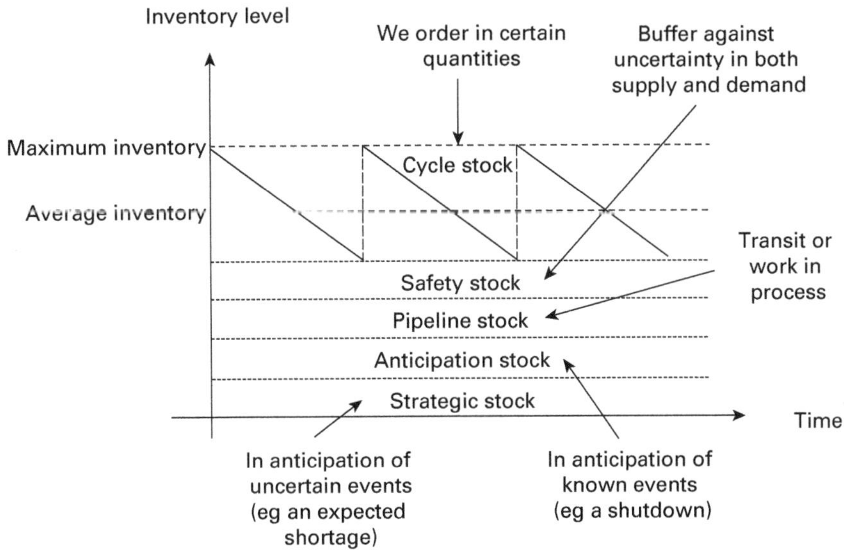

to produce in batches. If we produce once a month, the average cycle stock will be two weeks. If we produce once a week, the average cycle stock will be half a week. The EOQ teaches us that batch sizes go up as the changeover or order costs go up, and as the product cost goes down. They are primary drivers of the amount of cycle stock.

Safety stock is a buffer against uncertainty. In an ideal situation, your customer will just wait for you to order your raw materials, make the product, and ship the finished product to the specified location. The ideal situation is, unfortunately, the exception. In a make-to-stock environment, the customer expects you to have the finished product available in stock. In a make-to-order environment, the customer expects you to keep inventory of raw materials and components and is willing to wait for manufacturing and distribution to take place. If we take the make-to-order example, it implies you will have to order your raw materials and components in the absence of the actual customer orders. That demand uncertainty is covered in a safety stock. Safety stocks also cover supply uncertainty. Suppliers may be late or deliver less than expected. There may be a quality issue that makes part or all of the supply unavailable to production. These are examples of supply uncertainty covered in the safety stock.

Anticipation stock is typically the result of your supply planning process. You may build up stock to anticipate a seasonal peak, a tender or a shutdown. This type of planning decisions lead to so-called anticipation stock.

Pipeline stock is the result of lead times. If we ship things per truck, train or boat, it creates 'in transit' inventory. In the process of production we have work in progress (WIP), which is all inventory sitting on the production floor.

Strategic stock is carried to manage potential risks, eg a potential price increase or a shortage in a key raw material. In contrast to a planned shutdown, these events are uncertain. That defines the difference between anticipation and strategic stock. You can consider strategic stock more as hedging and as part of the risk management in your supply chain.

In addition to the above five, there are other reasons why companies carry inventory. Examples include a minimum order quantity imposed by a supplier, or the amount of inventory needed in a shop to create a nice display of the goods. Ordering or displaying five pieces may represent five months of stock if you use or sell only one per month. As a company, it is important that you list your key inventory drivers. Adapt the classification to something that works for you.

Inventory balances with cash. If we were able to sell off £20 million of inventory and get a cash payment, we'd have £20 million more cash in our bank account. In practice, we have payment terms with both customers and suppliers. Accounts receivable (AR) define the amount we still need to receive from our customers. The receivables are defined by the payment terms and the speed of collection. If customers need to pay within 30 days, but on average pay only after 45 days, we will have 45 days of sales for which we are waiting to receive the cash. If we can reduce that average from 45 days to 40 days, that creates an extra five days of cash in our bank account.

Accounts payable (AP) defines the amount we still need to pay to our suppliers. That again depends on the payment terms and our speed of payment. If we need to pay after 30 days but on average we pay after 45 days, it is worth 45 days of goods for which we have not yet spent the cash. If the supplier increases the pressure, our average may shift to 40 days. This requires an extra five days of goods for which we need to provide the cash.

The working capital is the cash we need to keep the operations running. It is the cash required to finance the inventory and the receivables from our customers, minus the cash we have still kept from our suppliers in the form of the payables. An increase in inventory or receivables increases the cash required. An increase in the payables towards our suppliers decreases the cash required.

Companies struggle with balance in the triangle

In the previous section we introduced the three corners of the supply chain triangle, and in this section we will show that companies struggle with balance in the triangle. Figure 1.5 shows a couple of examples.

Let's start at the top left corner. In a bid to reduce cost, purchasing has, in many companies, started sourcing in the Far East. It helps to lower cost, but what is often overlooked is that because of the longer lead times, the average inventory will increase. So we decrease cost, but at the expense of extra inventory. Likewise, production will strive for longer production runs, as longer production runs lead to higher efficiency, which leads to a lower production cost per unit. Longer runs will lower the unit cost, but again at the expense of extra inventory.

A second example is shown at the top right corner. When faced with peaks in demand, for instance through seasonality, an important design question is whether to accommodate the peak by pre-building inventory (the so-called 'level' strategy) or whether to build peak capacity so you can

FIGURE 1.5 Companies struggle with balance in the triangle

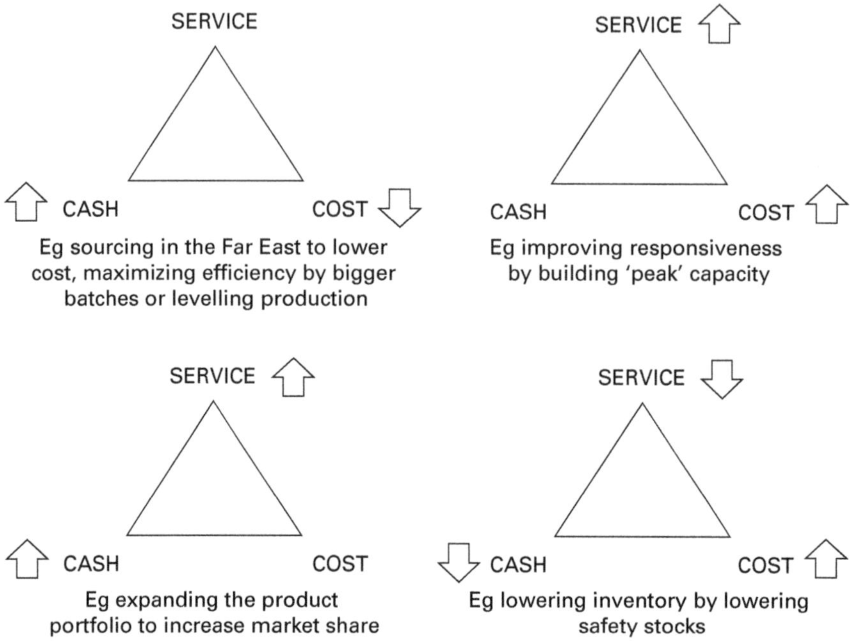

more closely follow the demand as it happens (the so-called 'chase' strategy). Building 'peak' capacity will improve the responsiveness to the customer, but it increases the overall investment, so it will increase the overall cost. Levelling the peak by pre-building inventory lowers the overall investment and allows production to run more smoothly. This will lower the overall cost, but at the expense of extra inventory. Though this seems intuitive, in practice it is hard to quantify the value of responsiveness. This gives leeway for operations to always go for the cost-optimal solution of pre-building inventory. The challenge with pre-building inventory is that you often can't accurately predict what a customer is going to buy three months from now. As a result, you risk having the wrong product, creating both an excess inventory (of the wrong product) and service issues at the same time.

A third example is shown on the bottom left. Marketing and sales may push for an expansion of the product portfolio in order to increase market share. A wider portfolio will add value for the customer and help to increase market share, but carrying more products will require more inventory. It may also negatively impact cost as more products may mean more changeovers or longer picking tours in a warehouse.

The fourth example is shown on the bottom right of Figure 1.5. The above examples all push inventories up. In my experience, companies have become more concerned with inventories since the 2009 financial crisis. As a result, over the last 10 years many companies have launched multiple working capital reduction projects in a bid to free up cash. Many of them start the year with ambitious programmes attacking the inventory from multiple angles, only to find out around summer that none of the initiatives is really on track or has delivered the anticipated benefits. Working capital reduction projects are high-visibility, so failing is not an option. As a result, to save face and possibly their bonuses, supply chain managers resort to the 'handbrake', which in inventory management means lowering safety stocks. Lowering safety stocks will lower the inventory, but it will also negatively impact the service, and, as service issues arise, trigger all kinds of operational firefighting costs.

So, in summary, a first key finding of Figure 1.5 is that the three corners of the triangle are connected. Decisions in one corner almost automatically impact on the other corners. A second key finding is that companies struggle to balance the triangle. We often take decisions with only one of the corners in mind, without assessing the impact on the full triangle. In the next section we explain why this is the case.

Traditional organizations cause tension in the triangle

Figure 1.6 shows a typical and traditional organization chart of a manufacturing company. We have a management committee existing of a CEO, a CFO, and four VPs responsible for purchasing, production, supply chain, and sales and marketing. Bigger corporations may have matrix variants, but even there the dominant power typically resides in the functional organization. Assume you're the VP of sales and marketing. You step into the car in the morning, and what is the first thing you think of? In general, sales and marketing people are driven by top-line metrics such as sales revenue and market share. What if you're the VP of production? Chances are you'll think of efficiency, as efficiency drives costs. Or if you're in procurement? Most probably your first thoughts are with your spend and how to get the spend down. So, in general, operations will be cost-driven. In many companies, supply chain will have a double function. On the one hand we are managing an operational process like the outbound logistics for which we are cost-driven. In more and more companies I see that supply chain has the responsibility for managing global inventories. As we have learnt above, managing inventory is about balancing it against service and cost. Finally, the CFO will

FIGURE 1.6 A traditional organization and the corresponding KPIs

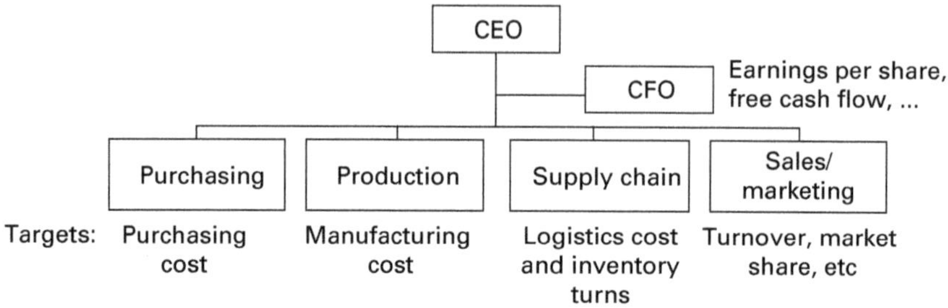

FIGURE 1.7 A traditional organization mapped to the supply chain triangle

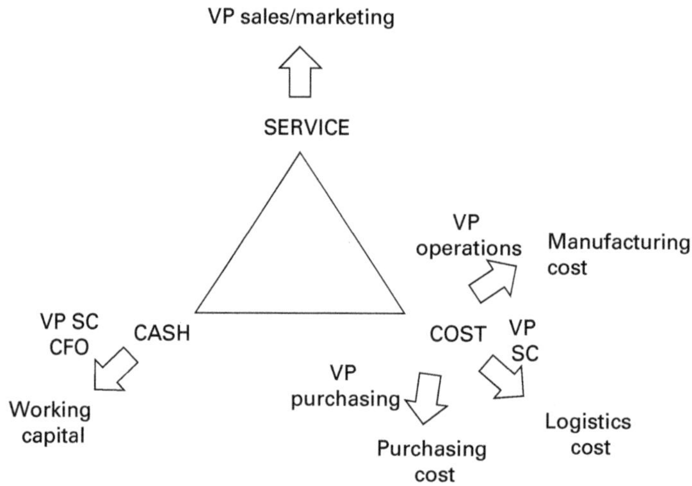

be driven by financial metrics like earnings per share (EPS) and free cash flow (FCF). EPS is the net income per share. Roughly speaking, the FCF is the cash flow from operations minus the capital expenditures. Refer to the appendix on accounting basics at the end of this chapter (page 30) for more details.

Figure 1.7 maps this traditional organization to the supply chain triangle. It shows that, in general, marketing and sales are pulling the service side of the triangle, whereas operations is pulling the cost side. In some companies, that is still the main dynamic. There is a tension between sales and operations, with the inventory as a buffer in between, making often huge swings as a result. In many companies, the CFO has become more concerned with working capital, making inventory a part of the equation, instead of just the result. Where accounts payable and accounts receivable are relatively straightforward, inventory is more complex. As a result, the CFO will look for a companion when trying to get the inventory under control. The likely candidate is supply chain, as the other functions typically have a conflict of interest. This is the moment that as a VP of supply chain you can get the target to reduce inventories by 30 per cent. You need to be careful about accepting the challenge. Reducing inventories is really about creating balance in the triangle, and balancing the triangle is not something you can do alone!

Increased tension in the triangle as growth stalls

When a company is growing and has healthy profits, there is little incentive for better alignment in the triangle. Yes, maybe working capital has increased and our inventory turns went down, but who will really complain if the company has grown by 20 per cent and has realized 10 per cent earnings before interest and taxes (EBIT). Some will probably even advocate that the functional KPIs and incentives have actually led to the good result. If I'm in sales, I will push back on any mingling on the service side in order to keep my room to manoeuvre. If I'm in operations, the extra volumes have helped me to create more efficiency. I'm happy for now and will push back on any projects that risk making my life more complex.

The trouble starts when growth stalls and profitability drops back. There may be different underlying reasons. The market in general may be slowing down, or may be disrupted by low-cost players or newer technologies. In any case, the trouble starts when a company or business unit is underperforming compared to the budget that has been put forward. Figure 1.8 shows a possible reaction.

In a typical response, the sales side will increase pressure on the service side. They will desperately try to get in any order. They are willing to make any promise that helps, including shorter lead times, expedited shipments, changes in the payment terms and some safety stock at the customer's site.

To sustain profits, operations will start a relentless focus on cost. To lower production costs, production prefers big runs and limited changeovers. To lower the purchasing cost, purchasing makes more commitment to the suppliers, typically increasing the inventory risk.

A business in trouble needs cash to turn around the situation. The cash may need to go into the development of new products, the exploration of new markets, rebranding, or a takeover. To generate the cash, we assign the

FIGURE 1.8 Increased tension in the triangle as growth stalls

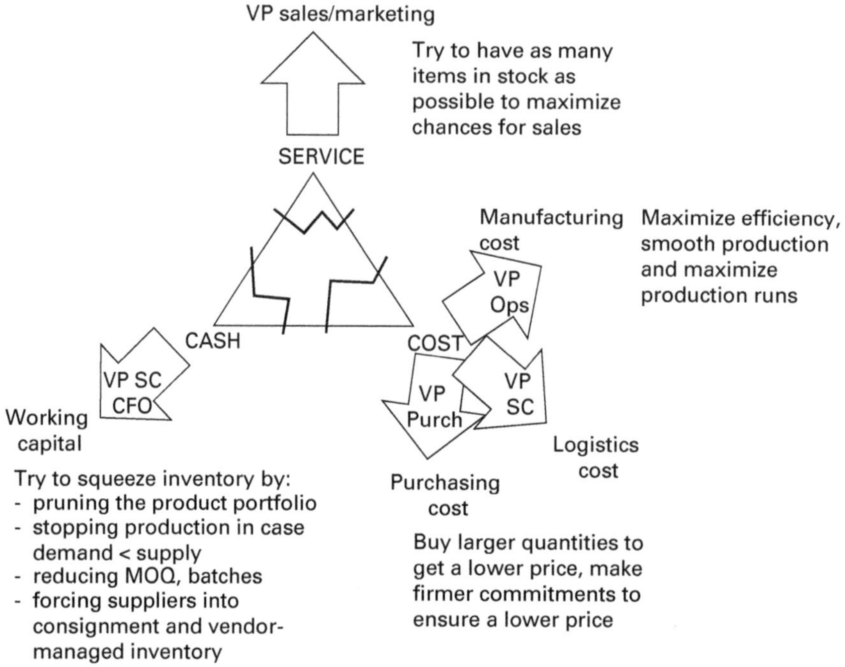

unlucky VP of supply chain the challenge of aggressively reducing inventories, the famous 30 per cent. Supply chain has its back against the wall. Simplifying the product portfolio will go against sales. Stopping production to control inventories will go against manufacturing. Supplier contracts have just been renegotiated, with a focus on cost instead of cash. We may find ourselves locked into an impossible situation.

The only way to get out of this deadlock is to make common choices, instead of having each of the departments just pulling harder on their side of the triangle. The choice may be to temporarily sacrifice profit and work at higher inventories to 'sweat it out' and sustain market share through a difficult period. If the market is severely disrupted by low-cost players or by newer technologies, it may be crucial to generate cash for new investments. As a result, we may aggressively cut inventories, sacrificing the top line to free up the cash to reinvent the company.

So, in summary, when times are good, there is little incentive to create alignment. When times are bad, alignment is key as we can no longer improve on all corners at the same time. It is another illustration of how companies struggle with the triangle, and how that even creates a dangerous 'catch-22' situation.

EXERCISE 1.1

A quick check of the balance in your triangle

We have developed a survey that allows us to map the balance in the supply chain triangle for a specific company. The survey is based on the principles of conjoint analysis. Conjoint analysis is a statistical technique often used in market research to understand the relative importance of different possible value drivers.

A possible example is the market research for a new mobile phone that could come in different options:

- 32Gb or 128Gb of RAM
- silver grey or dark grey
- 24-hour lead time or one-week lead time

Conjoint analysis will reveal what is more important to the people in the survey: the memory, the colour, or the lead time.

The way conjoint analysis does this is by making all possible combinations of the three attributes:

- 32Gb, silver grey, 24-hour lead time
- 32Gb, silver grey, one-week lead time
- 32Gb, dark grey, 24-hour lead time
- [...]
- 128Gb, dark grey, one-week lead time

Conjoint analysis is counter-intuitive; why would anybody ever opt for a one-week lead time instead of a 24-hour lead time? The trick is that you ask people to rank the different options, from most preferred to least preferred. If the person completing the survey is very hung up about the colour, for instance the silver grey, then the silver grey will be ranked at the top and the lead time will turn out to be less important. If a second person completing the survey is desperately in need of a phone, then the 24-hour lead time will be ranked at top and the colour or memory will turn out to be less important.

We can apply the same technique to analysing and revealing the balance in the supply chain triangle by considering the following as drivers and options:

- volume high/low
- margin high/low
- inventory high/low

In a conjoint analysis, we list all the possible combinations and ask people to rank them:

- high volume and high margin and high inventory
- high volume and high margin and low inventory
- high volume and low margin and high inventory
- [....]
- low volume and low margin and low inventory

Again, the conjoint analysis seems confusing, as you would say 'everybody will choose the high volume and high margin and low inventory option'. Yes, that's probably right. The interesting question, though, becomes: *what do they rank second*? High volume and high margin and high inventory? Or would it be high volume and low margin and low inventory? That tells something about the orientation of the person filling in the survey. In the case of the first answer, volume and margin seem to precede inventory. In the second answer, volume and inventory seem to precede margin.

Figure 1.9 shows the result of a survey of around 20 people primarily coming from supply chain. For such a homogeneous group it was surprising there was such a wide spread of the answers.

One person gives 80 per cent of the weight on margin, 0 per cent on volume and 20 per cent on inventory. The spread becomes all the more striking if we remove that one person as an outlier in Figure 1.10. The highest scores now become 0.63 for margin, 0.57 for inventory and 0.55 for volume.

FIGURE 1.9 Balance in the triangle for a random set of 20 respondents

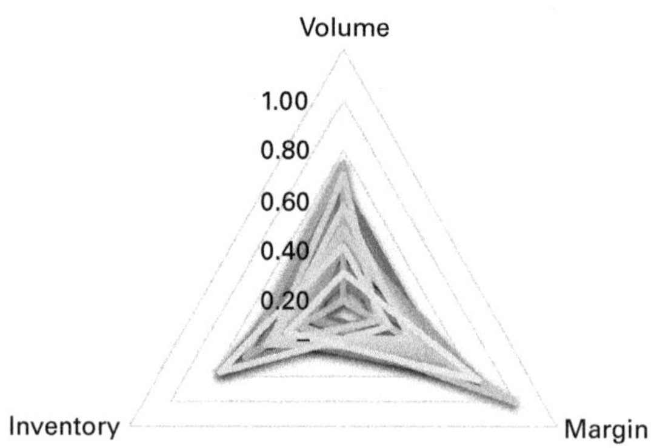

FIGURE 1.10 Balance in the triangle for a random set of 20 respondents, after removing one outlier

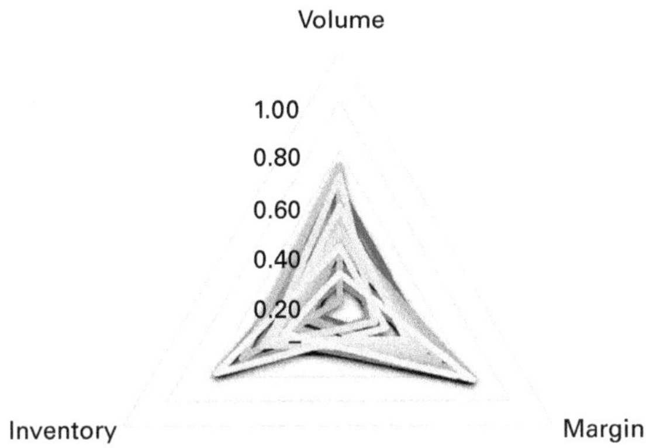

You might say that there remains a slight preference to focus on margins over inventory over volume, but the individual preferences are clearly very different.

Send out your own survey to a list of around 20 people in your company and get a better view of the balance in your supply chain triangle via the following link: www.strategydrivensupplychain.com/resources/surveys/balance-in-your-supply-chain-triangle

The supply chain triangle during COVID-19

The dynamics in the triangle have also been illustrated during the COVID-19 crisis. During the first wave, when the virus swept first through China, then through Europe and the US, we saw two types of companies: those positively affected by COVID-19, for instance companies active in food, in medical equipment, hand sanitizers, etc; and those negatively affected, such as companies in the automotive, aerospace and construction industries.

Let's consider those that were positively affected first. Many companies were surprised by the extra demand. In the run-up to the first lockdown, retailers reported a 20 per cent surge in demand.[6] In that period, retailers and their suppliers were scrambling to fulfil the extra demand. Companies were doing significant overtime, using expedited shipments to fight raw material shortages. We could say that at the start of the crisis the triangle was skewed towards 'service' and the 'top line'.

A couple of weeks later, demand started to stabilize, and companies were pondering how much of the extra sales was extra consumption and what part could be explained by hoarding by customers and consumers. As the initial rush faded out and employees started becoming exhausted due to overtime and the difficult working conditions, unions started talking about how to get appropriate compensation. As some demand could have been artificial, companies also started asking which inventories potentially were at risk, for instance for expiration. We could say that this is the moment where the balance in the triangle was restored and companies were looking across the service, cost and cash corners to optimize their decisions.

As countries reopened from lockdown, these same companies saw demand dropping below normal levels. This was, in hindsight, to be expected as customers and consumers were depleting the stocks they had been building up at the start of the crisis. As demand dropped, companies went into 'energy saving' mode, looking to reduce costs to sustain profits, and to reduce working capital to keep the cash generation up. Depending on how abrupt or gentle this move was, we could say the triangle was now skewed towards the cost and the cash corners.

At the time of writing, Europe was hit by a severe second wave, leading to a second series of national lockdowns, none of them as strict as in the first wave but still significant enough to create a new surge in demand and a rush on supermarkets, leading to a new skewing of the triangle towards the service side. With no vaccine available in the short term, the current expectation is we may have extra waves in the future. The impact on the triangle is illustrated in Figure 1.11.

Companies that were negatively affected by the crisis went through a different, though comparable, transition. As suddenly demand was faltering, they were cutting costs and trying to save on inventories to keep the company afloat. These companies were faced with two major uncertainties: how deeply would they be affected, and how long is this crisis going to last, which, combined, required powerful and drastic action. During the first wave and lockdown, these companies essentially went into hibernation, with minimal costs and cash burn.

Subsequently, these companies were discussing a V-shaped versus a U-shaped or a W-shaped recovery. As countries were coming out of the lockdown and economies restarted, these companies were seeing extra demand as their customers had to refill their buffers. This is the moment where these companies were doing overtime and using expedited shipments to fight raw material shortages. These dynamics are illustrated in Figure 1.12.

FIGURE 1.11 Motions through the triangle for companies 'positively' affected by the COVID-19 crisis

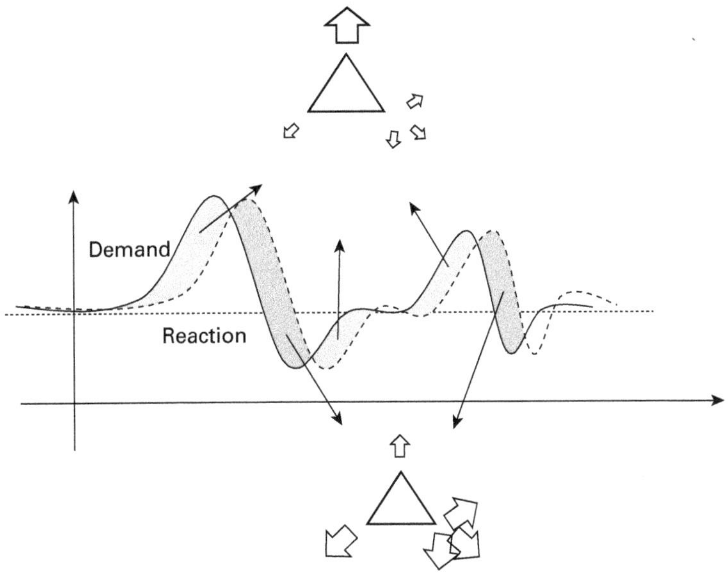

FIGURE 1.12 Motions through the triangle for companies 'negatively' affected by the COVID-19 crisis

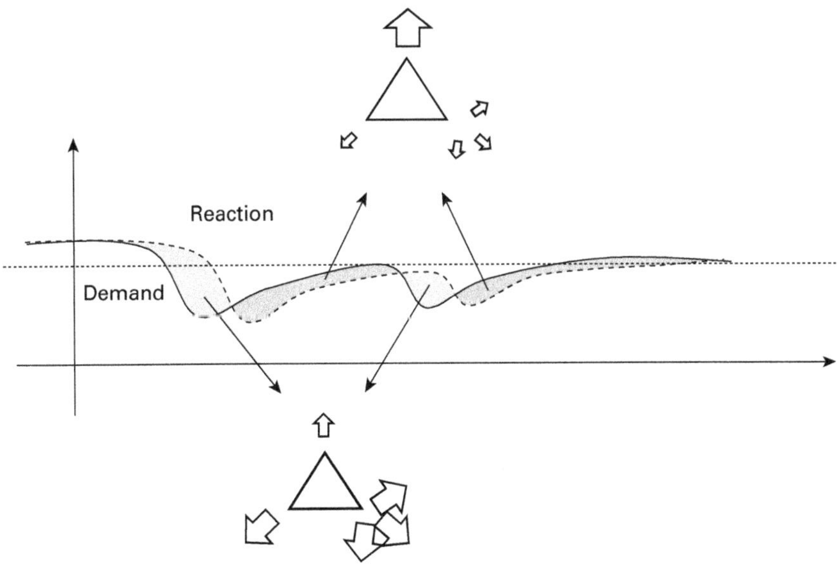

We believe COVID-19 could be a game-changer for supply chain. CEOs, boards, investors, everybody has understood that in general we have been slow to react, and that increased agility in the supply chain is not optional but mandatory.

Expanding the triangle from cash to capital employed

So far we have focused on the balancing of service, (operational) cost and cash. There are two possible extensions, shown in Figure 1.13. The first is accounting for non-operational costs like research and development (R&D) and selling, general and administrative (SG&A). These will be important in later chapters as we link the triangle to different strategies. The second is expanding from cash to capital employed, which is the financial term for the sum of the working capital and the fixed assets.

We already gave an example in Figure 1.5. When companies decide to install capacity to cover the peak demand (chase strategy) instead of levelling the demand and pre-building inventory (level strategy), they are in essence creating more service by increasing the fixed assets, as opposed to creating more inventory. Operating capacity at peaks typically also increases the cost. That is illustrated in Figure 1.14.

FIGURE 1.13 Expanding the triangle from cash to capital employed

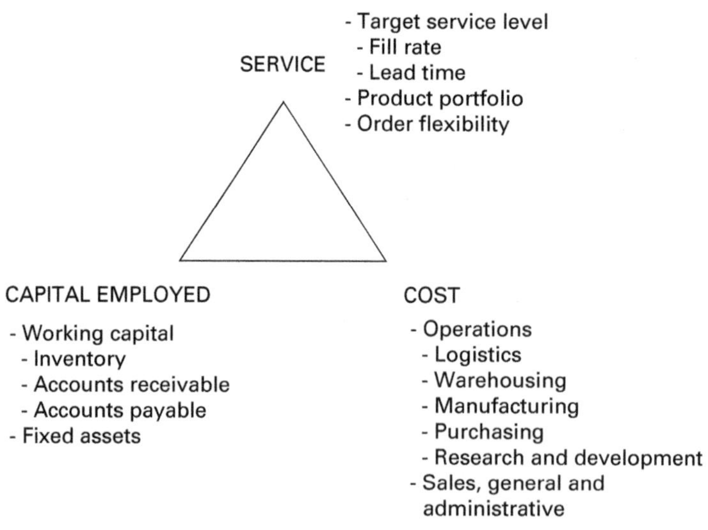

FIGURE 1.14 Balancing service and capital employed

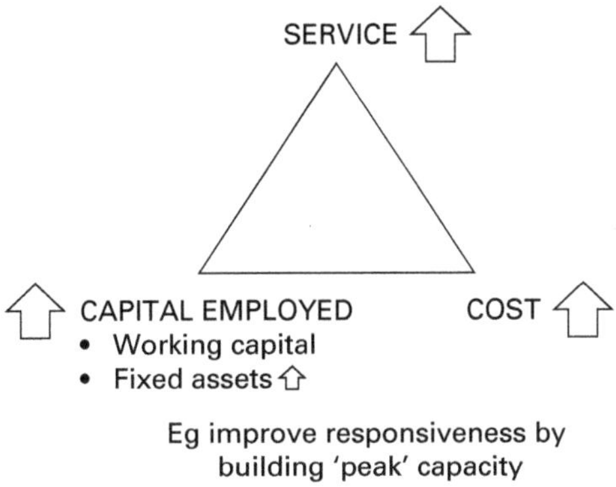

FIGURE 1.15 Fixed assets translate into the cost corner through depreciation

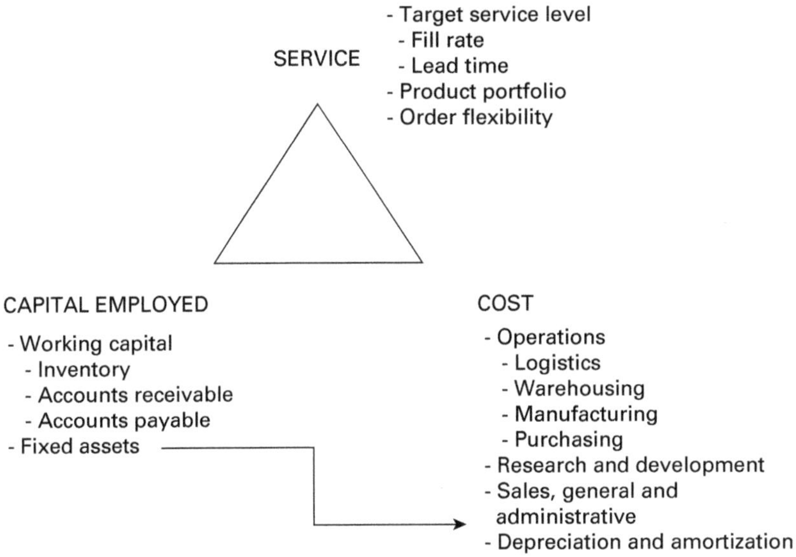

Fixed assets are depreciated. If we invest in a production plant or warehouse for £10 million, and we depreciate it over 20 years, then the annual depreciation will be £500,000. As a result, fixed assets always translate into the cost side of the triangle, as shown in Figure 1.15. Depreciation is not cash out, but it is accounted for in the EBIT or the operating income. We refer to our section on accounting basics at the end of this chapter for more details (page 30).

If companies invest in automation, they typically do so to replace the cost of manual labour with a lower cost per unit after the automation. Figure 1.16

FIGURE 1.16 Lowering the cost of manual labour by investing in automation

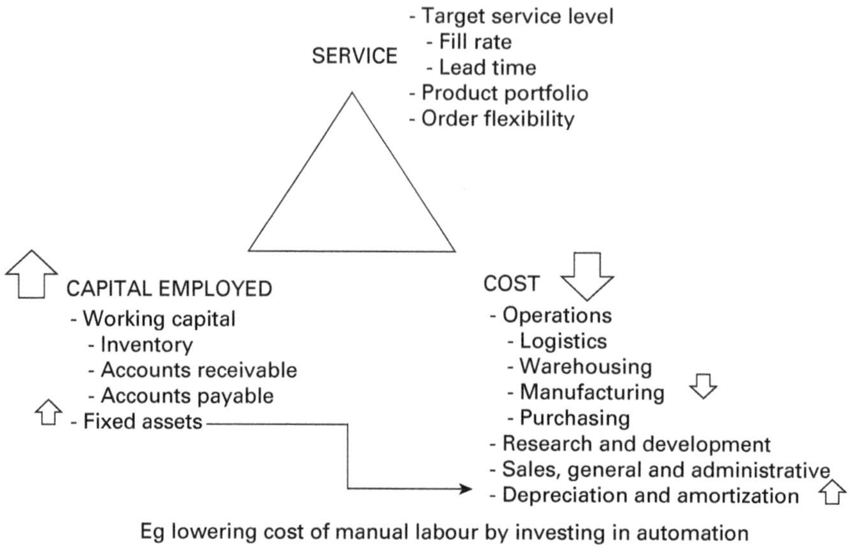

FIGURE 1.17 Inventory translates into the cost corner through write-offs

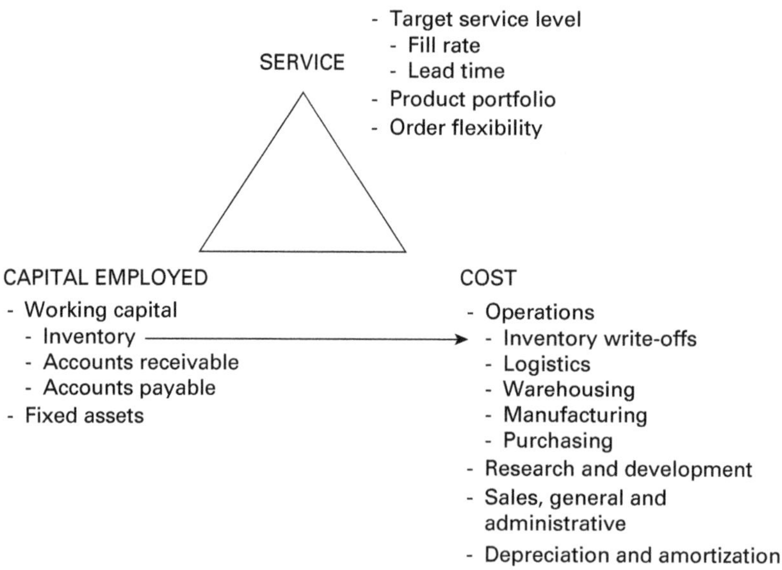

visualizes that the cost will only be lower if the annual depreciation is less than the annual saving on labour cost. Take our example of the £10 million investment which is depreciated over 20 years. Let's assume the investment is in automation. If the yearly saving in labour cost is £750,000, where the annual depreciation is £500,000, the investment makes sense. It will lower our cost to the expense of a higher capital employed.

Inventory also translates into the cost corner. First, more inventory requires a bigger warehouse and will increase the warehousing costs. More inventory may also lead to more write-offs. Write-offs are typically charged to the cost of goods sold. For that reason we have shown them in Figure 1.17 under the 'operations' costs.

EXERCISE 1.2

Analysing the balance in your triangle

Organize a workshop with key stakeholders from sales, marketing, supply chain, operations, purchasing and finance. Hand out Post-it notes and let individuals think for 10 minutes on what they see as 'the struggle in your company's triangle'. Draw a supply chain triangle on paper. Put service at the top, cost at the bottom-right, cash/capital employed at the bottom-left. Ask somebody to start sticking Post-it notes to it. Try to cluster Post-its around key struggles in the triangle.

Figures 1.18 and 1.19 show two simplified real-life examples from two different sectors. If you do it with a supply chain group you will see a different result compared to doing it with a cross-functional team. Try to gather a

FIGURE 1.18 Brainstorm result for a manufacturer of dairy products

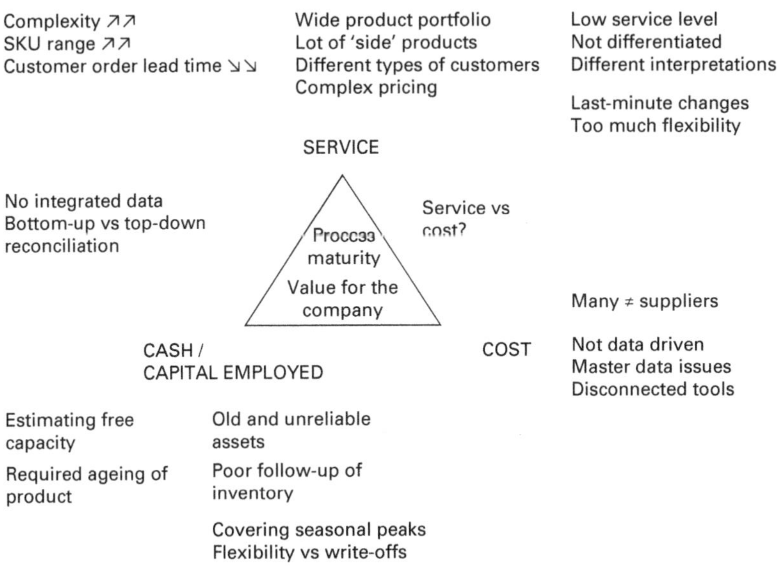

FIGURE 1.19 Brainstorm result for a manufacturer of pharmaceutical products

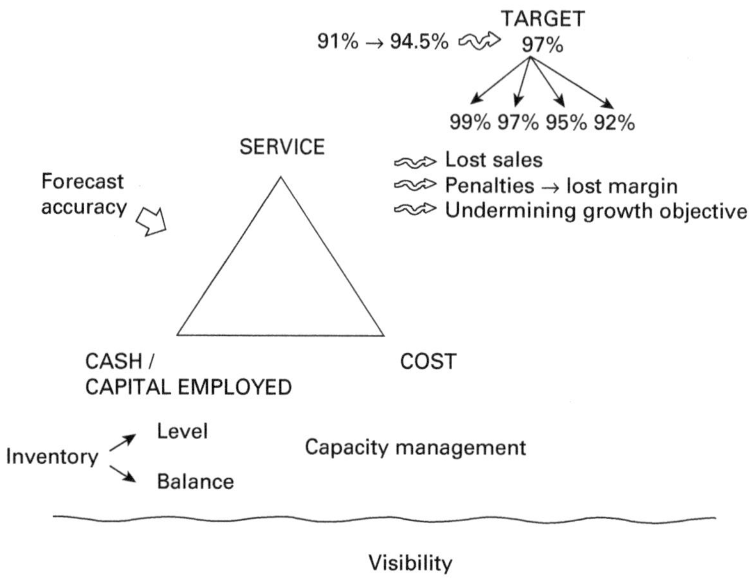

cross-functional team. A common awareness of what is going well or wrong in the triangle is the starting point for a common ambition to change things.

More examples can be found on this book's website at www.strategydrivensupplychain/resources/examples/balance-in-your-supply-chain-triangle

Share a picture of your exercise on LinkedIn with the hashtag #strategydrivensupplychain!

CASE STUDY

Indaver

WITH ANNICK VAN DRIESSEN, INTERNATIONAL DIRECTOR, SUPPLY CHAIN OPERATIONS, INDAVER

Indaver is a European player in responsible waste management for both industry and public authorities. Indaver takes care of the entire waste management chain of its customers, from onsite recycling to final treatment, saving customers time and worry. By recovering as many materials and as much energy as possible, Indaver contributes to the transition to a circular economy that uses materials and energy more intelligently. Indaver was originally founded by the Flemish government and 15 private companies to provide a solution to the waste of the chemical industry in the port of Antwerp. Since 2015 it has been part of the port and logistics firm Katoen Natie.

The supply chain department at Indaver is squeezed between a demanding market situation and highly complex operations. On the market side, the industry concept of Indaver is 'total waste management'. It implies that Indaver takes care of all the waste streams of its customers. For the industrial part, these customers are typically large chemical or pharmaceutical companies. The idea is to unburden the producer and relieve them of any concern about waste. The total waste management is arranged via long-term contracts, many of them resulting in exclusivity for Indaver. While commercially a big success, from a supply chain perspective the total waste management results in a very broad range of waste streams that, obviously, all need to be processed. The supply of waste is not as stable as one would expect. From time to time customers have major campaigns to clear waste, resulting in a significant amount of waste in a short period of time. Indaver makes a difference between process and batch-driven customers. Except for campaigns, the process customers are more stable; for the batch customers the type and amount of waste depends on the actual batch being run by the customer. There could be little to none in some weeks and multiple trucks or vessels in others.

On the operations side, the processing of waste is what we call 'asset intensive'. Industrial waste is processed in so-called rotary kilns. These are advanced furnaces that come at a significant investment cost. Once an investment has been made, these assets need to be loaded to the maximum capacity to earn a decent margin. The operating cost of these kilns is heavily influenced by the mix of the waste being processed.

As has been explained, the inflow of waste is neither stable nor highly predictable. An option would be to temporarily store the waste in a buffer, but historically the onsite storage capacity has been limited, to save on capital expenditure (CAPEX). Storage is seldom seen as a productive asset. Limited storage requires a kind of 'just-in-time' supply of waste in a specific mix. Knowing that Indaver doesn't control that supply, you feel the stretch that is put on the supply chain organization.

The underlying strategy in the past was to make sure that you contracted more waste than you could treat in your own waste facilities, and to use 'external treatment facilities' to process the 'net remainder'. You loaded your own assets with the optimal mix and contracted the remaining volumes on the external market. This worked well in a situation of overcapacity, where other waste treatment companies were happy to take on any extra waste to help them to cover their high fixed costs. Over the last two or three years the market has grown significantly and the excess capacity has more or less been absorbed. This means suppliers are less flexible about

FIGURE 1.20 The supply chain triangle at waste treatment company Indaver

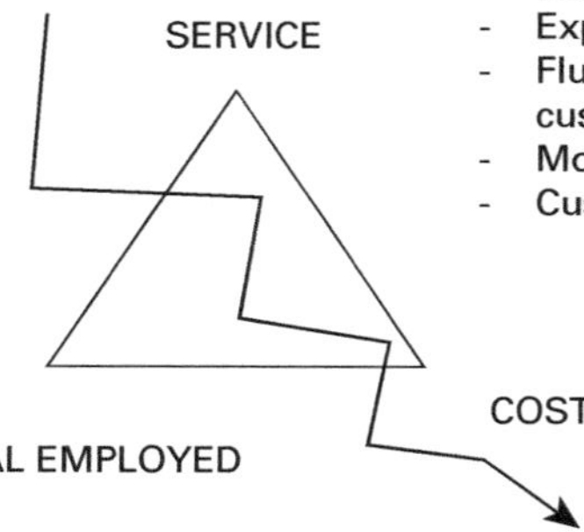

Total waste management
- Broad range of waste streams
- Long-term contracts with an obligation to take all the waste – all customers are 'key'
- Expectation of high responsiveness
- Fluctuations in waste due to campaigns, accidents at customer, etc
- More complex streams than in the past
- Customers produce more than planned → oversupply

Asset intensive
- Short on capacity if economy is doing well
- More complex streams → frequent unplanned shutdowns
- The mix of waste is important for cost and efficiency
- Continuous loading of assets is important for cost
- Waste buffer capacity scaled down to save on CAPEX
- External storage is limited and expensive (waste)
- External processing less flexible than 10 years ago
- Alternative routes subject to approval by governmental institutions (as it is waste)
- Efficiency internal installations overrated (actual < budget)

- A lot of last-minute changes and operational firefighting
  - due to changes on the demand side
  - due to unforeseen shutdowns
- A lot of Excel files, no single view on planning
- A lot of emails, phone calls, etc
- Continuous state of escalation from operations to waste treatment managing supplier relationships (to find alternative destinations)

taking on any type of waste at the very last moment, further complicating the challenge to the supply chain organization.

To make matters worse, as a result of the increasing complexity of the waste, the Indaver assets had frequent unforeseen shutdowns. Without much buffer, a hiccup in production almost immediately requires a plan to start rerouting waste to alternative destinations. And remember this is about waste, which comes with a lot of regulations. No type of waste can be transported anywhere without first getting approval from the relevant authorities. All of this further complicates the challenge to the supply chain organization.

Annick comments that the supply chain triangle has helped Indaver in two important ways. First, as shown in Figure 1.20, it has helped management to better understand and capture the supply chain challenge at Indaver, the fact of being caught between a demanding market and a complex operation. Second, it created this awareness across different functions and different levels in the organization. Supply chain is often considered technical and operational, so it's difficult to get the attention and buy-in from sales departments or the full executive committee. The triangle creates a common language to formulate a common understanding of the challenge ahead. A common understanding across departments and levels is a requirement to implement a successful solution.

Conclusion

In this chapter we introduced the supply chain triangle of service, cost and cash. We have shown how a traditional functional organization leads to tension in the triangle, as sales people are more service and top line driven, operations is more cost-driven, and finance has asked supply chain to keep control of the inventory as an important element of working capital or in short cash.

We have expanded the cash corner into a capital employed corner, by adding the fixed assets. Seasonal peaks can be covered by either inventory or investing in peak capacity. We can reduce cost by investing in new machines. These are example trade-offs that are better captured in this extended triangle.

We have closed the chapter by showing how the triangle can be used in your company to create alignment on the most pressing challenges in your supply chain. The triangle allows supply chain to be explained in a non-technical way to non-experts.

In the next chapter we will link supply chain to finance, using the triangle, and using the financial metric of the return on capital employed.

Appendix

Accounting basics: Inventory, working capital, and cash generation

In this appendix we will dig into some accounting basics, which are required for a good understanding of the main text in the book. To better understand the link between inventory, working capital and cash generation, we will introduce and explain the three key financial statements of any publicly listed company: the profit and loss statement (P&L), the balance sheet, and the cash flow statement.

The profit and loss statement

Figure 1.21 shows a simplified profit and loss of an example company. Let's discuss the different lines. Sales revenue minus the cost of goods sold defines the gross profit. The cost of goods sold (COGS) includes the direct material costs, which are the costs of the raw materials and components going into the finished goods and the direct labour cost, which is any cost that can be directly allocated to the production of a specific product, for instance the line operators. COGS also includes the manufacturing overhead, which can be variable (changing with the volume produced) or fixed (independent of the volume produced). The overhead can include the cost of the process engineering, the planning department, etc. Costs that are not linked to the manufacturing of the finished product are grouped into SG&A.

EBITDA are the earnings before we subtract interest, taxes, depreciation and amortization. If a company invests in a new production facility or a new warehouse, the cost of that investment is spread over its lifetime. This means we can invest €10 million this year and spread the cost over 20 years, ie €500,000 per year. This is called 'depreciation'. If a company invests time or money in the creation of new products or services (R&D), the cost of that investment can also be spread over the lifetime of the product. The yearly cost is called amortization. Notice that depreciation and amortization are not cash out as of year two. The only cash out is in year one, when we make the investment.

The P&L traces all the revenues and all costs during a period, typically a quarter, a semester or a year. Subtracting all the costs from the revenues that relate to a given period gives the net income or net profit. The earnings per share show the net income per share in the given period.

FIGURE 1.21 Profit and loss of an example company

Profit and loss (2020)			
Sales revenue	€	75,600	
Cost of goods sold (COGS)	€	–52,920	
Gross profit	€	22,680	30%
Selling, general and administrative (SG&A) expenses	€	–15,120	
Earnings before interest, taxes, depreciation & amortization (EBITDA)	€	7,560	10%
Depreciation	€	–3,024	
Amortization	€	-	
Earnings before interest & taxes (EBIT)	€	4,536	6%
Taxes and interest	€	–2,646	
Net income / net profit	€	1,890	3%
Earnings per share (eg 1,000 shares)	€	1.89	

Cost of goods sold (COGS) → Cost that can be directly attributed to the sale, eg purchasing cost

Selling, general and administrative (SG&A) expenses → Cost that can NOT be directly attributed to the sale, eg marketing costs

Depreciation → 'Investments' in eg warehouses are 'depreciated', for instance over 20 years. This implies we account for 1/20th of the total cost each year. A depreciation is not a 'cash out'. The actual cash has been spent when the warehouse was built.

The balance sheet

The balance sheet shows all that a company 'owns' at a specific moment in time (typically at the end of a year). What a company owns is called its 'assets'. They are shown in Figure 1.22. The current assets can be converted into cash on the short term, typically less than a year. Important components of the current assets are the cash we have in the bank and the accounts receivable (the money that has been invoiced to the customer, but has not yet been paid). Inventory is also part of current assets. Fixed assets are those that cannot easily be converted into cash, such as the plant, property and equipment in which we have invested in the past.

The balance sheet also shows the financing of these assets. This is shown in Figure 1.23. When starting a company, the owners will invest a certain amount of money. This is the 'paid-in capital'. When the company makes a profit, part of the profit can be returned to the shareholders via a dividend. The shareholders can decide to leave part of the profit in the company as 'retained earnings'. So part of the financing of the assets comes from the owners' equity (paid-in capital + retained earnings).

A second part of the financing is summarized as 'liabilities'. Current liabilities are due in the short term. Accounts payable, which is the money still to be paid to suppliers, are part of the current liabilities. Any type of

FIGURE 1.22 Explaining the asset side of the balance sheet of an example company

Balance sheet (31/12/2019)			
Assets		Liabilities and owners' equity	
Current assets		*Owners' equity*	
Cash	€ 6,600	Paid-in capital	€ 15,000
Accounts receivable	€ 6,200	Retained earnings	€ 800
Inventories	€ 5,000		
Total current assets	€ 17,800	*Total owners' equity*	€ 15,800
Fixed assets		*Liabilities*	
Property, plant & equipment	€ 20,000	*Current liabilities*	
		Accounts payable	€ 8,000
		Short-term bank loans	€ 4,000
		Long-term liabilities	
		Long-term bank loans	€ 10,000
Total fixed assets	€ 20,000	*Total liabilities*	€ 22,000
Total assets	€ 37,800		€ 37,800

Current assets can be converted into money in the short term. 'Current' refers to 'short-term'

Fixed assets are more difficult to convert in cash. They are 'long-term' assets

Accounts receivable = eg clients that pay at 30 days or 60 days, consumers who buy on credit of 30 days, etc

FIGURE 1.23 Explaining the liabilities and owners' equity side of the balance sheet of an example company

Balance sheet (31/12/2019)			
Assets		Liabilities and owners' equity	
Current assets		*Owners' equity*	
Cash	€ 6,600	Paid-in capital	€ 15,000
Accounts receivable	€ 6,200	Retained earnings	€ 800
Inventories	€ 5,000		
Total current assets	€ 17,800	*Total owners' equity*	€ 15,800
Fixed assets		*Liabilities*	
Property, plant & equipment	€ 20,000	*Current liabilities*	
		Accounts payable	€ 8,000
		Short-term bank loans	€ 4,000
		Long-term liabilities	
		Long-term bank loans	€ 10,000
Total fixed assets	€ 20,000	*Total liabilities*	€ 22,000
Total assets	€ 37,800		€ 37,800

The owners' equity consists of the cash investments made in the company by the shareholders + any earnings that have not been paid as a dividend

Current liabilities are payable in the short term

Long-term liabilities are payable in the long term

Accounts payable = costs that have been made and accounted for in the P&L, but that still need to be paid. Eg we pay our suppliers only after 30 days or 60 days short-term debt will also be part of the current liabilities. Investment in fixed assets (plant, warehouses, etc) is typically financed by long-term loans. These are part of the long-term liabilities.

EXERCISE 1.3

Understanding the P&L balance sheet

Take the latest financial reports from your company and two key competitors. From the P&L compare revenue, cost of goods, SG&A, EBITDA, depreciation and amortization, EBIT, net income, earnings per share. What do you learn about your profitability compared to your two competitors? From the balance sheet compare the following metrics:

Current ratio = current assets / current liabilities
Debt ratio = total debt / total assets

The current ratio is what we call a 'liquidity measure'. It explains how easy the short-term liabilities can be returned from the short-term assets like receivables and cash. A ratio below one indicates a lack of liquidity. The debt ratio indicates how much of the total assets is financed by debt (liabilities) versus equity. Less debt financing, or a so-called 'lower leverage', makes it easier to get extra debt financing.

The statement of cash flows

The 'statement of cash flows' explains the difference in the cash position at the end of the previous period and the end of the current period. As explained when discussing the P&L, depreciation of an investment is not cash out as of year two. As a result, when starting from net profit, we need to add depreciation (and amortization) if we want to know the actual cash generation (or consumption). If our accounts receivable have decreased, eg from €6,200 at the end of the previous period to €5,000 at the end of the current period, we have been able to 'collect' €1,200 of cash from our customers. As a result, a decrease in accounts receivable generates cash. An increase in accounts receivable will consume cash. Likewise, a reduction in inventory and an increase in accounts payable will generate cash.

Figure 1.24 shows the cash flow statement for our example company. The net income is €1,890. We have a depreciation of €3,024. Assuming the investment has been done in earlier years, this is not cash out, so we can add it to the net income. Apparently over this period, our accounts receivable have increased, inventory has increased, and accounts payable have decreased. As a result, the cash we generated of €1,890 + €3,024 has been consumed by the increase in the receivables and the inventory and a reduction in the payables. In fact, the cash generated is not sufficient. There is a deficit of –€1,586. This deficit will lower the cash we have available in the bank. If we don't have enough cash in the bank account, we'll need to extend our loans or ask shareholders to increase the capital to finance this deficit.

There is a saying that companies don't go bankrupt from making a loss – they go bankrupt from a lack of cash. The statement of cash flows is instrumental in understanding which factors are the cash generating and which are the cash consuming over a given accounting period.

Figure 1.24 shows the 'cash flow from operations'. We can also generate or consume cash from investing activities and from financing activities. The above-mentioned investment in a new production facility or warehouse will typically be explained in the 'cash flow from investments'. This is a second and separate part of the overall cash flow statement. If we make an investment of €10 million in year one, it will show the €10 million here. If we depreciate over 20 years, we only show €500,000 in the P&L. That €500,000 is not an extra cash-out, so it should be added to the net income in the 'operations' part of the cash flow statement.

FIGURE 1.24 The cash flow statement of the example company

Statement of Cash Flows (2020)	
Net Income	€ 1.890
+ Depreciation Expense	€ 3.024
+ Decrease in Accounts Receivable	€ –3.000
+ Decrease in Inventory	€ –2.500
+ Increase in Accounts Payable	€ –1.000
Cash Flow from Operations	€ –1.586

The net income or net profit is not equal to the cash we have generated!!

e.g. as already explained, a depreciation is not a "cash-out". The cash has been spent when the investment was initially done. As such, to calculate the actual cash generation, we add the depreciation expense to the net income.

If I decrease my inventory (e.g. From €5,000 at the end of 2012 to €4,000 at the end of 2013 ... then I generate cash. Likewise, if I decrease my AR (money to receive from customers) or increase my AP (money still to pay to suppliers), ... I also generate cash.

Roughly speaking, the free cash flow equals the cash flow from operations minus the capital expenditures. A capital expenditure is any investment in non-financial assets, like a new production facility or warehouse. It is called the 'free' cash flow as it represents the cash that is available to all security holders, the holders of equity and the holders of debt. It is the cash flow that can be used to pay dividends, and to pay interest.

The exact definition of the FCF takes the interest out, as interest is money returned to the holders of debt. That makes it a bit more complicated. The resulting definition is as follows

$$FCF = EBIT \times (1\text{-tax rate}) + D\&A - \Delta WC - CAPEX$$

Where EBIT × (1-tax rate) is also called the net operating profit after tax (NOPAT), D&A are depreciation and amortization, ΔWC are the changes in working capital and CAPEX are the capital expenditures as just explained.

If we make a large investment, all or part of the investment may be financed by a new loan, or a capital increase by the shareholders. This financing is typically shown in the cash flow from financing. That is the third and last part of the overall cash flow statement.

Figure 1.25 shows that the statement of cash flows can also be derived from comparing the balance sheet at the end of the previous and the current period. Depreciation shows as a reduction of the fixed assets. To come back to our example, each year we account for €500,000 in the P&L. In the balance sheet we reduce the value of the corresponding asset by €500,000 each year. The comparison also shows the increase in the receivables and the inventory, and the decrease in the payables. The cash deficit of –€1,586 shows as a reduction of the cash balance from €6,600 to €5,014.

EXERCISE 1.4

Understanding the cash flow statement

Take the latest two financial reports from your company and two key competitors. Try to derive the cash flow statement by comparing the balance sheets of the last two years, as shown in Figure 1.25. Compare your result with the cash flow statement in the financial reports. Try to understand any differences.

Take a step back and review the following questions: which activities have generated cash? Which have been consuming cash? Was there a net cash generation or consumption? Review for your company and the two key competitors.

FIGURE 1.25 Deriving the cash flow statement from the balance sheet at the end of the previous and the current period

Balance sheet (31/12/2019)			
Assets		Liabilities and owners' equity	
Current assets		*Owners' equity*	
Cash	€ 6,600	Paid-in capital	€ 15,000
Accounts receivable	€ 6,200	Retained earnings	€ 800
Inventories	€ 5,000		
Total current assets	€ 17,800	*Total owners' equity*	
Fixed assets		*Liabilities*	
Property, plant & equipment	€ 20,000	*Current liabilities*	
		Accounts payable	€ 8,000
		Short-term bank loans	€ 4,000
		Long-term liabilities	
		Long-term bank loans	€ 10,000
Total fixed assets	€ 20,000	*Total liabilities*	€ 22,000
Total assets	€ 37,800		€ 37,800

Balance sheet (31/12/2020)			
		Liabilities and owners' equity	
Current assets		*Owners' equity*	
Cash	€ 5,014	Paid-in capital	€ 15,000
Accounts receivable	€ 9,200	Retained earnings	€ 2,690
Inventories	€ 7,500		
Total current assets		*Total owners' equity*	€ 17,690
Fixed assets		*Liabilities*	
Property, plant & equipment	€ 16,976	*Current liabilities*	
		Accounts payable	€ 7,000
		Short-term bank loans	€ 4,000
		Long-term liabilities	
		Long-term bank loans	€ 10,000
Total fixed assets	€ 16,976	*Total liabilities*	€ 21,000
Total assets	€ 38,690		€ 38,690

–€1,586 Cash
+€3,000 Receivables
+€2,500 Inventory

+€3,024 Depreciation

–€1,000 in payables

Working capital

Working capital is defined as current assets minus current liabilities. Figure 1.26 shows that the working capital for our example company is €5,800. Throughout the year, our working capital will go up and down as the underlying components go up and down. The working capital represents the capital we need to have smooth operations. You can consider it the oil into our operational engine.

Figure 1.26 also shows that our working capital is in fact financed by the owners' equity and the long-term liabilities. These do not come for free. We typically pay interest on the long-term liabilities. If we pay 5 per cent to the bank, our shareholders will typically expect a higher return, such as 15 per cent. Without explaining the details, there is a financial metric that is called the weighted average cost of capital (WACC). This WACC weighs the different types of debt and their corresponding return. For manufacturing and retail companies, it typically varies between 8 and 12 per cent.

Figure 1.27 shows that the working capital in our company has increased over the last period, from €5,800 to €10,714. Our current liabilities decreased by €1,000. Our current assets increased by €3,914.

FIGURE 1.26 Deriving the working capital of the example company

Balance sheet (31/12/2019)			
Assets		Liabilities and owners' equity	
Current assets		*Owners' equity*	
Cash	€ 6,600	Paid-in capital	€ 15,000
Accounts receivable	€ 6,200	Retained earnings	€ 800
Inventories	€ 5,000		
Total current assets	€ 17,800	*Total owners' equity*	€ 15,800
Fixed assets		*Liabilities*	
Property, plant & equipment	€ 20,000	*Current liabilities*	
		Accounts payable	€ 8,000
		Short-term bank loans	€ 4,000
		Long-term liabilities	
		Long-term bank loans	€ 10,000
Total fixed assets	€ 20,000	*Total liabilities*	€ 22,000
Total assets	€ 37,800		€ 37,800

€17,800 – €12,000 = €5,800

FIGURE 1.27 Working capital ncrease in the example company

Balance sheet (31/12/2019)			
Assets		Liabilities and owners' equity	
Current assets		*Owners' equity*	
Cash	€ 6,600	Paid-in capital	€ 15,000
Accounts receivable	€ 6,200	Retained earnings	€ 800
Inventories	€ 5,000		
Total current assets	€ 17,800	*Total owners' equity*	€ 15,800
Fixed assets		*Liabilities*	
Property, plant & equipment	€ 20,000	*Current liabilities*	
		Accounts payable	€ 8,000
		Short-term bank loans	€ 4,000
		Long-term liabilities	
		Long-term bank loans	€ 10,000
Total fixed assets	€ 20,000	*Total liabilities*	€ 22,000
Total assets	€ 37,800		€ 37,800

Balance sheet (31/12/2020)			
Assets		Liabilities and owners' equity	
Current assets		*Owners' equity*	
Cash	€ 5,014	Paid-in capital	€ 15,000
Accounts receivable	€ 9,200	Retained earnings	€ 2,690
Inventories	€ 7,500		
Total current assets	€ 21,714	*Total owners' equity*	€ 17,690
Fixed assets		*Liabilities*	
Property, plant & equipment	€ 16,976	*Current liabilities*	
		Accounts payable	€ 7,000
		Short-term bank loans	€ 4,000
		Long-term liabilities	
		Long-term bank loans	€ 10,000
Total fixed assets	€ 16,976	*Total liabilities*	€ 21,000
Total assets	€ 38,690		€ 38,690

€17,800 – €12,000 = €5,800

+ €4,914 →

€21,714 – €11,000 = €10,714

WORKING CAPITAL AND SUPPLY CHAIN

Figure 1.28 shows the primary components of the working capital on which we have an impact from the supply chain:

- Inventory: Lowering inventories generates cash.
- Accounts receivable: Reducing payment terms to clients or improving collection speed generates cash.
- Account payable: Increasing payment terms to suppliers also generates cash.

Days of inventory on hand (DIOH), inventory turns, days of sales outstanding (DSO) and days of payables outstanding (DPO) are financial metrics that are commonly used to measure and follow up these key components of working capital. They are defined and applied to our example company in Figure 1.29. Notice that for DSO it is common to divide by the net sales, whereas for DPO, DIOH and inventory turns it is common to divide by the cost of goods sold. Different companies use different definitions, for instance excluding the labour cost and just looking at the direct material cost when calculating DPO. We suggest that you stick to commonly used standards, to make comparisons across companies easier.

Another commonly used metric is the cash conversion cycle (CCC). Figure 1.30 shows its definition and the application to our example company. CCC indicates the number of days between disbursing cash to suppliers and collecting cash from customers. It is a direct measurement of the key components of the working capital. Reducing CCC lowers the working capital and generates cash. Increasing CCC increases the working capital and consumes cash.

EXERCISE 1.5

Understanding working capital and CCC

From the latest two financial reports from your company and two key competitors, derive the working capital from the last two years as shown in Figure 1.30. Calculate and compare the cash conversion cycle using Figure 1.29 and Figure 1.30. Who has been generating cash from working capital? Who has consumed cash? Do we understand why, and how? Which is a sign of weakness or strength?

FIGURE 1.28 Supply chain components of working capital for the example company

Balance sheet (31/12/2019)			
Assets		Liabilities and owners' equity	
Current assets		*Owners' equity*	
Cash	€ 6,600	Paid-in capital	€ 15,000
Accounts receivable	€ 6,200	Retained earnings	€ 800
Inventories	€ 5,000		
Total current assets	€ 17,800	*Total owners' equity*	€ 15,800
Fixed assets		*Liabilities*	
Property, plant & equipment	€ 20,000	*Current liabilities*	
		Accounts payable	€ 8,000
		Short-term bank loans	€ 4,000
		Long-term liabilities	
		Long-term bank loans	€ 10,000
Total fixed assets	€ 20,000	*Total liabilities*	€ 22,000
Total assets	€ 37,800		€ 37,800

Sales, logistics, manufacturing and procurement primarily have impact on:

- Inventory
- Accounts receivable (defined by payment terms for customers and speed of collection)
- Accounts payable (defined by payment terms for customers and respecting due dates)

FIGURE 1.29 DSO, DPO, DIOH and inventory turns for the example company

$$\text{DSO} = \frac{€9{,}200}{€75{,}600\ /\ yr} \cdot 365\ days\ /\ yr = 44\ days$$

$$\text{DPO} = \frac{€7{,}000}{€52{,}920\ /\ yr} \cdot 365\ days\ /\ yr = 48\ days$$

$$\text{DIOH} = \frac{€7{,}500}{€52{,}920\ /\ yr} \cdot 365\ days\ /\ yr = 52\ days$$

$$\text{Inventory turns} = \frac{€52{,}920\ /\ yr}{€7{,}500} = 7\ /\ yr$$

FIGURE 1.30 Definition of the cash conversion cycle and its application to the example company

CCC = DSO + DIOH – DPO
= 44 *days* + 52 *days* – 48 *days*
= 48 *days*

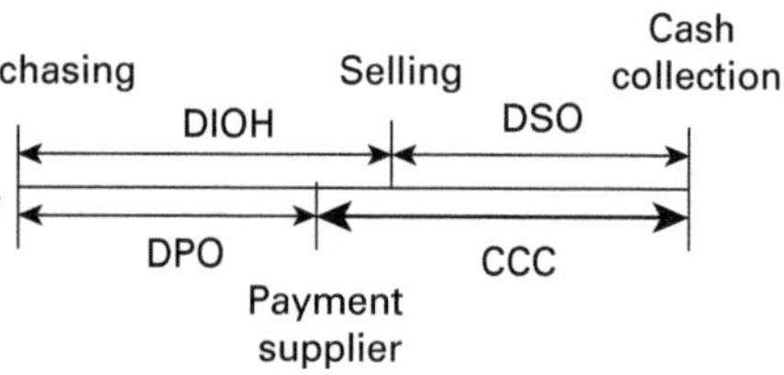

Notes

1 M Christopher (1998) *Relationships and Alliances: Embracing the era of network competition* (pp 272–84), Gower Press, Hampshire, England

2 P F Drucker, Management's new paradigms, *Forbes Magazine*, 1998, 10 (2), 98–99

3 D M Lambert (2008) *Supply Chain Management: Processes, partnerships, performance*, Supply Chain Management Institute

4 B DeSmet (2018) *Supply Chain Strategy and Financial Metrics: The supply chain triangle of service, cost and cash*, Kogan Page, London

5 S Axsäter (2015) *Inventory Control*, International Series in Operations Research and Management Science, Vol 225, Springer, Switzerland

6 J Eley, Record month for UK supermarkets as consumers spend extra £1.9bn, *Financial Times*, 31 March 2020, www.ft.com/content/cf153651-09f3-4cf5-a012-e4f823b648be (archived at https://perma.cc/TPL6-8RQS)

02

Finance in the supply chain triangle

In the previous chapter we introduced the supply chain triangle of service, cost and cash, or, more broadly, service, cost and capital employed. We described how companies struggle with balancing the triangle and how we believe the true mission of supply chain is to balance that triangle.

In this chapter we will show that balancing the triangle is about maximizing shareholder value, as measured by ROCE. That means that supply chain and finance have the same goal and that they have a common interest in aligning the three corners of the supply chain triangle. We show how ROCE can be used as a balancing metric or as a decision criterion to make trade-offs in the triangle. We also show how ROCE can be used to benchmark the value generated by different companies and to set targets for underlying financial metrics.

In the second part of this chapter, we compare ROCE to other common financial metrics like return on equity (ROE), return on assets (ROA) and earnings per share (EPS). We discuss growth, EBITDA and FCF, and link them to our supply chain triangle. We explain why FCF is so important to finance, how growth consumes FCF and how a healthy ROCE is the basis for a healthy FCF and a high company valuation. We conclude by proposing to follow up growth, ROCE and FCF as key financial metrics, independent of the sector and the size of the company.

Aligning the triangle is about optimizing the return on capital employed

Though people from different backgrounds – supply chain, finance, sales, marketing – recognize the tension in the triangle, the dominant thinking is that the tension is 'unavoidable' and that 'this is just how companies work'. I do get questions like 'Won't there always be conflicting objectives between sales, operations and finance?' and 'Isn't the conflict a source of creative energy?' Though rightful questions, I believe the answer is no, and the solution lies in taking an investors' perspective.

Figure 2.1 shows that service is a driver for sales revenue. Shorter lead times and improved reliability will lead to happy customers and repeat buying. We can also open extra locations, expand our product portfolio or improve our existing products. Those are other examples of service improvement and they too will be driving extra sales.

But as an investor I'm concerned with more than sales or sales growth. At least in the long term, I would also like to see a profit. Figure 2.2 shows how we can combine the service and the cost side of the triangle into a profit metric like EBIT. Different companies look at different metrics. Instead of EBIT, we could also look at EBITDA, gross margin or net profit. We will come back to those metrics and their differences later in this chapter.

But even then, as an investor, I am concerned with more than growth or EBIT. The reason is the following. If I have two companies generating 100 million of EBIT, where the first company requires 1 billion of capital and the

FIGURE 2.1 Service is a driver for sales revenue

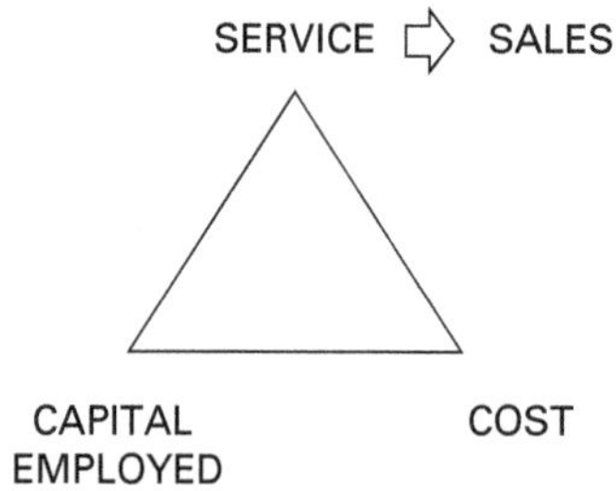

FIGURE 2.2 Service and cost combine into a profit metric like EBIT

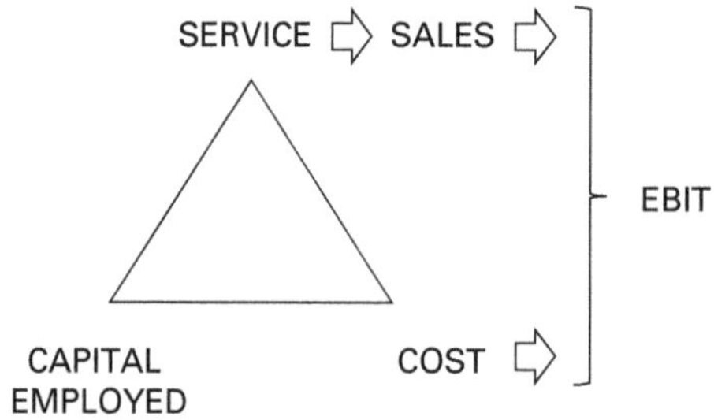

FIGURE 2.3 EBIT over capital employed gives a return metric like ROCE

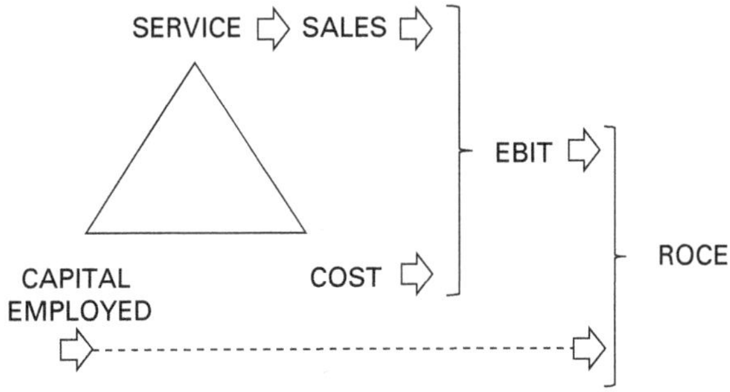

second only 0.5 billion, then of course I'd rather do the second investment twice. In the end, as an investor, I am concerned with the EBIT you generate over the capital employed, which is the definition of ROCE. As an investor, I will say it is OK if your EBIT is a bit lower as long as you need less capital. Or vice versa: it is OK if you need a bit more capital as long as you compensate with a higher EBIT. As an investor, I will judge you by the 'bang-for-the-buck', the EBIT you generate, over the capital employed. That is illustrated in Figure 2.3.

Figure 2.3 does two things. First, it links supply chain and finance. It shows that supply chain and finance have a common objective: creating value for the shareholder, as measured by ROCE. There is a common interest to balance the triangle of service, cost and capital employed. Second, it introduces ROCE as a balancing metric, as a criterion that can be used to make trade-offs in the supply chain triangle. We will show how this works by retaking some of the challenges introduced earlier in Chapter 1.

Using ROCE as a balancing metric and decision criterion

Let's review Figure 1.5 again, which shows the struggle with balance in the triangle, and see if ROCE helps us to come to a decision. We have repeated it here as Figure 2.4 for your convenience.

Let's start with the product portfolio expansion shown on the bottom left. On the one hand, expanding the product portfolio will lead to extra sales; on the other hand, it will increase the inventory. So what should we do? Is it worthwhile pursuing this?

We believe the dominant thinking in companies today is: 1) growth, 2) margin and 3) capital employed. Some companies are blinded by growth.

FIGURE 2.4 Companies struggle with balance in the triangle

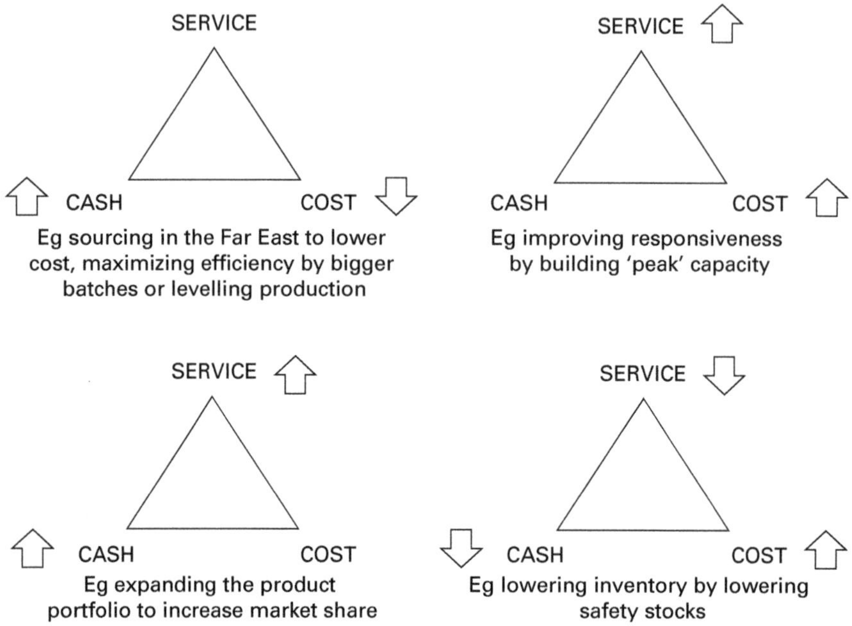

If the top line is under pressure, any initiative supporting growth will easily be approved. When growth is 'under control', companies will start looking at margins. If margins look promising, our expansion of the product portfolio is likely to be approved. Why wouldn't it? Well, if you introduce 20 per cent of new products it is likely that your sales will not increase by 20 per cent. This means you are introducing a long tail of more slow-moving products, so your inventory turns will go down (or your days of inventory on hand will go up). In many companies, the impact on working capital is only an afterthought. We only find out that our inventories went up a year down the road. If we want to stick to the same ROCE, we need to make sure our margins (percentage wise) are increasing, as our working capital will certainly be increasing. That puts a product line extension into a new context. The new question becomes whether a line extension will add ROCE and improve value generation, or whether it will lower ROCE and reduce the value generation.

We can apply the same reasoning to the 'sourcing in the Far East' example in Figure 2.4. What will be the impact on EBIT, and what will be the impact on the capital employed? If the net impact on ROCE is limited, we may include other factors like risk or flexibility. A local supplier may provide more flexibility over long-distance sourcing. Or take the example of 'improving responsiveness by building peak capacity' in Figure 2.4. What is the extra business we would be able to bring in, and at what margin? If I am in a tender-driven market, what is the margin to be earned on tenders versus recurring business? Or, if I'm in a seasonal market, how would extra capacity in the season lower my average inventory? Do I have lost sales or inventory write-offs that I would be able to avoid? In both situations the solution is to analyse the impact across the three corners on EBIT and on capital employed, and to use ROCE as the decision criterion. Will it improve my ROCE – yes or no?

Let's also revisit our dangerous catch-22 situation shown earlier in Figure 1.8. We have repeated it as Figure 2.5 for your convenience. The discussion on the catch-22 situation was that there is little incentive to think across the corners of the triangle when business is good, as there is little incentive for change. However, when business turns bad we often see a reflex of each different department pulling their side of the triangle harder, making optimization across the corners even more difficult at that moment.

FIGURE 2.5 Increased tension in the triangle as growth stalls

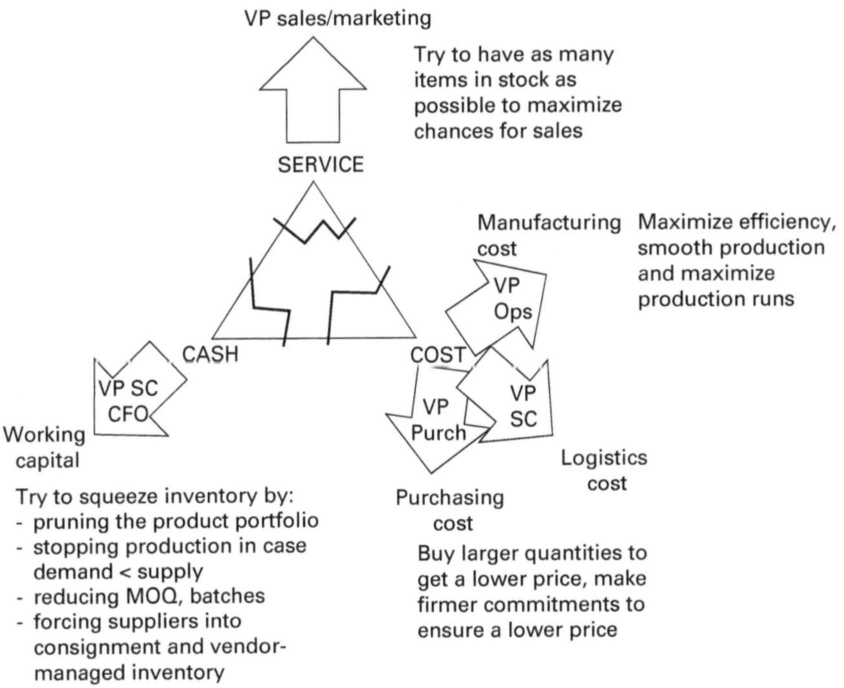

In general, in their quest for growth, we believe companies over the years add complexity to the service corner. They start offering more products, they offer them at a shorter lead time, they get more flexible in honouring customer-specific requests. Even in 'normal' times, when supply chain managers try to rationalize that service and product portfolio, to reduce inventories and to reduce costs, there is typically a lot of pushback from the marketing and sales side. We've all heard the argument multiple times that 'Yes, we know those products are not profitable but they are critical to customers A and B. If we cut those products, we're going to lose those customers.' The harder the pressure on the top line, as in Figure 2.5, the harder to get acceptance for cutting stock keeping units (SKUs).

So how do we solve this? We should start by recognizing that, yes, if we stop certain products, it will negatively impact the top line. If we can cut SKUs without impacting the top line it will be non-moving products that most probably carry some obsolete stock. In which case, we're simply cutting too late. Moreover, it's not only about top line or margin, it is about the margin we generate over the capital employed. Let's think through what happens near the end of the lifecycle of a product. On the one hand, the sales volumes start declining. At the same time, because of low-cost competition, the margins are typically eroding even faster. On the other hand, if we want to keep delivering the same service to our customers, we will need proportionally more inventory as these products become slow moving. So what does this mean? It means less margin for a higher investment. Less bang for more buck? That's not what I want as an investor!

ROCE will help me to analyse and optimize my product portfolio. I will always have products and customers that are positively contributing to my ROCE, whereas others are lowering it. In supply chain terms we often hear about 'good complexity' versus 'bad complexity'. Bad complexity lowers our ROCE and should be taken out. But not all complexity is bad. As supply chain people we'd often like to remove all complexity and simplify to the minimum in order to minimize costs and inventories. That is a bridge too far. ROCE will help you to define the limits.

But what if the business is heavily under pressure, as illustrated in Figure 2.5? Will the ROCE reasoning still hold? Yes, we believe so. The question becomes more strategic, though. If the business is really in trouble, the question becomes: how will we get ROCE back to the right level not in 3–6 months but in 3–6 years? A well-documented case is that of McBride. McBride is a producer of private label household and personal care products. The company is headquartered in the UK and listed on the London Stock Exchange.

In its 2015 annual report, McBride management announced a multi-year programme to restore its operational performance consisting of three phases: 'repair', 'prepare' and 'grow'.[1] The report states that 'over the past years McBride has built a level of complexity in its business which prevents the company from translating its scale into sustainable competitive advantage' and that the company 'will make these choices and drive our business decisions and actions with the single aim of restoring our operational performance and improving our cost competitiveness'. In a 'results and strategy presentation' from September 2016, the company reported a staggering '75 per cent of customers exited' and an 'SKU reduction of over 20 per cent and ongoing'.[2] These actions are part of the 'repair' phase reported under the heading of 'complexity'. The 2016 annual report shows net sales of £680 million versus £704 million, or minus 3.4 per cent.[3] The adjusted operating profit (adjusted EBIT), however, increases from £28.5 million (4 per cent) in 2015 to £36.2 million (9.5 per cent) in 2016.

The McBride example teaches us that when a business is under severe pressure, a mere 'pull' on each of the corners will not lead to a breakthrough. We believe it starts with affirming your strategy and your strategic choices, as McBride did in confirming it wanted to excel in manufacturing and achieve the lowest cost. We will discuss strategic choices at length in the next chapter. In that same chapter we will explain how the strategy defines how you will drive ROCE. In the case of McBride, that is done by simplifying the product and customer portfolio to the maximum and delivering the absolute lowest cost in that segment. Implementing those choices has an impact on the triangle and may, in the short term, impact the top line and service. Avoiding tough choices and bluntly stretching the triangle has little chance of improving ROCE, in the short term or the long term. It is merely a sign of poor management.

Using ROCE as a starting point for benchmarking

In this section we will show how ROCE can be used to benchmark the value generation of different companies. It is a more high-level and non-technical summary of Chapters 3, 4 and 5 of our first book, *Supply Chain Strategy and Financial Metrics*.[4] We will discuss EBIT and alternative margins metrics. EBIT is the numerator of ROCE. We will discuss metrics for the different components of the capital employed. Capital employed is the denominator of ROCE. We strongly recommend reviewing the appendix on accounting basics at the end of Chapter 1. We will assume a basic knowledge of financial metrics is present.

Margin metrics

ROCE uses EBIT to measure margins. Other common margin metrics are gross margin, EBITDA and net profit. In the next chapter we will argue why we believe gross margin is a good indicator of the chosen strategy. For that reason, we already include it in our comparison of Henkel and P&G. Next to gross margin and EBIT we could look at EBITDA. The difference between EBIT and EBITDA is depreciation and amortization. Companies can boost EBIT by underspending on depreciation and amortization. While it is a short-term booster of EBIT and of ROCE, underinvesting is detrimental to the long-term EBIT and ROCE as your assets will become outdated and unreliable. For that reason, looking at both EBIT and EBITDA is advisable. We didn't include EBITDA in our comparison of Henkel and P&G because the data was not readily available. Finally, we could look at net profit. Net profit is derived from EBIT by subtracting interest and taxes. Interest and taxes are financial in nature. In this book we want to focus on supply chain and operations so we will leave the net profit out of the comparisons; we leave that discussion to the finance books. So, in summary, from a margin perspective we take a look at:

- gross margin (as an indication for the chosen strategy, as will be explained in the next chapter)
- EBIT (as the numerator of ROCE)
- EBITDA (if easily available, as a cross-check that EBIT is not inflated by cutting back on investments)

Capital employed metrics

As explained earlier in our appendix on accounting basics, capital employed consists of working capital and fixed assets. Working capital is defined as current assets minus current liabilities. Three key components are: inventory; accounts receivable, as part of the current assets; and accounts payable, as part of the current liabilities. This key part of working capital can be measured through the cash conversion cycle:

cash conversion cycle (CCC) = days of inventory on hand (DIOH) + days of sales outstanding (DSO) – days of payables outstanding (DPO), with:

DIOH = inventory value / cost of goods sold × 365

DSO = accounts receivable / net sales × 365

DPO = accounts payable / cost of goods sold × 365

For inventory, another common metric is inventory turns, defined as:

inventory turns = cost of goods sold / inventory value

For many companies, the two main components of fixed assets are net property, plant and equipment (net PPE), and goodwill. Net PPE is the cumulative historical investment in physical assets minus the cumulative depreciation. Goodwill results from mergers and acquisitions (M&A) activity. If I buy a company for 100 million whereas the book value is only 50 million, then the delta can be booked as goodwill that is amortized over future periods. I'm typically prepared to pay more than the book value because I expect a certain amount of leverage; maybe the acquired company is active in a different continent where I expect to cross-sell my existing products. As such, it is an investment on which I want to generate EBIT. It should be leveraged equally well as a physical asset. In what follows we will measure the level of net PPE and fixed assets (and so, implicitly, the goodwill as the difference between the two), by looking at the net PPE turns and the fixed asset turns, defined as:

net PPE turns = net sales / net property, plant and equipment

fixed asset turns = net sales / fixed assets

The metrics are summarized in Figure 2.6

FIGURE 2.6 Key financial metrics on the margin side and the capital employed side

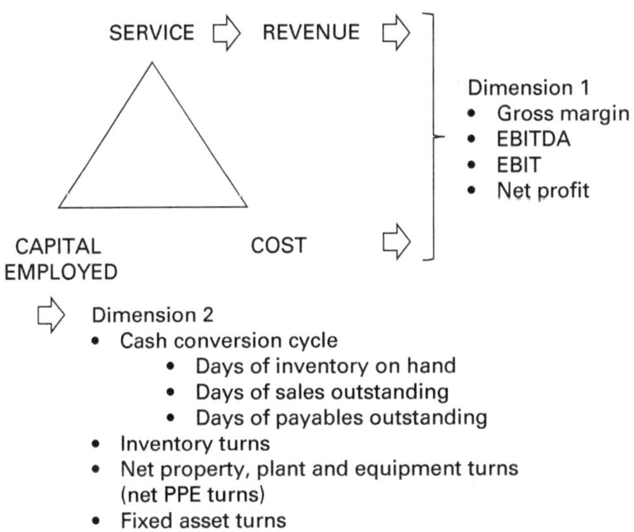

CASE STUDY

Benchmarking in one dimension: Henkel

WITH DR DIRK HOLBACH, CHIEF SUPPLY CHAIN OFFICER, LAUNDRY AND HOMECARE, HENKEL

Figure 2.7 shows the evolution of Henkel and P&G in the period 2007–15. Both companies are publicly listed so information is freely available from annual reports. This benchmark report is also available at www.strategydrivensupplychain.com/resources/benchmarkreport/Henkel-PG. Having the report open as you read through this section will make it easier to follow. You can also customize the report by selecting specific years, and adding or removing companies. Share your results and your thoughts on LinkedIn with #strategydrivensupplychain.

Looking at gross margin and EBIT, we see over the nine-year period that Henkel has been playing catch-up with P&G. Gross margins gradually improved to around a 50 per cent mark. EBIT dramatically improved in the period 2008–12 to stabilize at around 15 per cent. P&G found it difficult to sustain its 20 per cent EBIT after 2011. Still, if we judge by margins, many people would prefer P&G as an investment over Henkel.

The second row looks at inventory in both inventory turns and DIOH. For the turns we want to be as high as possible, as higher turns means less inventory. For DIOH we want to be as low as possible. We see that P&G has been improving its inventory position: inventory turns went gradually up, days gradually went down. Starting from the same turns or days in 2007, Henkel made exactly the opposite move. So here, once more, now judging by margins and inventory turns, two common and popular metrics, many people would prefer P&G as an investment over Henkel.

The third row looks at receivables and payables, and on the fourth row we combine DIOH, DSO and DPO into the CCC. For DSO, we like to have the lower value, as it means less financing of what customers have already bought. For DPO, we like it to be as high as possible, as it means more financing of the working capital by suppliers. Henkel is highest on both; the difference is around 20 days in 2007, and around 30–40 days in 2015, meaning that the CCC has gone down by 10–20 days as a result. The extension in payment terms to suppliers has been bigger than that to customers. Despite the weaker inventory position, the lead in DPO made Henkel better in working capital except for 2015, where P&G made a jump. That P&G jump in 2015 is a combined effort to further reduce inventory and DSO, and increase DPO. It almost feels like some kind of working capital reduction programme was running at P&G at that time. So, taking it all together, certainly when looking at 2015, we probably still prefer P&G as an investment over Henkel.

FIGURE 2.7 One-dimensional benchmark: Henkel playing catch-up on P&G

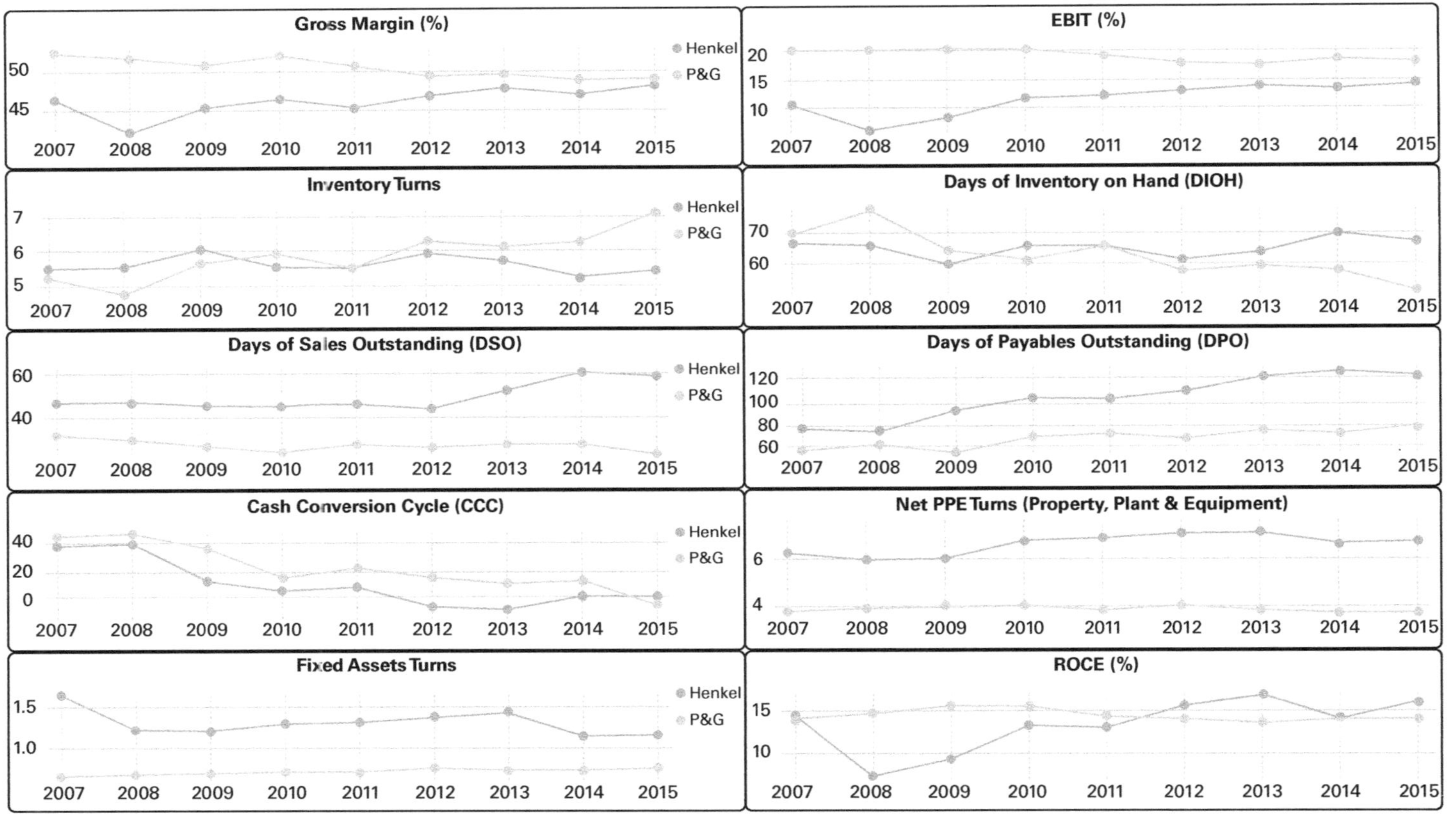

Rows four and five look at net PPE and fixed assets turns. This is where it gets interesting. Henkel is realizing all of the above results with roughly half of the net PPE and fixed assets compared to P&G. Both companies are loaded with a lot of goodwill, which shows from the difference in the net PPE and the fixed asset turns, but the ratios remain the same and the difference is both striking and relatively consistent. On net PPE, Henkel improved in the period 2009–13, whereas P&G was relatively stable. That translates to a comparable improvement in the fixed asset turns in that same period. The fixed asset turns take a hit in 2014, potentially after an acquisition. The lower fixed assets are a game-changer when it comes to ROCE. The CCC is close to zero, which means the main impact on capital employed comes from the fixed assets. Because of its significantly lower fixed assets, we can see from the ROCE graph that Henkel had already overtaken P&G by 2012 and remained better throughout the rest of the horizon. So which company would now be your preferred investment?

When asked about how supply chain has impacted the business and the business performance, Dirk Holbach, the CSCO of the Laundry and Homecare divisions, commented as follows:

> Supply chain impacts the business in two ways. First of all, we need to ensure agility. As a fast-moving consumer goods (FMCG) player, demand can change by a factor of two or three over a few days. Second, as a branded goods manufacturer, up to 40 per cent of sales are generated from products launched over the last three years. Our ability to launch new products quickly and reliably is key to our business strategy.

When asked which supply chain initiatives have supported the impressive business transformation shown in Figure 2.7, Dirk continues:

> In the period 2005–13 we worked on a number of key projects. First, we optimized our footprint and efficiency. We nearly halved the number of our factories from 50 to 27, and we reduced our headcount from around ten thousand to around six thousand. Second, we optimized our product portfolio. We reduced the number of SKUs by approximately 50 per cent, and by 2013 around 84 per cent of our sales was generated by the top 10 brands.

While Laundry and Homecare is only one of the three divisions, it is clear that this type of supply chain initiative has been key to the dramatic improvement in the years leading up to 2013. All of this, of course, had to be done while not compromising the required agility as a branded goods leader.

The next question is, of course, what the current initiatives are and how supply chain will continue to support the business results. Dirk answers:

> In recent years, Henkel has worked on the centralization of its supply chain activities for all three business units. This should allow a further harmonization and standardization of processes, which should further improve customer service levels and enhance efficiency. In fact, some processes like footprint optimization and the target setting and follow-up of KPIs have been fully centralized in Amsterdam, processes like net demand planning, production and supply planning have been centralized in six regional centres, while line scheduling is still organized in the factories.

When asked whether there are significant differences between the three business units, Dirk answers:

> We don't publish these figures in detail on a business unit level. In general, Laundry and Homecare does better on some aspects like the cash conversion cycle. Our fast movers are quite bulky in nature so we have to be very operationally excellent there. But, in general, Laundry and Homecare follows the general trend of the company and vice versa. In the financial report of 2016 Henkel announced four new strategic priorities running into 2020. One of them is 'increase agility'. Agility remains key and supply chain is key to agility. A second is 'drive growth' and a third is 'fund growth'. A further increase of efficiency and the further expansion of the global supply chain organization are key levers to generate the money required to fund our targeted growth. The fourth strategic priority is to 'accelerate digitalization'. Supply chain will also play a crucial role here, as we digitalize the relationship with our customers and consumers and translate that into improved agility and efficiency in the supply chain.

In summary, we can say that the consistent improvement in financials of Henkel is quite impressive. It is also clear from the figures and the comments of Dirk Holbach that supply chain is core to both the strategy and the financials. It has been instrumental in the improvements running up to 2013, and it remains core to the strategic priorities that were announced for 2020.

EXERCISE 2.1

Get to grip with your financials

- Calculate the ROCE for your business unit/company over the last 10 years.
- Look at the (one-dimensional) evolution of the underlying components:
  - margin: gross margin, EBITDA, EBIT, net profit
  - capital employed: inventory, accounts receivable, accounts payable, working capital, net property, plant and equipment, goodwill, fixed assets.

- Make a (one-dimensional) comparison with three sector peers/competitors.
- What do you conclude? Think about the comparison of Henkel and P&G. Any obvious margin differences or evolutions? What about working capital differences and evolutions? What about net PPE, goodwill and fixed assets? Who would you pick as the better investment over which period?

An easy benchmarking tool is available on the book website at www.strategydrivensupplychain.com/resources/benchmarkreport/. After creating an account, you can upload your company-specific data or synchronize it from an online source. You can then benchmark against sector peers in both one and two dimensions.

CASE STUDY

Benchmarking and target setting in two dimensions: Hero

The beauty of ROCE as a holistic metric doesn't stop with the one-dimensional benchmarking explained in the previous section. The real beauty starts when we start benchmarking in two dimensions.

Figure 2.8 shows a two-dimensional benchmark between Mondelez and Hershey. Each dot shows the combined performance of operating income (EBIT) and inventory turns. There are 10 dots for Mondelez and 10 dots for Hershey, corresponding with 10 years of historical performance. From the graph we see that Mondelez, on average, is doing better on inventory turns. From a ROCE perspective that is not necessarily a problem for

FIGURE 2.8 Operating income versus inventory turns for Mondelez versus Hershey

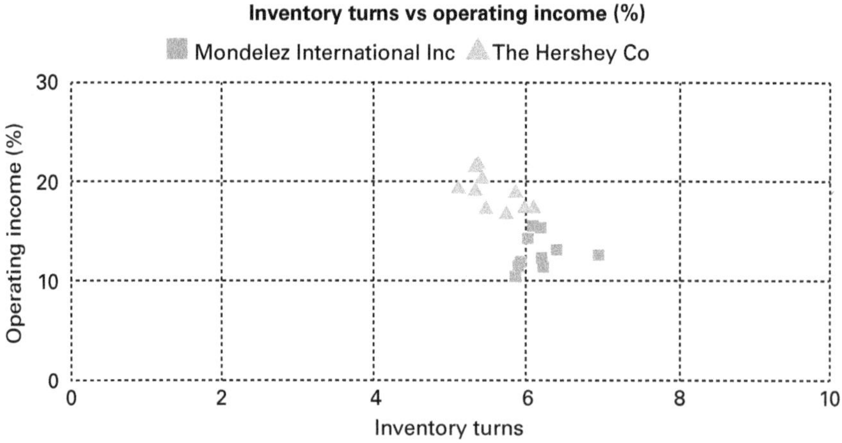

Hershey, as we see the operating income (EBIT) of Hershey is higher. As an investor, I am concerned with the EBIT over the capital employed, the combination of the two. In Figure 2.9 we build on that ROCE principle and add an indifference curve reflecting the best EBIT/inventory performance of Mondelez, which was reached in 2017, with a 15.35 per cent EBIT and inventory turns of 6.19. The indifference curve shows all the combinations of EBIT and inventory turns leading to the same EBIT/inventory or 'bang-for-the-buck' performance. More detail on how to draw these curves is included in Chapters 3, 4 and 5 of our first book, *Supply Chain Strategy and Financial Metrics.*[5]

As an investor, we would say that it is OK if you need a bit more inventory as long as the EBIT is higher, or vice versa – it is OK if the EBIT is a bit lower as long as you compensate by having less inventory. You can calculate and draw such indifference curves or 'bang-for-the-buck' lines for the minimum, median and maximum performance. The maximum performance is the most interesting, as this might become your internal reference to set targets. From Figure 2.9 we notice that many of the Hershey points are above the best performance curve of Mondelez. This implies, as we noted from Figure 2.8, that if Mondelez is doing better on inventory, that is not a problem for Hershey, as Hershey is doing better on EBIT and, as shown in Figure 2.9, from an overall 'EBIT/inventory' performance. While this sounds logical, it is disruptive, as the typical approach to benchmarking is to aim to be 'best in class' in any metric. When doing two-dimensional benchmarking we don't need to be best in class in all metrics; we want to be best in class in the balance between the two metrics.

FIGURE 2.9 Operating income versus inventory turns for Mondelez versus Hershey, including the best performance indifference curve for Mondelez

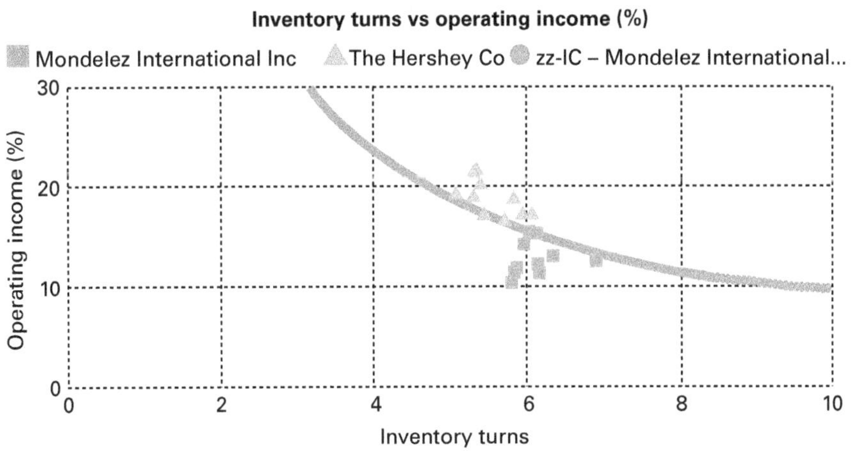

In Figure 2.10 we have added a third company, Hero, also a global FMCG player. Whereas Mondelez and Hershey seem somewhat different in balance but overall still in each other's neighbourhood, Hero is clearly lagging behind in both operating income (EBIT) and inventory turns. Ideally, we'd like to be at the top right of the graph; Hero is at the bottom left. When defining targets for operating income or inventory it

FIGURE 2.10 Operating income versus inventory turns: Hero versus Mondelez and Hershey

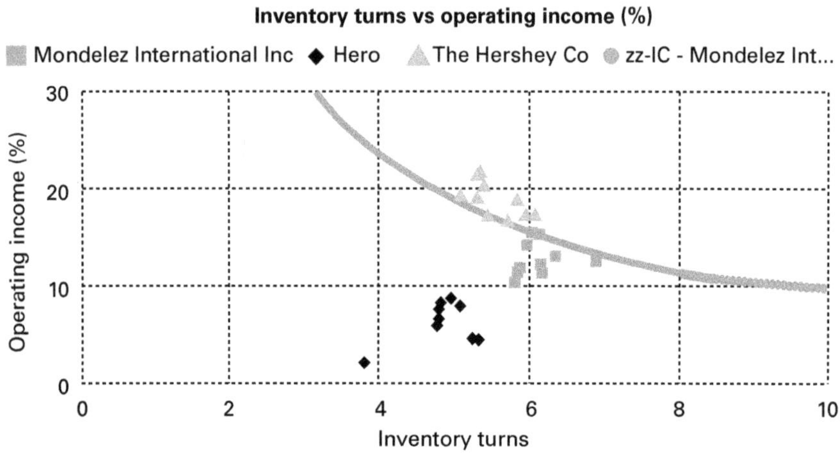

FIGURE 2.11 Operating income versus inventory turns: target setting for Hero based on best performance curve of Mondelez

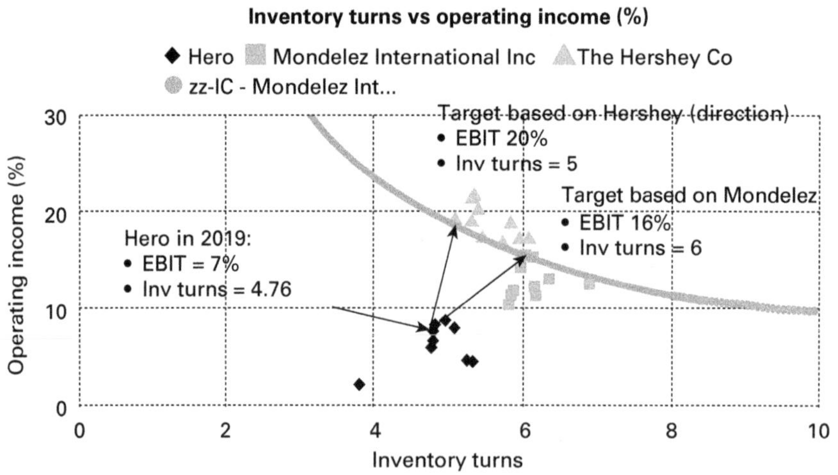

is again tempting to become best in class. However, no company is best in class in both operating income and inventory turns at the same time. That is not realistic. What we can do is use the best performance indifference curve of Mondelez as the reference, which is what we have done in Figure 2.11.

Figure 2.11 takes the 2019 performance of Hero, with an EBIT of 7 per cent and inventory turns of 4.76, and connects it to the best performance curve of Mondelez in two ways. One is going in the direction of Hershey, where the improvement is directed more towards EBIT improvement; a second is going in the direction of Mondelez, which is a more balanced improvement in both EBIT and inventory turns. A key question here is which one of the two to pick. In the next chapter we will explain what the position on the curve has to do with strategy.

Figure 2.12 illustrates that the same approach can be followed for other metrics, like net PPE turns. Here we see that the turns of Hero, which range from around 3 to around 3.5, are more in line with those of Mondelez, and there is a better overlap with those of Hershey, though the top performance of Hershey is extending up to net PPE turns of 4. We again show two possible directions for improvement. Starting from a Hero performance of 7 per cent EBIT in 2019, combined with net PPE turns of 3.18, going in the Hershey direction is now almost exclusively directed towards EBIT improvement, whereas improvement in the direction of the best performance of Mondelez is again more balanced over an improvement in both EBIT and net PPE turns.

FIGURE 2.12 Operating income versus net PPE turns: target setting for Hero based on best performance curve of Mondelez

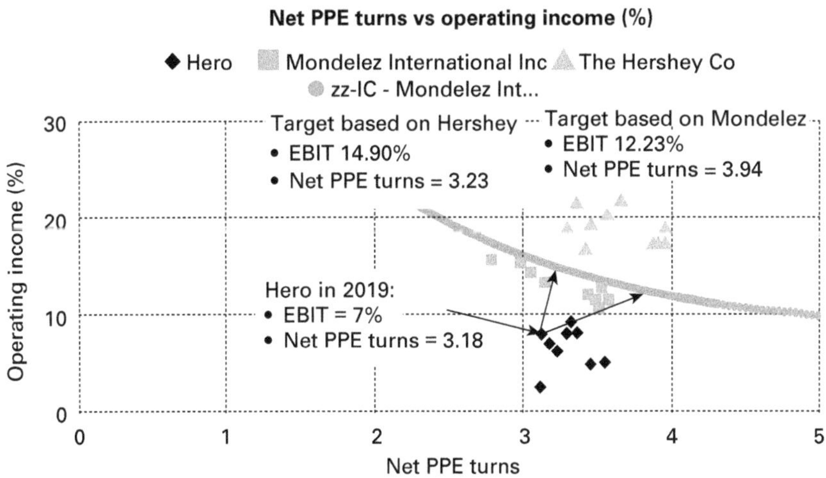

FIGURE 2.13 Target setting for inventory turns, CCC, net PPE turns and fixed asset turns

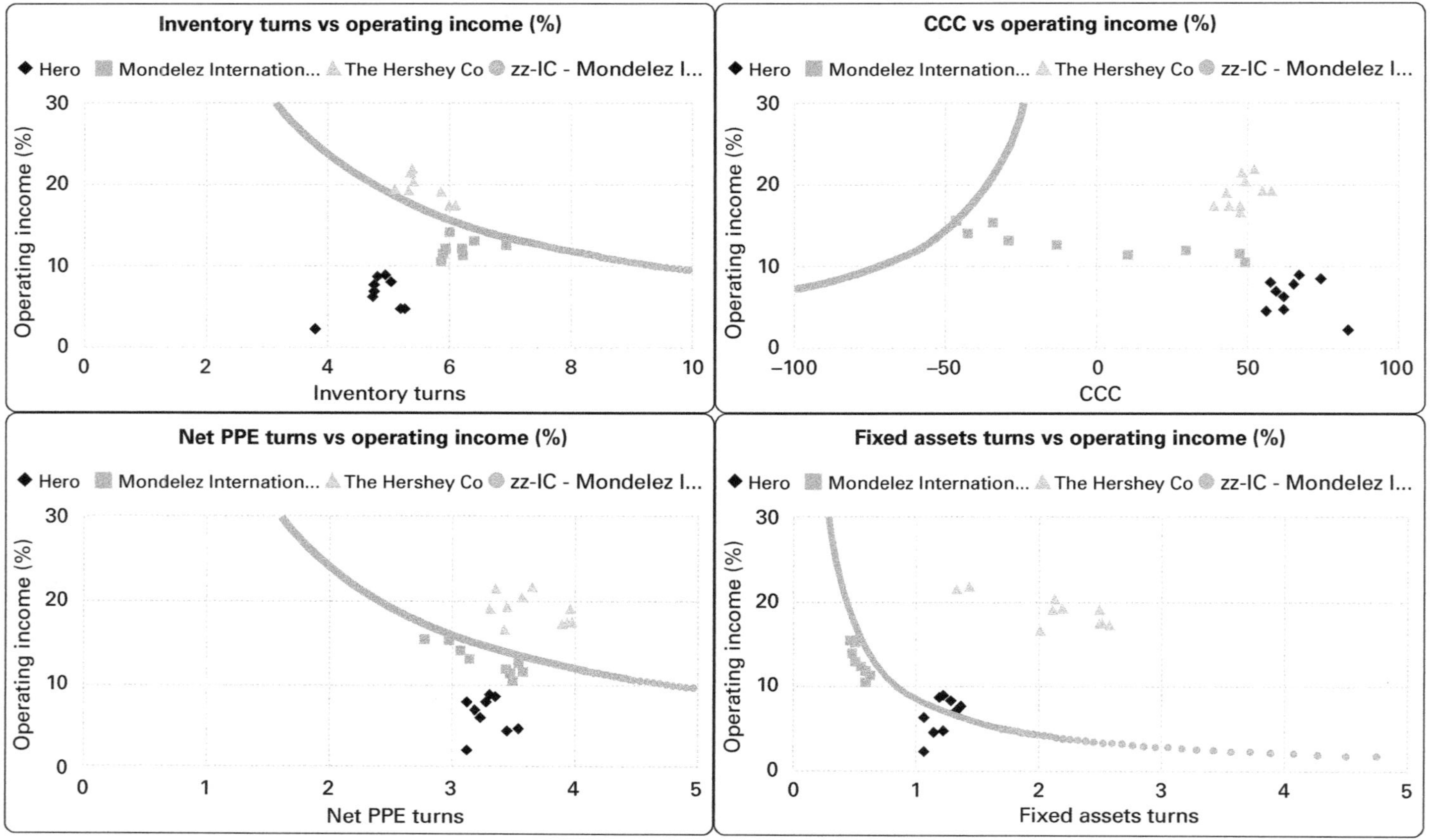

FIGURE 2.14 Picking the right benchmark when setting targets

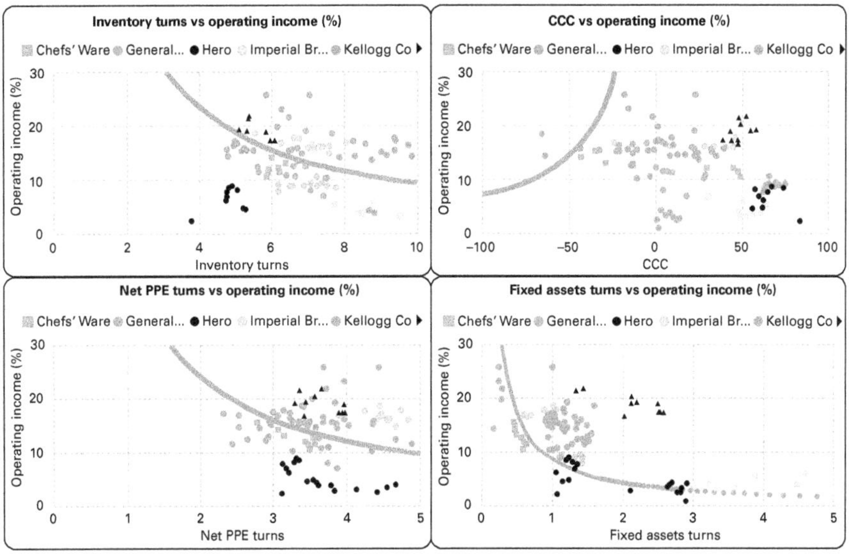

Name	Gross profit (%)	Operating income (%)	Inventory turns	DIOH	DPO	DSO	CCC	Net PPE turns	Fixed assets turns	ROCE (%)
The Hershey Co	42.44	16.70	5.74	63.56	44.54	28.52	47.54	3.42	2.01	34.37
Lotus Bakeries NV	40.58	17.81	9.37	38.96	66.29	36.64	9.32	3.14	1.16	20.27
PepsiCo Inc	55.08	15.58	10.36	35.23	79.68	33.18	−11.26	3.79	1.34	18.46
General Mills Inc	35.20	16.37	7.59	48.07	69.59	29.99	8.47	4.42	0.93	16.23
Nestle SA	50.77	15.83	5.26	69.38	153.84	40.75	−43.72	3.26	0.90	15.06
Kellogg Co	36.54	10.72	6.67	54.71	89.01	30.80	−3.50	3.65	1.07	13.11
Imperial Brands	21.55	9.18	6.20	58.90	15.93	31.94	74.91	14.11	1.10	11.22
Ter Beke	26.37	4.19	13.85	26.36	74.57	51.53	3.32	5.26	2.90	11.15
Hero	32.60	8.97	4.92	74.22	51.96	44.17	66.42	3.32	1.22	10.17
Chefs' Warehouse	25.25	3.96	10.19	35.82	26.82	39.18	48.17		3.23	8.98
Mondelez International Inc	39.07	13.16	6.40	57.06	122.89	36.76	−29.07	3.15	0.49	7.24
Kraft Heinz Co	36.19	23.19	6.30	57.96	86.30	12.37	−15.96	3.96	0.24	5.53
Treehouse Foods Inc	18.22	4.36	5.16	70.69	33.11	25.36	62.94	4.54	1.24	4.60

Figure 2.13 shows how this approach can be applied to different capital employed metrics, including inventory turns, CCC, net PPE turns and fixed asset turns. Comparable graphs can also be made for DSO and DPO.

Figure 2.14 shows a broader data set that includes many FMCG companies. The table at the bottom shows that Hero has a 10-year average ROCE of 10 per cent whereas Hershey is at 35 per cent. Picking Hershey as the reference is probably a bridge too far. Hero might formulate the ambition to go from 10 per cent to 15 per cent ROCE, realized by Nestlé. Once it has reached the level of Nestlé, it is probably ready to shift ambition to that of PepsiCo or Lotus, with a ROCE of around 20 per cent. When it has reached that level, Hero might be ready to target Hershey.

As with the other benchmarks, this benchmark report is also available from the book's website at www.strategydrivensupplychain.com/resources/benchmarkreport/FoodCompanies. Build your own benchmark reports by changing the selections on companies and/or the years to include. Share your outcomes and ideas on LinkedIn with #strategydrivensupplychain.

Check out our other sector benchmarks at www.strategydrivensupplychain.com/resources/benchmarkreport/

EXERCISE 2.2

Define your targets

- Now extend your analysis into two dimensions.
- Start with EBIT versus inventory turns. Add your own best performance line and that of two key competitors. Who is best in class in inventory? Who is best in class in EBIT? Who is best in class in value, EBIT/inventory? Whom would you take as a reference? What are the possible targets if you start from your own and latest best performance?
- Repeat the exercise for EBIT versus net PPE turns.
- Look at a list of sector peers. Where are you with your ROCE? What seems like a good first step? Who would be a reference company for that ROCE level? What seems like a logical next step?

An easy benchmarking tool is available on the book website at www.strategydrivensupplychain.com/resources/benchmarkreport/. After creating an account, you can upload your company-specific data or synchronize it from an online source. You can benchmark against sector peers in both one and two dimensions.

ROCE versus ROE and ROA

In the first part of this chapter we introduced ROCE as a balancing metric across the triangle and have shown how it can be used for benchmarking and target setting. In this second part we compare ROCE to other common financial metrics, starting with other return metrics, and then linking it to growth, EBITDA and free cash flow.

Though the return on capital employed seems the 'natural' financial metric to balance the triangle, as it naturally boils up from the margin (EBIT) and the capital employed presented in the triangle, other financial metrics like ROE or ROA seem more popular. So which return metric should we use, and how do they compare?

Let's start by comparing ROCE and ROE. Once more, we strongly recommend reviewing the accounting basics in the appendix to Chapter 1. Getting to grips with financial metrics and their differences is essential in better understanding how to drive value through the triangle.

ROCE and ROE are defined as:

ROCE = EBIT / capital employed, with capital employed = fixed assets + working capital

ROE = net income / owners' equity

ROCE has EBIT in the numerator versus net income for ROE. The difference is the interest and the taxes. EBIT is something operational, it starts from gross margin, it accounts for SG&A, and for depreciation and amortization, which is related to the depreciation of the fixed assets. The interest and taxes are something financial. So from an operational perspective we prefer to work with EBIT or EBITDA instead of net income.

ROCE has capital employed in the denominator. ROE has equity. As shown in Figure 2.15, equity plus long-term liabilities equals capital employed. Remember that capital employed is working capital plus fixed assets, and working capital is current assets minus current liabilities. Working capital is shown as the shaded area on the assets side of the balance sheets.

Figure 2.15 also shows that, for the same EBIT, increasing the leverage (increasing the debt over equity or D/E ratio) can increase the ROE. That is shown on the right-hand side of Figure 2.15. Some simple maths shows that the ROE will increase by increasing the leverage, as long as your net extra interest (interest after accounting for the tax advantage) is lower than the original ROE. Leverage and increasing ROE by increasing leverage are again financial, not operational. So from an operational perspective we prefer to work with capital employed instead of equity. Capital employed is about working capital and fixed assets, two very tangible things from an operational perspective.

Our first conclusion is that we prefer ROCE over ROE because it is more closely linked to operations. ROE includes the effects of the leverage, the amount of debt versus equity, and the interest and taxes that are financial in nature.

And what about ROCE versus ROA? ROCE and ROA are defined as:

ROCE = EBIT / capital employed, with capital employed = fixed assets + working capital

ROA = net income / total assets

FIGURE 2.15 ROCE versus ROE

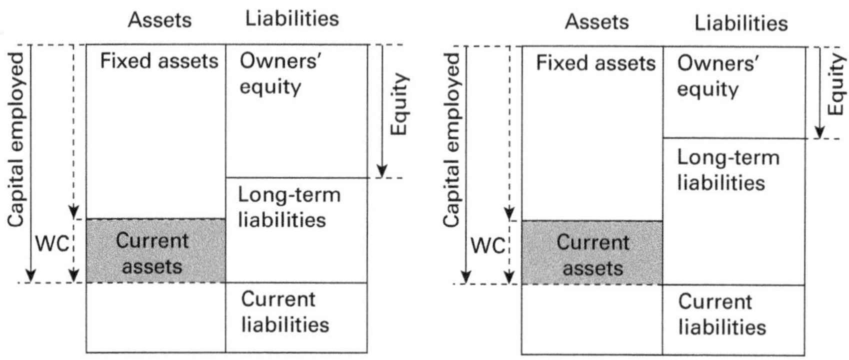

FIGURE 2.16 ROCE versus ROA

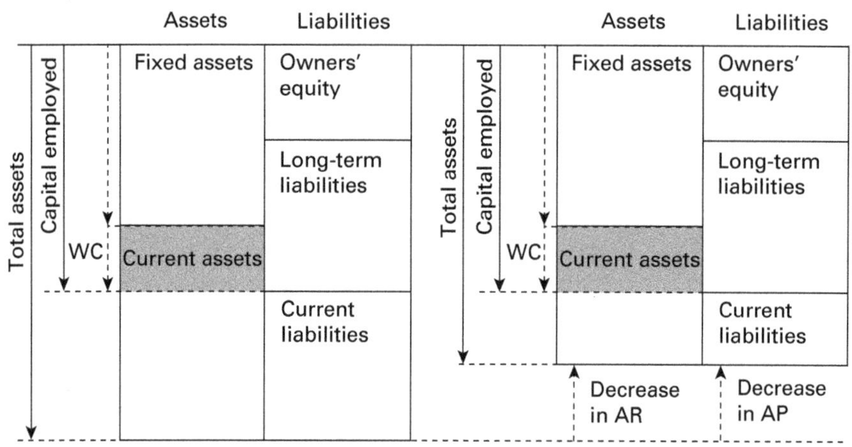

The difference in the numerator is the same as for ROCE versus ROE, EBIT versus net income. The difference in the denominator is now the capital employed versus the total assets. Figure 2.16 shows a situation where the total assets have been decreased by a decrease in accounts receivable and a corresponding decrease in accounts payable. Maybe we were pushed by key suppliers to reduce the payment terms and in a reaction have successfully reduced the payment terms to key customers as well. The net effect on the working capital (WC) is zero, so the ROCE is unaffected. However, the total assets have been reduced so the ROA increases. We don't really see an increase in value in the illustrated case, though. So, again, in this example we prefer ROCE over ROA. We prefer to discuss the capital employed, composed of the working capital and the fixed assets, both very tangible things, instead of the total assets.

CASE STUDY

Henkel: ROCE versus earnings per share

WITH DR DIRK HOLBACH, CHIEF SUPPLY CHAIN OFFICER, LAUNDRY AND HOMECARE, HENKEL

When discussing ROCE with Dr Dirk Holbach, the CSCO of Henkel Laundry and Homecare, he mentioned, 'We use ROCE at the board level, but at the management level we are incentivized on earnings per share. If you could prove to me that ROCE drives earnings per share then I might get the interest of our CFO.'

In a simple version, EPS = net income / number of shares. EPS is driven by ROE = net income / equity. If ROE goes up, then EPS will go up. That could be done by increasing the net income or by reducing the equity, for instance by a share buy-back and subsequent destruction of the shares.

In the previous section we explained that the difference between ROE and ROCE is the 'leverage', the amount of debt versus the amount of equity, typically measured through the D/E ratio. We explained that the ROE can be 'pimped' by 'increasing the leverage' if the net interest (interest after accounting for the tax advantage) is lower than the starting ROE. So the question is whether we can 'prove' that ROCE and D/E together define the ROE.

To study the relationship between ROCE, D/E and ROE, we analysed a set of 30 FMCG companies for which we calculated a 10-year average ROCE, ROE and D/E ratio.[6] Figure 2.17 shows the regression output for the unfiltered data set. On the top left we see the linear regression where we try to explain ROE based on ROCE. For a regression model to have predictive power, the R^2 should be at least 80 per cent. In this case it is close to zero, which means, with ROCE alone, we cannot explain any of the variance in the ROE.

On the top right in Figure 2.17 we see the linear regression where we try to explain ROE based on D/E. The R^2 is now 0.9, which is good. For this unfiltered data set, around 90 per cent of the variability in the ROE is explained by the D/E alone. However, in both graphs there are outliers. There seems to be a nucleus of points with an ROCE of up to 0.4 and an ROE of up to 1.6 and some more isolated points scattered around that. Figure 2.18 shows the results when we remove these outliers. We want to build a model for the core, not for the outliers.

When filtering for the outliers, we have 23 of the 30 companies left. ROCE is now between 5 per cent and 35 per cent, which are common percentages. The ROE is now between 0 and 1.2, the D/E between 0.5 and 8. Zooming in on the core reveals different behaviour. The importance of ROCE as an explanatory variable has increased, whereas the importance of D/E is reduced. With an R^2 of 0.53 (graph on the left) and 0.34 (graph on the right) none of the two (ROCE and D/E) are satisfactory on their own, so what we can do next is build a multiple linear

FIGURE 2.17 ROCE versus ROE and D/E versus ROE – uncleaned raw data

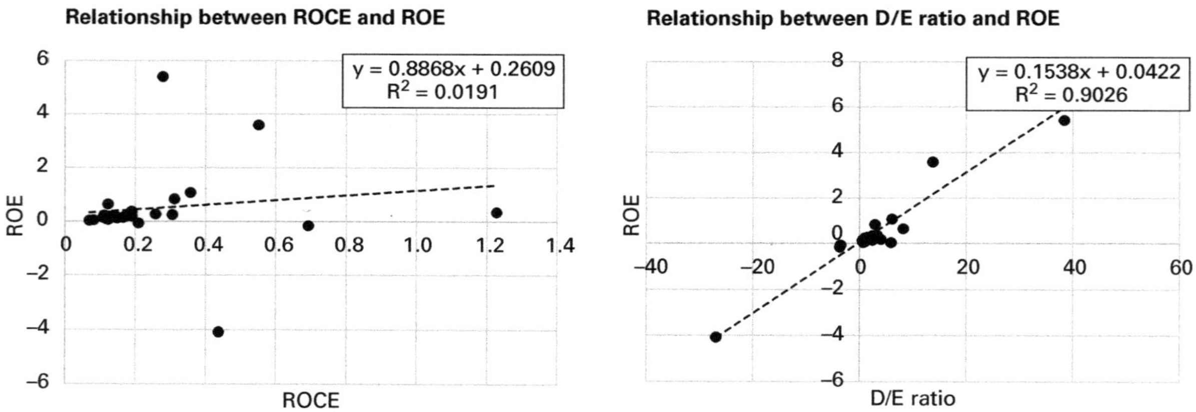

FIGURE 2.18 ROCE versus ROE and D/E versus ROE – cleaned data, outliers removed

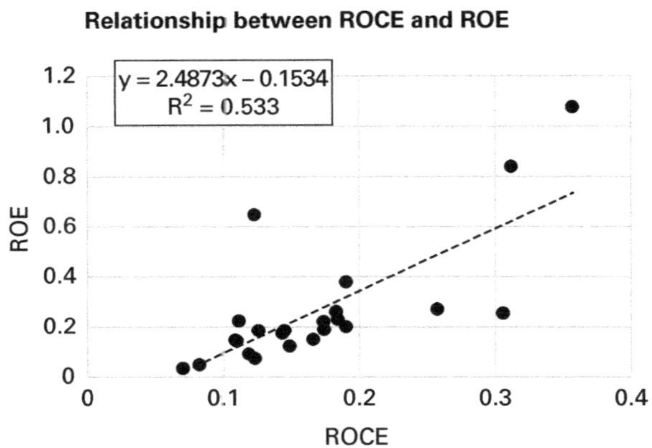

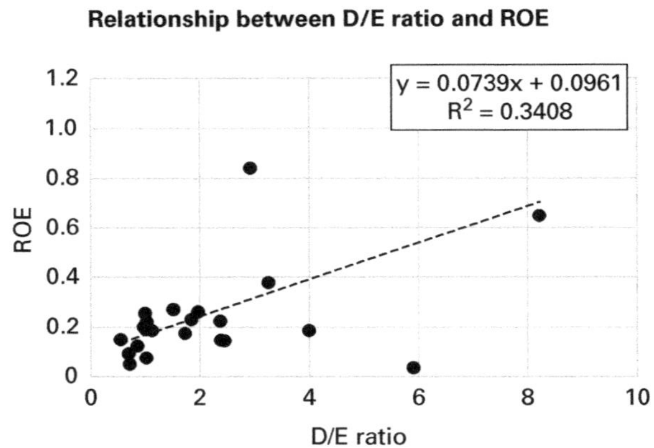

FIGURE 2.19 ROCE and D/E versus ROE – cleaned data, outliers removed

Relationship between ROCE, D/E ratio and ROE

Regression statistics						
Multiple R	0.91					
R Square	0.83					
Adjusted R square	0.82					
Standard error	0.11					
Observations	23					
ANOVA						
	df	*SS*	*MS*	*F*	*Significance F*	
Regression	2	1.18	0.59	50.18	0.00	
Residual	20	0.23	0.01			
Total	22	1.41				
	Coefficients	*Standard error*	*t stat*	*P-value*	*Lower 95%*	*Upper 95%*
Intercept	–0.30	0.06	–4.82	0.00	–0.43	–0.17
Average of ROCE	2.40	0.31	7.70	0.00	1.75	3.04
Average of D/E ratio	0.07	0.01	6.02	0.00	0.05	0.09

regression where we take both ROCE and D/E as inputs trying to model the ROE. That result is shown in Figure 2.19.

If you're not used to reading a regression output, let me help you through. The most important factor is to look at the R^2: that is, the predictive power of the regression model for the data set at hand. If there are multiple input variables, look at the adjusted R^2, which in this case is 0.82. It means that the model explains 82 per cent of the variance in the ROE. So where individually ROCE and D/E were explaining 0.53 and 0.34, together they explain 0.82, which is useful. The other interesting elements to look at are the 'coefficients'. Based on the coefficients, we can build the linear regression equation, which in this case is:

$$\text{ROE} = -0.30 + 2.40 \times \text{ROCE} + 0.07 \times \text{D/E ratio}$$

Using this regression formula, we can predict ROE, starting from ROCE and D/E. If the p-values shown next to the coefficients are less than 0.05 we say they are statistically significant, which is the case here. This means our regression model has practical relevance.

The coefficient of ROCE is 2.40, which we might interpret as ROCE being more influential than D/E, for which the coefficient is 0.07. But don't be mistaken. The coefficient of ROCE is larger because the range of ROCE is smaller. The minimum ROCE is 0,07 and the maximum is 0.36. The coefficient for D/E is smaller as the range of D/E is wider: the minimum D/E is 0.55 and the maximum is 8.22. To better understand the relative importance of ROCE versus D/E in predicting ROE, we can look at what impact the minimum and maximum ROCE (and D/E) have on ROE. For ROCE, the minimum and maximum lead to an impact of 2.40 x 0.07 and 2.40 x 0.36 on ROE, which is 0.17 to 0.86 or a range of 0.69. For D/E the minimum and maximum lead to an impact of 0.07 x 0.55 and 0.07 x 8.22, which is 0.04 to 0.57 or a range of 0.53. So we can say that ROCE is slightly more influential to ROE over the D/E ratio.

In summary, if we remove the outliers and focus on the core of the data set, we find good evidence that ROCE and D/E explain a significant part of the ROE. From the two variables, ROCE is slightly more influential. So, in answer to Dirk Holbach's question, yes, we believe ROCE is driving earnings per share, at least in the set of FMCG companies studied in this example. The underlying principle, that the difference between ROCE and ROE is the debt structure, makes us believe it can be generalized far beyond this example data set.

Mapping growth, EBITDA and free cash flow to the triangle

Despite our enthusiasm for ROCE, we rarely see it as a prominent metric in annual reports, in analyst briefings or in financial newspapers. When talking to a recently retired CFO, he was more concerned with growth, EBITDA and free cash flow than with ROCE. To understand the link with ROCE, let's map growth, EBITDA and free cash flow to our supply chain triangle, in a comparable way to how we mapped ROCE in Figure 2.3.

Figure 2.20 maps growth and EBITDA to the supply chain triangle. As explained in Figure 2.1, driving growth is typically done by driving service in the market. A broader geographical reach, a broader product portfolio, a newer, better performing version of a product... all of these can be considered extra service or extra value delivered to the customers.

EBITDA, like EBIT, can be derived from combining revenue and cost or combining the service and the cost side of the triangle. The former CFO I talked to preferred EBITDA over EBIT as it is a better proxy for cash flow. The D&A subtracted from the EBITDA to derive the EBIT doesn't have a cash impact. The D&A are also relatively fixed. They depend on CAPEX investments that have been done over the last few years. For bigger investments such as new production plants the depreciation can run over 20 or 30 years. The former CFO prefers to focus on the more variable pieces like the EBITDA (and the working capital and the CAPEX – we will come to that). Those are the ones to monitor and steer with.

FIGURE 2.20 Mapping growth and EBITDA to the supply chain triangle

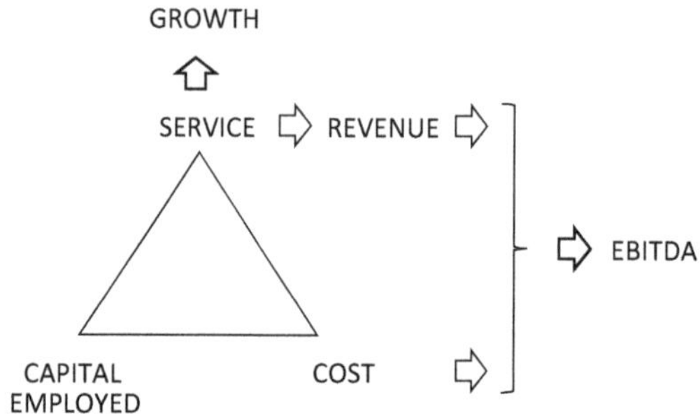

Out of growth, EBITDA and free cash flow, FCF is the more difficult to understand. As explained in our appendix on accounting basics in Chapter 1, FCF is roughly speaking equal to the cash flow from operations minus CAPEX. The more exact definition is:

$$\text{FCF} = \text{EBIT} \times (1 - \text{tax rate}) - \Delta\text{WC} + \text{D\&A} - \text{CAPEX}$$

where EBIT × (1 – tax rate) is also called the net operating profit after tax (NOPAT), ΔWC are the changes in working capital, D&A are depreciation and amortization, and CAPEX is the capital expenditure or investment in fixed assets. An increase in working capital is cash out, so it is subtracted. CAPEX is cash out as well, so it is also subtracted. D&A are not cash out so they can be added.

The free cash flow measures the amount of cash available for all security holders, including both equity holders and debt holders. The last one (cash available to debt holders) is the reason we use NOPAT instead of net profit as in the cash flow from operations. The cash flow from operations uses net profit, which includes interest on loans; for free cash flow, we use NOPAT.

$$\text{Cash flow from operations} = \text{net profit} - \Delta\text{WC} + \text{D\&A}$$

The cash flow from operations doesn't include CAPEX, which in the cash flow statement is part of the cash flow from investments. Once more we refer to the appendix on accounting basics in Chapter 1 for more details.

We can further simplify our equation for free cash flow as follows:

$$\text{FCF} = \text{EBIT} \times (1 - \text{tax rate}) - \Delta\text{WC} - \Delta\text{FA}$$

where ΔFA are the changes in fixed assets, equal to CAPEX minus depreciation and amortization. If CAPEX exceeds D&A, net fixed assets will increase.

$$\Delta FA = CAPEX - D\&A$$

And once we're there, we can further simplify our equation for free cash flow and say:

$$FCF = EBIT \times (1 - \text{tax rate}) - \Delta CE$$

with ΔCE being the changes in capital employed, consisting of the changes in working capital and fixed assets (being CAPEX minus depreciation and amortization):

$$\Delta CE = \Delta WC + \Delta FA$$

That brings us to what is shown in Figure 2.21. Free cash flow is derived from the 'margin side' of the triangle, through NOPAT, and from the capital employed side of the triangle, by looking at the changes in capital employed. The changes in capital employed are derived as the changes in working capital and fixed assets, with the changes in fixed assets being CAPEX minus depreciation and amortization.

FIGURE 2.21 Mapping growth, EBITDA and free cash flow to the supply chain triangle

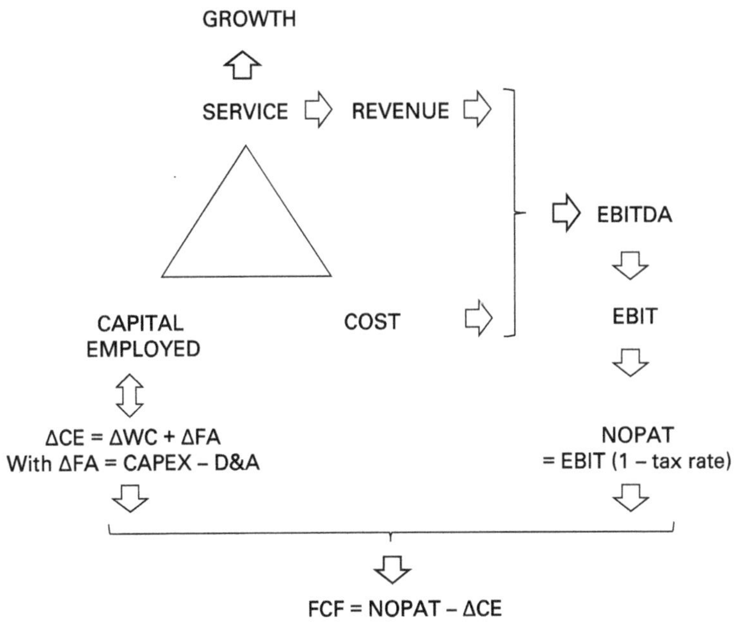

The importance of free cash flow

If we continue working with our definition FCF = EBIT x (1 – tax rate) – ΔCE, the fallacy of this definition is that it makes you think that free cash flow follows as the result of the elements on the right. So, depending on EBIT and the changes in capital employed, free cash flow follows as a result.

In practice, it works the other way around. We start from a required free cash flow. The CFO will look at what needs to happen on the debt side. Do any loans need to be repaid? Can these be financed by new loans, or do we need to reduce our overall debt levels? High debt levels typically lead to higher interest rates. Banks control that through the so-called covenants attached to the loans they provide. Higher interest rates may create pressure to reduce the overall debt level. Reducing the overall debt level will consume cash. The CFO will also look at what needs to happen on the equity side. What are the expectations on dividends from the shareholders? Is there any need for a share buy-back? Both again consume cash.

Free cash flow seems to be a key metric to those in finance. People seem to be hung up on it. And gradually I start to understand why. If you are the CFO, you don't want to ask shareholders to cut back on dividends. Nor do you want to go back to the banks to say the planned debt restructuring cannot happen as planned. As a CFO you don't want to make the investors and debt holders nervous. That would probably be your fastest way to the exit. Free cash flow is predominant and that has some ramifications.

So, in practice, free cash flow is predominant. It is a constraint to the operating plan. If the target is 100 million we go for 100 million. If the EBIT is less than expected, we will not cut back on free cash flow, but we will cut back on working capital or on CAPEX. Out of the two, my feeling is that working capital is the more popular. We rarely see working capital as a value-adding investment. As mentioned at the start of Chapter 1, inventory is poorly understood and too many people think it is 'elastic'. That explains why pushing inventories down is a favourite source of cash. This explains how we obtain pressure in our supply chain triangle as shown in Figure 1.7.

We see companies where the ability to invest in working capital and fixed assets through CAPEX is very limited. There are different possible reasons for this. If your EBIT is structurally too low and you have an important amount of debt and some demands of the shareholders, then little room for investment will remain. I've seen companies where the EBIT was healthy, but over two or three years the leverage needed to be significantly reduced. That can limit the cash available for investing in that two- to three-year period. I have also seen companies with a healthy EBIT, but where shareholders were siphoning a disproportionate amount of cash from the company through dividends to support their lavish lifestyle. That can also be a reason why the headroom for investments is limited. Of course, any of these are OK in the short term, but underinvestment leads to problems over the long term.

Mapping growth, free cash flow and ROCE to the triangle

In Figure 2.22 we have combined our ROCE reasoning from Figure 2.3 with the growth, EBITDA and free cash flow reasoning from Figure 2.21.

We believe in ROCE as a metric for the reasons explained earlier in this chapter. EBIT, working capital and fixed assets are very tangible things to steer with from an operational perspective. ROCE helps companies in their struggle to balance the triangle. If as a CFO you feel more comfortable in steering with EBITDA, working capital and CAPEX as the 'short-term components', that's fine, as long as you know where you're going from a long-term value or ROCE perspective.

As ROCE starts from EBIT we have kept EBIT instead of EBITDA as a margin metric in Figure 2.22. As explained earlier, D&A are relatively fixed in the short term, which means that in the short term controlling EBIT means controlling EBITDA and vice versa.

We understand that growth and free cash flow are important and are different in nature, so they need to be added. A common valuation method of companies is based on discounted free cash flows.[7] In this case, an analyst forecasts the business's free cash flow into the future and discounts it back to today at the firm's weighted average cost of capital (WACC). Growth is meant to increase the future free cash flow, and as such increase the value of a company. So growth is important. It needs to be planned and monitored. Next to being a 'short-term constraint' on 'changes in working capital and CAPEX', free cash flow also defines the value of the business. That further stresses the importance of the metric. It needs to be planned and monitored separately, not only in the short term, but also in the long term. So if we want to get finance and investors on board, we'll need to monitor more than just ROCE. We'll need to add growth and free cash flow at the minimum, as shown in Figure 2.22.

What also follows from Figure 2.22 is that ROCE and free cash flow are almost two sides of the same coin. ROCE looks at EBIT over a snapshot

FIGURE 2.22 Mapping growth, ROCE and free cash flow to the supply chain triangle

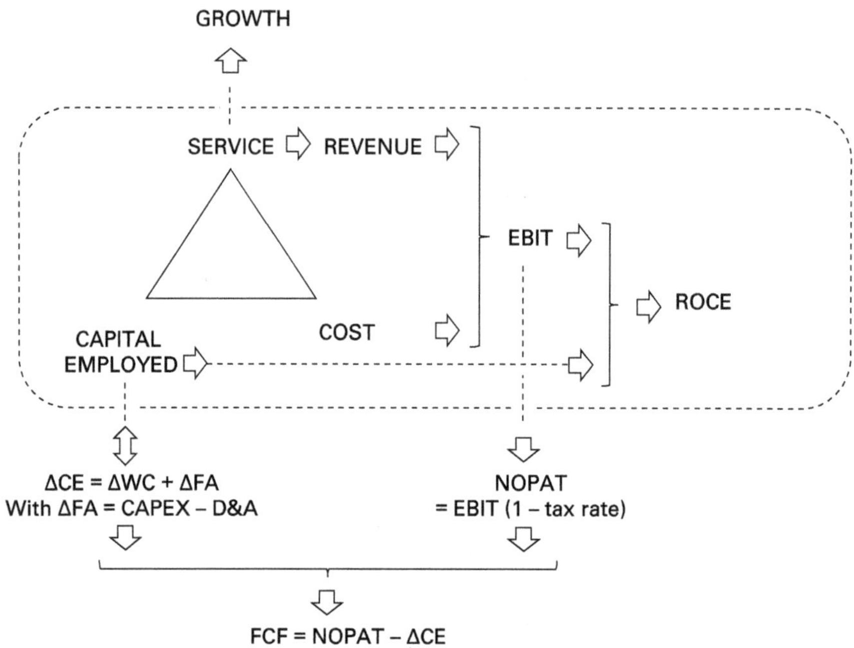

of capital employed, typically at the end of the year. Free cash flow looks at EBIT and the changes in capital employed. It is interesting to understand how growth impacts both ROCE and free cash flow from that perspective.

How growth impacts free cash flow and ROCE

Growth typically requires investments in new plants, new warehouses, working capital, new products, marketing... That may weigh in on EBIT and NOPAT. It may require an investment in working capital and fixed assets, so it may weigh in on capital employed. From Figure 2.22 it will be clear that growth weighs in on free cash flow. A disappointing EBIT may cause a strain on our growth plans and objectives.

Figure 2.22 also shows that growth will weigh on ROCE. If we invest in a new production plant, its full capacity will typically only be reached after a couple of years. We basically have full investment in the fixed assets, but we don't have the volume or EBIT yet to bring us to a decent ROCE. As we start up a plant, we typically also have a learning curve. That will further weigh on EBIT and as such on ROCE.

So, in short, growth consumes cash and reduces free cash flow. Growth requires investment in capital employed and has a learning curve, which weighs on ROCE. ROCE and free cash flow are almost like two sides of the same coin. They typically move together.

Conclusion

We started this chapter by linking the triangle to finance through the return on capital employed. We showed how ROCE can be used as a balancing metric across the three corners of the triangle and as a decision criterion to make trade-offs in the triangle. We used ROCE as the basis for financial benchmarking of companies and to set targets for the financial metrics related to ROCE.

Next, we compared ROCE to popular alternatives like return on equity and return on assets, and argued why we prefer ROCE. We mapped growth, EBITDA and free cash flow to our triangle, as these commonly appear in financial reporting. We explained the importance of free cash flow both as a short-term metric, limiting the room for changes in working capital and CAPEX, and as a long-term metric, defining the value of a company.

We concluded by showing that ROCE and FCF are like two sides of the same coin. ROCE looks at EBIT and a snapshot of capital employed. FCF looks at NOPAT = EBIT x (1 – tax rate) and the changes in capital employed. They tend to go together. Companies pursue growth to increase the future value of the company, but in the short term it weighs on FCF and ROCE.

In the next chapter we will introduce the strategy model of Treacy and Wiersema, which describes three archetypical strategies called 'operational excellence', 'customer intimacy' and 'product leadership'. We will analyse how these different strategies impact the balance in our supply chain triangle and how we drive ROCE as a company.

Notes

1 McBride plc, *Manufacturing our Future: McBride plc annual report and accounts 2015*, www.mcbride.co.uk/investors/results-centre/ (archived at https://perma.cc/4GQB-32FR)

2 McBride plc, *Preparing for Growth: McBride plc results and strategy presentation: September 2016*, www.mcbride.co.uk/media/dxsdgaae/mcbride-results-and-strategy-presentation-2016.pdf (archived at https://perma.cc/6SKY-FSLG)

3 McBride plc, *Preparing for Growth: McBride plc annual report and accounts 2016*, www.mcbride.co.uk/media/gkgj4tqv/mcbride-annual-report-2016.pdf (archived at https://perma.cc/24H9-9LE3)

4 B DeSmet (2018) *Supply Chain Strategy and Financial Metrics: The supply chain triangle of service, cost and cash*, Kogan Page, London

5 B DeSmet (2018) *Supply Chain Strategy and Financial Metrics: The supply chain triangle of service, cost and cash*, Kogan Page, London

6 The following publicly listed companies were taken into account for the FMCG benchmark: Procter and Gamble, Colgate-Palmolive, Estée Lauder, Johnson and Johnson, Avon Products Inc, Ecolab Inc, Coty, L Brands Inc, Clorox CO, Church and Dwight Co Inc, Sealed Air Corp, Nature's Sunshine Products Inc, Nu Skin Enterprises Inc, Revlon Inc, Inter Parfums Inc, Tupperware Brands Corp, Helen of Troy Ltd, Herbalife Nutrition Ltd, Hain Celestial Group, PepsiCo Inc, Coca-Cola Co, Nestlé SA, Unliver NV ADR, L'Oréal SA, Strauss Group Ltd, Kraft Heinz, Imperial Brands, Anheuser-Busch InBev SA/NV, Philip Morris International Inc, Celsius Holdings Inc

7 Corporate Finance Institute, What are the main valuation methods? https://corporatefinanceinstitute.com/resources/knowledge/valuation/valuation-methods/ (archived at https://perma.cc/2EWD-WZJJ)

03

Strategy in the supply chain triangle

In this chapter we will introduce the strategy model of Treacy and Wiersema and show how different strategies lead to different trade-offs in the supply chain triangle. We will show that different strategies are in fact different routes to generate ROCE, in a different balance between EBIT and capital employed. This implies that different strategies lead to different targets for key financial metrics.

We will expand on our two-dimensional benchmarking technique introduced in Chapter 2 and further explain that different strategies lead to a different positioning on the 'indifference curves'. We will revisit the example of Hero, and we will add McBride as a private label player to the benchmark of P&G and Henkel. These examples will help us in understanding how to account for strategy when defining targets for our financial metrics like gross margin, EBIT and the different capital employed metrics.

We conclude this chapter by introducing our strategy-driven scorecard. We will argue that many S&OP dashboards lack a strong financial and strategic perspective, and many 'financial' or 'business' dashboards lack a strategic and operational perspective. We need to become stronger in setting targets and then we need to become stronger in monitoring. We use our supply chain triangle as the starting point to ensure our dashboard helps in balancing the triangle.

The three strategic options of Treacy and Wiersema

Treacy and Wiersema argue that in any sector, a company can be a market leader by excelling in one of three dimensions only.[1] The company is a product leader, a leader by operational excellence, or a leader by customer intimacy. We will give our interpretation of these three extremes and then analyse the impact on the supply chain triangle.

Operational excellence

An opex (operational excellence) leader prevails by low-cost and hassle-free, no-nonsense, easy service. They focus on being the cheapest in combination with being easy to deal with. Commonly used examples are low-cost airlines like Southwest or Ryanair, which have disrupted the airline sector by a relentless focus on low-cost and hassle-free service.

Operational excellence as a strategy is not to be mistaken for 'lean' or operational excellence as a management philosophy to improve operations, and as originally described in the books of Womack and Jones.[2] Applying the principles of 'lean manufacturing' to both manufacturing processes and administrative processes will help to reduce throughput times and work in progress (WIP), and improve quality measures like first pass yield (FPY).[3] Regardless of your strategy, applying the principles of lean manufacturing will improve the operations in that it will improve service (eg through better quality), at a lower cost (eg less rework) and with a lower working capital (eg less WIP). Its principles of 'flow' and its techniques like 5S apply to a very broad range of production and administrative processes. In that sense, it is what you could truly call a 'best practice'. If operational excellence is my strategy, I will translate the outcome of any lean implementations into a lower price for my customer. If I'm a product leader, the goal may be different, eg reducing throughput times to reduce time to market, and any improvements in cost or working capital will be invested in better products instead of lower prices.

An opex leader has a relentless focus on lowering cost. In addition to lean, a second important principle or management philosophy is simplicity. Even without a lot of explanation, we feel intuitively that simplicity drives efficiency and that efficiency lowers cost, which in turn allows the price to be lower. Crawford and Mathews give the example of Dollar General as a price player.[4] They mention simplicity and values as two critical success factors for Dollar General. Simplicity translates into every aspect of the business. One example is limited price points. To keep things simple for the customers, and for the company, Dollar General features only 14 price points. This reduces check-out, accounting and inventory time. It allows suppliers to preprint item prices on the packaging. Another example is a limited choice. Dollar General limits itself to 4,500 SKUs, compared with about 35,000 offered by Wal mart. A comparable example in Europe can be given by Colruyt. Colruyt is a retail group headquartered in Belgium, of which the biggest branch is called Colruyt Lowest Prices. Their slogan is 'simply retail'.[5] The 'simply' refers to simplicity as a core principle to guarantee the 'lowest prices' in the name of the branch.

So where does that leave the service delivered by an opex leader? An opex leader doesn't give bad service; on the contrary, they focus on delivering excellent service, but it is excellence in the basics. Low-cost airlines like Ryanair or Southwest are known to have stripped the flying experience back to the basics. There are no meals or free drinks, and they will fly to smaller airports. Boarding takes place via mobile staircases instead of via jetways. They will cut back on numerous service parameters, except for something like on-time departure and arrival. In their book *Blue Ocean Strategy*, Chan Kim and Mauborgne argue that in many industries competitors have focused on outperforming each other to a level of irrelevancy.[6] Consider it a rat race up to a level where, as a customer, you become indifferent about any extras. Cutting down on 'less important' dimensions or on 'overperformance' is their technique to create a 'blue ocean' instead of competing in the 'red ocean' where all the big sharks are fighting for the same fish. Opex leaders will be extra-critical in evaluating the 'added value' generated by individual service aspects. They will ensure excellence in those service parameters to which customers are very sensitive, like 'on-time departure and landing' when flying. Meals, snacks and jetways will never substitute for leaving and arriving on schedule. Opex players have understood that very well. That's why they focus on 'low cost' but equally on 'hassle-free service'. The essence is in the focus they create.

Product leadership

A product leader prevails by having the newest and highest-spec product, again and again. They focus on generating a stream of innovative products or services that sell at a significant premium to early adopters and niche markets. Investment in R&D and sales is significant. In fact, with each new product, the product leader is betting their business, as high volumes are required to cover the heavy R&D and sales costs.

A tempting example is Apple. It is clear that Apple has been very successful in launching a series of new products over the last 15 years. It is a dangerous example, though. It is clear that Apple has been successful in launching an impressive series of products. Think about the iPod, the iPhone, the iPad, the iMac and many more. However, Apple wasn't necessarily the first on the market, nor did they have the 'best' product in terms of the 'highest specification'. Apple has primarily excelled in product design and in marketing. It didn't invent MP3 as a technology nor the MP3 player. It merely excelled in making it eye-catching and user-friendly, and in making it the hippest product around. This has been extremely rewarding. In August 2020 it was the first US company to hit a market capitalization of over $2,000 billion. It has by far exceeded any reasonable expectations. However, it's not what I see as a typical product leader.

On one of my trips to China I met the CEO of Sea and Sun Technology GmbH.[7] As its website tells us, the company has a worldwide reputation in the development of innovative products and solutions in water measurement. If you are looking for the most precise equipment for measurements at an unexplored depth, Sea and Sun Technology will be your partner. The biggest asset of the company is its knowhow of water measurement. Knowhow is typically an accumulation of decades of experience. Successful companies of this type have typically survived many technological evolutions.

It is typical for a product leader to be in niche markets. For Sea and Sun Technology these are oceanography, limnology, offshore and hydrology. In general, only niche markets really benefit from the higher specification. Mass markets are not willing to pay the associated premium. They will go with a more average specification, possibly with a previous version of the technology, coming at a lower cost. Not getting to the big volumes may frustrate the product leader, but you can't have it all. As a niche player you will have smaller volumes but bigger margins. If you want the bigger volumes, you will typically achieve them via an operational excellence or a customer intimacy model.

In general, I prefer smaller companies like Sea and Sun Technology as examples of a product leader over bigger companies like Apple. They better illustrate that companies can be globally successful by simply having the best product. There are no side effects from the sheer size that may influence their performance or what they can do in the market.

Customer intimacy

Customer intimacy leaders prevail by having the best knowledge of their key customers, and by providing the best total solution to their challenges. They relieve their key customers of the job of selecting the appropriate products and combining them into a solution. They will proactively define the appropriate answers even before customers have fully realized the question was so relevant.

Coming to a 'total solution' is challenging. It is common for customer intimacy players to work with partners, offering complementary products or services, to come to that total solution. Typical examples come from the maintenance domain; this could be maintenance of your machines or maintenance of your buildings. Instead of selling spare parts or maintenance, repair and overhaul (MRO) materials,[8] a customer intimacy proposition can be to provide maintenance services, including preventive maintenance, or to guarantee uptime, because, in the end, your customer just wants their machines to be up and running. Next to selling robots, ABB Robotics delivers the following services: inspection and diagnostics, preventive maintenance, refurbishment and reconditioning, condition monitoring and diagnostics, lifecycle assessment.[9] A company like Bosch focuses on software solutions for so-called 'predictive maintenance'.[10] Like preventive maintenance, the idea is to intervene at the 'right' time. They don't wait until a breakdown occurs; likewise, they avoid stopping the machine if it's not needed. The idea of 'predictive' maintenance uses the (big) data of the equipment to predict the 'right' time. These are examples where solutions are delivered. They may combine software services with maintenance services and spare parts services into an 'uptime solution'.

An often-quoted company with a customer intimacy position is IBM. IBM has, throughout its existence, had an important focus on innovation. In 2012, IBM had topped the annual list of US patents for the 20th consecutive year.[11] However, the newest products might not be what IBM is most known or recognized for. In the end, it was Microsoft that pioneered a Windows-based operating system for personal computers in the 1980s. It was Digital Equipment Corporation (DEC) that pioneered the so-called minicomputers in the 1970s. It was Google that took the real advantage of making the internet accessible. The biggest success of IBM has probably always been to provide a full range of IT solutions to customers and to be the trusted partner of the CIO. They are the best at understanding the information technology needs of bigger corporations and in providing the tailored solutions to serve them. That makes bigger corporations spend large sums of money on IBM products and services.

Compared to a product leader, a customer intimate company will have a lower R&D cost, but a higher sales cost. It invests more time in building the 'best total solution'. It has more sales people, who spend more time talking to their key customers, to ensure that 'best total solution' is well understood and fine-tuned, and finally sold and implemented. Customer intimate companies draw value from this positioning. If their customers assembled the solution themselves, by shopping at low-cost players for each of the underlying products and services, they might end up with a lower cost solution, but they would need to put in the effort, which also has a cost, and they would probably have more issues when implementing the solution compared to the customer intimacy player, who has done this multiple times before. This is the reason why customers are willing to pay a little more to customer intimacy players compared to operational excellence players. Customers are willing to pay a premium for a 'one-stop shop' solution builder with expertise in solving their problems.

Strategy is about making choices

The good thing about the strategy model of Treacy and Wiersema is that it shows that companies must make a choice. We would all like to have the lowest price in the market, with the newest and the most customer intimate offerings. Treacy and Wiersema help us in understanding that this is impossible. If you don't make a choice, be aware that your competitors will. By creating focus on one of the dimensions, they will outperform you. Soon you find yourself being outperformed on each of the dimensions by different competitors. That will leave you stuck in the middle, unappealing to customers, to employees and to investors. We hate to make choices, but we simply must.

EXERCISE 3.1

Quick check for your strategic positioning

When working with companies, we notice they are intrigued by strategy and making strategic choices (or the lack thereof). A good way to start the debate on strategy is by using our online exercise that reveals the strategic positioning. You can use the following link to launch your own survey: www.strategydrivensupplychain.com/resources/surveys/treacy-and-wiersema

You will be asked to select the five statements, out of a total of 24, that most closely reflect what your business is standing for. If you are a company with multiple business units, either pick one business unit, or do the exercise twice. Comparing the outcome for different business units can be very revealing. You must select exactly five. You need to make a choice. We have adapted this exercise from Kurt Verweire.[12] We will extend his work on how to link the strategy model of Crawford and Mathews to that of Treacy and Wiersema in Chapter 5.

Depending on your five selected statements, you could score three on product leadership, one on customer intimacy and one on operational excellence, as shown in Figure 3.1. We recommend you do this exercise with a cross-functional team of marketing, sales, operations, finance and R&D. That will be the most revealing and lead to the best debate. As illustrated in Figure 3.1, your colleague might select different statements and score a two on product leadership, two on customer intimacy and one on operational excellence.

Treacy and Wiersema advocate two things. First, you don't want to be stuck in the middle. Market leaders make a choice and are to be found on one of the extremes. Second, if you ask 10 employees you want their thinking to be aligned – there's only one strategy for the company. You don't want R&D to aim for product leadership, operations for operational excellence and sales for customer intimacy.

FIGURE 3.1 Revealing your strategy in the Treacy and Wiersema model

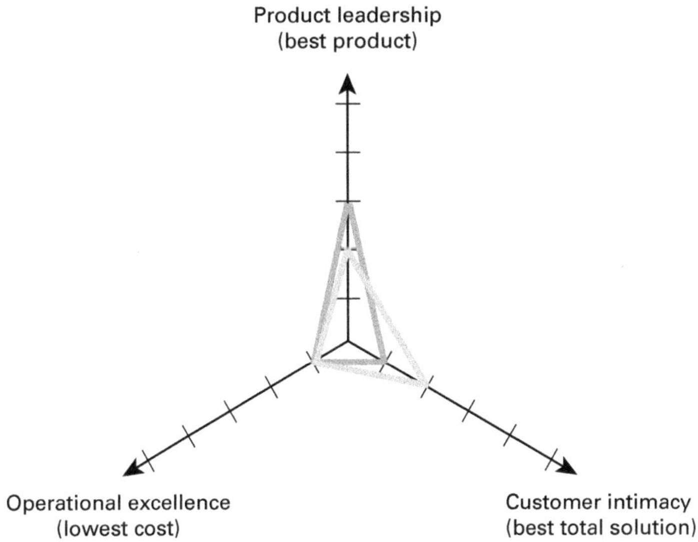

Based on the inputs from the online exercise, organize a workshop with key stakeholders from sales, marketing, operations, purchasing and finance. Give recommendations on the following questions:

- Have we made clear choices in our strategy/value proposition? Yes/no? Explain.
- Do the different functions in the company/business unit have the same view? Yes/no? Explain.
- What is your proposed strategy in the models of Treacy and Wiersema?
- What choices must be clarified in order to get to a sharper profile?

CASE STUDY

Waste treatment company Indaver

We carried out this exercise with the waste treatment company Indaver, introduced in Chapter 1. The key concept of 'total waste management' sounds a lot like a 'customer intimacy' positioning. We understand our customers' problems and have developed a total solution. We may work with partners to come to that total solution. In that sense, Indaver doesn't necessarily need to have the capability to process any type of waste stream. It can work with partners to come to that total solution.

One of the obvious questions was whether this was going to come out as a result, and whether different functions would have the same view. A second question was whether that strategy would be the same for the industrial waste business and the municipal waste business. Without knowing the sector, one could think of the municipal business being more tender-driven and cost-driven, so maybe operational excellence would be the more logical choice.

The results are shown in Figure 3.2. First, for industrial waste, which was our focus at the time, the choice of customer intimacy is relatively pronounced. Second, there is a big similarity between the industrial waste and the municipal waste business.

FIGURE 3.2 Revealing the strategy in the Treacy and Wiersema model for Indaver

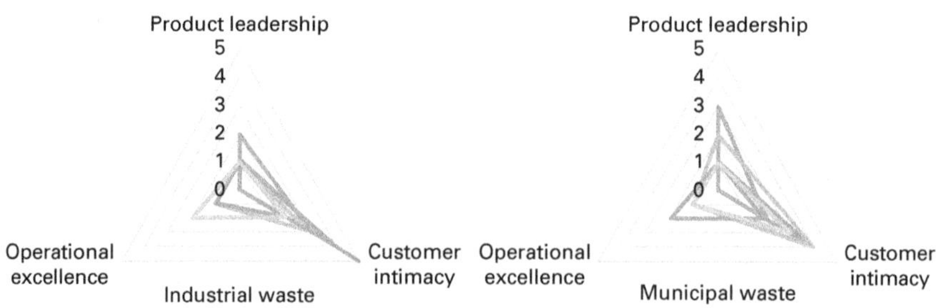

In the case of Indaver, the exercise didn't trigger a strategy debate. The conclusion was that the strategy is clear. However, it triggered a debate about whether strategies come with an impact. Total waste management means a broad range of waste streams, with an obligation to take them. Coupled to the challenges on the processing side, explained in Chapter 1, improved supply chain processes and systems were clearly needed to realize that strategy.

CASE STUDY

Food cooperatives

Another interesting exercise was done with a group of food cooperatives where I was invited as a guest speaker. Food cooperatives are in a challenging situation. There are thousands of farmers, millions of consumers, but only a handful of retailers, which as a result are very powerful in the chain. As governmental regulations get stricter, costs for the farmers are rising, but because of the power of the retailers they face difficulties in raising their prices. They are squeezed in the middle.

I used the model of Treacy and Wiersema to explain to them they'll have to make a choice if they want to stand out, and that Belgium, with its high wages and scarce land, was probably not well positioned to compete on price. Competing on quality and innovation, or on a total solution for the retailer, are probably more obvious choices. If they wanted to compete on price, they should go to Eastern Europe where wages are lower and enough farmland is available to really achieve scale.

When explaining the need for choices, the audience was deeply touched. The reason was that it felt like a conflict with the founding principle of solidarity. Farmers organize in cooperatives for mutual support in good times and bad times. It is like their insurance policy. The cooperatives also have the obligation to take and process the product from their members. Making a choice felt like having to make a choice among the members and possibly dropping some of them. That would be considered treason to the founding principle of solidarity.

Though it was discomforting, I continued to challenge their mindset. I encouraged them to think about either splitting up into more focused cooperatives or maybe organizing as chapters, where different chapters had a more pronounced focus. Everybody in the world knows jamón ibérico or Wagyu beef. Consumers are willing to pay significantly more for premium quality food. Many cooperatives leave the assembly of meat and vegetables for ready-made meals to companies like Greenyard. Maybe these are options to be explored. Organizing into more focused groups would work much better. Solidarity should not be a hurdle or an excuse to prevent them making choices and being successful.

FIGURE 3.3 Revealing the strategy in the Treacy and Wiersema model for food cooperatives

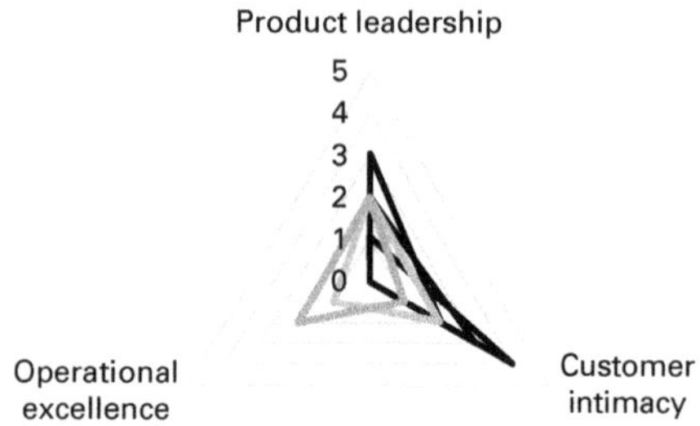

Figure 3.3 shows the results of the Treacy and Wiersema exercise performed with this group, which consisted primarily of CEOs and chairs of the board. Though there were many more attendees, only six people filled it in. That might indicate some felt insecure about thinking about strategy or revealing their strategy to their peers. That is awkward. Anybody can distinguish the strategies of Ryanair and Etihad. It illustrates the misconception that strategy is something secret, for the boardroom or the executive committee only.

Of the six people who filled it in, three were from one cooperative (in black) that was playing in the field of product leadership and customer intimacy. In the follow-on discussion it proved to be a success story of a cooperative auction that started focusing on premium quality products in particular assortments: strawberries, cherries, tomatoes, peppers, etc.[13] The auction has seen significant growth and profitability. The other three cooperatives were more stuck in the middle, left with an undifferentiated positioning. Though it wasn't clear how they were going to do it, the need to make a choice was apparent at the end of the evening. I have had comparable experiences in other sectors and with other companies. If your positioning is not clear, it will come up in this exercise, with different people and departments having different opinions. If that is where you are, starting a discussion on making tough strategic choices is what needs to be done.

Mapping Treacy and Wiersema to the supply chain triangle

If Treacy and Wiersema help us to understand the need to make choices, let's continue with mapping how these choices impact the balance in our supply chain triangle. Figure 3.4 has extended the supply chain triangle in a third dimension. Instead of three corners we now have three axes where we can score a lower/higher service, cost and capital employed. For capital employed

FIGURE 3.4 The supply chain triangle in three dimensions

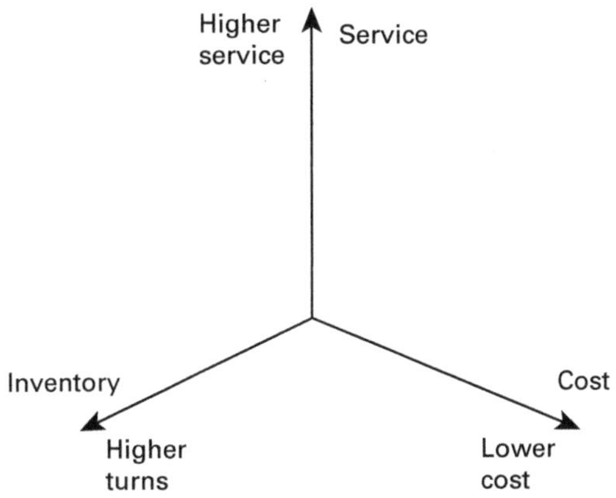

we will start by looking at inventory. We assume a higher service, lower cost, and higher inventory turns (meaning less inventory) to be the desired direction, so these are pointing outwards.

Let's start at the service angle. From the previous section it is clear that the opex leader has the most basic service. They deliver excellent service, but in a stricter set of service parameters. The more difficult question is how to position the customer intimacy player versus the product leader. Another difficult question is how to measure service. In the previous chapter we talked about 'service level' and about the 'product portfolio'. For the product leader, we should probably add the 'product quality' or 'product performance' to the service dimension. All of this is intellectually appealing but difficult to measure, and especially difficult to benchmark across companies.

When performing the financial benchmarks introduced in Chapter 2, we came to appreciate gross margin as a measure for service. The gross margin compares the selling price to the cost of the goods. The higher the premium that the customer is willing to pay, the higher the implied service or value. It tackles two problems at once: we've made the service measurable, and it is easy to benchmark gross margin across companies. Figure 3.5 shows the updated supply chain triangle. Given the cost of goods is now included in the service measurement, we will exclude it on the cost axis. That will allow us to focus the cost axis on anything that is added on top of the cost of goods sold. This involves costs like R&D and SG&A. That will be helpful, as we know from the previous section that R&D costs are important for the product leader, and selling costs are important for the customer intimate company.

FIGURE 3.5 The supply chain triangle in three dimensions with gross margin as the service metric

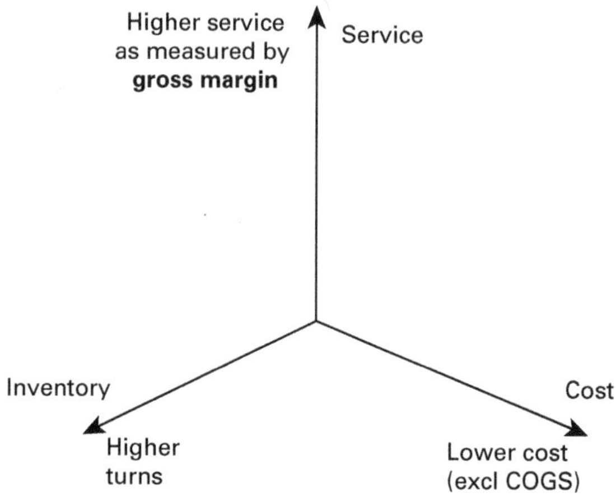

Figure 3.6 shows how we position the three strategies on the resulting service axis. Opex players rank the lowest. They excel in the basics. Their gross margin will be the lowest. If you look at the cost of goods, their mark-up is minimal as they want to assure the lowest price offer in the market. The customer intimacy player ranks next. As we've argued in the previous section, customer intimate companies drive a premium compared to the opex players. The premium comes from the convenience (for customers) of having the one-stop shop plus the expertise (on which customers can draw) of developing a total solution that is fit for purpose. The largest gross margin will be generated by the product leaders. The superiority of their products means that they have few to no competitors. That gives them a strong position from which to negotiate. As they focus on niches where the higher specifications of their products make an important difference, customers are willing to pay a high premium to get the best and the latest product. They can apply value-based pricing instead of cost-plus pricing. Niche business is extremely profitable. The challenge for product leaders is to create scale and to stay ahead.

Figure 3.7 maps the three strategies to the cost side of the triangle. Again, the opex leaders are the easiest. They will have the lowest cost, as every fibre in their organization is focused on delivering the lowest cost to be able to offer the lowest price in the market. The difficulty is again with differentiating the product leaders from the customer intimacy players. In the previous section we have discussed how customer intimacy players have a

FIGURE 3.6 Mapping Treacy and Wiersema to the service axis of the supply chain triangle

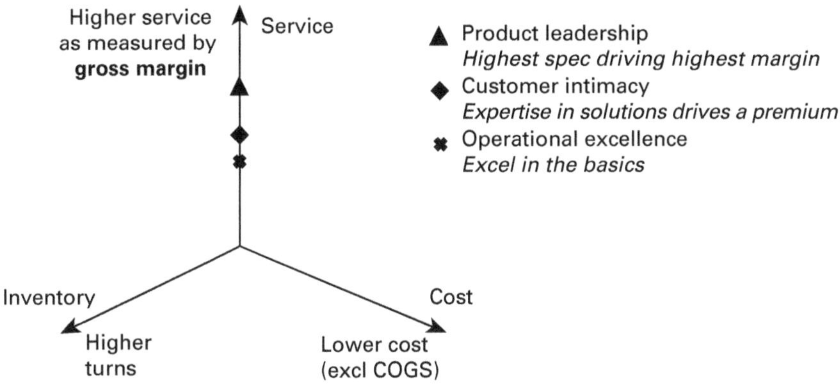

FIGURE 3.7 Mapping Treacy and Wiersema to the cost axis of the supply chain triangle

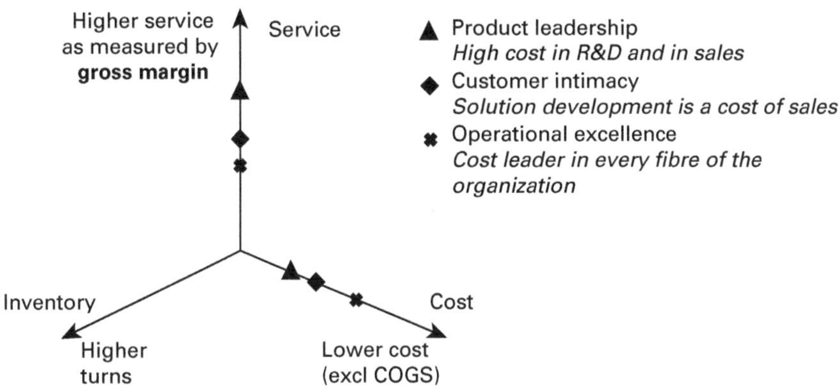

significantly higher sales cost compared to the opex leaders. Developing the best total solution requires time and expertise, and comes at a significant sales cost. As mentioned on the service axis, the good news is that customer intimacy players are able to drive a premium from this. So, what about the product leaders? Product leaders typically have less complex product portfolios compared to the customer intimacy players. Their complexity is in the products themselves, rather than the number of products. Explaining complex products and their advantages to niches still requires a significant sales cost. Moreover, product leaders have significant R&D expenses, and for that reason we have put the product leaders at the highest overall cost.

The good news is that the product leaders have headroom for this, as they can drive the highest gross margin from offering their unique products in niche markets.

Figure 3.8 maps the three strategies to the inventory axis. The opex players have the highest inventory turns. Remember from the previous section that simplicity drives efficiency at the opex players. They will avoid complex products and will avoid a long tail of slower-moving products. As a result, they will have the highest inventory turns. As already mentioned, the complexity of customer intimacy players will be in the broader product portfolio, required to come to the best total solution. Managing a broader range of products adds complexity, but in our experience companies have found ways to manage this. If you segment your customers and products into A/B/C, and have a good statistical and collaborative forecasting process, you should be able to control the required levels of inventory and cost. Controlling complexity is required, because the premium you get as a customer intimacy player is continuously challenged by the opex players in the market. In our experience, the toughest inventory challenge resides with the product leaders. Purchasing as a product leader is challenging. R&D has probably forced you to work with niche suppliers in the quest for the newest and the best. Getting consistent quality and service from a wide range of niche suppliers is challenging. Frequent updates and revisions of components and raw materials are common. It is a common cause of slow-moving and obsolete inventories. On the other hand, for the more common inputs, as somebody more focused on niches, your volumes may be small compared to the mass market players focusing on cost or a broader offering. If you're small, you don't have leverage, again creating a challenging situation when trying to streamline your supply chain. You may be confronted with long lead times and high minimum order quantities. From a production side, working with the newest, the latest and the most complex is challenging. You're quite sure to carry higher levels of work in process and have higher levels of rework compared to the industry average. From a sales side, predicting how niche markets will react to the newest product is daunting. You easily make mistakes, and half of the mistakes end up in inventory (the other half in operational firefighting and lost sales). This explains why we expect product leaders to have the highest inventories and have put them as the ones with the lowest inventory turns in Figure 3.8.

FIGURE 3.8 Mapping Treacy and Wiersema to the inventory axis of the supply chain triangle

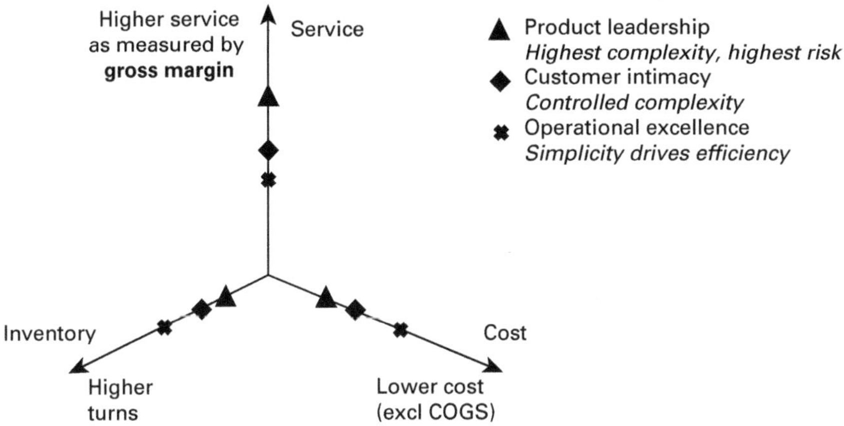

FIGURE 3.9 Different strategies lead to different positions in the supply chain triangle

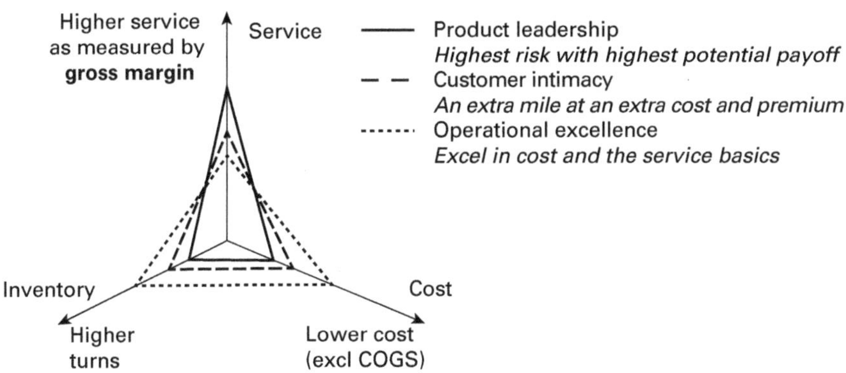

Figure 3.9 shows the overall summary. Different strategies lead to different positions in the supply chain triangle. In their drive to provide the lowest price in the market, opex players will drive out complexity to have the lowest cost and the lowest inventory. We believe inventory can be extended to capital employed. They will have fewer assets and make sure that the utilization rate is higher, again to ensure the lowest cost as a prerequisite for the lowest price in the market.

The more difficult discussion is in positioning the customer intimacy players versus the product leaders. The best total solution of the customer intimacy players drives a premium from the customer but that premium is under continuous pressure from the opex players. Yes, customers are willing to pay more for a one-stop shop and for the expertise going into the total solution that is fit for purpose, but in the age of internet transparency they will watch the premium to stay in sync with the market. This requires customer intimate companies to keep control of the complexity, and closely monitor their added value. Compared to the opex players, more products require more space in the warehouse, and a more diverse set of tools and machines to deliver the broader range. Again, we believe the inventory can be extended into the capital employed.

Product leaders have the unique advantage that their products are simply better than those of the competition. If they find the right applications where the higher specifications translate into a significantly higher value, they are in a good position to charge a superior premium. However, product leaders are also high-risk businesses. Delivering superior products is risky. You must commit the cost of developing and selling the product, but one or two mistakes can bring companies into the danger zone. We've discussed our experience that product complexity is more difficult to handle than product portfolio complexity. This translates into lower turns for product leaders. Again, we believe this extends into the capital employed. If you want to make a top-notch product, you need top-notch equipment. Making the highest spec product requires the highest spec infrastructure. The highest spec infrastructure tends to have fewer applications. All this is driving up the investment in fixed assets.

From where we started out with discussing inventory as a measure of complexity, we believe it can be extended into capital employed, which is working capital plus fixed assets. That extended version is shown in Figure 3.10.

FIGURE 3.10 Different strategies lead to different positions in the extended supply chain triangle

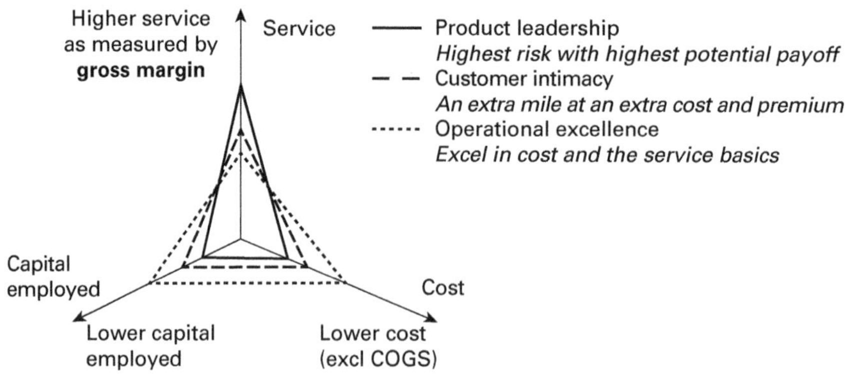

Different strategies are different routes to generate ROCE

In a next step, let's link the triangle back to ROCE. As we show in Figure 3.11, the 'service' and the cost translate into EBIT. The ROCE principle teaches the following. As an investor I will say to the product leader, it's OK if you need more capital, as long as you compensate with a higher EBIT. Or vice versa to the opex leader: it's OK if your EBIT is lower as long as you compensate by having less capital employed. As an investor, I will be indifferent, as long as I get the same bang-for-the-buck.

Operational excellence players will typically work at a minimum EBIT. Why? Because they want to have the lowest price in the market. Any improvement in cost is likely to be translated into a lower price in the market, assuming enough competition in that market. From a ROCE perspective that is fine, as those opex players typically work with a minimal capital employed. Likewise, product leaders have more complexity and require a higher capital employed. From a ROCE perspective that is fine, as product leaders can typically drive a higher margin from their customers because of the unique performance of their products. So different strategies not only lead to a different balance in the triangle; different strategies are

FIGURE 3.11 Different strategies lead to different ways of generating ROCE

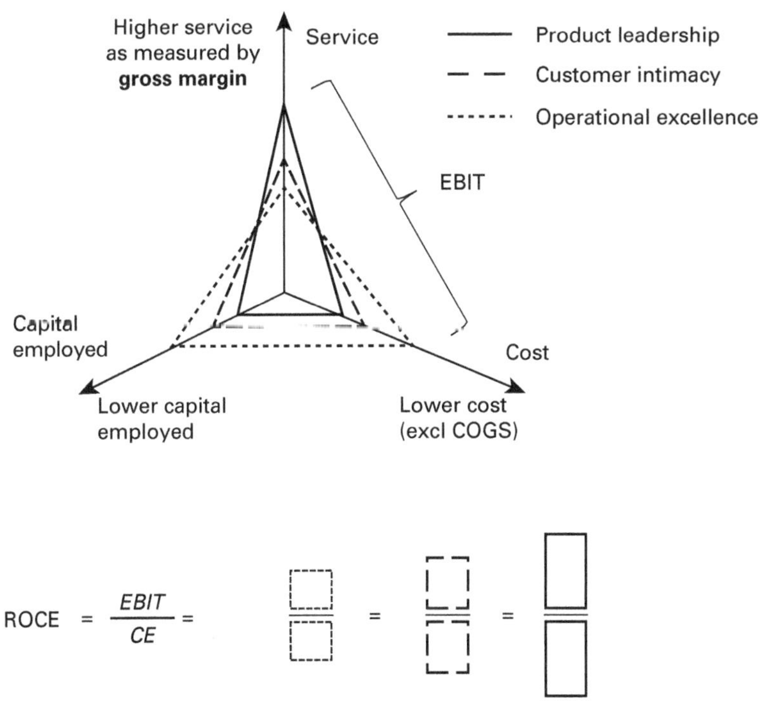

indeed different routes to generate the same ROCE. As an investor I'm indifferent about the chosen strategy; I'm primarily concerned about the bang-for-the-buck.

The effect of strategy is even more subtle, though. The product leader needs to deliver a higher EBIT, to compensate for the extra capital employed, but as is also shown in Figure 3.11, this needs to be done starting from a higher cost. So the product leader actually needs to earn a double premium: one to account for the extra cost, and one to account for the extra capital employed. This is refined in Figure 3.12.

This dynamic of the 'double premium' is poorly understood and often ignored. To come back to our earlier discussion on extending the product portfolio, the extension needs to earn a double premium. The first premium must cover the extra operational costs of managing an extended portfolio. Be aware that not just your total cost will go up, but your cost per unit will go up as well. Managing a broader portfolio will lower your efficiency. A second premium is required to cover the extra capital employed, for instance for the

FIGURE 3.12 Extra complexity needs to earn a 'double premium'

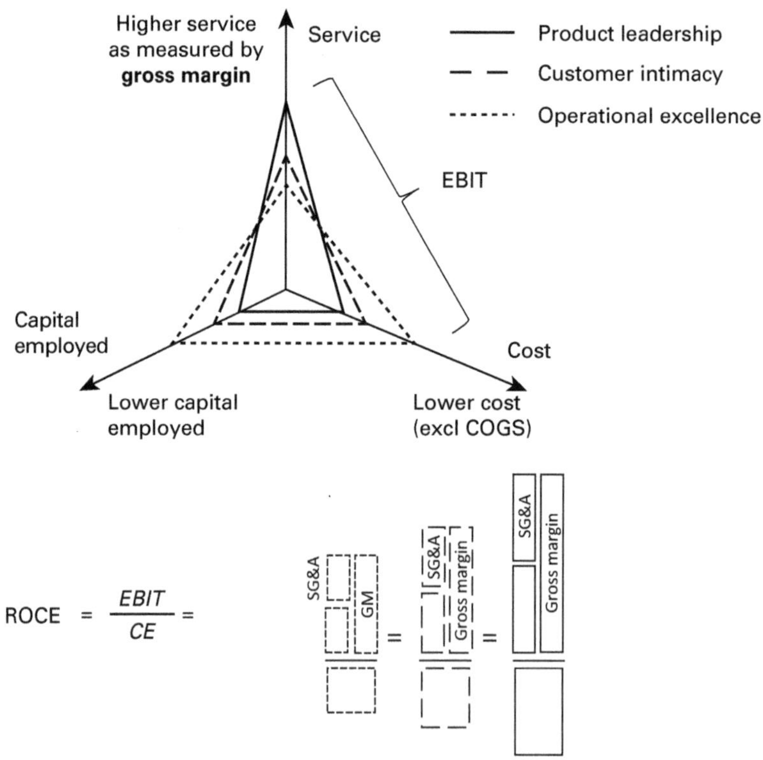

extra inventory. Here, too, be aware that not just your total inventory will go up, but your inventory turns will go down, as we are gradually introducing a long tail of more slow-moving products.

CASE STUDY

Strategy-driven benchmarking and target setting: Hero Group

Remember that in Chapter 2, when setting financial targets for Hero, we still had two options left: the Hershey direction, somewhat more aggressive in EBIT improvement, and a bit less in capital employed, and the Mondelez direction, with a more equal improvement in EBIT and capital employed. We have repeated Figure 2.11 as Figure 3.13.

With the knowledge of Figure 3.11 we can now better explain that the position on the curve is not arbitrary. The position on the curve has to do with the chosen strategy. In the markets we have analysed, successful product leaders are typically in the 15–30 per cent EBIT range, successful customer intimacy players in the 7–15 per cent EBIT range, and successful operational excellence players can be in the 2–7 per cent EBIT range. The 'indifference curve' will help you to define the corresponding level of inventory, receivables, payables, net PPE, fixed assets... in short, the corresponding level of capital employed.

Looking at Figure 3.13, we see Hershey is well in the 15–20 per cent EBIT range. We believe it can be classified as a true product leader. Remember from Figure 2.14 the Hershey Co has a staggering ROCE of 34 per cent, well above any other company in the benchmark. If you go to the Hershey website you'll find that 'relentless

FIGURE 3.13 Strategy-driven target setting: Hero Group

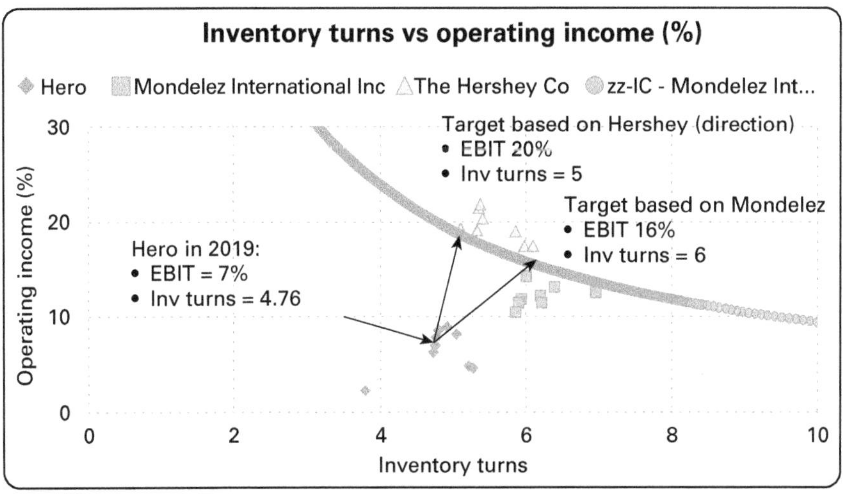

innovation is their foundation'.[14] There is also a very strong sense of heritage of the founder Milton Hershey, a social entrepreneur 'avant la lettre'.[15] Strong innovation reinforced by a strong brand and reputation is what product leadership is about. For Hershey that translates into a strong financial position 'all the way up' on the 'indifference curve' in Figure 3.13.

So what is Mondelez? Well Mondelez is a brander as well, but we believe it differs from Hershey in two ways. First, the Mondelez website talks about the following purpose:

> We will lead the future of snacking around the world by offering the right snack, for the right moment, made the right way. That means delivering a broader range of delicious, high-quality snacks that nourish life's moments, made with sustainable ingredients and packaging that consumers can feel good about.[16]

The broader range is striking. That goes into the direction of a customer intimacy positioning, a 'best total solution' rather than a 'relentless focus on innovation' as is more common at a true product leader. Second, Mondelez differs from Hershey as its ROCE of 7 per cent, shown in Figure 2.14, is simply much lower than that of Hershey. Mondelez is simply less successful. Judging by Treacy and Wiersema, we could even question whether the strategic positioning of Mondelez is clear enough. What is it after? Delivering the best possible snacks in the world? Or delivering a total range for its customers (retailers and distributors) and consumers? Judging from Figure 3.13, with its 10–15 per cent it might be in the EBIT range of a customer intimacy player, but to boost its ROCE it would have to be more efficient in inventory turns and make sure that it shifts to the right of Figure 3.13.

If we then return to the positioning of the Hero Group in Figure 3.13, that position is of course the most challenging and even slightly problematic. From the Hero website, it is clear Hero positions itself as a product leader, making high-quality, natural and healthy products.[17] In that sense, the 'logical' direction for target setting would be the direction of Hershey, with a strong improvement in EBIT, rather than a big improvement in inventory turns. That is the atypical choice. If you disregard the strategic context, people will feel more comfortable with a more balanced improvement in both EBIT and inventory turns, as that seems 'more realistic'. However, it is not what we feel comfortable with that counts, it's what we're after. If we want to differentiate by quality, innovation and brand, then we need to drive the corresponding premium. We believe the right direction for Hero is straight up, aiming for a 20 per cent EBIT with some limited improvement in inventory turns.

CASE STUDY

Strategy-driven benchmarking and target setting: Henkel, P&G, McBride

In Chapter 2, we introduced a one-dimensional benchmark of Henkel and P&G. We showed how Henkel had been playing catch-up with P&G on gross margin and on EBIT to overtake it as the company with the higher ROCE in 2012, where the ROCE advantage from Henkel lies in a significant higher efficiency in both net property, plant and equipment (net PPE) and fixed assets. We used the case to illustrate that in general we often ignore or are unaware of the importance of the capital employed when analysing the value generated by a company.

In Figure 3.14 we show the two-dimensional benchmark of Henkel and P&G, and we have added McBride as a third company. Where Henkel and P&G are branders, so typically pursuing a product leadership position, we introduced McBride in Chapter 2 as a private label player in household and personal care products. Private label players focus on the lowest cost and the lowest price. Their customers, the retailers, use private label products to compete on price with the branded products in their stores. We also discussed in Chapter 2 how McBride started a 'war on complexity', with the primary goal of boosting its value generation. You can find this two-dimensional benchmark on the book website at www.strategydrivensupplychain.com/resources/benchmarkreport/mcbride-henkel-pg

Figure 3.14 gives a different perspective to the fixed asset turns shown on the right versus the inventory turns shown on the left. On the right we see a nice and logical positioning, with P&G all the way up on the indifference curve, the position of the true product leader, Henkel more in the 10–15 per cent range, positioned close to the curve, more typically in a customer intimacy range, and then McBride positioned to the far right, with minimal EBIT but compensating with dramatically higher fixed asset turns compared to P&G and Henkel. It's hard to say whether Henkel truly wants a customer intimacy positioning; its website talks about 'a winning portfolio, competitive edge in the areas of innovation, sustainability and digitalization'.[18] The website of P&G is clear and concise.[19] It aims to provide 'superior products + superior packaging + superior brand communication + superior retail execution + superior consumer and customer value'.

The graph on inventory turns, shown on the left of Figure 3.14, gives a different picture. The situation here is problematic, especially for McBride. We see that with other private label players as well. The portfolio of private label players can be prohibitively complex, as products are customer-specific. If you don't watch out, every customer has a different bottle, a different cap, a different formulation, a different label... exploding the complexity compared to a brander. Though some of

FIGURE 3.14 Strategy-driven target setting: Henkel, P&G, McBride

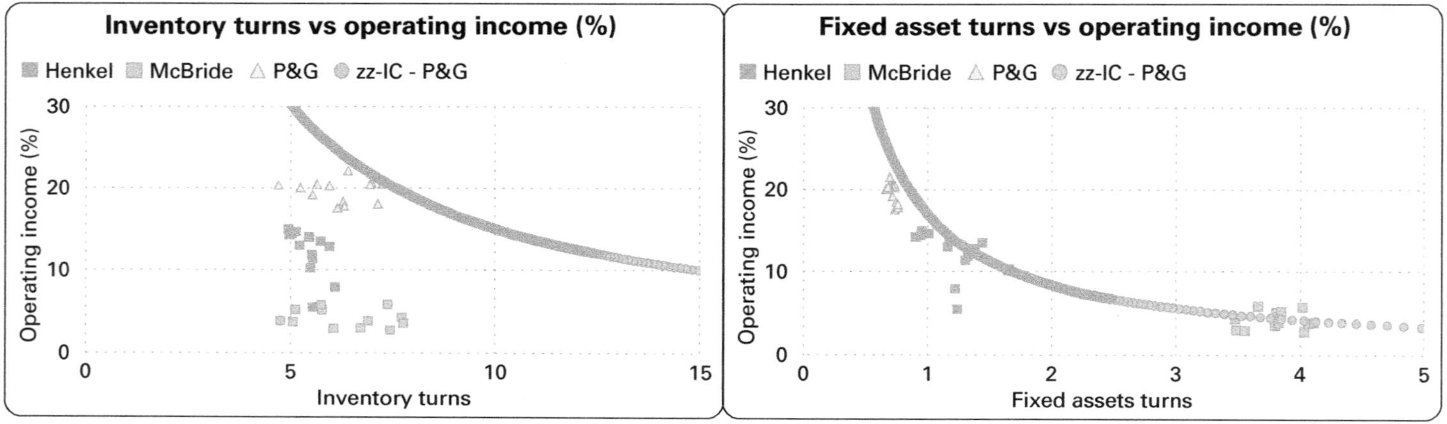

that is inevitable, a private label company should not be run with a customer intimacy mindset. That is what McBride did for part of its history. A private label company should be run with an operational excellence mindset, and that is exactly the strategic repositioning of McBride we described in Chapter 2. Private label companies should also try harder to get rid of their inventories. I need to challenge my customers by saying, 'What is that inventory doing in your warehouse anyway? It has the label "Carrefour" on it – who else is going to sell it?' Private label players should demand a vendor-managed inventory (VMI) type of replenishment from their customers, and they should focus on big customers and big volumes as these drive the efficiency required to drive the lowest cost. We believe many companies lack the courage to make the necessary strategy choices. We will describe those as common 'strategy fails' in the next chapter.

The above examples (Hershey–Mondelez–Hero, P&G–Henkel–McBride) should clarify a couple of points. The place on the curve is defined by strategy. Product leaders are in the higher EBIT range, and using the indifference curve we can find the corresponding capital employed ranges. Operational excellence players will be in a lower EBIT range and the more aggressive capital employed ranges can also be found through the indifference curve. Second, it is actually very helpful to visualize different types of competitors, with a different strategy, to get a good understanding of what are typical ranges within your specific sector. That will help in further defining where you believe you are good and where you need to improve. Finally, Figure 3.14 further clarifies that you don't always need to be best in class. Product leaders need to be best in class in margin but will be worst in class in capital employed... by design. For opex players it will be the other way around. Customer intimacy players will be stuck in the middle. All of them need to be best in class in value, however.

EXERCISE 3.2

Strategy-driven target setting

- Identify in your sector what you'd consider as a typical example of:
  - product leadership
  - customer intimacy
  - operational excellence
- Add these companies to your benchmark of Chapter 2
- Do you see these companies taking different positions on the EBIT and capital employed dimensions?

- What do you learn about typical ranges for EBIT, inventory turns, net PPE turns, etc?
- What does it teach you with respect to the targets you defined in Chapter 2? Are you in any way more comfortable not to be best in class in all of the dimensions?

An easy benchmarking tool is available on the book website at www.strategydrivensupplychain.com/resources/benchmarkreport/. After creating an account, you can upload your company-specific data or synchronize it from an online source. You can benchmark against sector peers in both one and two dimensions.

Building a strategy-driven scorecard

In our experience, companies are weak in setting targets for metrics like inventory turns. Either they just try to do a bit better compared to last year, or finance has done a (one-dimensional) benchmark and stretches the supply chain to become best in class. We hope that the techniques developed in this chapter will help companies in doing a better job in defining the right targets and that companies will account for the chosen strategy in a better way. We hope you'll dare to make choices, not just in your strategy but also in the financial targets. It is OK to be worst in class in inventory, as long as you're best in class in EBIT. That is exactly the position of a company like LEGO when you analyse the toy industry. We have come to call this technique strategy-driven benchmarking and target setting. It is an important building block for the strategy-driven supply chain. Compared to our first book, *Supply Chain Strategy and Financial Metrics*, the tools and techniques have matured, and we have made them more easily accessible via this second book's website. We hope it will help companies to do a better job and make more pronounced choices.

Once we have defined our targets, we should also follow them up. Here we see that reporting is fragmented. Many S&OP meetings report on on-time, in-full delivery performance and, forecast accuracy and inventory turns, but they typically lack both the financial and strategy context. At the same time, we see many financial or business reviews that are heavily focused on the financials, but they are often focused on the past, more like a 'variance' analysis, rather than forward looking. They also often miss the strategic and more operational context.

In this section we use our supply chain triangle to build a 'balanced' and 'strategy-driven' scorecard. When Kaplan and Norton first talked about 'balanced' they meant balancing financial KPIs against KPIs on intangible assets like human capital.[20] While that is relevant, our balancing is different in nature; it is balancing the three corners of the supply chain triangle. We have argued at length in Chapter 1 that companies struggle to balance that triangle and, in Chapter 2, that ROCE is a promising balancing metric. We will also merge operational KPIs, which we will position as causal or leading metrics, and financial metrics into one dashboard, further merging supply chain and finance into one balanced and comprehensive overview.

Next, we will make the scorecard strategy-driven. Different strategies focus on different value drivers. Efficiency may be key to an operational excellence player but for a product leader the primary KPI would rather be the time to market and the percentage of revenue coming from new products. That doesn't mean a product leader doesn't need to be efficient. It means the product leader doesn't differentiate in the market with its efficiency; it differentiates with its capability to innovate and bring superior products to the market. It will survive a drop in efficiency as it has superior margin, but it may not survive launching failed products. It is important we reflect this strategic perspective in our strategy-driven scorecards.

We start in Figure 3.15 by defining metrics on each of the corners of the supply chain triangle. For cost and capital employed, we use the metrics introduced in the appendix in Chapter 1. On the 'service' corner, we use the value drivers linked to the strategy model of Crawford and Mathews, which we will define in more detail in Chapter 5. For each of the possible value drivers we listed one possible metric. Strategy is about making choices. As we will explain in Chapter 5, Crawford and Mathews translate that as follows: we can choose one driver on which we want to dominate, a second on which we want to differentiate, and for the rest we will play at par. If we want to dominate on price, then the price point in the market and the delta with the competition will be our first and primary KPI. If we want to dominate on product quality we may look for a metric that captures the performance of our product on a certain specification. It could be the light output as measured by lumen, or the 'autonomy' if it is about a battery, or the 'range' for an electric vehicle. We might also look at more indirect measures, like the time to market or the percentage of sales coming from new products. If we need to 'collapse' our dashboard and show only one or two KPIs, then the strategy will be leading in which KPIs we show and which ones we don't.

FIGURE 3.15 Layer 1 of the KPI dashboard: value, cost and capital employed

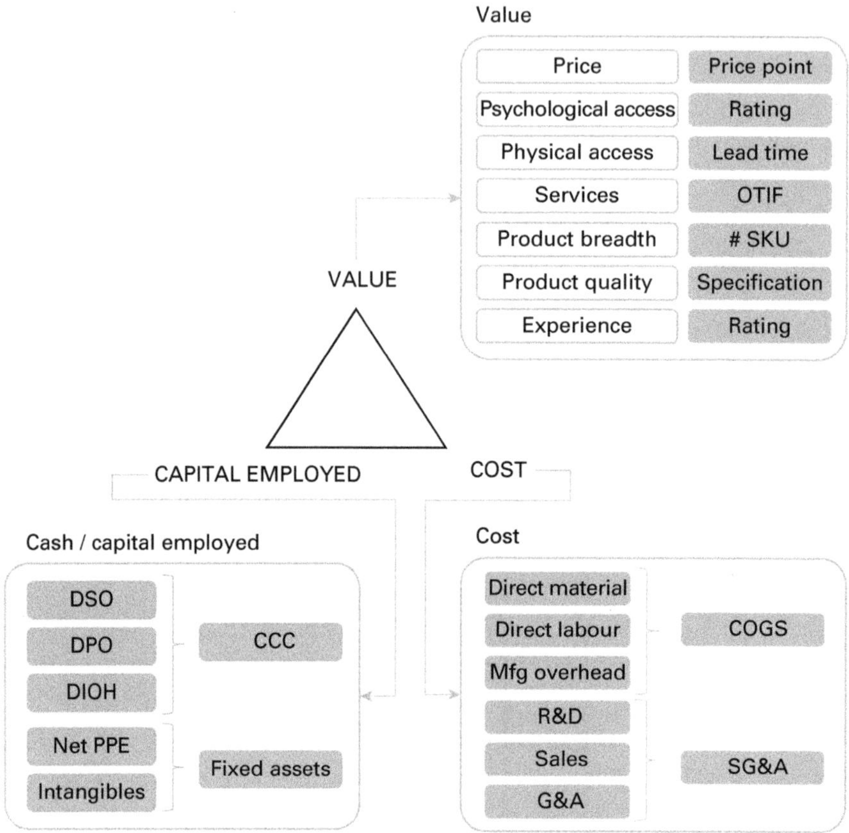

We continue building our strategy-driven scorecard in Figure 3.16. For that we build on the basic reasoning from Figure 2.21. Service is a driver for top line. Top line and cost give the bottom line. Bottom line over the capital employed gives a return. The changes in capital employed and EBIT (actually NOPAT) lead to free cash flow.

Finally, in Figure 3.17 we can add a layer of operational process metrics. These process metrics can be called 'causal' or 'diagnostic' metrics. If something goes wrong in the financial metrics, we can look for the root cause in the operational processes. In that sense the operational process metrics are causal. If we take the example of the forecast accuracy, an improvement in forecast accuracy will lead to improved OTIF (as not all forecast gaps can be closed from inventory or rush orders), improved costs (as we have fewer rush orders) and improved inventories (as there is less overproduction and

FIGURE 3.16 Layers 1 and 2 of the KPI dashboard: top-line, bottom-line, return and cash flow metrics

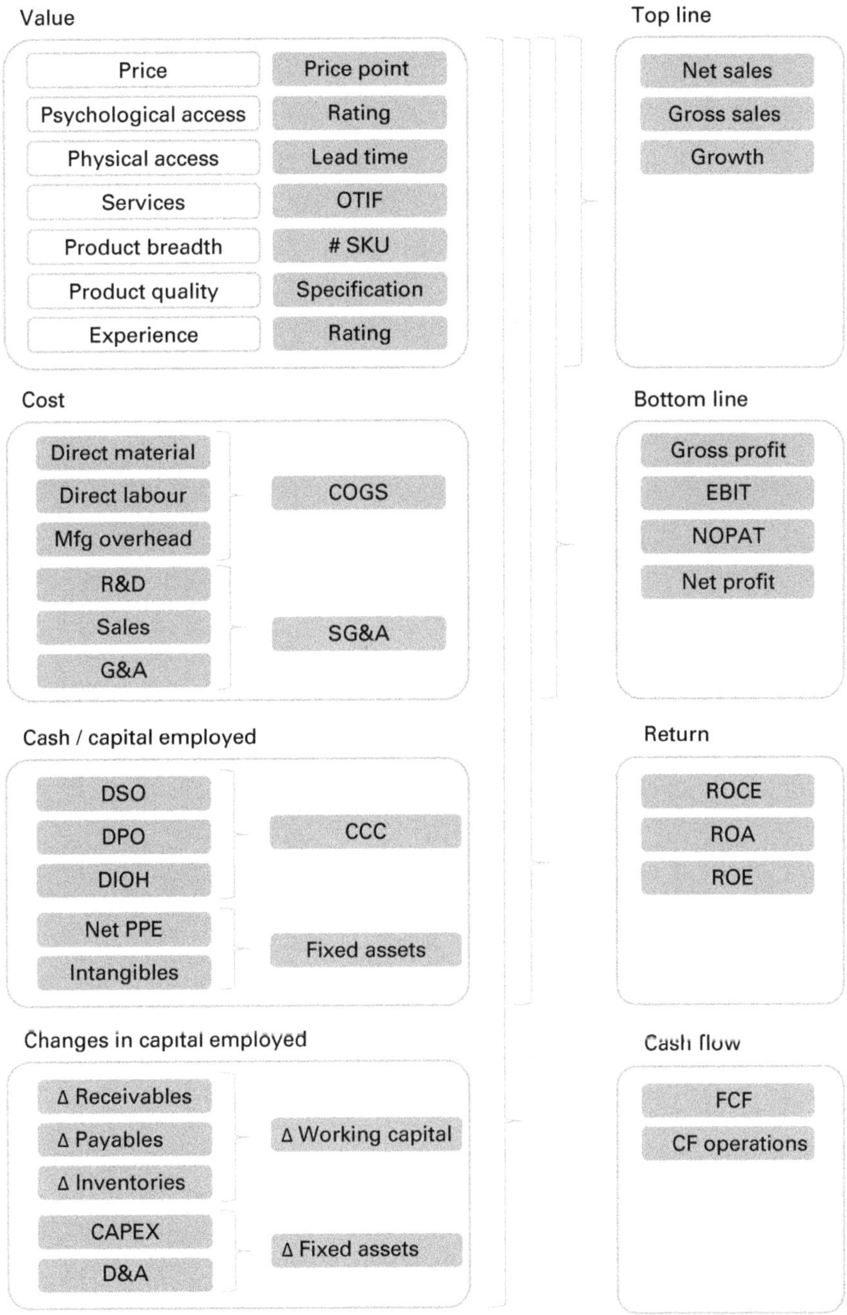

FIGURE 3.17 Layers 1, 2 and 3 of the KPI dashboard: process or diagnostic metrics

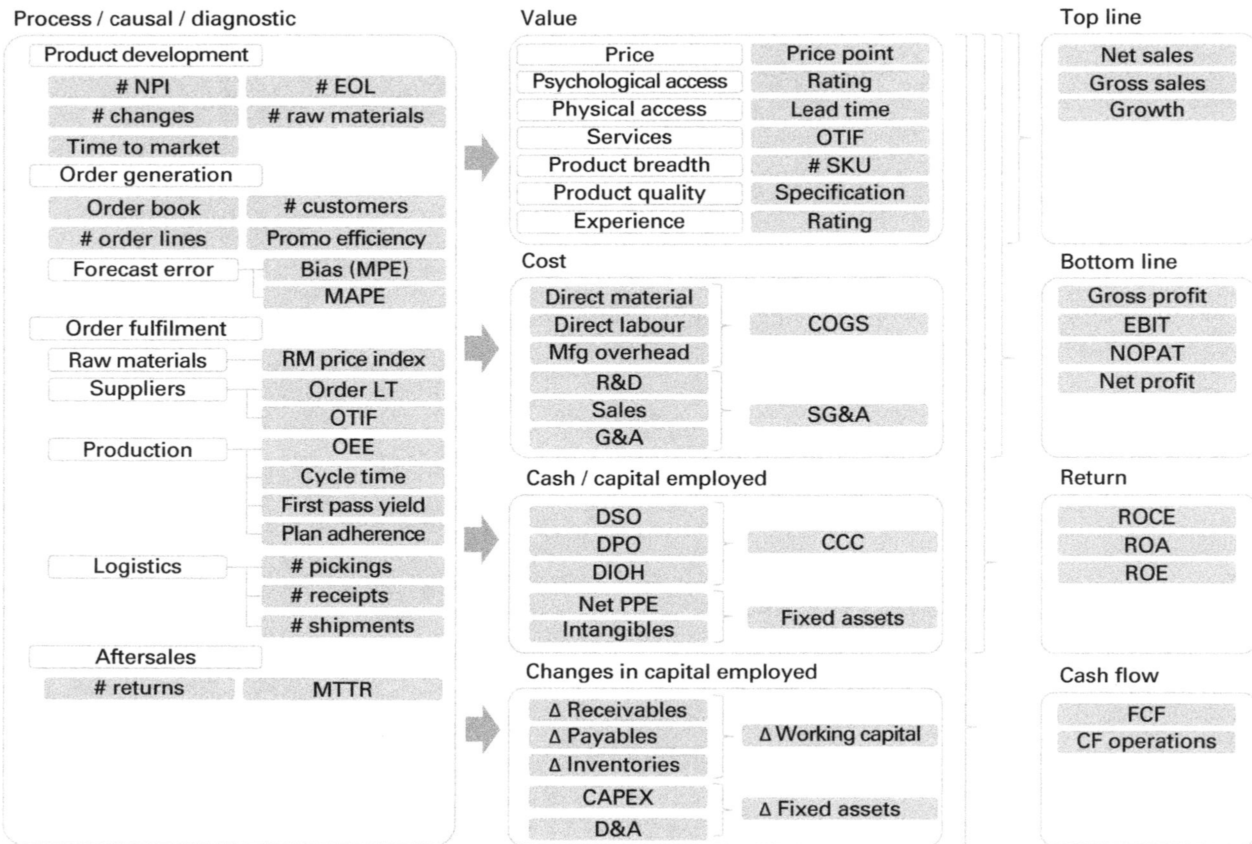

we can lower the safety stocks). As such, an improved forecast accuracy has a triple effect on ROCE. Production metrics like cycle time and first pass yield behave in the same way.

Strategy impacts the balance and the target setting in our scorecard. If I add more products to the product portfolio, my forecast's accuracy will go down, as I will introduce more 'mix variability', as we will call it in Chapter 6. So, yes, I will need more inventory, have a higher cost, and it will be more difficult to score the same service level. Don't panic. Works as designed. We know that a customer intimacy player will have a higher cost and a higher capital employed compared to an operational excellence player. The challenge for the customer intimacy player is in driving a double premium from the customer, as explained in Figure 3.12. A first premium needs to cover the extra costs, a second premium the extra capital employed. Equally likely, I know the forecast accuracy at a customer intimacy player will be lower than that at a lowest cost player. If I'm Delhaize and I have 15,000 SKUs in my store, my forecast will be less accurate than that of a hard discounter like Aldi who has only 2,500 SKUs, all of which are fast-moving. That is illustrated in Figure 3.18. For the financial metrics the target setting while accounting for the strategy can be done based on the two-dimensional benchmarking technique introduced above. For operational metrics we see companies typically don't account for the strategy and simply want to be 'best in class' as well. As with the financial metrics, that is not only meaningless, it is outright dangerous. If Delhaize would want to be best-in-class in forecast accuracy the best thing to do, as for inventory turns, would be cutting slow movers. Needless to say, this outright conflicts with the strategy of being an upscale supermarket. Delhaize may want to be best in class among its strategy peers. That is a whole different thing, and for operational KPIs, that type of information and benchmarks are often missing. That makes the target setting and benchmarking for operational KPIs a whole lot more difficult. Nonetheless, look for comparable references, comparable in the sense of size, complexity, strategy, etc. Even if the sector is somewhat different, the resulting benchmark will be a lot more meaningful. And don't overly focus on the KPIs. Different companies often use different definitions, making truthful comparisons hard. Instead, focus on comparing the processes, the capabilities. Regardless of the KPIs and the current performance, if you feel the capabilities can be improved, they will improve the corresponding KPIs and performance.

FIGURE 3.18 Making our scorecard strategy-driven

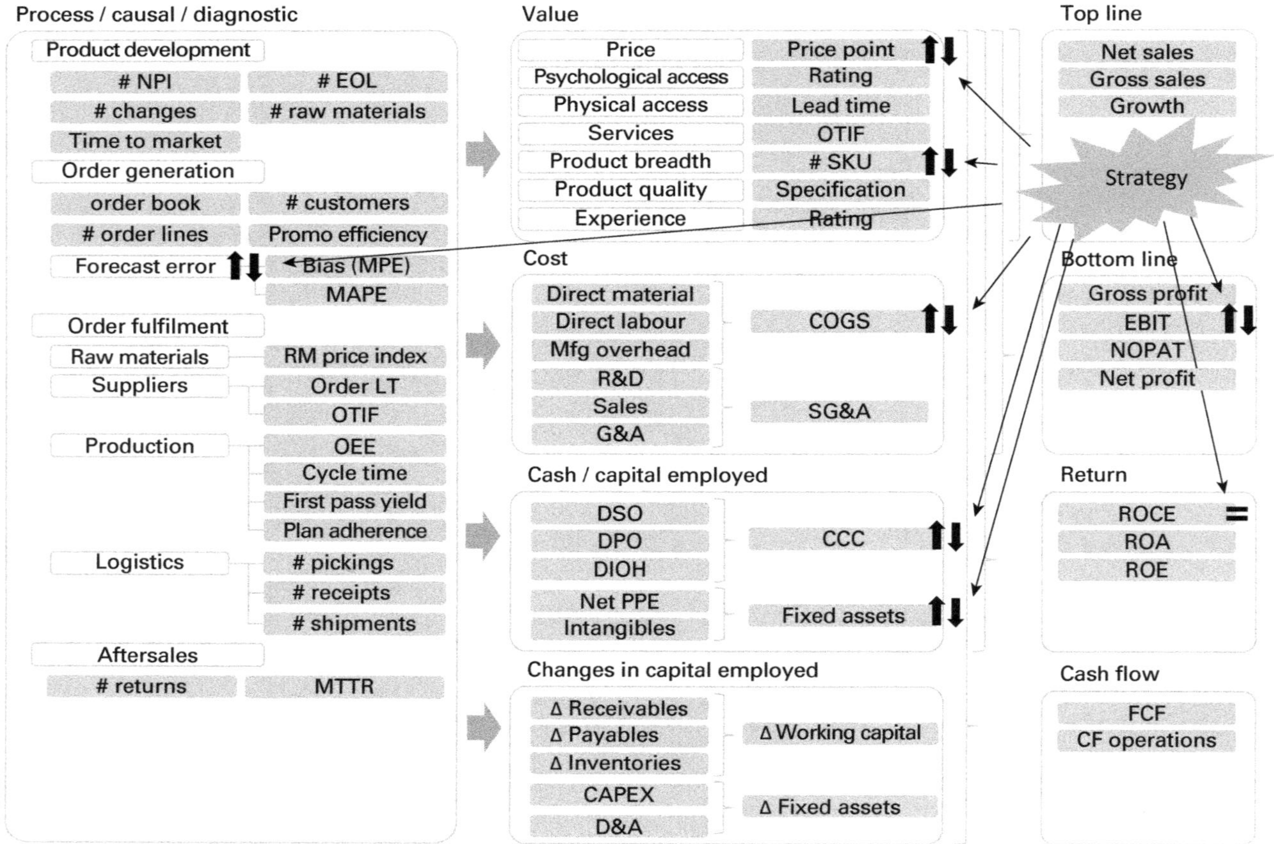

CASE STUDY
Strategy-driven scorecard at a product leader

The building blocks for a strategy-driven dashboard are shown in Figure 3.19. We measure value drivers, cost, capital employed and changes in capital employed. These drive top-line, bottom-line, return and cash flow metrics. Process metrics are causal and diagnostic to the financial KPIs.

Figure 3.20 shows how we used some of these building blocks to build a ROCE dashboard for a product leader company. The targets for the key financial metrics (gross profit/COGS, EBIT/SG&A, DPO, DSO, DIOH, CCC, fixed assets and ROCE) have been defined using the technique described earlier in Chapter 2 and included in the budget. We show the actual performance, the delta with the budget, and the delta with the previous year. Companies that have a good planning processes can show both the actual performance and a latest estimate for the current quarter or the current fiscal year.

Looking at Figure 3.20, you probably wouldn't want to be in the supply chain department of this company. With an OTIF performance of 90 per cent, which is 5 per cent below target, and an order fulfilment lead time of three weeks, which is one week above target, two of your important KPIs seem to be blood-red. However, if we put this into the correct business context it turns out to be a completely different story.

The story behind the figures is that the company had huge success with a major new product. With five or six major vendors, being on different technologies, our company seemed to have won the lottery, as for multiple reasons our technological choices gradually turned out to deliver superior performance, making the full market

FIGURE 3.19 The three layers and nine essential blocks of our strategy-driven scorecard

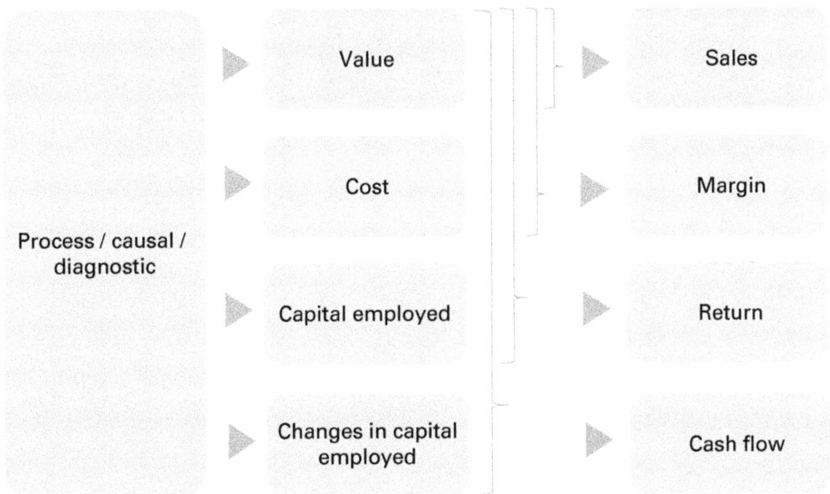

FIGURE 3.20 iPad example of a strategy-driven scorecard for a product leader

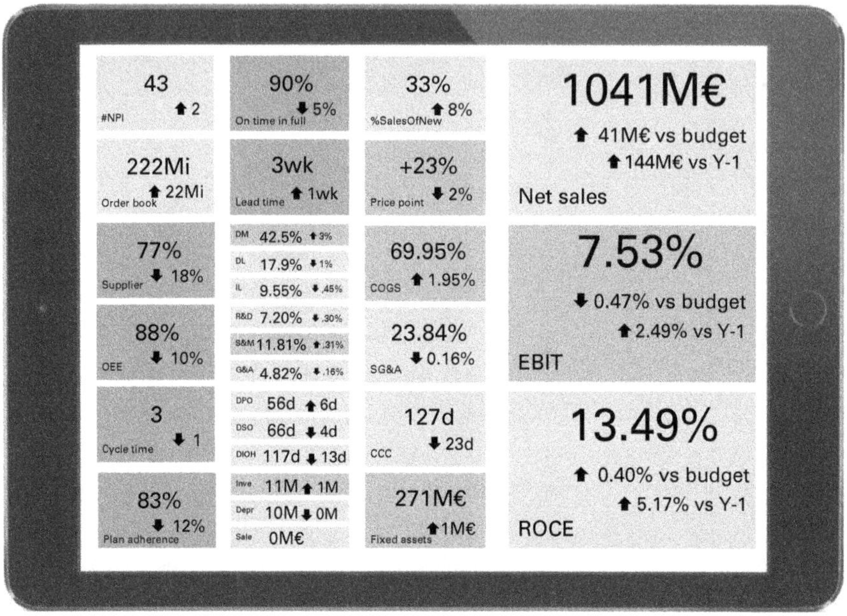

shift towards our products, because of our superior standards. We see that this new product is propelling our sales ahead of the targets and significantly beyond last year's performance. In the %SalesOfNew box we see that the sales percentage of new products, which is an important KPI for us as a product leader, is significantly ahead of schedule. As a product leader, this is what we dream of.

The business 'problem' or 'challenge' is that some of our key suppliers are unable to follow the growth rate. Given that we did not anticipate this would happen, they are doing what's possible to scale up. However, as always, getting new equipment in and ready takes time, and is causing some delay. The problems at key suppliers explain the low supplier OTIF, and that also weighs on our OTIF delivery performance and customer order lead time. All the expedited shipments and last minute production changeovers are weighing on our cost of goods sold, which weighs on the EBIT, which at 7.53 per cent is below what we had budgeted, but is way ahead of last year's performance. From a ROCE perspective, we still are on schedule, given that the somewhat lower than planned EBIT is compensated by lower working capital.

Imagine you try to build that 'business story' by having only a fraction of the KPIs. Although we seldom see all KPIs from Figure 3.20 together in one dashboard, if we want to better understand the dependencies and the impact of strategy it is clear this is what we need. It is our definition of a 'strategy-driven' and 'balanced' scorecard.

Conclusion

In this chapter we've introduced the idea that strategy is about making choices, and that different strategies lead to a different balance in the supply chain triangle. Different strategies are in fact different routes to generate ROCE, in a different balance between EBIT and capital employed. We used that insight to further refine our technique for benchmarking and target setting introduced in Chapter 2. Different strategies lead to different positions on the 'bang-for-the-buck' lines in our two-dimensional benchmark graphs.

We concluded our chapter by introducing our strategy-driven scorecard. Once we have successfully done strategy-driven benchmarking and strategy-driven target setting, it is important we follow up our financial metrics in a balanced way, with a balance across the supply chain triangle, that we link operational metrics and financial metrics and that we prioritize metrics in function of our chosen strategy.

In the next chapter we will provide practical examples of how we believe companies fail in strategy and making strategic choices. We will discuss cases of companies that changed strategy, and companies that chased strategic changes for the wrong reasons, and we will illustrate how different strategies lead to a different balance in the triangle in food retail companies.

Notes

1 M Treacy and F Wiersema (1995) *The Discipline of Market Leaders: Choose your customers, narrow your focus, dominate your market*, Basic Books, New York

2 J P Womack, D T Jones and D Roos (1990) *Machine that Changed the World*, Simon and Schuster, London; J P Womack and D T Jones (2010) *Lean Thinking: Banish waste and create wealth in your corporation*, Simon and Schuster, London

3 First pass yield, also known as throughput yield, is defined as the number of units coming out of a process divided by the number of units going into that process over a specified period of time. Only good units with no rework or scrap are counted as coming out of an individual process. For more information we refer to T Pyzdek and P A Keller (2014) *The Six Sigma Handbook*, McGraw-Hill Education, New York

4 F Crawford and R Mathews (2007) *The Myth of Excellence: Why great companies never try to be the best at everything*, Crown Business, New York

5 www.colruytgroup.com/wps/portal/cg/en/home/about-us (archived at https://perma.cc/4D9B-XV2P)

6 W Chan Kim and R A Mauborgne (2005) *Blue Ocean Strategy*, Harvard Business Review Press, Brighton, MA

7 www.sea-sun-tech.com/technology.html (archived at https://perma.cc/NKA8-L87K)

8 MRO involves fixing any sort of mechanical, plumbing or electrical device should it become out of order or broken (known as repair, unscheduled or casualty maintenance). It also includes performing routine actions that keep the device in working order (known as scheduled maintenance) or prevent trouble from arising (preventive maintenance).

9 new.abb.com/products/robotics/service/maintenance (archived at https://perma.cc/R63U-WM5J)

10 www.bosch-si.com/manufacturing/solutions/maintenance/predictive-maintenance.html (archived at https://perma.cc/U2DR-LY55)

11 www.research.ibm.com/articles/patents.shtml (archived at https://perma.cc/5CM3-SJYK)

12 K Verweire (2014) *Strategy Implementation*, Routledge, Abingdon

13 In the Netherlands, an 'auction' is a cooperative company formed by farmers or growers. Their products are jointly sold to the market (retailers, wholesalers, etc) through this company, using an auction mechanism.

14 www.thehersheycompany.com/en_us/innovation.html (archived at https://perma.cc/FNZ9-M88G)

15 www.thehersheycompany.com/en_us/our-story/milton-hershey.html (archived at https://perma.cc/DE7G-WNBN)

16 www.mondelezinternational.com/About-Us/Who-We-Are (archived at https://perma.cc/KE7K-VF65)

17 www.hero-group.ch (archived at https://perma.cc/22UM-URAE)

18 www.henkel.com/company/strategy (archived at https://perma.cc/2X3C-9MD5)

19 www.pginvestor.com/company-strategy/default.aspx (archived at https://perma.cc/JKC2-K6J9)

20 S Kaplan, S Robert and D P Norton, The balanced scorecard: Measures that drive performance, *Harvard Business Review*, 2005, July–August

04

Strategy in the supply chain triangle: cases

In this chapter we want to provide practical examples on how companies struggle with making clear strategic choices. We will start by what we call common 'strategy fails'. We will also review four case studies in detail. The first two are about two technology companies making or trying to make a strategy shift. The third is about the multi-year transformation of Johnson Controls from a diversified group with multiple strategies into a more focused total solution player in the construction market. We conclude by looking at how strategy plays in the food retail market, at how different strategies lead to a different positioning, and how that translates into different ways to generate a comparable ROCE.

Five myths about strategy

Treacy and Wiersema teach us that you need to make a choice. In the previous chapter we have discussed how different strategies lead to a different balance in our supply chain triangle. We showed that different strategies are just different routes to generate the same ROCE, in a different combination of EBIT and capital employed.

While people tend to accept this, my experience over the last two to three years has been that, if strategy is about making choices, companies are bad at strategy. We hate making choices. We think choosing is losing. We'd rather be stuck in the middle with an undifferentiated positioning rather than taking the risk of choosing the wrong option. I will share some of the common problems with strategy I have encountered so far. As we will further elaborate in Chapters 5 and 6, clear choices are needed to define the correct supply chain.

Combining branded and private label

Since our first book, I ran into multiple companies that combine branded and private label. With one of them the story was that they had some excess capacity and the private label was brought in to fill the assets. Another company simply wanted to grow. Given private label is small to non-existing in South America, they simply bought a branded business over there.

The reasoning for both cases sounded logical and acceptable. For the first one, basics in finance teach us that as long as the variable costs are covered, bringing in extra business is always beneficial as it contributes to covering the fixed assets. For the second one, the reasoning was that growth would lead to better negotiation power with key suppliers and as such improve the bottom line.

Treacy and Wiersema clearly advise us not to do this. If you want to be a market leader, you need to make a choice. In the terminology of Treacy and Wiersema, branders can be seen as product leaders. A brander like P&G invests a lot in innovation. They have key knowledge areas that they try to deepen and combine into new products. Branders also invest a lot in marketing, in building brands that last. Once people have put their trust in brands, they are more loyal. Private label can be seen as operational excellence. Retailers compete with the branders using private label products. That competition is on price. I give you a good-quality product, but at a significantly reduced price compared to the branders. The challenge for the branders is to stay ahead in product quality and in trust. This target positioning is reflected in Figure 4.1.

Market leaders have what Jim Collins calls a 'cult-like culture'.[1] Once they have made a strategic choice, every fibre in the organization is focused on executing that choice. Think about what happens when we take somebody from Southwest or Ryanair and place that person at Etihad. That person dies on the spot. How can you throw money out of the window like that! Or vice versa, take somebody from Etihad and put them at Ryanair. That person also dies on the spot. How can you ever be that rude to your customers! You would do better to take somebody from Ryanair and put them at Aldi or Lidl. Or you could switch the person from Etihad with somebody working at Harrods in London. The strategy is dominant, not the sector.

FIGURE 4.1 Branded versus private label in the supply chain triangle: in theory

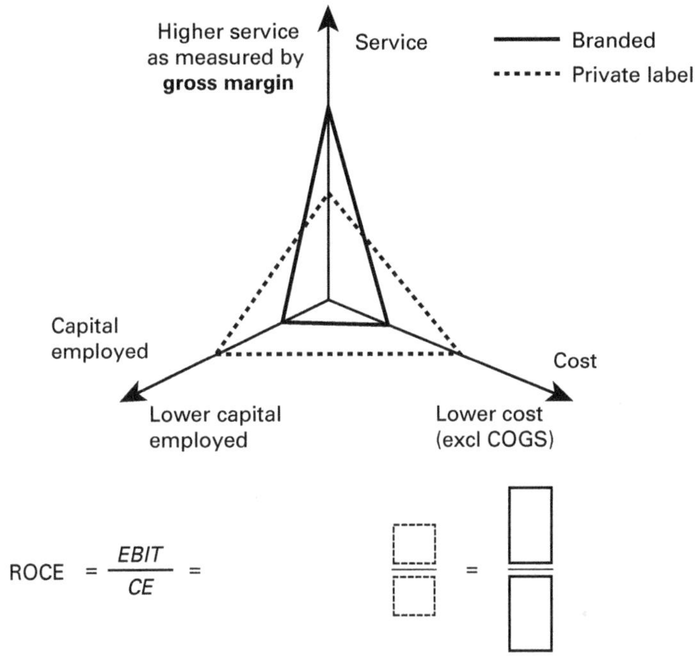

Still, this is exactly what we expect organizations to do if we ask them to combine branded and private label. Either you have strong personalities, maybe split personalities, to handle that, or you're going to run into trouble. Without looking into the details, my expectation is these companies end up with a complexity problem in the private label business and a margin problem in the branded business. When provoking one of the CFOs with that statement, I saw in his eyes that I was spot on.

When looking at private label, we know margins are going to be lower. Retailers use these products to compete on price so there will always be price pressure. The challenge with private label is the complexity. I have customer specific SKUs. In the best case it is just another label. But most likely Delhaize or Food Lion would like to have different packaging than Carrefour or Kroger, and maybe a different type of formulation or recipe. Retailers are not just competing with the branders. They are also competing with each other. Without even noticing, complexity is creeping in.

To make things worse, private label is typically also more difficult to handle. I no longer control the timing of the promotions. Retailers may even be late to announce or suddenly want to react to the promo of a brander with some of their private label SKUs. Working for the hard discounters like

Aldi and Lidl is no walk in the park. There is little information sharing. They have very strict service requirements and back that up with penalties in case you fail to deliver according to the agreement. Hard discounters also want to minimize their working capital, so they will ask you to keep inventory and drive payment terms to the extreme, driving up your working capital. Instead of the targeted situation from Figure 4.1, we may end up in the situation displayed in Figure 4.2. When comparing the private label business to the branded business we have a lower gross margin, but with a higher cost, and with more capital employed, so we have less EBIT, for more capital employed or less bang for more buck. That's not exactly what I as an investor was looking for.

The belief that we should be able to combine both businesses is quite persistent and even dogmatic. When talking to a chief supply chain officer (CSCO) recently, he told me, 'This has been discussed with the family owners and they decided that combining branded and private label is a strategic choice for our company.' That makes me ponder who is getting what wrong here. In any case, I tell those chief operating officers (COOs) or CSCOs that we'll need to educate sales colleagues about the different balance and the need to restore it, as shown in Figure 4.3.

FIGURE 4.2 Branded versus private label in the supply chain triangle: in practice

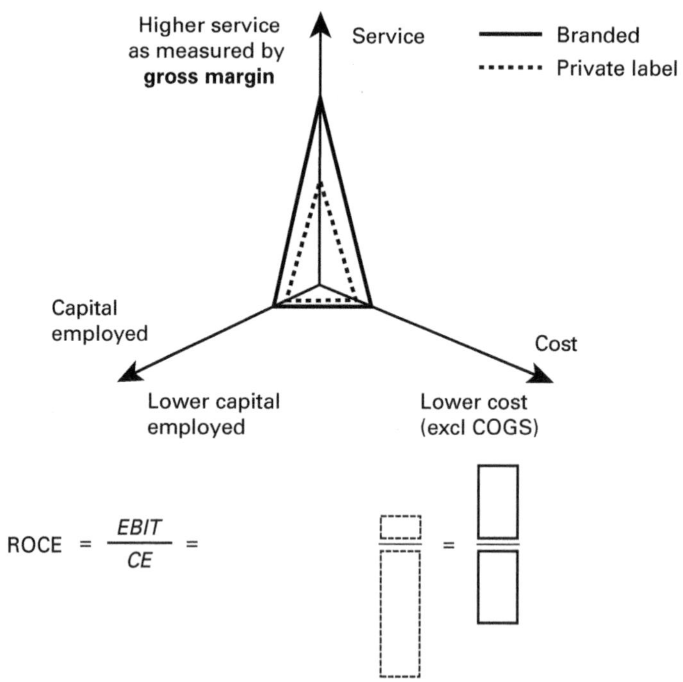

Let's start with working capital and, more specifically, inventory. I challenged the private label player by asking, 'What is this inventory doing at your place? It has the customer's name on it!' You shouldn't accept inventory of private label products. This is the ideal case for concepts like VMI. You don't want to get punished for not delivering on-time, in-full from your warehouse. The only metric that really matters is the on-shelf availability of your products at your customers. To get there, you need a different type of collaboration. Sales will tell you that the customer is not open to it. That's fine, but then you need to charge him for the extra inventory. It's either one or the other; you can't have it both ways. The same for payment terms. It's OK for you to have more working capital, as long as you compensate with a higher EBIT, so think about how you are going to charge the customer. Sales will tell you that the customer is not open to it. You'll need to educate sales that you don't want to support a business that structurally drives less value. You will not be attractive to investors, nor to talent, and eventually not even to new customers.

Then let's look at the costs. For private label to generate value, it should be simple. That's the idea of operational excellence. In Chapter 2 we discussed

FIGURE 4.3 Branded versus private label in the supply chain triangle: restoring the balance

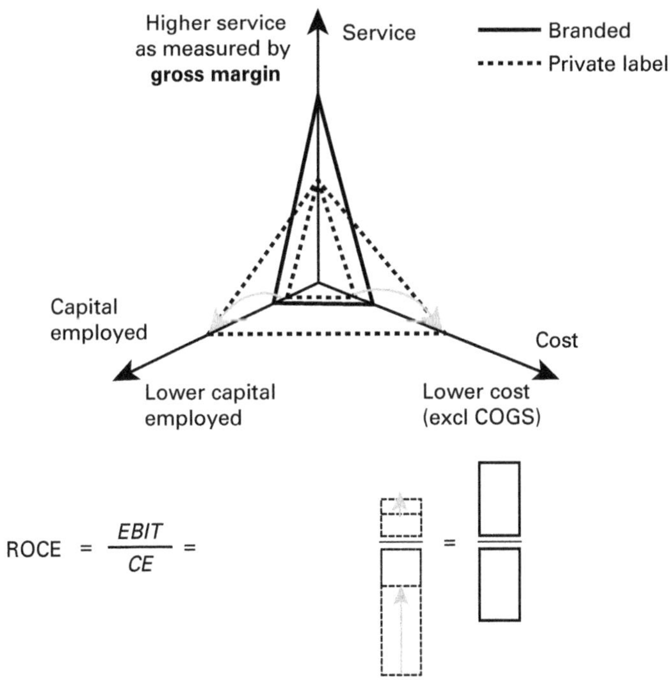

how McBride plc cut back on complexity; 100 customers should not result in 100 different caps and 100 different bottles, and maybe you don't even need all 100 customers. To achieve a low cost, you need to achieve high efficiency. To achieve high efficiency, you need to achieve high volume and high predictability. So, cut out any smaller volumes, focus on the head, cut off the tail. And make it predictable. No orders today for tomorrow. We require you to deliver a forecast for the next three months, the forecast for the next month is binding, so whatever happens we will deliver exactly that amount to your doorstep. I get pushback here from supply chain people. This is not going to work. The bigger retailers have multiple regional distribution centres (DCs) to which we deliver. I agree they have multiple DCs, but I disagree that it's not going to work. Get over it. Make a split based on the latest forecast per DC. Incentivize your customer based on forecast accuracy. Be creative, be bold. Accepting the status quo is accepting that private label is structurally less attractive. Rethink the boundaries!

Strategy evolves with the lifecycle of the product

It is a common perception that as a product or technology commoditizes, the dominant strategy changes to operational excellence. I believe that's true. The problem arises when companies are indecisive in where they want to play. Do they want to play in the innovation arena, with top-notch R&D, highest performance, highest specification products, or do they want to play in the operational excellence arena, with a focus on simplicity, scale and efficiency? Many companies never really ask this question. As a product or technology commoditizes, they simply 'stay on board'. The reason is that selling off the business would create a hole in their top line, and most probably conflict with their growth ambition.

Still, this is exactly what product leaders like 3M do. 3M was once in VHS video cassettes; it quit the business long before video started to decline. In his book *International Business Strategy*, Alain Verbeke states that 3M eliminates any business that cannot sustain annual sales growth of 10 per cent and profit targets of 25 per cent.[2] So 3M decided to sell off the business at a moment it could still get good money for it. They focus on innovation and the growth phase. They leave the mature phase of the market to others.

Figure 4.4 shows the 3M 'technology platforms' as displayed on the 3M website.[3] The subscript of the title says 'Explore 3M's core technologies to see how our ideas live on, in connection with others, to help solve problems around the world.' This indicates that 3M is not afraid of stepping out of a

FIGURE 4.4 3M technology platforms

Explore 3M's core technologies to see how our ideas live on, in connection with others, to help solve problems around the world.

Ab Abrasives												
Ad Adhesives	**Em** Electronic Materials										**Di** Display Components	**Hd** Healthcare Data Management
Bi Biomaterials	**Fi** Films	**Nw** Nonwovens							**Ms** Modeling & Simulation	**Ac** Acoustic Management	**Ec** Energy Components	**Lm** Light Management
Ce Ceramics	**Fl** Fluoro-materials	**Pm** Performance Materials	**Am** Additive Manufacturing	**Pc** Precision Coating & Web Processing	**Rp** Radiation Processing	**An** Analytical Science	**Pr** Process Design & Control	**Cv** Computer Vision	**Ro** Advanced Robotics	**Bd** Biodetection & Microbial Management	**Eg** Engineered Graphics	**Mf** Mechanical Fasteners
Co Advanced Composites	**Mm** Metamaterials	**Po** Porous Materials & Membranes	**Mo** Molding	**Pd** Particle & Dispersion Processing	**Su** Surface Modification	**Cp** Converting & Packaging	**Sd** Sustainable Design	**Ds** Data Science & Analytics	**Se** Sensors	**Cs** Connected Systems	**Fe** Flexible Electronics	**Sw** Skin & Wound Management
Do Dental & Orthodontic Materials	**Nt** Nano-technology	**Rm** Release Materials	**Mr** Micro-replication	**Pp** Polymer Processing	**Tf** Thin Film & Plasma Processing	**In** Inspection & Measurement	**We** Accelerated Weathering	**Es** Electronic Systems	**Ss** Software Solutions	**Dd** Drug Delivery	**Fp** Filtration & Purification	**Tm** Thermal Management
Materials			**Processing**			**Capabilities**		**Digital**		**Applications**		

SOURCE 3M

market; they do that by design. The core technologies are the breeding ground from which new products will be created. 3M has confidence 'there will always be problems around the world that need a solution'.

So coming back to our original question, yes, the strategy can evolve with the lifecycle of the product, but Treacy and Wiersema tell us that your company's strategy does not. So how do you want to become a market leader? By being at the start of the product lifecycle, as an innovator, earning a premium from the early adopters and niches, stepping out at the moment something becomes mainstream? Or as an operational excellence player, never the first on the market, but a follower that waits until the market is a certain size, until technological innovation is slowing down and a good version of the technology becomes available at a decent price, to then go for the volumes, and beat the competition on price? Strategy literature in general tells us you need to make a choice. Do you have the guts to do so?

We changed our strategy

I have seen companies changing their strategy. Sometimes deliberately and well advertised in annual reports. Sometimes almost unknowingly, as a kind of a natural reaction to the changing competitive landscape. Let's reflect on that through the eyes of Treacy and Wiersema, and through the lens of the supply chain triangle.

We just gave the example of transitioning from product leadership to operational excellence, as a technology evolves through its lifecycle. In practice it is even more common to transition from product leadership to customer intimacy. One of the examples would be the former 'control rooms' division of Barco, a company featured in more detail later in this chapter. Barco historically was active in control rooms, as it is a specialist in projection technology. Control rooms historically were made from so-called 'rear projection cubes'. By putting a projector at the back, and making a system of cubes, companies could build a wall of cubes of virtually any size. Figure 4.5 shows an example of such a rear projection cube.

What is happening to this market? It is being disrupted by LED technologies. Early LED screens didn't have the same resolution and came with thick borders. However, as the technology matures, it becomes far easier, and far cheaper, to build a LED wall rather than a wall of rear projection cubes. Who are the champions in LED? Not a 1 billion company like Barco, but Korean giants like Samsung. What was the almost 'natural' reaction of

FIGURE 4.5 Rear projection DLP cube, EC-2004 Series from Eyevis

Barco? Well, we have an existing relationship with customers needing a control room. Let's try to build on that relationship and start building a total solution. Barco started talking and offering products and services for anything that is 'before the wall', like high-speed networks and controllers that need to move a massive amount of high-resolution imaging data. The 2013 annual report talks about the plan to 'grow beyond visualization and video walls to offer customer-integrated systems for collaborative decision-making'.[4] So what Barco did was switch from a product leadership to a customer intimacy strategy, as suggested by the 'integrated systems'.

Though this seems logical, there are two problems with this type of move. First is getting the EBIT right. A product leadership business should get to a 50 per cent gross margin. If the business starts suffering because the product is no longer really leading, it is hard to sustain that. Let's say the gross margin starts dropping to around 40 per cent, which following our earlier discussions in Chapter 3 might rather be the number of a customer intimacy player. We still have the cost structure of the product leader, though. So unless we start cutting costs in R&D and operations, we will simply be eating our EBIT. And remember that in the meantime we will need to start building that total solution as well. Not that obvious.

Second is getting the capital employed right. A product leadership business is already heavy on working capital. What I see happening is that we are going to add the broader product range on top, without cutting out the original complexity. So if we already had an EBIT problem, we just added a capital employed problem, resulting in an even bigger ROCE problem.

So what would be the options according to Treacy and Wiersema? The most logical choice for Barco would be to step out of the market. That's probably what a company like 3M would do, long before LED starts hitting the market. 3M would pull back, start from its core competencies, and recombine those core competencies, attacking new markets with new products.

A second choice could be to switch to operational excellence, as I have seen with a company like Agfa-Gevaert, when it comes to 'analogue film'. Think about the old X-ray scanners where your bones are displayed on a blue film. Agfa-Gevaert makes that film and the cassettes to develop them after the X-ray scan has happened. As medical systems are going digital, analogue film is facing a slow but certain death. That death can take 20 years, however. Developed countries will be the first to switch to digital systems, and they switch quickly. It can take years for developing countries to switch. The saying at Agfa was 'the last one [in the market] turns off the lights'. As players are quitting the market, there is an opportunity to either buy and consolidate the activities, or try to grab the market share that becomes available at that moment. If you can cut complexity, consolidate volumes and organize in an operationally excellent way, there can be many years of good business in there. As these markets keep declining, you'll need to prepare for multiple restructurings, though. Treacy and Wiersema would ask you 'Is this your skill?' or 'Is this your DNA?' Is this what you're good at? In the case of Barco, it's most probably not.

The third choice would be the customer intimacy. But instead of 'keeping the old' while 'bringing in the new', the better choice would probably be to 'sell the old', for instance to an opex player that wants to 'turn off the lights' in that rear-projection market, while 'building the new'. You might think about the type of deal you want to negotiate, some kind of benefit sharing in the first few years, but in any case you try to relieve the organization of the 'old complexity' so it has headroom to start building the 'new complexity'. You're no longer a designer, producer and marketeer of rear-projection cubes; you have become a specialist in control room solutions, with privileged access to a partner that is producing one part of the solution.

Growth is not a strategy

In the section on branded versus private label, we gave the example of a private label player that had growth as a strategy. The idea was that growth would lead to a better negotiation power and as such improve the bottom line. Judging by Treacy and Wiersema, I would say that is a tactic at best, but it is not a strategy. The strategy question would be, 'How are you going to differentiate? How are you going to stand out? What will be your source of competitive advantage? Product? Price? Or best total solution?'

When I was talking to the VP Finance responsible for M&A, he admitted that from a financial point of view the strategy of the target (branded versus private label) was of little consideration. They were more interested in looking at the price to be paid, the discounted cash flows, the cost of capital, the risk factor, etc.

In his HBR article 'The new M&A playbook', Clayton Christensen teaches us to compare the 'business models' of the two companies to be merged.[5] He captures the 'business model' in four elements. The first is the customer value proposition (product/price/total solution). The second is the profit formula, made up of a revenue model and a cost structure that specify how the company generates profit and the cash required to sustain operations (cf Figure 3.12). The third is the resources – such as employees, customers, technology, products, facilities and cash – that companies use to deliver the customer value proposition. The fourth is the processes such as manufacturing, R&D, budgeting and sales. We have already discussed how different these are (or should be) for a branded goods manufacturer and a private label player.

So when it's about M&A or about organic growth, the strategy will always be dominant in defining how we drive that growth. It should not be the other way around.

The curse of segmented supply chains

The answer to the above questions, combining branded and private label, combining innovation and commodities, has been 'segmented supply chains'. Though I agree that different strategies lead to very different supply chains and there is no one size fits all, we should think about whether these segmented supply chains are a gift or a curse.

If the two businesses are completely separate, run on different assets, by different planning teams, the issue is not really with supply chain. The issue then shifts to marketing, to R&D, or to sales. How will they prioritize one over the other? Often, these different businesses share at least some of the supply chain people and some assets. If that is the case, think about how you want to differently control the assets for the different businesses. If you need to combine branded and private label, my advice has been to concentrate the private label products, for instance, in the beginning of the week. The amount of changeovers and the efficiency should be much higher for the private label products, as we know we won't get to the same margins as for the branded business. For the branded business, some smaller runs and more frequent changeovers are OK. The margins of the branded business should allow for that. More flexibility is needed, as we may want to launch a test of a new product in a small batch first. We may have temporary products or packaging variants for temporary promotions. All of these are part of the branded DNA.

Segmented supply chains should not, however, be used as an excuse to avoid strategic choices. As mentioned earlier, we hate to make choices and think choosing is losing. We'd rather be stuck in the middle with an undifferentiated positioning rather than taking the risk of making the wrong choice. Most often, the choices are obvious. Go back to your roots. Those define your DNA. Stay true to yourself. Don't try to be all things to all people. Though supply chain doesn't have the clout in the organization to force choices, it should also not provide excuses for not having to make them. In that sense, I believe segmented supply chains are more of a curse than a blessing.

This concludes our section on typical 'strategy fails'. In what follows, we will zoom into the strategy transformation of Barco, Casio and Johnson Controls. We will analyse how strategy plays in food retail and how different strategies lead to a different financial structure there.

CASE STUDY

Technology company: Barco

Any technology-related sector is a dream for applying Treacy and Wiersema. You can have product leaders, which are continuously on the edge and live from the newer, better, and higher spec technologies. You can have customer intimacy players, who solve the broad technological challenges for their customers. You will have the cost players, which strip down products to their core, work with older but still recent versions of the technology, making products that are 'good enough' and which come at prices that can't be beaten.

In this section we will look in more detail at Barco, a Belgian company active in high-end projection and visualization. Barco is headquartered in Kortrijk in Belgium and listed on the Euronext stock exchange in Brussels. The public listing means financial information is available for over 15 years. The financial reports of the company cover the strategy, any acquisitions or divestments, any changes in strategy. Any information we share is drawn from information available to the public.

The interesting aspect of Barco is that it went through a clearly communicated strategy shift. The shift came in response to the significant downturn Barco experienced during the financial crisis. Figures 4.6 and 4.7 show sales and EBIT (before restructuring and goodwill impairment) in the period 2004–14. We see at least three distinct periods: the period 2004–07, where EBIT was between €60–80 million, and sales were between €600–800 million; the crisis period 2008–10, where 2009 was the absolute dip, in both sales and EBIT; and the period 2011–14, where sales exceeded €1 billion for the first time in the existence of the company, and where the EBIT rebounded between €80 million and €100 million, except for 2014. Looking back, 2010 was a year of transition. The data shown in Figures 4.6 and 4.7 has been taken from publicly available financial reports of Barco.

The shift in strategy was linked to a change in CEO. Eric Van Zele became CEO in 2009, at the deepest moment of crisis. As an alumnus of Stanford, he is familiar with the model of Treacy and Wiersema. He used the model in public presentations to first explain that, as a product leader, Barco had fallen behind on operational excellence, so a catch-up had to be done. Second, he announced a shift from product leadership into customer intimacy, having observed that, of all the beautiful technologies originally invented at Barco, not enough was reaching more mass markets.

The 2013 annual report provides the most elaborate documentation of the shift.[6] It discusses the shift from the 'high end' to inclusion of the 'mid-segment' and 'volume markets'. High end remains the roots of Barco. The 2013 report talks about 40 per cent

FIGURE 4.6 Barco sales, 2004–14

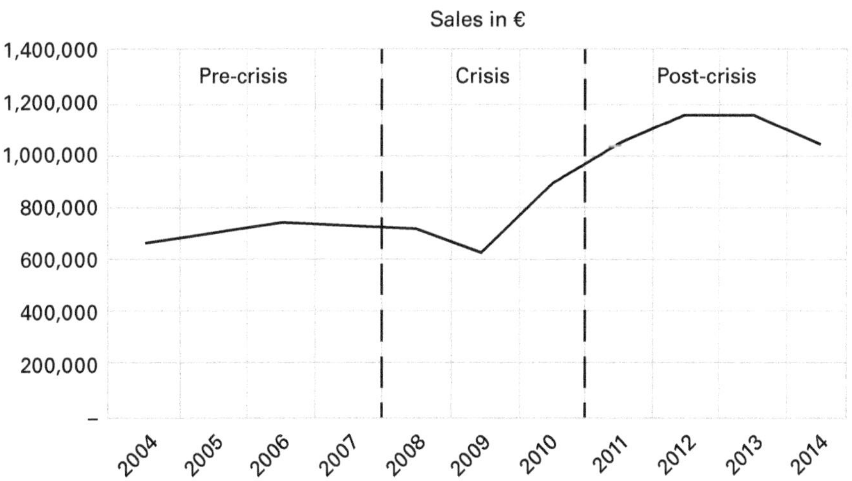

FIGURE 4.7 Barco EBIT, 2004–14

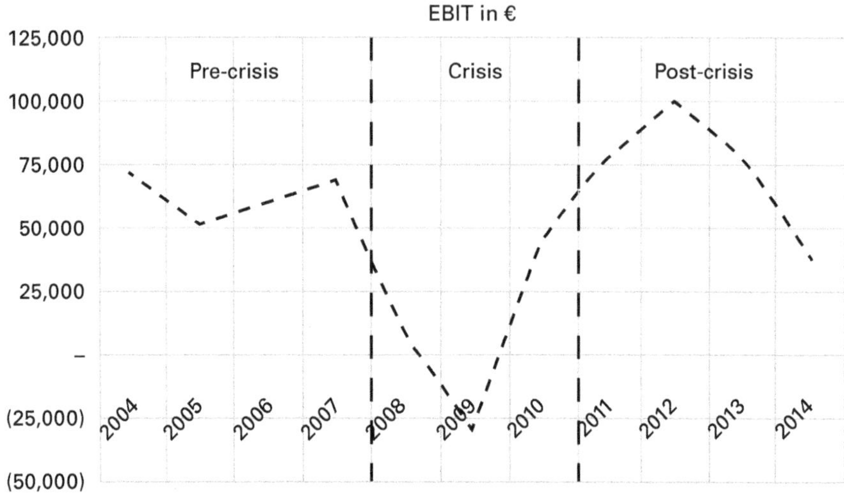

market share in projection solutions for entertainment, and 45 per cent market share for diagnostic and modality imaging in healthcare. The claim of the top segment is supported by the mentioning of 223 technology patents and by sustained R&D spending. The move into mid-segment projection solutions was exemplified by the acquisition of a Norwegian company called Projectiondesign, a provider of mid-range projectors. The move into the volume markets was announced through the launch of a 'range of single-chip DLP projectors to facilitate collaboration in meeting rooms'. So when it comes to projectors, the range was extended into meeting-room projectors, where Barco started competing with a whole new range of competitors like Optoma, Benq, Acer, InFocus, Casio, Viewsonic, Epson, and many more.

The 2012 annual report talks about 'customer intimacy' and the objective to expand the product portfolio with mid-range products, with a strong focus on a two-tier channel model, as opposed to the direct model in the high-end market. The year 2012 was when Barco launched its 'ClickShare' product.[7] By entering a ClickShare dongle into your laptop via USB, you can connect wirelessly to a projector by just a push of the button.[8] It's another illustration that the strategy shift was serious, and not just idle talk.

Connecting the strategy shift to our supply chain triangle, we'd expect the shift to customer intimacy to be accompanied by a drop in gross margins, requiring a drop in spending on R&D and SG&A, and, if the shift is well organized, an increase in inventory turns, cutting some of the complex products to make room for expanding the portfolio into the mid-range. Figures 4.8 and 4.9 show the evolutions in the period 2004–14. Table 4.1 shows the averages.

FIGURE 4.8 Barco gross profit, R&D and SG&A, 2004–14

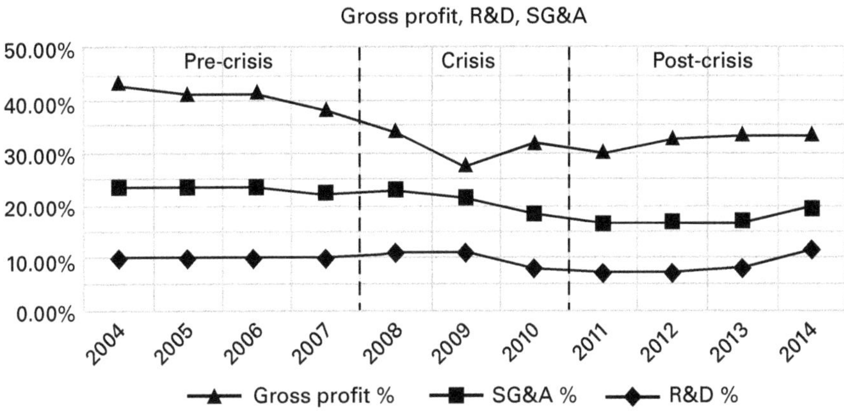

FIGURE 4.9 Barco inventory turns, 2004–14

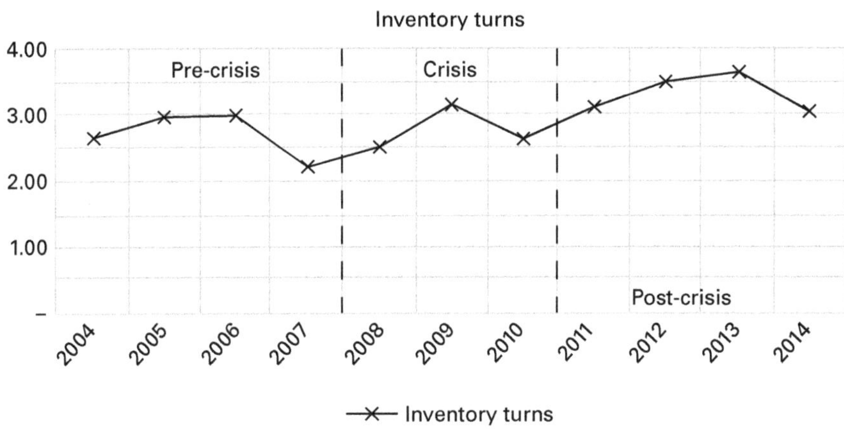

TABLE 4.1 Barco key figures, 2004–07, 2008–10, 2011–14: part 1

	2004–07	2008–10	2011–14
Gross profit %	40.92%	31.27%	32.34%
R&D spending %	9.51%	9.85%	8.39%
SG&A spending %	23.16%	20.87%	17.49%
Inventory turns	2.71	2.78	3.32

Gross profit drops from 41 per cent to 32 per cent before/after the strategic shift. R&D spending drops from 9.5 per cent to 8.4 per cent (1 per cent drop). The biggest impact is in the SG&A spending, which drops from 23 per cent to 17.5 per cent. Inventory turns improve from 2.7 to 3.3, which is an improvement, but only limited. The explanation is in the strategy. Instead of a 'full shift' towards customer intimacy, it seems more like the customer intimacy comes 'on top of' the product leadership. We will keep our positions in the niche markets, and in parallel expand into the mid-range and the volume markets. The data for Figures 4.8, 4.9 and Table 4.1 have been taken from publicly available financial reports of Barco.

Connecting back to the ROCE principle in our supply chain triangle, we'd expect a customer intimacy player to generate ROCE with a lower EBIT, but using less capital employed (in comparison to the product leader). Figure 4.10 shows EBIT and ROCE over 2004–14. Table 4.2 shows the averages. The average ROCE of 12.25 per cent in the pre-crisis period is based on an average EBIT of 8.82 per cent. ROCE in the post-crisis period averages 11.25 per cent, which is exactly 1 per cent lower, based on an EBIT of 6.66 per cent, which is more than 2 per cent lower. Looking at the inventory turns, it seems the company has not been cutting sufficiently in the product complexity, to make room for the extension into the mid-range. Making tougher choices here would have supported a further reduction of the capital employed and as such a further increase in ROCE. The data for Figure 4.10 and Table 4.2 have been taken from publicly available financial reports of Barco.

The above case has been reproduced from our 2018 book, *Supply Chain Strategy and Financial Metrics*.[9] We have chosen to keep the original story intact, as it is a truthful narrative of the type of discussions held at the company and the moves that have been made. But it is equally interesting to continue the story and give you the sequel.

FIGURE 4.10 Barco EBIT and ROCE, 2004–14

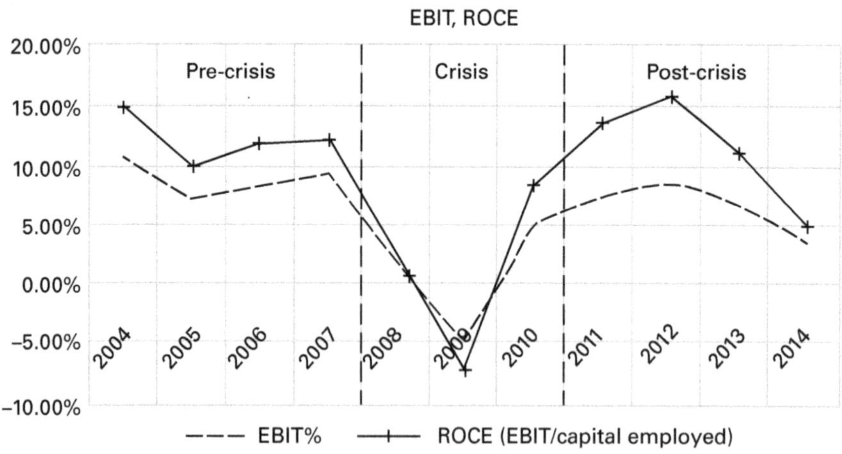

TABLE 4.2 Barco key figures, 2004–07, 2008–10, 2011–14: part 2 (*EBIT before restructuring and goodwill impairment)

	2004–07	2008–10	2011–14
EBIT, in €000 (*)	63,109	8,167	73,963
EBIT % (*)	8.82%	0.54%	6.66%
Capital employed, in €000	516,648	493,445	680,973
ROCE %	12.25%	0.98%	11.25%

It starts with a bad performance in 2015, as was already visible from Figure 4.10, where the EBIT trend was clearly down. That trend was confirmed in 2015 with an EBIT of a mere 0.17 per cent. Coincidence or not, in 2016 Barco transitioned from Eric Van Zele to Jan De Witte as the new CEO.

Before joining Barco, Jan De Witte worked for P&G and McKinsey, and for the previous 15 years for GE Healthcare as the President and CEO of Global Performance Solutions. GE is known for its ruthless focus on performance. Each year, their iconic CEO Jack Welch would fire the bottom 10 per cent of his managers and rewarded those in the top 20 per cent with bonuses and employee stock options. Around the same period as Jan De Witte joined Barco as its new CEO, Charles Beauduin, a Belgian entrepreneur with a strong focus on operations, became the major shareholder and chair of the board. You feel this will go in a different direction...

The 2016 annual report talks about 'enhancements in gross margin', 'keeping OPEX [operational expense] under control' and a 'focus on technology that truly enables customer outcomes'. The 2017 annual report continues with 'executing our renewed strategy, which includes an increased focus on our performance' and 'of course, we retained the zeal for innovation so typical of Barco'. The 2018 report concludes with talking about a 'balanced focus on operational excellence and intensified management attention on business and cost efficiencies', while 'continuing to invest in innovation to secure our long-term growth prospects'.

The change in CEO and chair led to a 'focus to perform', as the strategic plan was called. You see a combination of 'back to the core', being the 'product leadership DNA', the innovation, but in a GE or operationally excellent, no-frills way. The result is shown in Table 4.3.

In the period 2017–19, Barco went back to the gross profit levels of 2005–07, its heyday of product leadership. EBIT was restored to 8.55 per cent, also comparable to the 2005–07 levels. Under the operational excellence push it has become much more efficient in working capital. An average CCC of 170 went down to an average of

TABLE 4.3 Barco key figures, 2005–19 (*EBIT before restructuring and goodwill impairment)

	2005–07	2008–10	2011–13	2014–16	2017–19
Gross profit %	40%	31%	32%	34%	39%
EBIT (*)	60,336	8,167	85,874	25,495	91,084
EBIT %	8.22%	0.54%	7.67%	2.37%	8.55%
CCC	170	154	111	96	77
Fixed asset turns	3.04	3.36	3.21	2.45	2.87
ROCE	13.46%	1.52%	15.30%	3.60%	12.05%

77. That is quite impressive. It went backward on fixed asset turns, though, lowering ROCE to 12.05 per cent.

It is tempting to feel sympathy for the Barco story and have some understanding that a change of CEO and chair leads to a change in course. However, that's not what Treacy and Wiersema advise. It is not what in their understanding builds market leaders. Also, as investors, there's not necessarily much to be happy about. As shown from Table 4.3, for every three-year period where we get to a 12–15 per cent ROCE, there seems to be a three-year period of a 1–4 per cent ROCE. This, too, is not what Treacy and Wiersema would define as the performance of a market leader. It is bleak compared to the consistent 15–20 per cent EBIT performance and the consistent 12–16 per cent ROCE of P&G in Figure 2.7. We need to seriously question whether it is acceptable that strategies change with the CEO or chair, or whether it would be more logical for strategies to survive the change in CEO and chair, and that both individuals are just passers-by who inherit, strengthen and develop it, to then pass it on to the next people in post.

CASE STUDY

Technology company: Casio

If Barco tried to switch from product leadership to customer intimacy or operational excellence, some companies make the exact opposite movement. A remarkable example is Casio. In its 2016 annual report, Casio claims high profitability through innovative products.[10] With a 12 per cent operating margin and a return on equity of 15.4 per cent, that's a credible claim. It reports 85.4 per cent of the net sales are from consumer electronics, 12.1 per cent from system equipment (including projectors) and 2.5 per cent from others. The report showcases six global 'timepiece brands', including G-Shock (absolute toughness) and Pro Trek (ideal for the field). The strategy talks about 'promoting the introduction to upscale retailers'. Next to this, the report talks about 'expanding scientific and localized calculators', 'expanding high-unit-price keyboards featuring high-quality, rich tones and rhythms', 'wrist devices for fishing, trekking and cycling', and 'laser and LED hybrid projectors with 20,000 hours' light source lifetime'. This reads and breathes a product leadership strategy – high-end niche products being sold through upscale retailers.

Casio was a completely different company before the financial crisis. As Pierre-Yves Donze describes in his book on the history of the Japanese watch industry, the dominant strategy of the Japanese watch companies, Seiko, Citizen and Casio, was to offer high-quality goods for a cheap price.[11] He describes how they were dominated by a real technological paradigm that had not changed since the 1950s, in which the competitiveness of a firm relied on the quality – hence the necessity to innovate and develop new technologies – and the cost – that is, relocating plants to low-wages countries – of their products. Their Swiss- and Hong Kong-based rivals started from a marketing strategy, constructing brands, careful positioning of their products, and watching the right distribution channels. Contrast that with the 2016 annual report and it is clear the company has made a shift.

The strategic shift is well documented in the 2008 annual report.[12] It describes how 'Fiscal 2008 was our 50th anniversary, and fiscal 2009 is our first year of a new phase of innovation under the name of The Rebirth of Casio'. The discussion of its 'medium and long-term management strategy' continues that efforts will be made to 'ensure high profitability', to 'create new strategic businesses' and to 'strengthen our financial structure'. Under 'ensure high profitability' it mentions the goal of achieving an overall operating income margin of 10 per cent or more. The main contributors to these are mentioned as lowering the cost of sales through improved productivity, and strengthening global market presence to create economies of scale. Under 'creating new strategic businesses' it mentions that 'we will have to develop new business areas in addition to our existing segments, drawing strengths from the unique technological base, which other companies cannot match, focusing even more management resources on the development of promising new business areas, creating new business with tough earnings structures and getting them up and running as soon as possible'. Where operations has to contribute to improving the profitability, the real strategic choice here is the shift to product leadership (develop new business areas, drawing strengths from the unique technological base, which other companies cannot match).

Let's get back to our supply chain triangle. A shift from operational excellence to product leadership should provide a dramatic shift in gross margin. As gross margin increases, this creates more room for spending on R&D and SG&A. As described above by Pierre-Yves Donze, Japanese watch makers may always have had smart

R&D but have underinvested and been weak in marketing and sales. Making catchier products and investing in marketing and sales should drive the extra gross margin. Catchier products, with a higher rate of innovation, with misses from time to time and longer distribution channels, might increase the inventory required and decrease the inventory turns. Figures 4.11 and 4.12 show exactly these movements. The numbers used in the figures and tables in this section have been taken from the publicly available annual reports of Casio since 2004.

Table 4.4 shows that the average gross profit increases from 29 per cent to 42 per cent. The R&D spending remains relatively constant at around 2–3 per cent. The SG&A

FIGURE 4.11 Casio gross profit, R&D and SG&A, 2004–16

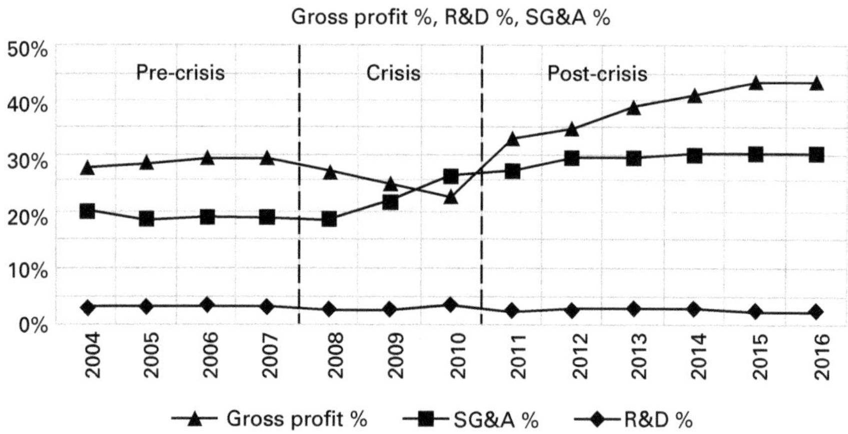

FIGURE 4.12 Casio inventory turns, 2004–16

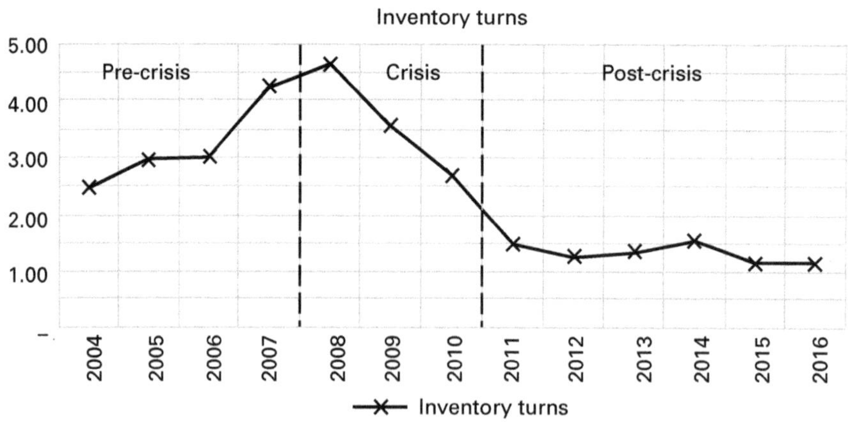

TABLE 4.4 Casio key figures, 2004–08, 2009–12, 2013–16: part 1

	2004–08	2009–12	2013–16
Gross profit %	28.66%	29.10%	41.87%
R&D spending %	2.82%	2.60%	2.38%
SG&A spending %	19.15%	26.39%	30.32%
Inventory turns	3.48	2.27	1.31

FIGURE 4.13 Casio EBIT and ROCE, 2004–16

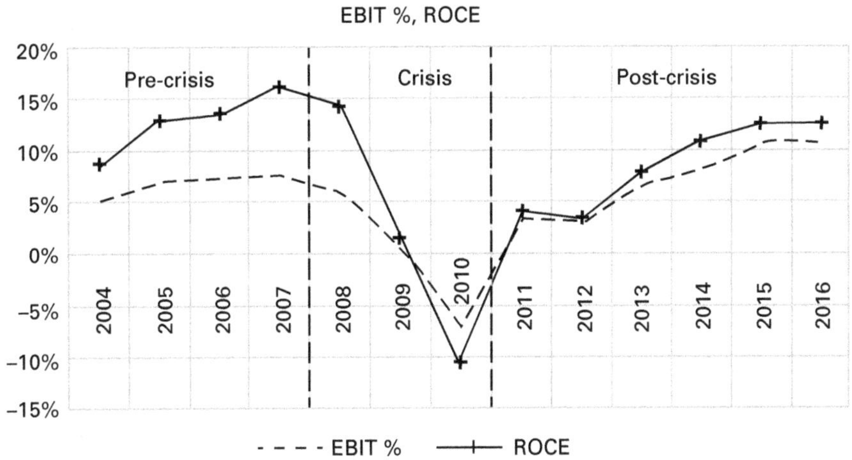

spending increases dramatically, from 19 per cent to 30 per cent. The inventory turns decrease, from an average of 3.5 to an average of 1.3. Compared to Barco, the 2–3 per cent spending on R&D seems low, and the SG&A of 30 per cent seems high. Also the turns of 1.3 seem low. More extensive benchmarks are required to develop industry standards.

Let's turn to the expected ROCE impact. If we switch from operational excellence to product leadership, we expect the EBIT percentage will significantly increase, but as the complexity increases, we need more capital employed. Figure 4.13 and Table 4.5 show that the EBIT percentage increases from 6.7 per cent to 9.2 per cent, which is a 2.5 per cent increase. ROCE decreases from 13.1 per cent to 11 per cent, which is a 2.1 per cent decrease. At first sight, the spending on SG&A seems heavy, negatively impacting ROCE. You have the feeling that, as they may have underdone it for a prolonged period in the 1980s and 1990s, they are now overdoing it. At the same

TABLE 4.5 Casio key figures, 2004–08, 2009–12, 2013–16: part 2

	2004–08	2009–12	2013–16
EBIT, in Mio Yen	39,094	(1,047)	30,039
EBIT %	6.69%	0.11%	9.18%
Capital employed, in Mio Yen	299,587	277,782	270,894
ROCE %	13.13%	-0.40%	10.97%

FIGURE 4.14 Casio gross profit and SG&A, 2004–19

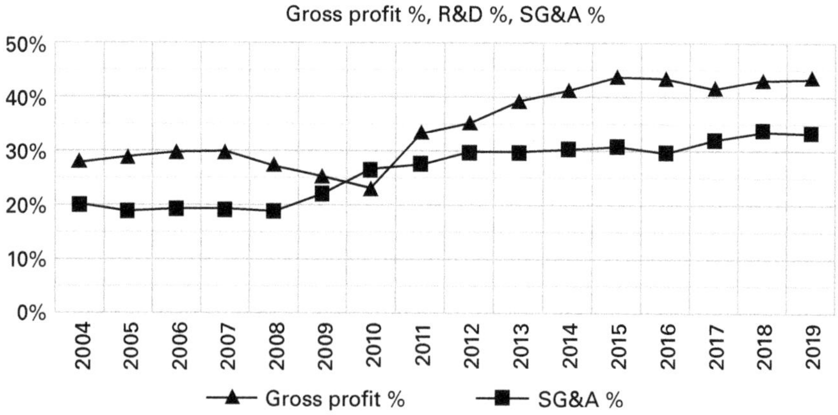

time, looking at the inventory turns, the turns seem below par, even for a product leader. This may be a signal that they have let the complexity grow out of control, putting a stretch on the capital employed.

This case study was also included in our 2018 book, *Supply Chain Strategy and Financial Metrics*.[13] We have chosen to keep the original story intact, as it neatly describes how a company like Casio tries to get out of the commodity space and more into the advanced and luxury space. In the meantime, we can extend the story with another three years of financials. So how did the story continue? How did Casio fare?

Figures 4.14 to 4.16 and Table 4.6 show that Casio has been quite consistent in executing its strategy. Gross profit levels have remained stable at over 40 per cent. Inventory turns have remained low at around 1. ROCE has been stable at around 10 per cent.

As Table 4.6 shows, it has been very consistent. Note that the 33 per cent SG&A in 2017–19 is including R&D expenses. The 11 per cent ROCE, however, is lower than the 13 per cent ROCE Casio was generating in the period 2004–08. Only time will tell if

FIGURE 4.15 Casio inventory turns, 2004–19

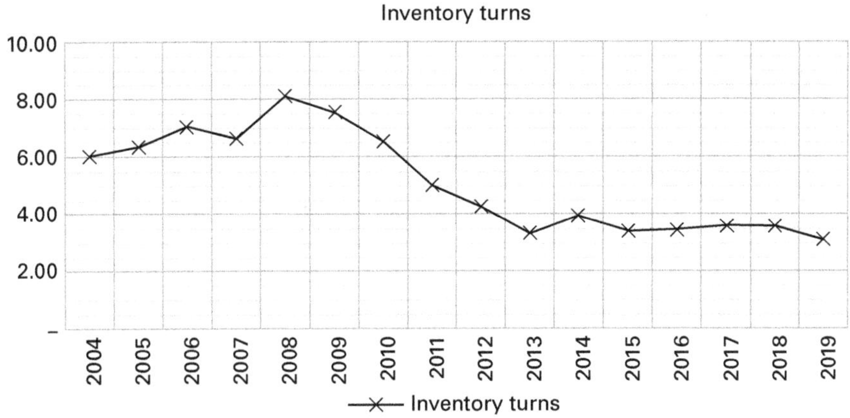

FIGURE 4.16 Casio EBIT and ROCE, 2004–19

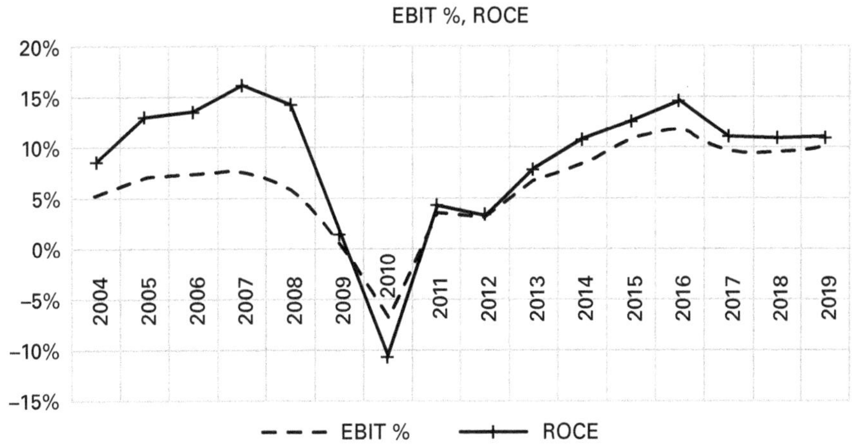

TABLE 4.6 Casio key figures, 2004–19

	2004–08	2009–12	2013–16	2017–19
Gross profit %	29%	29%	42%	43%
SG&A %	19%	26%	30%	33%
EBIT %	6.69%	0.11%	9.46%	9.69%
ROCE	13.13%	–0.40%	11.48%	11.02%

Casio succeeds in driving more value from its new strategy. Treacy and Wiersema, in any case, warn us. Once an operational excellence player, always an operational excellence player, a bit like when Barco almost automatically reverted to its product leadership DNA when a new management team took over. The Japanese are known to think determinedly in the long term. In that sense we might conclude that if one company could succeed in changing its DNA, it's probably going to be a Japanese company. If only we could 'fast forward' to 2024 to see how the strategy move further plays out for Casio. That's the hard part of strategy. It only really plays out over a longer term.

CASE STUDY
Johnson Controls

WITH FRANK VORRATH, VICE PRESIDENT, GARTNER, SUPPLY CHAIN SERVICE DELIVERY FOR EMEA AND APAC (FORMER VICE PRESIDENT, GLOBAL SUPPLY CHAIN, JOHNSON CONTROLS INC)

This case will dig into the multi-year transformational change of a multi-industrial company driven by the complexity of three different strategic positions.

Johnson Controls International plc is a multinational conglomerate headquartered in Cork, Ireland. The company is a global diversified technology and multi-industrial leader serving a wide range of customers in more than 150 countries. It employs 130,000 people in more than 1,300 locations across six continents. Johnson Controls International plc was formed via the merger of the American company Johnson Controls Inc with Tyco International, which was completed on 2 September 2016. The forming of Johnson Controls International plc is the result of a multi-year transformational change process. In this section we want to revisit the reasoning behind the transformation and analyse what value has been created as a result.

Prior to the merger with Tyco International, Johnson Controls Inc was organized in several business units, as follows.

Building Technologies and Solutions (BT&S, previously Building Efficiency). The Building Efficiency business unit designs, produces, installs and services heating, ventilation and air conditioning systems, industrial refrigeration, building management systems, fire and security systems and mechanical equipment for commercial and residential buildings. BT&S supply chains have a configuration of make to stock (MTS), configure to order (CTO) and engineer to order (ETO). Using the terminology of Treacy and Wiersema, the BT&S strategic position can be seen as customer intimacy providing integrated, customized and tailor-made product solutions and selling them globally through various sales channels. In 2014–15, BT&S generated a segment EBIT of 8–9 per cent.[14] One of the main characteristics of the business is that it is driven by long lead times and backlog orders.

Power Solutions. The Power Solutions business unit designs and manufactures automotive lead-acid, lithium-ion cells including complete batteries, absorbent glass matt batteries and enhanced flooded batteries. Power Solution's supply chains have a configuration of make to order (MTO) for the automotive original equipment manufacturing and MTS for the aftermarket and retail business. The Power Solution strategic position can be seen as product leader providing best in class products mainly for AGM and EFB batteries enabled by an unmatched competitive global production capacity. In 2014–15, Power Solutions generated a segment EBIT of 16–17 per cent.[15] One of the main characteristics of the MTS aftermarket and retail supply chain is that it's highly cash consuming as a result of a strategic decision to balance demand and supply through a pre-built manufacturing process as well as high inventory storage during the spring and summer months followed by the main sales only during the winter months.

Automotive Experience. The Automotive Experience business unit supplies automotive seating to car manufacturers. It is the largest tier 1 supplier for seating in the world. The seating division designs and manufactures automotive seats and supplies them in a just-in-time model to car manufacturers. Automotive Experience's supply chains have a configuration of MTO for the automotive original equipment manufacturing and MTS for the aftermarket business. The Automotive Experience strategic position can be seen as operational excellence leader focusing on efficiency, productivity and cost enabled by a world-class just-in-time manufacturing process and competitive sourcing. In 2014–15, Automotive Experience generated a segment EBIT of 4–6 per cent.[16]

In 2015, Johnson Controls started considering strategic options for Automotive Experience, reportedly to 'exit low-margin businesses and focus on businesses where it could attain a leadership position'.[17] The *Financial Times* quoted Alex Molinaroli, Chief Executive, as saying that 'the group was unwilling to provide the capital the business needed to develop new products such as lightweight materials'.[18]

In general, we believe low margins and heavy investments in the automotive business triggered a strategic review of the entire business of Johnson Controls Inc, which in the meantime seems to be unwinding in four major phases:

- Phase 1: Spin off of the automotive business into Adient plc, finalized October 2016.[19]
- Phase 2: Creation of a global leader in 'building systems' through a merger with Tyco International, finalized in September 2016.[20]
- Phase 3: Exit the power solutions business, finalized November 2018.[21]
- Phase 4: (Expected) M&A activity to strengthen building and technology business to increase the overall company revenue back to $30 billion or more.

As reported by the *Financial Times*, at the heart of the Tyco deal is 'a bet that a series of economic and technological trends should provide higher-than-average returns for a group with advanced expertise in building systems'.[22] Analysts report to the *Financial Times* that the Internet of Things (IoT) is triggering 'a convergence where fire and safety will be more closely linked to the other controls – air-conditioning, heating and ventilation'. Next to the above there are geographical synergies, with Johnson Controls (JC) being strong in China and the US and Tyco reinforcing the position in Europe.

The strategic transformation positions Johnson Controls International (JCI) as a global customer intimacy leader linked to an integrated service offering of their building and technology product portfolio in order to create long-term sustainable shareholder value as an industrial company.

An obvious question to ask is, 'Did Johnson Controls create value along the way?' Companies may report EBIT per segment, but typically don't report capital employed per segment, which makes it hard to estimate the ROCE of individual segments. As Johnson Controls has been splitting off businesses, and in the case of Automotive moving some parts into a separate company called Adient, it is a unique opportunity to reveal and better understand the impact on the capital employed. Figure 4.17 summarizes which financials we have averaged over which periods: JC pre-merger (with the three businesses as described above), Tyco pre-merger, the new JCI post-merger, with Automotive spun off in a separate company called Adient, and then finally JCI after spinning off the high EBIT power business.

Table 4.7 shows that if one of the original concerns was to improve EBIT, spinning off Automotive into Adient and merging with Tyco have been worthwhile. Adient has realized a 2.4 per cent EBIT, whereas JC post-merger, the new JCI, in 2016–17 realized 8.7 per cent EBIT, well above the 4.9 per cent EBIT of JC pre-merger.

However, we should look beyond EBIT, into capital employed and ROCE. Yes, the automotive business has a low margin, but the inventory turns are 21.8, and net PPE turns are 8.8, which is very high. ROCE, however, remains stuck at 5.7 per cent.

FIGURE 4.17 Financials for pre-/post-merger and pre-/post-divestments

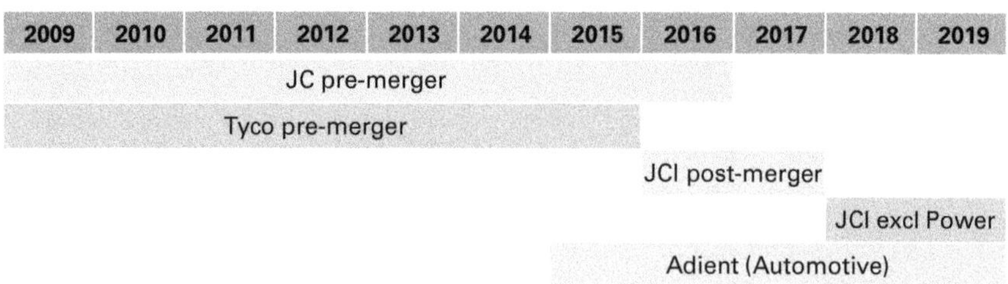

TABLE 4.7 Financials metrics for pre-/post-merger and pre-/post-divestments

Financial metric	JC pre-merger	Tyco pre-merger	JCI post-merger*	JC excl Power	Adient
Gross margin	15.7%	36.7%	28.8%	32.4%	7.5%
EBIT %	4.9%	9.3%	8.7%	7.3%	2.4%
Inventory turns	14.7	9.2	5.9	8.8	21.8
CCC	23	52	73	50	–4
Net PPE turns	6.8	6.0	4.4	7.1	8.8
Fixed asset turns	2.1	1.1	0.6	0.7	2.5
ROCE	9.9%	9.3%	5.5%	4.9%	5.7%

The situation is more difficult for the new JCI, however. EBIT is good at 8.7 per cent, but inventory turns are lower than the pre-merger JC and the pre-merger Tyco, working capital (CCC) is larger, net PPE turns are lower and fixed asset turns are lower, resulting in a 5.5 per cent ROCE, which is well below the 9.9 per cent and 9.3 per cent of the pre-merger JC and Tyco. Inventory turns, CCC and net PPE turns improve after divesting the power business, but fixed asset turns remain very low at 0.7, further reducing ROCE to 4.9 per cent, which is below Adient's ROCE of 5.7 per cent!

The ROCE shown in Table 4.7 is based on EBIT excluding 'transaction, integration and separation costs' and 'significant restructuring and impairment costs', which over 2014–17 are reported to be $1.4 billion and $1.7 billion, or together $3.1 billion, or around 10 per cent of the annual net sales.[23] This is another $3.1 billion of value that is lost in the transformation process, which casts another doubt on the value generated through this transformation.

Although in the short term no value has been generated, we do accept that strategies need to be evaluated in the longer term, say a 5–10- or sometimes even a 15-year period. From that long-term perspective, the resulting Johnson Controls International will certainly be a more focused company, a pure customer intimacy player focused on the expected revolution of IoT in building systems, and will have moved away from the more traditional multi-industrial conglomerate it once was. Judging by the thinking of Treacy and Wiersema, this promises to be a good thing. They argue that you can't mix the culture of a low-cost airline or hard discounter with that of a service or a product leader.

The new Johnson Controls aligns much better with these principles compared to the old multi-strategy, multi-industry conglomerate, which Treacy and Wiersema would call a dilution of focus. However, the challenge will be to transform the culture and supply chain capabilities of people, processes and technology from being very focused on lean principles and strong cost management to a more agile and aligned culture with the supply chain capabilities of a customer intimacy player. The challenge and opportunity are to execute the plans in the chosen strategic direction, which is promising but more from the long-term perspective, while generating enough shareholder value along the way. The leadership of Johnson Controls will be under pressure to justify the decline in shareholder value compared to the pre-merger period, while facing uncertainties in the marketplace that will create potential headwind to generate value.

So, although we believe Johnson Controls has done the right thing, we believe it has done so based on the wrong assumptions. As outlined at the start, much of the reasoning seems to be based on quitting a low-margin business (Adient) and a capital-intensive business with high margin (JC Powersolutions), and the rationale that both businesses will be disrupted by new mobility concepts and changing business models . Taking a more strategic and a value perspective reveals that it is perfectly OK to have a 3–5 per cent margin, if you compensate that with a lower capital employed, but with the overall disruptions in the automotive industry and the very capital-intensive investments on the horizon you will have to make deliberate decisions and that's what the leadership of Johnson Controls did. Adient, the new automotive spin-off, currently delivers a higher ROCE and more value than the new JCI but has to make the required investments which are very capital intensive over the coming years to compete in a new world of smart connected ecosystems and new mobility concepts. The challenge to the new JCI is important. As Table 4.7 shows, its ROCE has dropped instead of increased, and moreover it has spent $3.1 billion to realize the transformation. So, clearly, a lot of value has been destroyed along the way, and it is uncertain when the shareholders will see it back. It all comes down to how disciplined JCI is about executing the chosen strategic direction, but still, we need to say kudos to the Johnson Controls leadership. Being a more focused company, making deliberate choices playing to its strengths on which markets to play and how to position, based on long-term trends, we do believe this is what strategy is about, and strategy-driven organizations are better equipped to drive sustainable business performance as a strong foundation for intrinsic shareholder value.

CASE STUDY
Food retail companies

Where, for manufacturing, we looked at cases where companies changed their strategy over the last 10 years, we didn't find this type of example in retail. The retailers we analysed showed a more consistent strategy and (sometimes lack of) performance over a longer period of time. So to analyse retail we looked for typical 'operational excellence', 'customer intimacy' and 'product leadership' players, analysed their 10–15-year financials, and tried to see if a different strategy leads to a different balance in the supply chain triangle.

When looking for opex players or cost leaders, we need to look for hard discounters. Marc Sachon from IESE defines the key success factors of the German hard discounters as: a limited assortment of products, an increased percentage of private labels offered at low prices, maintaining a high quality/price ratio, and super-efficient operations.[24] Sachon mentions that at Aldi 90 per cent of products in the standard catalogue are distributed via cross-docking facilities. Cross-docking minimizes the warehousing space required and saves on logistics handling. If you have ever shopped at Aldi or Lidl, you will notice the ample use of pallets in the shop, as opposed to racks or shelves. This saves significantly on handling by in-store personnel. The use of pallets requires a high rotation of the goods, which links back into the limited assortment, which focuses on fast-moving products. As Sachon argues, the 'hard-discount model is a prime example of strategic coherence: there is a perfect fit between business strategy, operations strategy and day-to-day operations'. In terms of Treacy and Wiersema, it is operational excellence taken to its extreme.

According to the *Financial Times*, Aldi and Lidl are by far the biggest hard discounters in Europe.[25] Unfortunately, both companies are privately owned, by the German families Albrecht and Schwarz, so there are no public financial statements available. The next in line is Edeka. Edeka is focused on Germany and consists of several cooperatives of independent supermarkets all operating under the umbrella organization. Its headquarters are in Hamburg. Another discounter is Dia (Distribuidora Internacional de Alimentación), which was founded in Spain in 1979 and 'introduced the discount store model in the Spanish food retail market' as they say themselves.[26] For Edeka we have financials for 2009–18, except for 2016. We found management reports but no financial reports for 2016 and 2019. For Dia we have financials for 2015–19 but only used 2015–17 in the analysis. It has been widely reported that 2018 was an *annus horribilis* for Dia that plunged it into a dispute between debt and equity holders on how to keep the company afloat.[27] We believe 2015–17 are more stable and are representative of the discount model.

When looking for publicly listed 'product leaders', we've landed in the US at three companies: Whole Foods Market, The Fresh Market and Sprouts Farmers Market. On its website, Whole Foods Market brands itself as America's healthiest grocery store.[28] It exclusively features foods without artificial preservatives, colours, flavours, sweeteners and hydrogenated fats. It focuses on organic products, which means crops are grown without toxic and persistent pesticides. The Fresh Market brands itself as your neighbourhood food market and premium quality local produce store.[29] It claims to provide the freshest and tastiest produce all year long, and to have locally sourced seasonal selections. It states that its meat is hand-cut and trimmed by expert butchers who are on duty at all times in all stores and that the premium choice includes only the top 10 per cent of all beef in the US. As you read on, the product leadership positioning is clear. Finally, Sprouts Farmers Market markets itself as the neighbourhood grocery store offering thousands of natural, organic and gluten-free items.[30] Where The Fresh Market seems more about the best, Sprouts Farmers Market, like Whole Foods Market, is more focused on health. An example is grass-fed beef products. Most grass-fed cattle are leaner than feedlot beef, lacking marbling, which lowers the fat content and caloric level of the meat. Meat from grass-fed cattle also has higher levels of CLA and omega-3 fatty acids. In short, it's healthier. For Whole Foods Market we have financials for 2006–16, when it was taken over by Amazon. For The Fresh Market we have financials for 2011–15, when it was taken private by Apollo Global Management, an investment fund. For Sprouts Farmer Markets we have financials for 2011–19. The fact that two of these companies have been taken over shows the interest in this upscale type of retail formula.

Whole Foods Market, The Fresh Market and Sprouts Farmers Market are all heavily focused on fresh food categories. The traditional supermarket will extend the product range into canned and packaged goods, and various non-food items such as cleaners, personal care, baby items and pet items. If you're looking for the 'best total solution' as a consumer, you'll have to deal with the traditional supermarket, carrying anywhere from 10,000 to 30,000 SKUs, to ensure you get all your shopping for your daily needs done in one place. We have looked at Walmart, Ahold, Delhaize, the merged Ahold-Delhaize, Colruyt Group and Kroger as traditional supermarkets. Though Walmart is known for 'low prices', we believe it better fits into the 'supermarket' category, both from an assortment and from a financial perspective. In 2016, Delhaize was bought by Ahold. Both Ahold and Delhaize have activities in both Europe and the US. Albert Heijn is the biggest brand of Ahold, mainly focused on the Netherlands. Brands in the US are StopandShop, Giant, Martin's and Peapod. Delhaize grew from the Delhaize stores in Belgium and is known in the US through Food Lion. Colruyt Group is the biggest food retailer in Belgium, with limited activity in France. With $110 billion of revenue, Kroger is one of the major food retailers in the US. For all of these companies we gathered the financials for 2007–19, except for Delhaize, where we have it for 2007–14.

Table 4.8 summarizes key financial metrics of the listed retailers. As we map the retailers to our supply chain triangle, and more specifically to Figure 3.12, a first thing we would expect is that the product leaders have the highest gross margin, the customer intimacy players (traditional supermarkets) an average gross margin, and the (hard) discounters the lowest gross margin. That is confirmed in Table 4.8. Our 'product leaders' are at +30 per cent, the supermarkets range from 26 per cent down to 22 per cent. DIA comes at 21 per cent and Edeka at a staggering 12 per cent. At the bottom of Table 4.8 we have clustered the companies accordingly to get to an average for gross margin, EBIT and so on. That helps in getting to the conclusions.

Though there are big individual differences, the averages at the bottom show the product leaders, as expected, have the higher EBIT of 5 per cent, with 3.88 per cent for the customer intimacy and 1.92 per cent for the discounters. As we further relate to Figure 3.12, we can look for differences in inventory, working capital, fixed assets, or more generally in capital employed. We'd expect the (hard) discounters to be the most efficient, and the product leaders to have the highest levels.

TABLE 4.8 Key financials for a set of retailers

15 yr avg	Gross profit %	EBIT %	Inventory turns	CCC	Fixed asset turns	ROCE
Whole Foods Market	34.95%	5.23%	18.57	12.69	3.39	15.84%
The Fresh Market	33.38%	6.27%	15.62	13.53	3.43	23.11%
Sprouts Farmers Market	30.21%	3.58%	13.87	9.42	2.87	11.38%
Ahold	26.25%	3.33%	15.43	(10.58)	3.02	9.39%
Delhaize Group	25.04%	2.70%	11.07	4.28	2.65	7.00%
Walmart	24.87%	5.04%	8.34	8.38	3.27	17.97%
Colruyt Group	24.87%	6.09%	10.67	(5.67)	4.51	28.41%
Kroger	22.30%	2.24%	13.00	8.90	4.83	11.83%
DIA	21.37%	2.88%	11.35	(51.47)	3.66	18.24%
Edeka	11.58%	0.96%	28.32	(21.97)	7.68	12.30%
>30%	32.84%	5.03%	16.02	11.88	3.23	16.78%
22–30%	24.67%	3.88%	11.70	1.06	3.66	14.92%
<22%	16.47%	1.92%	19.84	(36.72)	5.67	15.27%

If we start with inventory turns, we see the supermarkets have the lowest turns (of 11.70). This has to do with the assortment. As we explained, the mentioned product leaders are heavily focused on fresh, which obviously has a short shelf life, so you simply can't keep a lot of inventory. The supermarkets extend into canned and packaged goods, and various non-food items such as cleaners, personal care, baby items and pet items. That drives inventory turns down.

Our expectation is confirmed, however, when we look at the working capital as measured by the cash conversion cycle (CCC). The CCC is 12 days at the product leaders, goes down to 1 day at the supermarkets, and becomes negative to −37 at the (hard) discounters. A comparable pattern is confirmed for fixed asset turns. The product leaders have the lowest turns of 3.23, the customer intimacy players do a little bit better with 3.66 and the (hard) discounters do significantly better with 5.67. Notice the 7.68 of Edeka here. The average ROCEs are 17 per cent, 15 per cent and 15 per cent, which are good.

The results for Edeka may be influenced by the fact that it is a cooperative. A cooperative typically doesn't have profit as a motive but it would rather redistribute its profits by charging lower transaction fees to its cooperative owners. Second, we assume Edeka owns the central logistics but not the stores. We assume the stores are owned by individuals in a kind of franchise model. That would mean that, compared to the traditional retailer, it owns only 'half of the assets', as it doesn't own any stores nor the inventory in the stores. Traditionally, we would say 'Oh yes, so these things are not really comparable'... well, that depends, from a ROCE perspective it remains comparable. Edeka is generating 12 per cent ROCE, which is well above that of Ahold,

FIGURE 4.18 Different strategies lead to different positions in the retail supply chain triangle

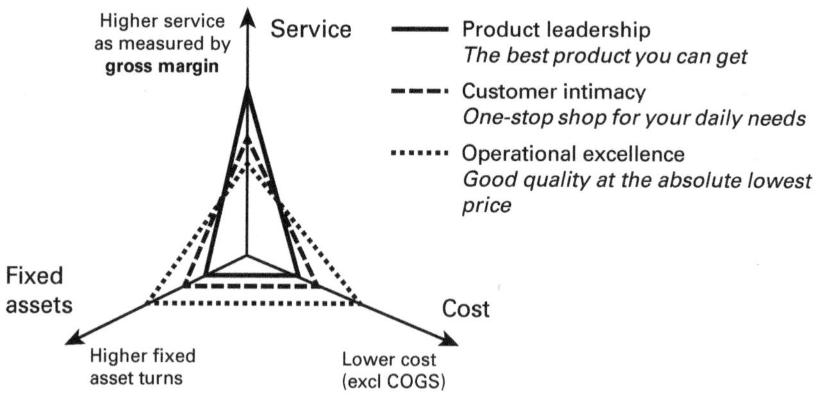

Delhaize and even Kroger. As an investor I don't care if the operating model is different, as long as I get the same bang-for-the-buck.

So, we do get confirmation in food retail of what we expected in Figure 3.12 and is summarized in Figure 4.18. Different strategies are different routes to generate a comparable ROCE, 15–17 per cent in this case. Operational excellence starts from lower gross margins and a lower EBIT, but compensates by having less working capital and fixed assets. Product leaders are most heavy in working capital and in assets, but compensate by superior EBIT, starting from superior gross margins.

Conclusion

We started this chapter by summarizing how we see companies struggling with making strategic choices. If strategy is about making choices, companies are bad at strategy. People hate to make choices, and tend to think choosing is losing. We summarized what we have called 'five common fails' in strategy.

We recapped some example cases from our first book and have extended them with more recent history. In the case of Barco it illustrates that with a change of CEO and chair of the board, the company shifted strategy once more, back to its original positioning of around 10 years ago. In the case of Casio, the management has persisted in the strategy change but so far it has not delivered on its promise. The Casio ROCE is still lower than before its strategic shift.

We added the case of Johnson Controls, where we describe the disentanglement of a large industrial conglomerate into more focused pieces. Though that should be a recipe for success, that success is not yet proven in the short term. More than $3 billion went into the restructuring, making it uncertain for shareholders whether and when they will see their value back.

We concluded with an updated retail benchmark. We discuss different strategic positions in food retail and do find evidence that different strategies are different routes to generate ROCE, in a different balance between EBIT and capital employed.

The combined examples strengthen our belief that, indeed, different strategies lead to a different balance in the triangle and do lead to different supply chains. In the next two chapters we will try to further zoom in on those underlying supply chains. In Chapter 5 we refine the 'service' side of the triangle by introducing the strategy model of Crawford and Mathews.

That allows us to be more precise in defining the 'value proposition' of a business. In Chapter 6 we start from that refined value proposition to analyse the impact on the supply chain.

Notes

1. J Collins (2001) *Good to Great*, Collins, Glasgow
2. A Verbeke (2013) *International Business Strategy*, Cambridge University Press, Cambridge
3. www.3m.com/3M/en_US/company-us/about-3m/technologies/ (archived at https://perma.cc/Y622-CMV7)
4. Barco, *Annual Report 2013*, www.barco.com/en/about-barco/investors/company-results (archived at https://perma.cc/ER6Y-DNET)
5. CM Christensen, et al, The new M&A playbook, *Harvard Business Review*, 2011, 89 (3), 48–57
6. Barco, *Annual Report 2013*, www.barco.com/en/about-barco/investors/company-results (archived at https://perma.cc/G8QD-GSJF)
7. Barco, *Annual Report 2012*, www.barco.com/en/about-barco/investors/company-results (archived at https://perma.cc/G39P-6BSB)
8. www.youtube.com/watch?v=3R-AbOkN_98 (archived at https://perma.cc/M6ZF-7GCK)
9. B DeSmet, (2018) *Supply Chain Strategy and Financial Metrics: The supply chain triangle of service, cost and cash*, Kogan Page, London
10. Casio, *Annual Report 2016*, world.casio.com/ir/library/results/ (archived at https://perma.cc/UN5V-FCJJ)
11. P-Y Donze (2016) *Industrial Development, Technology Transfer, and Global Competition: A history of the Japanese watch industry since 1850*, Taylor & Francis, Abingdon
12. Casio, *Annual Report 2008*, world.casio.com/ir/library/results/ (archived at https://perma.cc/UHT2-GX8A)
13. B DeSmet, (2018) *Supply Chain Strategy and Financial Metrics: The supply chain triangle of service, cost and cash*, Kogan Page, London
14. Numbers taken as 'segment income/net sales' from the 2015 annual report, http://investors.johnsoncontrols.com/financial-information/johnson-sec-filings (archived at https://perma.cc/UZ2T-7WTU)
15. Numbers taken as 'segment income/net sales' from the 2015 annual report, http://investors.johnsoncontrols.com/financial-information/johnson-sec-filings (archived at https://perma.cc/WZB2-77EQ)
16. Numbers taken as 'segment income/net sales' from the 2015 annual report, http://investors.johnsoncontrols.com/financial-information/johnson-sec-filings (archived at https://perma.cc/AAQ5-4TT4)

17 Trefis Team, How Johnson Controls' exit from the automotive seating business impacts its stock, 17 June 2015, https://www.forbes.com/sites/greatspeculations/2015/06/17/how-johnson-controls-exit-from-the-automotive-seating-business-impacts-its-stock/ (archived at https://perma.cc/AAS2-8ZKV)

18 R Wright, Johnson Controls considers sale of car seat unit, *Financial Times*, 10 June 2015, www.ft.com/content/b41a590e-0f7e-11e5-897e-00144feabdc0 (archived at https://perma.cc/Z94A-ELAQ)

19 http://investors.johnsoncontrols.com/about-the-spin-off (archived at https://perma.cc/3V5K-DPWL)

20 www.johnsoncontrols.com/media-center/news/press-releases/2016/09/06/johnson-controls-and-tyco-complete-merger (archived at https://perma.cc/P4DN-3B2E)

21 www.johnsoncontrols.com/media-center/news/press-releases/2018/11/13/johnson-controls-announces-agreement-to-sell-power-solutions-business (archived at https://perma.cc/3B5F-T743)

22 R Wright and J Fontanella-Khan, Johnson Controls and Tyco look to complement each other, *Financial Times*, 25 January 2016, https://www.ft.com/content/66486650-c37c-11e5-b3b1-7b2481276e45 (archived at https://perma.cc/9W3N-H6TX)

23 Figures were taken from the corresponding financial reports from the Johnson Controls website on 18 July 2018, http://investors.johnsoncontrols.com/financial-information/financial-reports (archived at https://perma.cc/3CA9-CKR4)

24 M Sachon (2010) *The Hard Discount Model in Retailing*, Consultant Report, IESE Business School

25 A Felsted, Supermarkets: Day of the discounters, *Financial Times*, 10 December 2014, www.ft.com/content/be5e8d52-7ec6-11e4-b83e-00144feabdc0 (archived at https://perma.cc/KY6A-8XR6)

26 www.diacorporate.com/en/about-us/history/ (archived at https://perma.cc/2M8F-KZDF)

27 LetterOne and Santander reach agreement over Dia debt, *Financial Times*, 20 May 2019, https://www.ft.com/content/1c52f4c8-7b1d-11e9-81d2-f785092ab560 (archived at https://perma.cc/K4PV-PLKU)

28 www.wholefoodsmarket.com (archived at https://perma.cc/3W2U-84EG)

29 www.thefreshmarket.com (archived at https://perma.cc/E2UC-HZ29)

30 www.sprouts.com (archived at https://perma.cc/NDC9-XTQB)

05

The strategy-driven supply chain

In the previous chapters we introduced the strategy model of Treacy and Wiersema and showed how different strategies lead to a different balance in the triangle. Different strategies are in fact different routes to generate the same ROCE. In this chapter we will take that argument a level deeper.

We start by introducing the concept of value drivers by showing the possible value drivers derived from Treacy and Wiersema. We expand the set of possible value drivers by introducing the strategy model of Crawford and Mathews, which allows us to paint a wider range of strategic options. Treacy and Wiersema introduce the need for choices and their model is good for rough choices. Crawford and Mathews allow further fine-tuning of the choices, which is often required if we want to start adjusting the corresponding supply chain.

Near the end of this chapter we introduce the value proposition and the corresponding supply chain as the yin and yang of business strategy. Together they define how you will drive value for the shareholder as measured by ROCE. We contrast this strategy-driven supply chain approach with the more traditional strategy approach that is unclear about the choices being made, and which results in targets for financial metrics that can be conflicting and which provides little guidance in how to set up the underlying supply chain.

Redefining the service corner into the value corner using Treacy and Wiersema

Figure 5.1 shows our starting point. It is a recap from Figure 1.13. Let's start by revisiting the service corner. In Chapter 1 we said that we should take a broad perspective of service. In supply chain it is common to narrow service

FIGURE 5.1 Starting point for building the supply chain and financial KPI dashboard

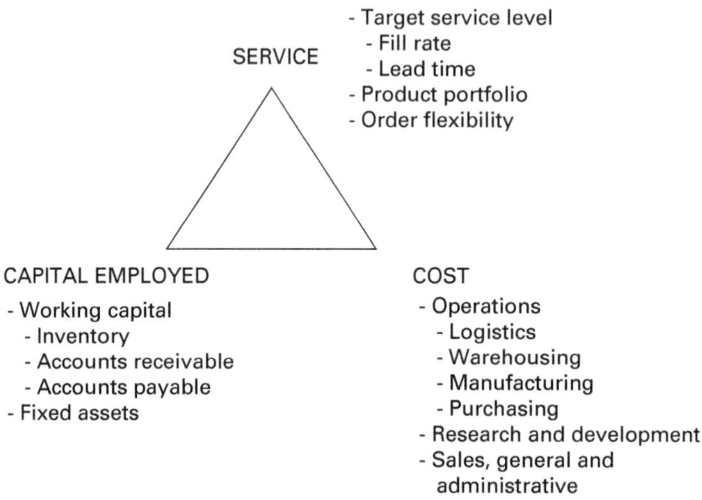

to on-time, in-full (OTIF) delivery performance. That is one aspect of service, but there are many more. Think about the product portfolio. Delivering a wide range of products creates a cost in the supply chain, but it is also a service that you deliver to the customer. In fact, it is one of the unique selling points of a customer intimacy leader. Or think about order flexibility. If customers can order at any time, in any quantity and with any type of delivery requirement, that will again create a cost in the supply chain. Some customers will value that, and will be willing to pay more, as it allows them to lower their inventories and still be responsive to their customers. If you are an operational excellence player, you will try to avoid these costs, to guarantee the lowest price. If you are a customer intimacy player, responsiveness may be part of the 'best total solution' you deliver to your customer.

From these examples, it is easy to make the bridge to the three strategic options of Treacy and Wiersema. From a customer perspective, we know that some customers will simply only value the lowest price. They will expect a basic set of services, the qualifiers, but will not be tempted nor be willing to pay for any extra services. Think about flying with a low-cost airline. You will not be interested in what drinks or quality snacks will be available on the flight. You just want the lowest price. These needs are of course best served by the operational excellence players in the market.

Other customers will value the product quality and specifications. To be a product leader, you need to work with product leaders in your supplier base. You can only build the best and the highest specification if you start from the best and the highest specification. Given that you typically already pay a premium for the product, adding extra services on top is easily done. The price difference with extra services is less important compared to buying a commodity product. Moreover, as a product leader you have a high gross margin, so you more easily commit to extra costs. An example could be transport by air instead of sea freight, to reduce your lead time. As a customer, the product quality is your primary reason to buy, you will add services on top, as long as the costs stay reasonable.

Finally, some customers will value a total solution, a one-stop shop. They will be best served by the customer intimacy players. That total solution will consist of a combination of a broad product portfolio and any 'value-added' services. An example of a value-added service could be an onsite technical service manager analysing his customers' problems and defining appropriate solutions. Where for a product leader the service comes 'on top', for a customer intimacy player the service is really an essential part of the total customer solution.

From the three strategies, we have just derived four possible 'value drivers': the price, the product quality, the product portfolio and value-added services. Figure 5.2 summarizes how the three different strategies create value for the customer in three different ways. The opex player will dominate on price and can have an average product quality and product range, and even the absolute basic when it comes to services. The product leader and the customer intimacy player take a different position. A product leader will dominate on product quality, while a customer intimacy player will dominate on product range and/or differentiate on value-added services.

We remember from the discussion in the previous chapters that different strategies come at a different cost and with a different level of capital employed. Instead of only showing 'service' in the narrow definition on the 'service

FIGURE 5.2 Different ways to create value based on the four value attributes of Treacy and Wiersema

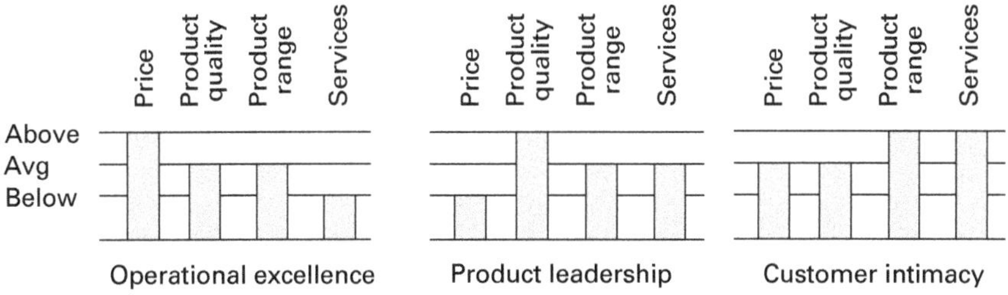

corner', we suggest that the four value drivers above are listed. If we know our current and our target performance for each of the four value drivers, then we will better understand our strategic position, and the resulting balance in the supply chain triangle. If I'm aiming for a product leadership position, I know I will carry more inventory compared to an opex player. This idea is illustrated in Figure 5.3. To avoid any confusion about the 'narrow' versus 'broad' definition of service, we have renamed the service corner the value corner, as it lists possible value drivers.

Our finding from Figure 5.2 about 'value drivers' and different strategies as 'different positions' or 'priorities' on those value drivers is comparable to the findings and work of Crawford and Mathews.[1] In their book *The Myth of Excellence* they identify five possible value drivers, and argue that a 5–4–3–3–3 profile is optimal if you want to reach excellence. We introduce their model in the next section, and map it to what we have derived so far. It will allow us to further refine our definition of the 'value' corner of our triangle.

FIGURE 5.3 The three strategies of Treacy and Wiersema are different ways to create value

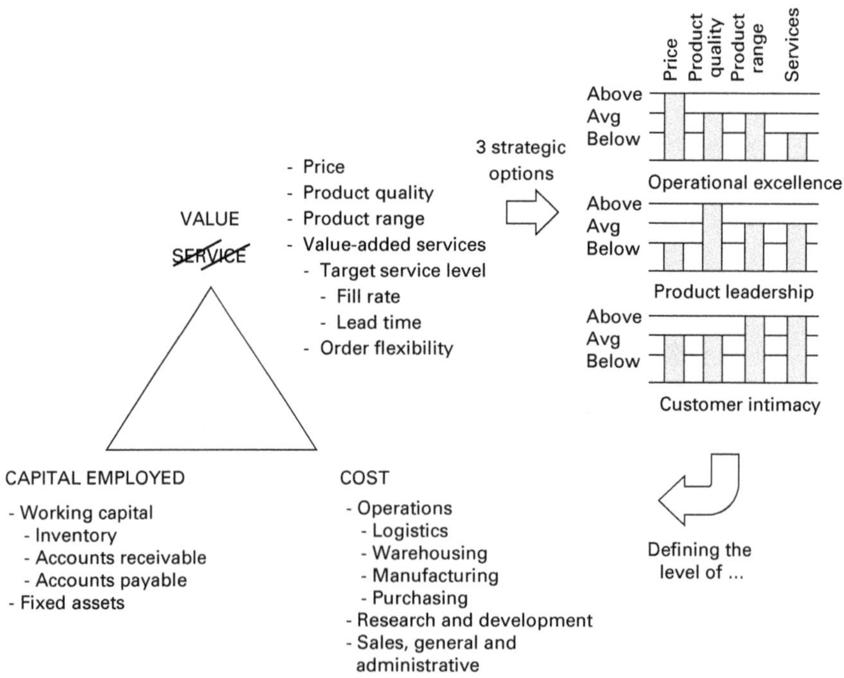

Redefining the service corner into the value corner using Crawford and Mathews

Crawford and Mathews studied the value propositions of manufacturing and retail companies. Their findings were twofold. First, any value proposition is based on the five primary value drivers shown in Figure 5.4: price, product, access, service and experience. Second, they argue that a 5–4–3–3–3 profile is optimal, meaning that you should dominate on one attribute, you should differentiate on a second, and that you will (at least) be at par for the other three.

Let's discuss the five attributes in more detail, revisit the 5–4–3–3–3 argument, and then link the findings back to the model of Treacy and Wiersema and to our supply chain triangle.

Exploring the five value drivers of Crawford and Mathews

PRICE

Let's start with price. Dominating on price means customers buy from you because you have the lowest price in the market. Next to having the lowest price, Crawford and Mathews stress the importance of honesty and consistency. They even argue that you don't necessarily need to have the lowest price. As long as you have a consistent low price, and are honest in your pricing,

FIGURE 5.4 An example optimal profile for the five value drivers of Crawford and Mathews

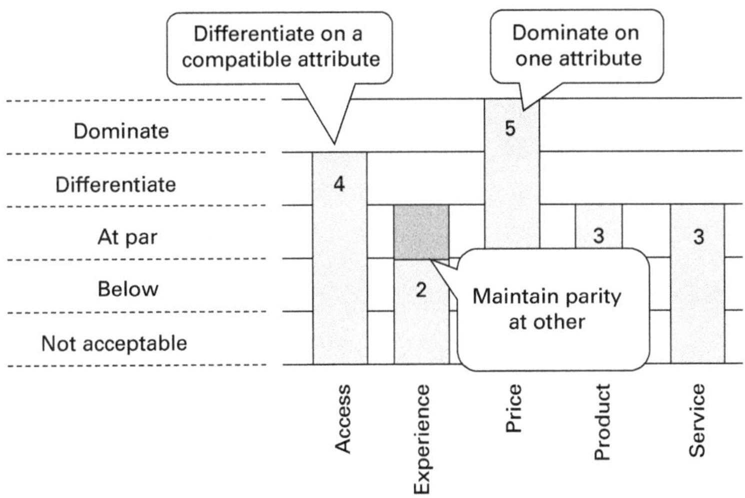

you will create a loyal customer base around that low-price proposition. Consistency means you continuously monitor and adapt your prices to remain in sync with the market. Honesty means you will not try to exploit your customer, for instance by reducing prices on one product, while making complementary products more expensive.

An example of consistency and honesty is a so-called 'every day low price' pricing strategy, as practised by Walmart, and as opposed to a so-called 'high–low' pricing strategy. With 'every day low price', a company, typically a retailer, guarantees to continuously keep prices down, as opposed to a 'high–low' pricing, where the price is low during a period of promotion, and high when not running a promotion. Crawford and Mathews argue that 'low price' customers prefer the consistency and honesty of the 'every day low price' above the lack of transparency of 'high–low' pricing. We wouldn't go that far. Low-cost retailers like Aldi and Lidl do use promotions to further enhance their lowest price image. They will typically do it on temporary products or assortments while ensuring an every day low price on their base assortment. A company like Lidl has been criticized by its customers for not carrying enough inventory of the lower priced promo products. Customers feel tricked if they arrive the first morning of the promo to find only three of the promo flat screen TVs are left in stock. It confirms that honesty and consistency are important, but lowest price definitely comes first. The hard discounters will keep exploring the limits on how to grow market share while keeping costs down to ensure the lowest price. Linking back to Treacy and Wiersema, it is clear that the lowest price ties seamlessly into operational excellence.

PRODUCT

Crawford and Mathews talk about three aspects in the product dimension: quality, depth and breadth. The quality ties into the product leadership strategy of Treacy and Wiersema. Customers buy from you because you simply have the highest quality product. That's why people buy a Ferrari or a Lamborghini when they want to buy a sports car. Next to an exquisite design, it is above all a fabulous sports car and the reference in its category. Depth and breadth are two aspects of the product portfolio or the assortment. Breadth refers to the one-stop shop of customer intimacy. Many DIY chains try to offer a full range of tools and consumables for any type of changes you want to make in your home. In addition to companies that carry a full range, you have specialist stores. If I'm a specialist in power tools, my assortment will be less 'wide', but I will have more choice than any of my competitors in the specific assortment of power tools. We call that 'depth'. From a supply chain perspective, the challenge of 'breadth' and the challenge of 'depth' are the same. I will have a large number of SKUs with most probably a long tail of more slow-moving products. That has been the trigger in our new book to also link 'depth' to a customer intimacy position. You could say it also delivers a total solution, be it in a more specific area. I will deliver you any power tool you could possibly need. In our first book we still linked 'depth' to product leadership, as it is more specialist. We now prefer to reserve product leadership for a positioning where the number of SKUs is more limited, but the products themselves are typically more complex, as they need to deliver a better and higher performance.

ACCESS

Crawford and Mathews talk about physical access and psychological access. In a retail world, physical access means the average distance to one of your stores, as exemplified by McDonald's or Starbucks. Take an average city from anywhere in the world, count the number of McDonald's or Starbucks outlets, and you'll know what physical access means. For a manufacturing company it will be the number of distributors or distribution centres across the globe and the resulting customer order lead time. Increasing physical access comes at a cost, so it conflicts with low cost. An operational excellence player will never be dominant on physical access. A product leader doesn't need to excel on the physical access. Customers are willing to wait or to travel for these products, because of the difference in quality. As a result, we link physical access to the customer intimacy position of Treacy and Wiersema. Proximity is part of the total solution that is being delivered.

Psychological access means 'How easy is it for me to find what I'm looking for?' In a retail environment it means 'easy in and out', which is supported by relatively compact stores, where you have an easy overview of the store, with the same layout across different stores, so you more easily find your way in each of the stores belonging to the same chain. Psychological access in retail is focused on the 'efficiency of the customer'. From that perspective, it matches well with an operational excellence proposition of the retailer. The same holds true, for instance, in low-cost airlines. Imagine that, instead of numbered seats, you just get on the plane and take the last seat available. We avoid complicated boarding procedures and save time for both the airline and the customers. The parallel to a manufacturing environment could be something like e-ordering. Instead of calling a customer service desk, faxing or emailing, an electronic data interchange (EDI) connection will make my life easier. It will be more efficient for me as a customer. It will also be more efficient for my supplier. If I do need to call to a customer service manager, the question could be, 'How long does it take to get it done?' The shorter the call, the more efficient for both the customer and the supplier. In general, hassle-free service at the customer side goes well with efficiency at the supplier side, so we will link psychological access to the operational excellence position of Treacy and Wiersema.

SERVICE

Service is the broadest and the hardest attribute to explain. Crawford and Mathews start by talking about 'knowledgeable sales persons providing helpful advice'. This breathes 'customer intimacy'. We have an intimate knowledge of the customers' problem and are there to help them with advice on how to solve it. That easily translates from a retail world into a manufacturing world and vice versa. A second example from Crawford and Mathews is 'customization' or 'tailoring'. A retail example could be a counter service, where a consumer can order a custom portion of his favourite product. The manufacturing example is customer-specific products, designed to tackle a customer-specific challenge. This again breathes 'customer intimacy'. Other aspects mentioned are 'hassle-free return' – no complicated procedures for returning products but trusting the client and helping them out by sending a replacement without questions. This type of returns policy is easier if there is some kind of long-term relationship and if there is some margin in that relationship. An operational excellence player has to control all of their costs in order to guarantee the lowest price, including any returns. If you get grounded when using a low-cost airline, don't expect an elaborate staff available to help you with rebooking or returning your money. A product leader will probably provide a hassle-free return, though the price of the products may justify maintenance contracts or insurances, which will cover the costs. It is probably the customer intimacy player who needs to earn this from the relationship rather than any maintenance contracts or insurances. A fourth element we want to add to the service dimension is 'availability'. For Crawford and Mathews 'availability', the fact that you have the product available, is part of the product dimension. We like to classify it as a service. Zara is a product leader, focused on a fast time to market and a high innovation rate. It deliberately limits the number of pieces of an individual item.

Consumers know that if they return next week the inventory may be depleted, so it makes them buy what they like immediately. For your local retailer of your favourite brand of shirts or shoes always to have the common sizes available requires extra inventory. This is an extra cost they hope to win back by your loyalty because of this service. Availability is not in the product, it is in the way the company organizes its supply chain and in the cost and inventory it is willing to carry to deliver that service. All of these service attributes best tie into the customer intimacy position of Treacy and Wiersema.

EXPERIENCE

In a retail environment, Crawford and Mathews talk about the attractiveness of the store, how employees dress to reflect the atmosphere, or how music and video are used to enhance the experience. Next to providing the best quality products, shopping at Harrods in London is an experience. If you buy a Ferrari, you can expect it to be delivered under a (Ferrari) red cover, accompanied by a bottle of exquisite champagne and an invitation for a series of driving lessons on a racing circuit. 'Experience' is ideally suited to further enhance the value of the products from product leaders. The cost of creating the extra experience can be small compared to the cost of the product. The experience has a high chance of appealing to the vanity of the buyer, significantly increasing the emotional value and as such the willingness to pay the premium price. In theory, you can offer common products based on a differentiation in experience. In practice, for an average product, consumers will be more price-sensitive and will more easily skip the experience factor to get the same product at a lower cost, particularly now that the internet has made prices very transparent. For a manufacturer, experience is often in the relationship with the customer. We can send sales people or technical service people over to the customer to celebrate the delivery or the installation of the actual product. Even when not strictly necessary, doing this will create a level of excitement that can be classified as experience rather than service. Again, an operational excellence player will avoid this type of cost to guarantee the lowest price. It is typically the product leaders who can further enhance the perceived value of the product and are in a position to provide this type of 'experience'.

Figure 5.5 summarizes the five attributes of Crawford and Mathews and the main characteristics discussed. Figure 5.6 summarizes our mapping of the five attributes to the three strategic options of Treacy and Wiersema.

FIGURE 5.5 Summary of the five attributes of Crawford and Mathews

Price	Access	Service	Product	Experience
Lowest price Consistency Honesty	Physical	Advice Customization Availability	Quality	Attractiveness Excitement
	Psychological		Breadth Depth	

FIGURE 5.6 Mapping the five attributes of Crawford and Mathews to the three strategies of Treacy and Wiersema

Product leadership

Price	Access	Service	Product	Experience
Lowest price Consistency Honesty	Physical	Advice Customization Availability	Quality	Attractiveness Excitement
	Psychological		Breadth Depth	

Operational excellence **Customer intimacy**

Integrating Treacy and Wiersema into Crawford and Mathews

As shown in Figure 5.4, Crawford and Mathews argue that a 5–4–3–3–3 profile is optimal. This means you can dominate on one of the dimensions, differentiate on a second, and be at par with competitors on the remaining three. From that perspective their message is comparable to that of Treacy and Wiersema: 'You have to make choices.' If you try to be the best on all of the dimensions, you may find yourself outcompeted on each by different competitors who focus on one dimension only. In addition, a sharper focus brings a clearer message to the customer about who you are, and a clearer message to your employees, who need to execute upon your promise. Companies hate to make choices and may believe that 'choosing is losing'. However, strategy is about making choices, and choices must be made if you truly want to be a market leader.

There are two important differences, though, in these two approaches. First, Crawford and Mathews advocate that any combination of 5–4–3–3–3 can give a competitive edge. So you could have 5–4–3–3–3, 5–3–4–3–3, 5–3–3–4–3 or any other of the total 20 possible combinations. Treacy and Wiersema stick to only three possible strategies. From that perspective,

Crawford and Mathews have a broader palette to paint the competitive situation. Some of them are helpful, and we will give one example.

In one of my strategy sessions with a food retailer, it was helpful to take a look at product leaders. The product leaders focus on delivering the highest quality meat, fish, vegetables, dairy products and so on. When screening a selection of product leaders in more detail we saw that some of them were more focused on combining the product with 'experience' while others combined it with 'service'. The 'experience' players had attractive stores, with nice decorations, an eye-catching display of the products, with ample opportunity to taste the products and with an in-house restaurant allowing you to discover the best and the newest. In a certain sense this was attracting the wealthier consumer looking for inspiration and willing to pay more for a premium product in an attractive setting. The 'service' players had basic stores, a somewhat broader assortment, and even more knowledgeable personnel delivering the necessary advice to ensure the product is used and appreciated in the best possible condition. These competitors were more focused towards the 'professional', for instance restaurant owners looking for the best product and professional advice. These professionals don't want to pay for fancy store decoration. They want the best product at the lowest possible price and with some professional advice on what to try and how to combine. This is just one example where we believe the approach of Crawford and Mathews allows more nuance in the strategic positioning of yourself and your competitors, in comparison to Treacy and Wiersema.

A second difference between Crawford and Mathews and Treacy and Wiersema is in how the dimensions combine, as shown in Figure 5.6. From our perspective, it is problematic to combine 'product quality' on the one hand, and 'product breadth/depth' on the other hand, into one 'product' dimension. The two serve very different purposes, as shown by the product leadership versus customer intimacy positions in the model of Treacy and Wiersema. We like the principle of the 5–4–3–3–3 and having more than three possible strategic options; however, we do believe that any strategy model should contain the three strategic options of Treacy and Wiersema as 'archetypes'. These archetypes have proven their value in strategy formulation over the last 20 years. Likewise, combining 'physical access' and 'psychological access' into one 'access' dimension is problematic. Whereas psychological access as 'efficiency for the customer' combines very well with an efficiency mindset or an operational excellence position on the suppliers' side, improving the physical access increases the cost and investment, which is more a service improvement, which better ties into customer intimacy. To combine the best of both worlds, and to make the model of Treacy and

Wiersema fit nicely into that of Crawford and Mathews, we suggest splitting the five dimensions of Crawford and Mathews into seven dimensions, as shown in Figure 5.7. These seven dimensions then easily combine into the three strategies of Treacy and Wiersema, as shown in Figure 5.8.

A 5–4–3–3–3 profile now becomes a 5–4–3–3–3–3–3 profile. Figure 5.9 shows our definition of the three 'archetypes' of Treacy and Wiersema. An opex player dominates on price and will differentiate on psychological access. In a recent exercise with an opex player, a dimension like experience was even ranked 'below par'. Once a company is 'below par' it needs to 'mind the gap' as falling too far behind may compromise its leadership position. The archetypical customer intimacy players dominate on product breadth or depth and differentiate on service. They deliver the one-stop shop, and bring the expertise to assemble the products into the best total solution. The archetypical product leaders dominate on product quality and differentiate on experience. They deliver the newest and highest specification products and turn this into an experience driving a superior premium from their customers.

The good thing about the Crawford and Mathews model is that it easily allows the definition of variants, like the one described above, where a product leader was focusing on service instead of experience as a differentiator. Having seven value attributes is more complex, but you can't have it all. If you want to put nuance in the strategy modelling, and have multiple options, you'll have to carry some complexity in your strategy model.

FIGURE 5.7 Extending Crawford and Mathews from five to seven attributes

Price	Psycho-logical access	Physical access	Service	Product breadth/ depth	Product quality	Experience
Lowest price Consistency Honesty	Easy Hassle-free Successful	Location Number of real estate	Advice Customization Availability	One-stop shop Broad/deep range	Highest spec	Attractiveness Excitement

FIGURE 5.8 Linking the seven attributes from the extended Crawford and Mathews to Treacy and Wiersema

Price	Psycho-logical access	Physical access	Service	Product breadth/ depth	Product quality	Experience
Lowest price Consistency Honesty	Easy Hassle-free Successful	Location Number of real estate	Advice Customization Availability	One-stop shop Broad/deep range	Highest spec	Attractiveness Excitement
Operational excellence		**Customer intimacy**			**Product leadership**	

FIGURE 5.9 The 5–4–3–3–3–3–3 profile for operational excellence, customer intimacy and product leadership

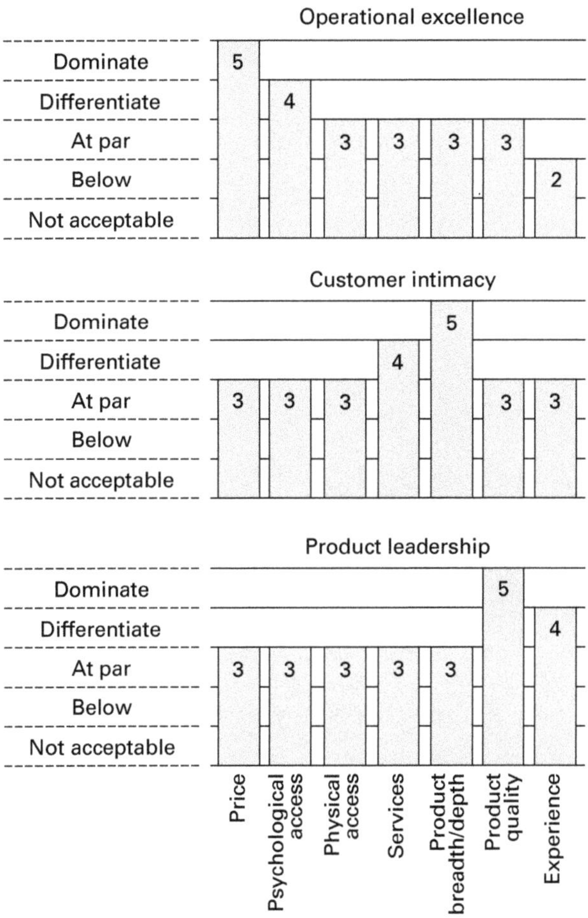

As discussed before, showing all of the value drivers on the value corner of the triangle, showing where we are today, and where we want to be, gives a better understanding of the current and targeted strategic position of our company. The strategy is essential in understanding the related and required cost and capital employed. The strategy defines the balance in the triangle. If I want to be a product leader, I know I will carry more inventory and a higher cost than the operational excellence player. This is summarized in Figure 5.10. It nicely summarizes how we have used the model and approach of Crawford and Mathews to extend our original result based on Treacy and Wiersema, as shown in Figure 5.3.

FIGURE 5.10 Mapping Crawford and Mathews into Treacy and Wiersema and the supply chain triangle using seven value drivers

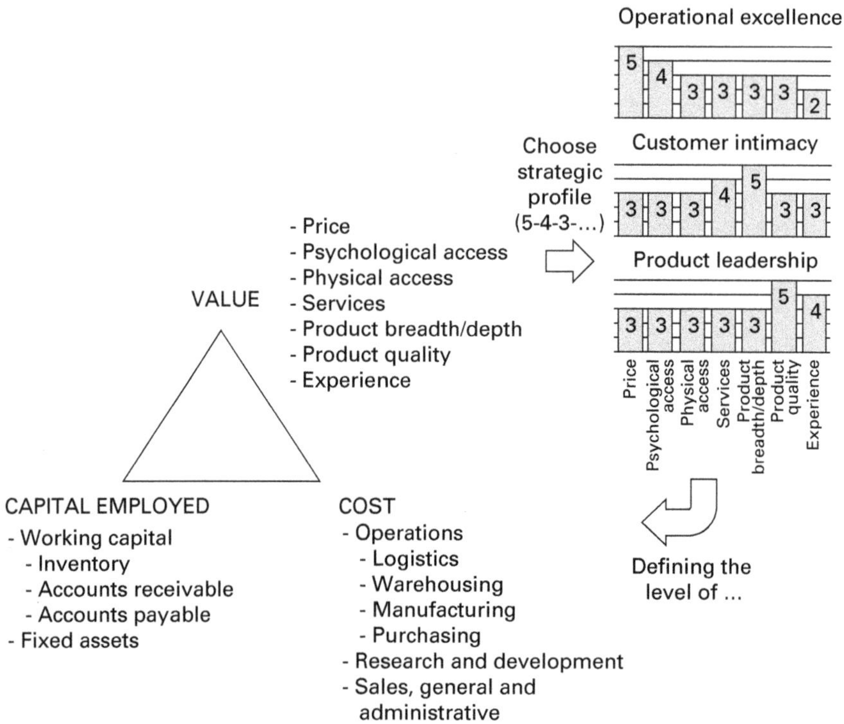

EXERCISE 5.1

Understanding Crawford and Mathews for your industry

Gather a cross-functional group of marketing, sales, R&D, supply chain operations and finance. List the seven value drivers on a sheet of paper: price, psychological access, physical access, services, product breadth/depth, product quality, experience.

Take 10–15 minutes to first individually think about what you believe defines these value drivers in your industry. You may note down your ideas on Post-it notes. Then start mapping the Post-its to the corresponding value driver on the sheet of paper.

You can expect some discussions. Promotions, for example. Is that a service? Or is that to deliver lowest price? For some activities the answer may be 'It depends' – it depends on the chosen strategy. If I'm a hard discounter then promotions will be used to support my lowest price positioning. If I'm a brander or product leader, then promotions may be used to stimulate customers to try something new. So a promotion is not a strategic choice. A promotion is a 'tool' that companies will use differently depending on the strategic choice they have made.

You can expect a comparable discussion on the 'online' channel. Is that part of the 'physical access'? The answer is twofold. On the one hand, yes it is, and in many markets not having an online channel is below par and could be a source of competitive disadvantage. On the other hand, the question is, 'How do you use the online channel?' You may use it to offer a long tail, which creates product breadth, and that may support your customer intimacy. Or, as a product leader, you may use the online channel to give extra product information about the origins of the product, comparisons with other products, etc.

When 'defining' a value driver, it may be helpful to define 'sub-drivers'. For services we have already listed personalization, availability and advice as subcategories. Try to structure the information in such a way that it is comprehensive.

Share a picture of your exercise on LinkedIn with the hashtag #strategydrivensupplychain! We will gather examples of this exercise on the book website at www.strategydrivensupplychain.com/resources/examples/crawfordmathews

EXERCISE 5.2

Defining your 5–4–3–3–3–3–3 profile

The first crucial step is making sure everybody has the same understanding of the different value drivers for your industry, so if you haven't done the previous exercise yet, start there. Once everybody has the same understanding of the value drivers, you can start discussing how you as a company are going to prioritize. What is your five, what is your four, where will you play at par? A typical question here is 'Should we take the *as is* or the *to be*?' This reveals companies may have an idea (or not) of where they want to be, but they are not there yet. Start with discussing the *to be*. If everybody agrees on where you need to go, then reflect on where you currently are, the *as is*.

Continue with your cross-functional group. Ask everybody to think about where they will put the five, where they will put the four, and for what reason. Then ask people to start putting out their fives and fours. Ask questions, five times why. Even at this stage you will see different people place the five differently because they still have a different understanding of what, for instance, psychological access means. This is not bad, it is good – the model and the approach help to bring that debate to the table.

Try to conclude, not necessarily with a consensus. You may agree to disagree. Making an explicit choice and sticking to it may be more important than the choice itself.

Share a picture of your exercise on LinkedIn with the hashtag #strategydrivensupplychain! We will gather examples of this exercise on the book website at www.strategydrivensupplychain.com/resources/examples/crawfordmathews

EXERCISE 5.3

Analyse your competitive landscape: defining competitive actions

What needs to be done to dominate, differentiate or play at par is defined by the competitive landscape, which evolves over time.

For the axis on which you dominate (5) and the axis on which you differentiate (4), list what your competitors are doing. Define your action plan for how you will differentiate, and how you will dominate.

Doing 'more' typically comes at an extra cost and possibly extra capital employed. So it will be good to mention areas where you will do less. If strategy is about making choices, it is as important to say what we will not do or will no longer do. This is where it gets hard. So for the axes where you put (3), think about where you can scale down, where you may currently be above par. Is that really required? The answer is yes if, not only for cost and capital employed, it is also required in order to get a sharp enough image for the customer and for the people in your company who need to realize your value proposition.

Share a picture of your exercise on LinkedIn with the hashtag #strategydrivensupplychain! We will gather examples of this exercise on the book website at www.strategydrivensupplychain.com/resources/examples/crawfordmathews

CASE STUDY

Food retail: Colruyt Lowest Prices

Colruyt Lowest Prices is one of the retail brands of the Colruyt Group. Colruyt Group is a Belgian €10 billion group active in retail and renewable energy. The group has grown from the Colruyt Lowest Prices brand, which built its success by implementing the discount store concept and guaranteeing the 'lowest price' through its 'red phone' and 'red prices'. If you have seen the same product at a lower price at a competitor, you can call the 'red phone' and Colruyt adapts its price, into the so-called 'red price'. When you walk into a store you can see the red labels, which indicate that the price has been adjusted, quite often in response to a promotion at a competitor.

When it comes to Treacy and Wiersema, mapping Colruyt Lowest Prices is relatively straightforward. It is a prototype of an operational excellence player. The interesting exercise for Colruyt Group, however, has been to map their other food retail branches on the Treacy and Wiersema model: Spar, Okay, BioPlanet, Cru, etc. Whereas Colruyt Lowest Prices is quite pronounced on the operational excellence axis, Spar and Okay are more pronounced on the customer intimacy axis, and Cru on the product leadership axis.

When it comes to Crawford and Mathews, the interesting debate within Colruyt Lowest Prices was whether to give a five to price or to psychological access. The debate was on the *dienstbaarheid, serviabilité* (the helping or serving attitude). Are 'price' and 'helpfulness' on the same level? If we try to combine them… is it 'helpful efficiency' or 'efficient helpfulness'? Which of the two is leading? Where that may seem like a detail, it is the essence. When having these discussions with management teams I put a challenge to them, saying, 'If it is not clear to you, how should it be clear to the thousands of people you employ?' If I'm employed in one of the hundreds of stores, how do I balance efficiency and helpfulness? You want your strategy execution to be consistent. Consistency starts with making clear choices. The management team at Colruyt Lowest Prices decided on five for price and four for psychological access. The baseline is 'helpful efficiency'. If you have lowest price in your brand, I believe this is a logical choice. But it is excellent to have the debate and the discussion.

If you are a multi-BU company like Colruyt Group, the model of Crawford and Mathews also helps in fine-tuning the strategy across multiple brands. Spar and Okay both focus on 'customer intimacy'… but in what way are they different? You certainly don't want to have two of your own brands cannibalizing each other. Where do we put the five? Where do we put the four? Okay prioritizes 'fast and easy', in combination with 'cheap'. It has smaller shops, easily accessible parking, and a limited assortment so that consumers don't lose time hesitating and having to make a choice. When discussing the value drivers, it becomes clear they go for 'psychological access' as a five, and 'price' as a four. So it's actually not necessarily customer intimacy, it's rather operational excellence but with the focus on the 'helpfulness' coming first. Comparing the positioning of multiple business units within your own company, or comparing with competitors, is very helpful in improving the understanding of your own positioning.

Traditional business strategy

When reading annual reports, I see a lot of statements like 'We want to grow', 'We want to improve our profitability' and 'We want to improve our free cash flow'. While all these goals are of course good, they don't say anything about how we want to be successful in the market, how we are going to differentiate, and how that is going to help us to drive these improvements. That is in essence the difference we see between 'traditional business strategy' and leveraging the principles of the 'strategy-driven supply chain'. We will illustrate the lack of choices by studying Bekaert's 2019 annual report.[2]

Bekaert is a global leader in the transformation of steel wire and the application of advanced coating know-how. The company has a €4.3 billion turnover and is active in different businesses including rubber reinforcement (steel going into tyres), ropes and advanced cords, steel wire solutions (agricultural, consumer, construction) and specialties (building products, fibre technologies, combustion technology and sawing wire).

Page 10 of the 2019 annual report talks about 'Our strategy'. The bottom section repeats 'Our strategy', which starts: 'Continuously driving value creation for our shareholders by cost effectively creating superior value for customers is our strategy.' Let's analyse this sentence: driving value for the shareholder, check – we believe every company wants to do this. By being cost effective, check – different strategies will lead to a different cost level, but we believe every company wants to be cost effective. Third, by creating superior value for customers, check – we don't know of any company that does not want to deliver (superior) value for its customers; the question is, which type of customers, valuing which type of drivers.

Page 11 of the 2019 annual report continues with 'Our long-term strategies'. There are five core strategies that 'reflect the direction and priorities over the longer term':

1. Drive the customer into the heart of our business.
2. Value-driven growth.
3. Technology leadership and speed.
4. Leverage scale, reduce complexity and reach lowest total cost.
5. Engage and empower people.

If we think Treacy and Wiersema, number 1, 'Drive the customer into the heart of our business', reads as customer intimacy. Other hints of customer intimacy are on page 10, which says: 'We seek to be the best in understanding the applications for which our customers use steel wire. Knowing how our steel wire products function within our customers' production processes and products helps us to develop and deliver the solutions that best meet their requirements and, through that, we create value for our customers.'

Through the eyes of Treacy and Wiersema, number 3, 'Technology leadership and speed', reads as product leadership. Other hints are on page 10 as well; when introducing Bekaert it says 'Bekaert is a world market and technology leader in steel wire transformation and coating technologies'. So, who are they? They are a technology leader.

Though we seem to have the complexity of customer intimacy and product leadership, we still go for number 4, 'Leverage scale, reduce complexity and reach lowest total cost', which reads as operational excellence.

As explained earlier, the danger of not making clear choices is twofold. First, individual departments such sales, R&D and operations might start initiatives that six months down the road are conflicting. It doesn't give any direction, nor does it tell staff how to trade off the impact of different initiatives. Second, you risk being left with an undifferentiated positioning. If a competitor puts all its efforts into technology leadership, it is most probably going to outperform you. If another competitor strips the complexity of your portfolio and focuses on the fast-moving core, it will undercut your prices by up to 20 per cent. In short, you are left vulnerable to disruption.

Figure 5.11 shows the 10-year financials of Bekaert. The interactive version is also available on the book website at www.strategydrivensupplychain.com/resources/benchmarkreport/bekaert

What is immediately striking is the 10 per cent and 15 per cent EBIT of 2009 and 2010, which Bekaert has been chasing ever since, but has not been able to repeat. The 2011 financial report[3] talks about a strong start, with the best quarter ever, to be followed by global financial turbulence and economic uncertainty, most notably drastic business evolutions in the solar energy market that occurred suddenly and unpredictably. Bekaert was delivering 'sawing wire' for the cutting of solar panels and in 2009 and 2010 had benfited from the huge boost in demand for solar panels, often driven by subsidies from national governments. In 2011 that bubble was bursting, and as you can see from Figure 5.11, Bekaert has been struggling ever since to get back to the same gross margin or EBIT levels. It feels wrong for such a diversified company to feel the impact of just one imploding market. You would expect a diversified company to be more resilient.

FIGURE 5.11 Bekaert ten-year financials

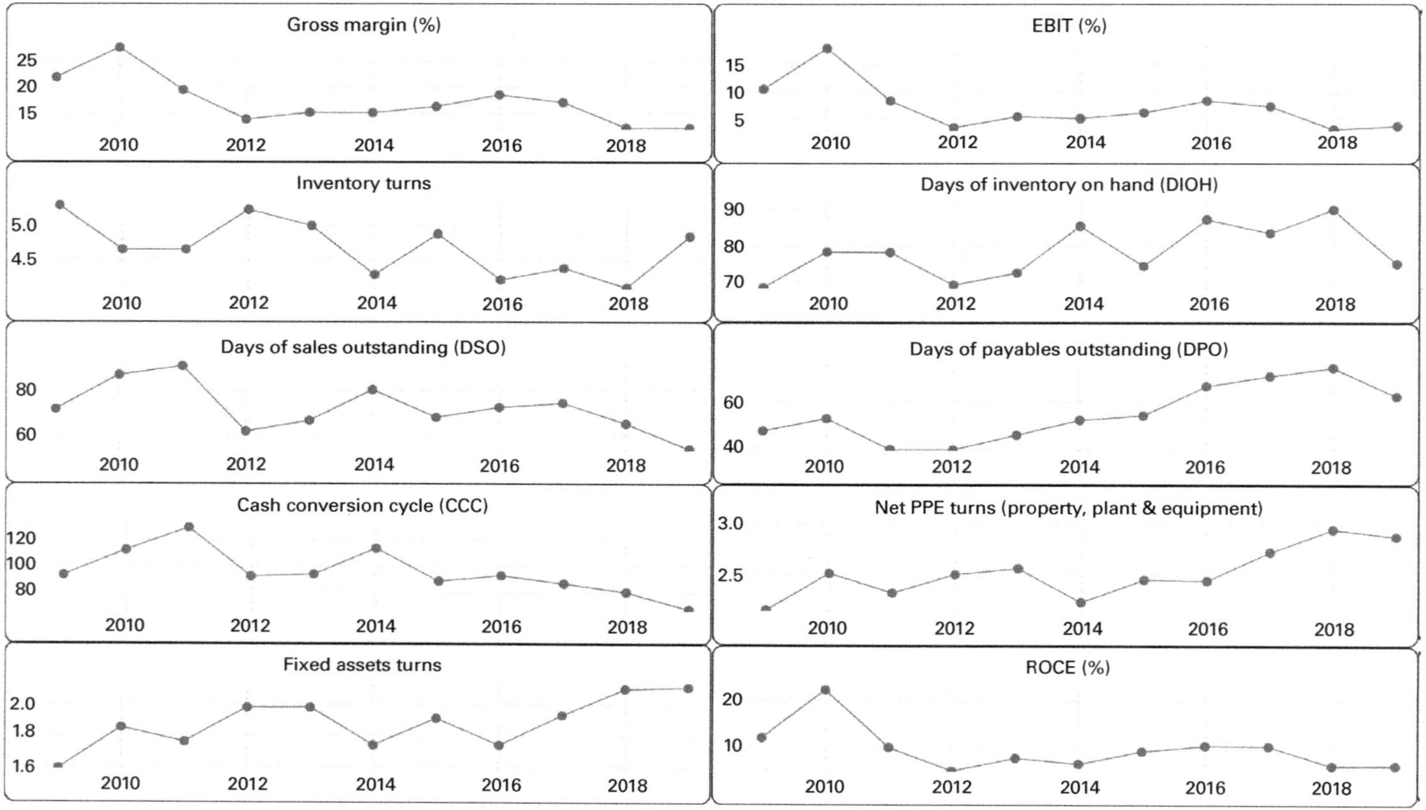

What you can see is that in 2012, probably in response to the adverse business conditions, Bekaert worked on working capital reductions and improvement of fixed asset turns. But it hasn't helped to pimp ROCE with an EBIT of less than 5 per cent. It may have helped free cash flow at that time. You see a clear second focus on being more efficient in working capital on net PPE and on fixed assets starting in 2016. The weak EBIT, however, has not allowed ROCE to rise above the 10 per cent mark.

So how does it get out of this type of situation? Well, Treacy and Wiersema would tell us: make a clear strategic choice. If this is not possible on a company level, then do it on a segment or a business unit level.

We believe the DNA of Bekaert is that of product leadership. As mentioned earlier, Bekaert is a technology leader in steel wire transformation and coating technologies. Given the efficiency gains shown in Figure 5.11, the logical consequence would be that it primarily needs to work on EBIT improvement. Figure 5.12 shows the required EBIT percentage for Bekaert to get to 15 per cent ROCE. That might not necessarily be easy but at least it plants a flag to show what the company needs to reach.

We also believe Bekaert has fallen prey to some of the strategy fails described in the previous chapter. Around half of its business is in rubber reinforcement. Without being experts in the field, we can imagine the technological advantage is less than 20 years ago, and Bekaert, knowingly or not, has shifted into a customer intimacy positioning. Treacy and Wiersema will tell us that will come at a lower margin and that the lower margin needs to be compensated with a lower capital employed. You can't tell that from the aggregated company figures, but a question is whether that has happened.

FIGURE 5.12 Required EBIT percentage for 15 per cent ROCE

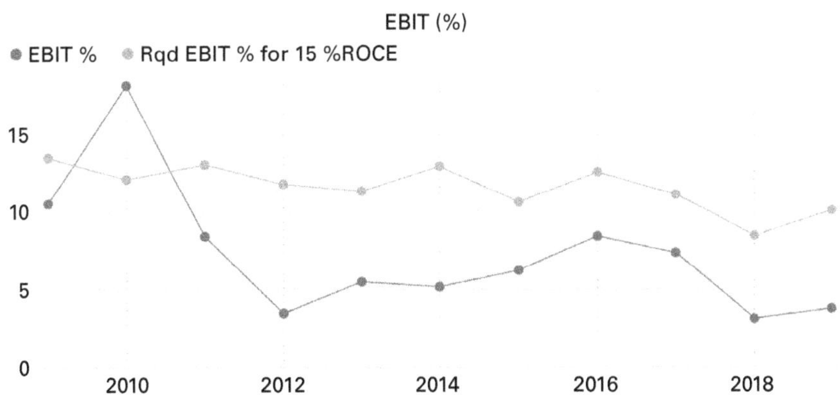

We don't see strong choices like 3M is making as a product leader, stepping out of markets if the advantage of the early innovation is gone and markets start stabilizing. Judging by the numbers shown in Figure 5.11, Bekaert has been trying, but has not succeeded, to realize a breakthrough.

The strategy-driven supply chain

As explained in the Bekaert example, in 'traditional business strategy' we risk getting stuck in setting targets instead of really making strategic choices. Yes, we want to grow, but how will we drive that growth – with better products, with better solutions, or by having the lowest price? That traditional 'conflicting target-setting' strategy approach is shown on the left of Figure 5.13.

The right side of Figure 5.13 illustrates what we call the concept of the 'strategy-driven supply chain'. We start by making choices in the value proposition. These choices will translate into choices in the supply chain. The supply chain of a product leader will be less cost efficient than that of the operational excellence leader but it will be more responsive. A product leader supply chain also comes with a higher investment. But, as we've explained in Chapter 3, a product leader will compensate with a higher margin. Product leaders will drive a double premium: one to compensate for the extra costs, and one to compensate for the extra capital employed. So translating the strategy into a value proposition and into the corresponding supply chain tells us how we are going to drive ROCE for our shareholders.

There are a couple of extra things we can learn from Figure 5.13. The first is that there is no such thing as 'translating a business strategy into a supply chain strategy'. I see, in many companies, strategic decisions being taken without having supply chain on the table. Strategic decisions to enter a new segment, to make an acquisition, seem to be the prerogative of marketing and sales or general management. Well, Figure 5.13 teaches us that as long as I don't know the corresponding supply chain, I don't know the level of cost and capital employed, so I cannot tell how I'm going to drive value as measured by ROCE for the shareholder, which means my business strategy is not finished. A business strategy consists of a value proposition and the corresponding supply chain. One cannot exist in isolation of the other. Only when they come together do we understand how we are going to drive value. The value proposition and the corresponding supply chain are the yin

FIGURE 5.13 The strategy-driven supply chain

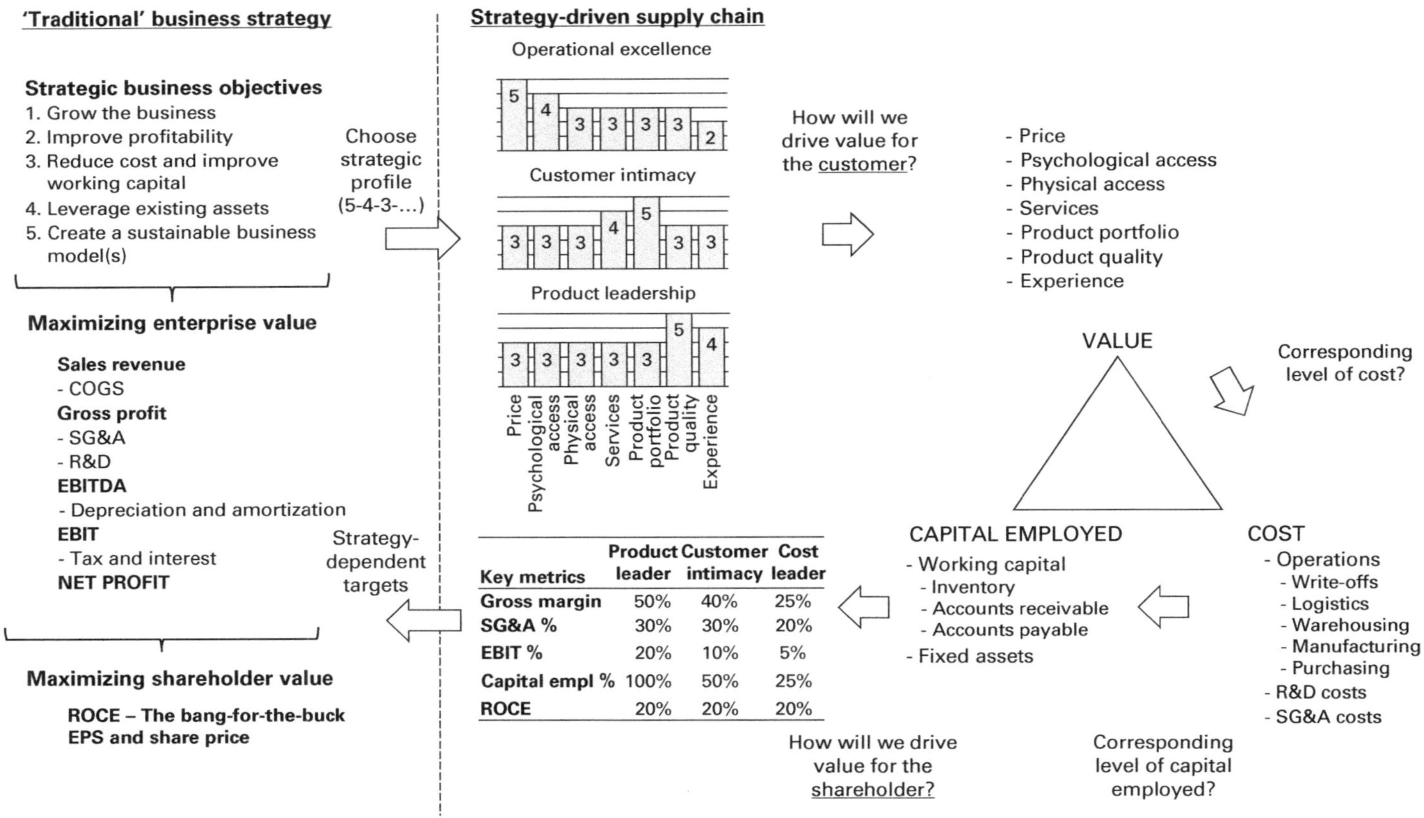

and yang of business strategy. The value proposition doesn't necessarily come first. Hard discounters have started more from the operational supply chain and how to optimize that, rather than starting from the value proposition, so both should be considered equal parts.

The second thing to learn from Figure 5.13 is that every strategy deserves an excellent supply chain. As we will discuss further in the next chapter, people mistake supply chain for cost and efficiency, so they might say, 'Supply chain is most important for an operational excellence player.' That assumption is wrong. The supply chain of the operational excellence player is the most simple; those of the product leaders and the customer intimacy players are more complex. They have complex products or product portfolios, combined with more difficult sales forecasting and a higher degree of innovation. Every strategy certainly needs an excellent supply chain, only that supply chain will be quite different and have a different focus.

A last thing to learn from Figure 5.13 is that supply chain cannot make up for a failed value proposition. In Chapter 4 we applied Treacy and Wiersema to the food retail sector. We discussed how the traditional supermarket is an example of the customer intimacy model as it provides the convenience of the one-stop shop. You can shop for all your groceries for the full week. The supermarket offers A, B and C brands, which you may combine for different occasions. The broader assortment drives a higher capital employed, but if executed properly it is compensated for by the customer with a higher margin. In the last five years, Carrefour had to restructure many of its hypermarkets, where next to food, you could also buy electronics, clothing, etc all under one roof. Consumers have lost interest in this concept. The rise of online shopping and home deliveries means that, when buying electronics, people would rather make a comparative study online and then have their choice delivered to their doorstep. In many cases I would see the pressure on supply chain being raised with questions like 'Why do we have so much inventory in the hypermarkets? Can't we do with less?' If an average supermarket has 10,000–15,000 SKUs, a hypermarket could easily have up to 30,000 SKUs. The long tail only becomes longer, which means per definition the inventory turns will be lower in the hypermarket. If executed correctly, the customer is willing to pay a premium for that. If the customer doesn't want to pay that premium, you can squeeze some percentages out of the supply chain, but supply chain cannot make up for a failed business model.

CASE STUDY

LEGO®

WITH RUEDIGER FUCHS, HEAD OF CORPORATE SUPPLY CHAIN, BAHLSEN (FORMER SENIOR DIRECTOR OPERATING MODEL INNOVATION, LEGO®)

This case digs into the effect of resolving conflicting KPIs in the triangle across different functions within LEGO®, putting mechanisms in place to create awareness about these conflicts, which is a critical factor to enable multi-year (double-digit) growth.

Did you know that LEGO® was almost bankrupt in the early years of the new millennium? The company was focusing on many different products and channels outside of its core business, eg producing clothes, running hotels and theme parks, and over time it lost the confidence and ability to excel with the product which is its DNA: the brick.

Apparently, it was necessary to feel this pressure and pain of almost closing down the business in order to become decisive about the company's own core capabilities, and about how many 'where to plays' and 'how to wins' can be driven at a time. This started as one of the most remarkable transformations of a company, resulting in many changes, tough calls on eliminating or selling parts of the product portfolio and assets, and setting up the company in its core DNA for long-term success.

This turnaround was managed in a very remarkable way and has set up LEGO® for successful growth. But, once you are successful again, how can you keep momentum? How can you keep growing and achieving scale and hence further improve your key results like EBIT and ROCE, which you will probably find in 98 per cent of all company strategies?

The solution is in the 'triangle', as Bram DeSmet describes it, and even more, it is in the way you apply this knowledge and how you work with it – every day.

'Welcome to Japan!' the local LEGO® general manager told me during my visit, 'You will see things are very different over here. Completely different, highly demanding consumers compared to Europe, a very different trade landscape, different price points, etc, require a very different value proposition. And, by the way, local production would be great so we can further customize our product portfolio to Japan and beat competition on service level and cost.'

Although this statement is made up from different conversations with different general managers across the world while I was working in the Operating Model Innovation role, it is supposed to give an example of the challenges companies are facing every day, from many of their employees and mostly with very good intentions.

So – is that the time to fundamentally change your strategy (which, for LEGO®, is clearly a product leadership strategy), completely target and adapt to this local environment (eg in Japan), invest in further assets and even start a journey towards customer intimacy?

There is always a trade-off between the incremental sales that can be achieved and the scale a company is losing in product development, marketing and operations. Many companies do not address these conflicts, and hence dilute their value proposition over time, with severe impact on EBIT margin and ROCE.

You cannot question strategy every day; you need to focus on execution with millions of related decisions by thousands of employees. We have seen in the example above how a successful value proposition can be diluted by the many decisions and choices, every day. LEGO® is managing these internal battles arising from conflicting choices very well, by consciously addressing them and spending the time to define and agree the parameters on how to run the business in all the relevant functions, by addressing the conflicts between functions proactively and by resolving trade-offs and hence driving coherent choices.

This task is about applying the triangle in practice, with your own company-specific settings and choices. Many great company leaders do this unconsciously by taking decisions every day, in order to protect core business or to keep scale. Being conscious about these choices makes you an even more successful leader.

It is a big challenge to define and align the way to steer a company, eg to convert your business model into operating model choices, or defining the targets of the KPIs in the triangle. Once this is done, the even bigger challenge is to find a way to communicate and deploy this new way of running the business in a successful way.

Only companies who find a way to protect their business from dilution through internal everyday choices (assuming you get the right strategy for your business environment) are rewarded with multi-year growth. Here are a few examples from LEGO®:

- Although there are very high lean standards and a high cost consciousness, LEGO® is focusing on developing its brand, on a high product innovation frequency and is hence following a product leadership strategy. Many, especially Asian, competitors are playing in the cost leadership sector and are trying to get share with different price points. There are many internal conversations on how to relate to this and it needs convincing arguments to stick to the strategic choice made.
- As for many companies with global growth plans, there is a risk of weakening the value proposition during globalization due to the many compromises made, eg in product portfolio, route to market or supply chain choices. LEGO® is consciously focusing on these threats by addressing the conflicts to keep scale. A model similar to the triangle and a supporting team are helping in internal

communication on how to make these trade-off choices, with high awareness all the way up to senior leadership and high top-down support.

- LEGO® has a highly seasonal business skewed towards key gifting events, and at the same time the product portfolio changes significantly every year in order to be relevant for the consumer. A big challenge for the supply chain is the conflicting targets of high product availability on the shelf and high risk of product leftovers at the end of the product lifecycle (which is often only one year).
- Another conflict is inventory cost versus cost of manufacturing bricks, which was solved by prioritizing moulding machine utilization over inventory carrying cost. Product design principles are applied to manage this conflict, eg a high level of common bricks, which can also be used for a later product. Hence the resolution is not only a supply chain choice, but also affects the whole product innovation department.

Net: LEGO® is benefiting already from many years of consecutive growth as a result of creating awareness in the organization about strategic choices, translating this into business-governing KPIs and identifying the relation between the KPIs. In contrast to other companies, LEGO® has found a way to teach the organization how to apply these strategic choices in everyday business and by working across functions prioritizing company goals. By identifying these conflicting KPIs, different functions within the company can agree on coherent choices and related trade-offs in order to keep scale.

This is what you can take out of this case for yourself:

1. Choose a model that has been described in this book.
2. Understand how it works and why, and apply it to your business.
3. Set your target KPIs.
4. Identify and resolve conflicts between them.
5. Involve your organization by making the conflicts transparent and explain them.
6. Take joint, integrated decisions, having the strategic direction of your company in mind.

This will help to defend your strategic choices, especially against internal threats, every day.

Conclusion

In this chapter we have started by redefining the 'service' corner of our supply chain triangle into a 'value' corner. We started by deriving four possible value drivers from the model of Treacy and Wiersema: price, product quality, product range and value-added services. We married that to the model of Crawford and Mathews, by splitting their five value drivers into seven: price, psychological access, physical access, service, product breadth/depth, product quality and experience. We adopted the approach of Crawford and Mathews to look for a 5–4–3–3–3–3–3 profile when defining a strategy. You can dominate on one driver, differentiate on a second, and at best be on par at the remaining drivers. By splitting the five value drivers into seven, we can still derive the three strategic options of Treacy and Wiersema, though we are no longer limited to only three. From that perspective you can say we have extended the model of Treacy and Wiersema by using an extension of the model of Crawford and Mathews.

We then introduced the concept of the 'strategy-driven supply chain', which shows that the value proposition and the corresponding supply chain are like the yin and the yang of the business strategy. Only together do they define how you can drive value for the shareholder as measured by ROCE. In the traditional strategy development we see a lack of choices and targets for financial metrics that can be conflicting, all of which leaves little guidance on how to design the supply chain. But not only does it leave the supply chain without guidance, it also leads to a lack of differentiation and most often to a lack of value generation.

In the next chapter we will use our refined 'value' corner to study how to design the corresponding supply chain in more detail. So far, we believe everybody gets the concept; the concept is important as it changes the thinking about strategy and supply chain. In the next chapter we will make it more practical and give more practical guidelines on how to design your supply chain, in alignment with your value proposition, what are the key drivers, and what are the key pitfalls.

Notes

1. F Crawford and R Mathews (2007) *The Myth of Excellence: Why great companies never try to be the best at everything*, Crown Business, New York
2. Bekaert, *Annual Report 2019*, https://annualreport.bekaert.com/ (archived at https://perma.cc/Z2MB-6YC6)
3. Bekaert, *Annual Report 2011*, www.bekaert.com/-/media/Annual-Report-2011/Bekaert-Annual-Report-2011.pdf (archived at https://perma.cc/RYG6-UNAE)

06

Designing your strategy-driven supply chain

In the previous chapter we refined our instruments to define our strategic value proposition by splitting the model of Crawford and Mathews into seven value drivers. We introduced the principle of the strategy-driven supply chain that states that different value propositions lead to different supply chains, with a different level of cost and a different level of capital employed.

In this chapter we will refine that 'mapping' exercise, from the strategic value proposition to the supply chain. We call it 'strategy-driven supply chain design'. We start by discussing supply chain design fails, like we discussed strategy fails in Chapter 4. We argue that too many supply chains are designed based on cost. We then introduce how the markets you operate in and your chosen strategy drive a given level of complexity and variability, and how our desired responsiveness translates that into a given level of cost and capital employed.

Near the end of the chapter we illustrate the SCOR model, which has driven improvements in supply chain as a profession, but lacks the complexity and variability dimensions and may contribute to the mistake of designing supply chains overly on cost. We will also reflect on the impact of sustainability on our supply chain triangle and supply chain design.

Eight fails when it comes to supply chain design

While the concept of the strategy-driven supply chain, introduced in Figure 5.13, may be logical, we see many 'fails' in practice. In Chapter 4 we introduced common 'strategy fails' and explained that companies are bad at making choices, as we think choosing is losing. In this chapter we introduce eight supply chain design fails. As the strategy is often not clearly pronounced, supply chains tend to be designed on cost, which may be good for an operational excellence player, but which tends to create problems if your strategy is different.

We grossly underestimate the impact of complexity

In one of my consulting assignments I was hired as an external advisor to the different supply chain managers of a company. During one of the consulting sessions, one of the supply chain managers came in depressed, shoulders down, with a sad face and a deep sigh. So I asked, 'What's up Frank?' He replied, 'I have a problem with my inventory.' To which I answered, 'I'm not sure you do.' Which made him look surprised, as if he had just seen a ghost.

So I continued: 'If you're still doing the same sales as five years ago, but you're doing that with 50 per cent more SKUs and you need to deliver those with a shorter lead time, then you shouldn't be surprised your inventory went up. On the contrary, you should go back to your boss and say that if that trend continues then your turns of next year will probably still be lower.'

I gave my gut feeling but when Frank started to analyse, he found evidence that over the years the number of SKUs had increased, lead times had been reduced and not a lot of effort had gone into a more modular design of the products or into some kind of postponement.

Though that didn't simplify Frank's task, it led to a different debate, and it shows how even supply chain managers underestimate the impact of complexity on the supply chain, let alone how this would be understood by R&D, marketing or sales. There is an education job to be done.

Over-constraining the supply chain

I see many of our customers that have multiple production plants, but each product can be produced in only one plant. That is simple but not very flexible, designed for cost instead of responsiveness. Drop it like it's hot. It doesn't mean you have to produce in multiple plants at the same time. It's about creating the option to do so. At a product leader like 3M, each technology is in at least three plants, and each plant has at least three technologies. That's not the most cost effective, but it does provide flexibility. If 3M has to phase out a technology, it can do so without major restructuring. We have discussed in the previous chapter that phasing in and phasing out technologies is key to the business model of 3M. If demand in one of their niches explodes, 3M will be able to scale up faster. In 2010 the European Commission introduced a European format for licence plates. That led to a boost in demand for reflective coatings. Guess who was able to deliver when the market went crazy? Yes, you're right, 3M.

Another example of over-constraining the supply chain is a long approval process to switch customers from one plant to another. Do something about it. Maybe it is due to a lack of consistency in the quality across plants; if so, then address it. Maybe it is due to regulatory processes; in which case, force double or triple sourcing on your key customers. Don't wait. Do it now. If you wait, you will always be too late.

Alternative sources come at a different cost. Production costs may be different, transport costs may be different. I have seen a company where the alternative sources and alternative prices were put in the customer contract. Don't do that. You don't want to have customers or sales define what will be the source of supply.

If you want to be able to plan your supply chain, try to relax as many constraints as possible, drop them like they're hot, try to create degrees of freedom. Don't make it more complex than it already is. Don't over-constrain your supply chain.

Squeezing buffers out of the supply chain

A specific case is that of Indaver, the company introduced in Chapter 1. Waste processing is capital intensive. Investing in a new rotary kiln requires volume to load it continuously. What we overlook is that waste supply isn't stable. There are days and weeks where supply is half or double. If we want to feed the rotary kiln in a continuous way, we need to be able to buffer the waste as it is coming in. When reviewing the investment proposals, storage space is seen as 'dead weight' with 'no value add' so we try to minimize it. This is because we underestimate the impact of variability.

And it is not getting any better. Due to the lack of new investments in Europe, all rotary kilns are reaching a certain age. As a rotary kiln begins to wear out, there are more unplanned shutdowns, which adds to the variability. Even if the supply of waste was 100 per cent stable, we would require a buffer to temporarily store the waste we have not been able to process because of the unforeseen shutdown. But the supply of waste is not stable.

So, imagine what happens if we have a peak of waste coming in, and an unforeseen shutdown at the same time... after having squeezed our buffers out of the original design... yes, this creates problems in the supply chain.

Creating our own bullwhip

The bullwhip effect[1] states that a small variation in demand gets amplified as it travels up the supply chain, all the way to the suppliers. Many companies create their own bullwhip, or their own variability. A common example is end-of-quarter sales peaks, caused by end-of-quarter incentives to sales people. Publicly listed companies selling into a distributor network are known to stuff the channels with incentives like price reductions to make their quarterly target. This is useless and meaningless. It destroys value. Rushing the end-of-quarter peaks through the supply chain comes at an extra cost and at extra inventory or extra capacity. If that is to sell products at a reduced price, products that if they stayed in inventory could have perfectly well been sold or delivered the month after, then we can rightly say it is useless, meaningless and destroys value. Still it is common.

In pharma companies I have seen regional inventories managed by sales people. I've seen sales people calling in panic to production planners when their inventory was below safety stock. In a sales-driven company this can result in sales doing the planning and getting an emergency order squeezed into the planning. The safety stock is there to be used. If you order every month, then one out of two months you should end up in the safety stock; if you don't, then you are most probably over-forecasting. It is a second example of how we create our own nervousness and bullwhip by a lack of understanding of how a safety stock works.

Supply chains are designed for cost instead of responsiveness

A couple of years ago, Barco, the technology company featured in Chapter 4, launched one of its, in the meantime hugely successful, products for meeting collaboration.

When discussing the corresponding supply chain, I told the then COO, 'Johan, you have a problem.' 'Why?' he asked. The manufacturing was outsourced to a third party, and to save on inventory, purchasing had negotiated a three-month consignment stock. As such, he felt quite safe.

So I continued and said, 'What happens when you negotiate a contract based on cost?' Question 1 will be 'Can you give me more volume?' Question

2 will be 'The forecast of month 1 is fixed, month 2 +/–10 per cent, month 3 +/–20 per cent.' If I negotiate on price, the supplier will try to get extra volume and will try to reduce the uncertainty. Low cost requires high volume, high predictability.

I continued, 'This is a new product; if the forecast is 100, there is only one certainty, you will not sell 100 – you will either sell 10 or 1,000. Let's say your forecast is 100 and you sell 10. You're not allowed to change forecast for the current month, only –10 per cent for month 2 and –20 per cent for month 3... so in three months' time (accounting for the delay of the three months' consignment) you find yourself sitting on 270 units, which at an actual sales of 10, is 27 months. Guess who will be under pressure for having an inventory problem? In the other situation, let's say your forecast is 100 and you sell 1,000. You have just squeezed a supplier to come up with lower prices and now you need to go back and ask for more volume. What will be the answer? Well, yes, of course I can do some more, but definitely not at the same price.'

This story is anecdotal for how we design supply chains for cost, maybe to pimp the business case, even at a product leader company like Barco. In the case of the specific product, the actuals will rather have been 1,000, which was good news. But Barco also ventured into products, where the actuals were rather 10, and where important write-offs had to be taken. The uncertainty is part of the business model of a product leader.

In other companies I see purchasing negotiates on price, and the supplier comes with minimum order quantities. Or, when we launch a new product, production wants to produce it in an optimal quantity, meaning a large batch. If demand is slow to pick up, or doesn't pick up at all, it means we are often confronted with slow-moving stock or write-offs after the first order or production batch. Though this is common, it is cynical. It's not how we drive value in the triangle.

Reducing inventories equally across the board

A couple of months ago a COO, a manufacturing director and a supply chain manager asked me for advice on how to tackle a challenging growth problem in one of their factories. The good news was that one of their product ranges was hugely successful. That had led to quite a challenging situation in operations. Operations had doubled its production in a three-month timeframe. Scaling up that fast requires a lot of training and is partly done with interims. That was eroding the efficiency and negatively affecting cost, resulting in pressure from the business. Their biggest hurdle was the inventory, and how to define a realistic level of inventory. Finance was putting a lot of pressure on working capital and they had the feeling they were continuously working against their limit.

The case triggered two reactions from my side. First is that operations and supply chain should quantify and review the options for responsiveness upfront with the business. If there are different customer-product segments, which are the segments we want to manage in a more efficient way, and which are the segments where we want to be more responsive? Try to quantify options for responsiveness: what if we need to double the volumes in three months' time, in six months' time, or in one year? What is the impact on cost and on capital employed? If we need to be able to double in three months' time, then maybe we need to buy strategic stocks of key components or raw materials.

Second is that operations and supply chain should not allow finance to define inventory targets on this level of detail. When we discussed free cash flow in Chapter 2, we understood there are times where generating FCF is a priority for the company. But starving a growing business of inventory is like accelerating in a car with the handbrake on. It gets very smelly and it's not very good for the engine. Operations and supply chain should simply not accept this. They should force a different type of debate with finance and the business and come to a more meaningful discussion and decision on 'which are the businesses we will manage more efficiently and what are the limits within which we can operate those', versus 'which are the businesses we want to strategically invest in or protect, even in times when generating free cash flow is a priority'. Though obvious, I miss this type of debate, even in professionally led companies.

Redesigning one step in the supply chain at the expense of another

Obvious cases are where distributors push back their inventories to their suppliers. Multi-echelon inventory management teaches us that this doesn't make sense. Inventory has the highest service impact at the customer-facing location. They can push back for two reasons. One is working capital or inventory risk, but then they talk about consignment or about taking back unsold inventory. A second reason could be physical storage space. If a distributor refuses to carry inventory because he doesn't have the space, then charge him for doing so in his place.

Another case I've seen is a retailer redesigning its shops to improve experience. If, after analysing your value proposition, you have decided you want to dominate or differentiate on experience, that is a fair thing to do. What the retailer almost overlooked was the impact on central logistics. The retailer was realizing around 30 per cent of its annual turnover in one big seasonal peak. The current stores could hold inventory in the build-up to that seasonal peak. The redesign of the stores would basically take that extra storage out. This implies that instead of flattening the peak and pre-building the inventory in store, central logistics had to deliver everything just-in-time, which, though not impossible, had a huge impact on the number of trailers, the number of loading docks, the number of drivers, the number of warehouse operators that needed to be active during that peak. Any decision is good if it is thought through over the full chain. This company almost missed an essential bit.

Disinformation towards key suppliers

I have seen companies with outsourced manufacturing that either don't have an S&OP process with their supplier or are not sharing information freely. Let's start with the first. I see that when it comes to outsourced manufacturing many companies only have an operational process, looking at the orders for the coming two to three weeks, and typically these are managed using Excel, which is an outdated and rudimentary solution. Companies spend money on IT systems within the company boundaries, but sometimes underinvest in integration with key suppliers. For the internal assets we have a tactical process that should allow us to better anticipate upcoming changes in demand or supply. Though that seems logical for the internal assets, we don't do that for the external assets.

At some companies I've seen, we have the tactical process, but we are not sharing information freely. We're behind on schedule but we're not going to share that with the supplier. Er, I say, 'Why?' We don't want them to start hesitating. Er, 'Why?' As mentioned before, we still design our supply chains on cost instead of flexibility. You should know the forecast is always wrong. The supplier should know that as well. You should design your contracts and processes to deal with that uncertainty. It also has to do with a lack of trust. If you've outsourced your manufacturing, you should stop talking about a supplier. Whether you like it or not, you really are supply chain partners. You need to create the corresponding trust.

Eight dos and don'ts from eight fails

If we try to summarize these eight fails into eight dos and don'ts when designing your supply chain, they become the following:

- Don't underestimate complexity. Do face it and embrace it.
- Don't add complexity. Do try to simplify and create degrees of freedom.
- Don't ignore variability. Do design the right buffers in your supply chain.
- Don't increase variability. Do try to reduce it.
- Don't design on cost. Do design your supply chain for responsiveness.
- Don't wait until it's too late. Do discuss options for responsiveness upfront.
- Don't look at just your part of the supply chain. Do always look end-to-end.
- Don't fool yourself by fooling your partners. Do build trust and transparency.

These eight fails reveal three important drivers for supply chain design: complexity, variability and our desired responsiveness. They also contain three important lessons: try to simplify – reduce your (self-induced) complexity; try to stabilize – reduce your (self-induced) variability; and take an end-to-end instead of narrow focus.

When summarizing the eight fails, we try to be provocative. 'Don't add complexity' should be 'Don't add "non-value adding" complexity'. 'Don't increase variability' should be 'Don't increase self-induced variability'. 'Don't design on cost' should be 'Don't design on cost unless your strategy is operational excellence'. We do it to make you think and to give you one-liners you can use to provoke your organization. We somehow need to wake up to a new reality. Sometimes that is easier when some of the nuance is left out in the beginning.

In what follows, we'll start by exploring how the markets in which we are active and our strategic positioning in those markets define the three design drivers: complexity, variability and our desired responsiveness. Next, we will try to discuss how these three together define our cost and capital employed. Near the end of the chapter we review the three important lessons learnt (simplify, reduce complexity, stabilize), as an extra dimension, when designing our strategy-driven supply chain.

EXERCISE 6.1

Identifying the fails in your current supply chain(s)

For each of the eight fails, dos and don'ts, review your supply chain(s) and comment on whether you recognize the fail, in what way, and what you think could or should be done differently.

- We underestimate complexity...
- We make it more complex than it already is...
- We underestimate variability...
- We create our own variability...
- We focus on cost when designing our supply chain...
- We are bad at discussing the impact of flexibility with finance and the business...
- We optimize one part of the supply chain at the expense of another...
- We are not transparent towards our supply chain partners...

Strategy-driven supply chain design

Figure 5.13 contains the 'principles' of the strategy-driven supply chain. We need to start from a value proposition. A value proposition needs to contain choices and the value proposition translates into a given level of cost and capital employed in the supply chain. In the remainder of this chapter we will try to further map that latest step – how do I get from the value proposition to the cost and capital employed in the supply chain?

Our approach for strategy-driven supply chain design is summarized in Figure 6.1. It builds on the findings from the eight fails introduced earlier in this chapter. As illustrated in Figure 6.1, we will discuss how our markets and our chosen strategy define a given level of complexity and variability. We will discuss how companies can design their desired response, and how that response comes with a corresponding level of cost and capital employed. A higher complexity and a higher variability drive up the level of cost and capital employed for the same level of responsiveness. We can design our supply chain to be highly efficient or to be highly responsive. But, above all, we need to ensure it is effective, that it drives the intended response in the market, aligned with what the market requires and aligned with our strategic positioning. We need to ensure our supply chain is fit for purpose.

FIGURE 6.1 Strategy-driven supply chain design: summary

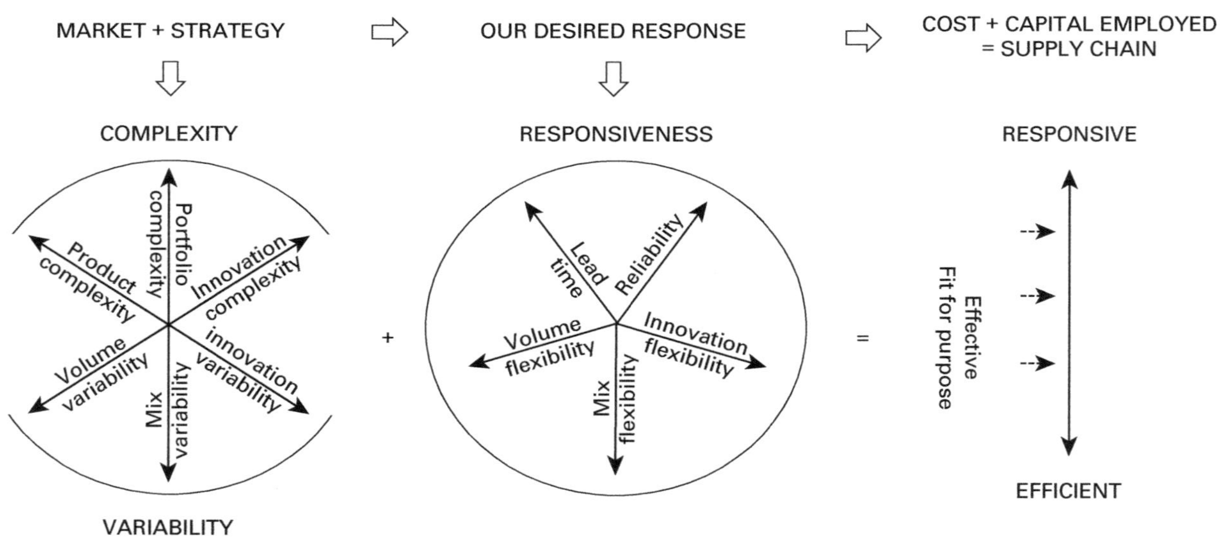

Complexity and variability

A first step in a strategy-driven supply chain design is to understand your level of complexity and your level of variability. These are driven both by the market and by your strategic positioning in that market. Let's start by discussing complexity and then continue with variability. Both are shown in somewhat more detail in Figure 6.2.

We see three drivers of complexity: product complexity, which is typical for product leaders, product portfolio complexity, which is typical at customer intimacy players, and innovation complexity, which is found at both, as we make changes to our product or to our portfolios. Part of the complexity is driven by the market. If I am in fashion or consumer electronics, the product lifecycles will be shorter than in B2B chemicals. So these

FIGURE 6.2 Strategy-driven supply chain design: assessing complexity and variability

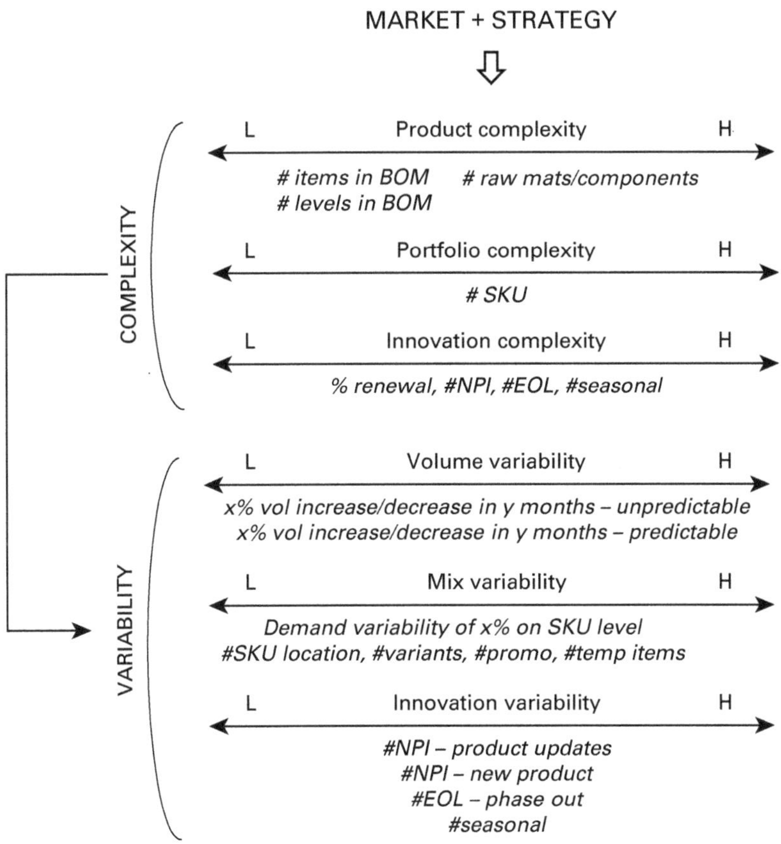

markets structurally have more 'innovation complexity'. Part of the complexity is driven by the strategy. Product leaders, in comparison to operational excellence players, will always have more complex products and a higher rate of product changes. Customer intimacy players, in comparison to product leaders and opex players, will always have a broader product portfolio and hence more portfolio complexity. In Figure 6.2 we have indicated possible metrics to measure and reveal your level of complexity.

As shown in Figure 6.2, the complexity almost automatically translates into variability. We talk about volume variability, mix variability and innovation variability. Volume variability is the need to scale up or scale down the volume of the supply chain, either in a predictable or in an unpredictable way.

A typical example of predictable volume variability is seasonality. If you are making BBQ sauces or air conditioning, there will be a strong seasonal peak in the summer. One of our customers makes the best pralines in the world. They have a strong seasonal peak at the year end, around Christmas and New Year's Eve. Food retailers have a strong seasonal peak around Christmas as well.

Volume variability from the 'unpredictable' variant is typical for product leaders. Think about the Barco example discussed earlier in this chapter. Or imagine you are Apple and you are going to launch a new product called the iWatch. How many are you going to sell? If the forecast is 100, it could as well be 10 as it could be 1,000. You can try to reduce the uncertainty by performing market testing and the like, but product leaders will always experience a significant amount of 'unpredictable' volume variability.

So, if some volume variability, like 'seasonality', can be linked to the market, some volume variability will be linked to your strategy positioning. If I'm a brander and I'm launching new flavours of BBQ sauces right in the middle of the peak season... I have just increased my volume variability. Regardless of the mix, I also have the question of how much I'm going to sell. Is this going to be a success? If I'm a brander that is driven by innovation, that is part of my business.

Volume variability can also be driven by external factors like a competitor going bankrupt, an outbreak of COVID-19, changes in import tariffs or in public opinion. You could say these are also more 'market' related rather than 'strategy' related. Next is what we call 'mix variability'. Maybe my overall volume is relatively stable or at least predictable, but my biggest challenge is changes in the mix. Part of it may again be driven by the market. If I'm a player in the automotive aftermarket, then my product portfolio will most probably be way larger than the average portfolio in an FMCG company. Part of it is driven by the strategy. If in that market I want to be a 'total solution' provider, in comparison to an operational excellence player, my product portfolio will be larger.

Take the example of Federal Mogul automotive aftermarket, now part of Tenneco. Federal Mogul formulated the ambition to have a 95 per cent coverage in selected product groups such as spark plugs, brakes, wipers, etc.[2] This means that it has a range that serves 95 per cent of existing cars in the market. That coverage of 95 per cent was one of the keys to the value proposition and the competitive positioning of Federal Mogul. The proposition was not to be the cheapest but rather to deliver a full range. That easily led to 100,000 SKUs being stored at multiple locations. Maybe the overall sales volume could be predicted relatively well. Maybe some product groups like spark plugs had predictable volume variability, having higher sales in wintertime. But the biggest challenge is certainly the mix variability – how to predict which SKUs will be sold more or less and in which location.

So as with volume variability, we believe part of the mix variability is linked to the market, and part is linked to the strategy. Customer intimacy players, who try to differentiate based on portfolio and a total solution, typically have a higher mix variability compared to other players in the same market.

Finally there is innovation variability. When it comes to new product introductions (NPI) there is a difference between 'product updates' and 'new products'. There is a difference between launching a new flavour, a new packaging of an existing product, or launching a brand new product that has less comparison to previous products. Think about the initial launch of the iWatch at Apple. It is not only about introductions, but also about end-of-life (EOL) management of SKUs that will be stopped. My strategy should define the size of my product portfolio. It will be more limited at operational excellence players or product leaders. My EOL management or phase-outs are key to keep the size of my portfolio under control. We will discuss that in the next chapter when we discuss the sales and operations planning process.

As with the other variabilities, part of the innovation variability is defined by the market. Again, if I'm in fashion or consumer electronics, the innovation variability will be higher than in many B2B markets. At the same time, product leaders, compared to operational excellence players, will have a higher innovation rate in their products, and customer intimacy players will have a higher innovation rate in their product portfolios.

EXERCISE 6.2

Identifying your level of complexity and variability

Start by analysing the impact of your market on the three types of complexity and the three types of variability. Do you think your market, in comparison to others, is low, medium or high. Try to give an example of markets that you rank lower and those that you rank higher. You may learn from analysing the markets that are ranked higher. You may, for instance, learn from the fashion world how they deal with the volume uncertainty in a new collection.

Then take your value proposition that you defined in the previous chapter. How does your strategy influence the three types of complexity and the three types of variability? You may try to name competitors that are lower and competitors that are higher. Try to put numbers on the KPIs shown in Figure 6.2.

CASE STUDY

Dreamland

WITH ANDRÉ CERON, DIRECTOR OF LOGISTICS

Dreamland promises 'to inspire children and their parents, and to connect in a playful way'. It is a chain of stores for 'family fun', offering a large range of assortments ranging from toys, games, multimedia, school and books up to garden furniture, etc. Dreamland is part of the Colruyt Group, introduced in the previous chapter.

When it comes to variability, Dreamland can be ranked high to very high on each of the three dimensions: volume variability, mix variability and innovation variability.

As a retailer focused on children, Dreamland realizes around 55 per cent of its annual sales in around 10 weeks. A first crucial period is 'back to school', which runs from mid-August to mid-September, and a second crucial period is 'Saint Nicolas', which is 6 December. The sales volume during these peak periods is four to five times the sales volume during the off-peak periods. From a volume variability perspective, this counts.

Dreamland has 60,000 items in the combined offline and online offering. There is a long tail of items that provides a significant challenge with mix variability. Think about comic books. These come in series. Recent titles may sell more frequently but older titles very easily become very slow-moving. As if that was not enough of a challenge, the combination of an offline and an online channel is adding to the mix variability. We know that Black Friday will create a peak in our sales, but apparently it is very difficult to predict whether it will be in the offline or the online channel.

Finally, Dreamland also has important product portfolio variability. Thirty per cent of the portfolio is changed year on year. Part of this has to do with many seasonal assortments like Halloween, back to school and Christmas. The other part has to do with the short lifecycles of many of the products; think, for instance, about multimedia.

On a scale of variability, it is one of the most complex businesses we have encountered. We will come back to the impact on cost and capital employed after we have discussed how to define responsiveness and how the desired level of responsiveness really defines the cost and capital employed.

Responsiveness and the corresponding cost and capital employed

As we indicated in Figure 6.1, it starts with understanding our complexity and variability. The next step is defining our desired response, and that response will translate into a certain level of cost and capital employed. This is further detailed in Figure 6.3.

A first crucial parameter in defining responsiveness is the order fulfilment lead time. That is also linked to the so-called 'manufacturing strategy' of make to stock (MTS) or make to order (MTO), or hybrid variants like assemble to order (ATO) or the so-called 'postponement'. In MTS we produce to forecast. We assume the customer is not willing to wait. In a MTO strategy, we wait for the customer to order, and we only start manufacturing when we have received the customer order. We may order components and raw materials based on a forecast. For assemble to order we have basic parts or semi-finished products available and just do a final assembly or operation. That reduces the lead time compared to an MTO situation. In a 'postponement' strategy we do a final assembly in the warehouse. A famous and well-documented example is from HP, where the right power box and cables are added to the printer before shipping the product.[3] That avoids storing different printers for the UK in Europe, as it has different sockets.

Different markets have different standards and those standards may show regional differences. In Europe ordering a car comes with a three- to six-month lead time. You could say it is MTO. The advantage of the longer

FIGURE 6.3 Strategy-driven supply chain design: desired responsiveness, and corresponding cost and capital employed

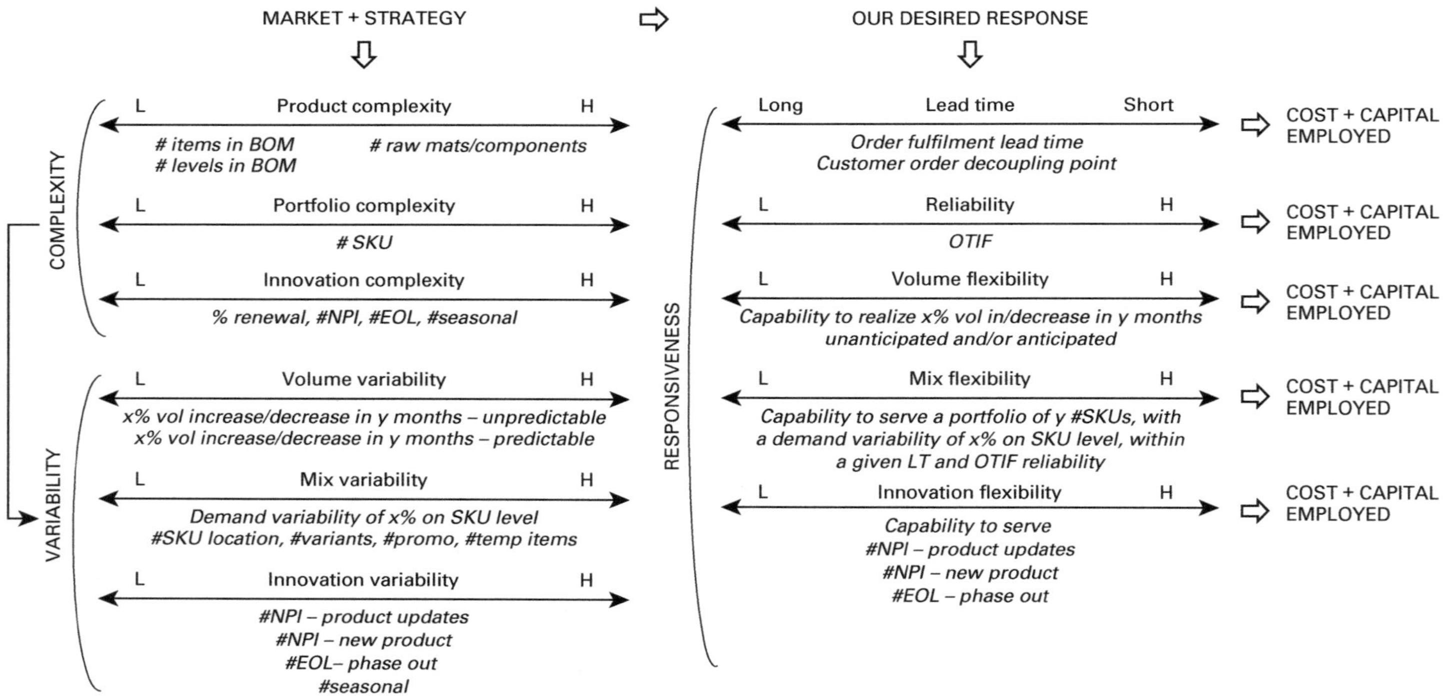

lead time is you can configure your own car from a long list of options. In the US that same car market is MTS. If you want to buy a car in the US, you go to a dealership, you pick your choice and you drive out your new car.

A shorter lead time is driving up both cost and capital employed. The obvious is the extra inventory in an MTS situation. That inventory increases if we further shorten the lead time. In a distribution network design it is common to evaluate scenarios. Delivering in Europe with a one-week lead time can be done from a central location. If we shorten the lead time to 72 hours, 48 hours or 24 hours, we will need to deploy more inventory in more regional hubs, further driving up the cost and the capital employed. Longer lead times typically allow me to organize more efficiently, shorter lead times drive extra costs. Lead time is also a crucial parameter in home delivery. Do I want to deliver the same day, the next day or within the next three days? A shorter lead time will require more inventory in more regional hubs and it will drive up warehousing and transportation costs.

Try to think through how lead time is driving cost and capital employed in your specific market. How does this link to your strategic positioning? Do you want to play at par? Do you want to differentiate? Or do you want to dominate on lead time? What does that cost? What is the required investment in working capital and fixed assets? When we talk about 'desired responsiveness', don't mistake that for 'whatever the customer or the sales rep desires'. The 'desired response' is the one realizing our carefully thought through strategic positioning. That is the difference between a sales-driven and a strategy-driven supply chain!

A second crucial parameter in defining responsiveness is reliability. Reliability is commonly measured through the on-time, in-full (OTIF) delivery performance. We outlined some common questions when defining OTIF as a KPI in Chapter 1: on time versus delivery date or shipment date, and on the requested date versus the promised date; and in full to an order level, an order line level or a requested quantity level? In general, we believe reliability is more important to customers than lead time. The problem with a lack of reliability is that I quite simply can't rely on it. It obliges me to either start ordering earlier or take extra inventory to buffer for the uncertainty. In many markets we believe customers don't mind ordering a bit earlier if they are sure they will get their product. That doesn't mean reliability is an obligation, however. If you sell Christmas trees, you don't want to have 98 per cent reliability or availability. That would leave you with a lot of leftovers after the Christmas period. A company like Zara is known to create scarcity, as scarcity makes people buy immediately on the spot.

In Chapter 5 we mentioned that reliability is a service we deliver to our customers. So, as with lead time, think about how this links to your strategic positioning. Do we need to play at par, do we want to differentiate or dominate? Greater reliability typically comes at a higher inventory or excess capacity, so it is not for free! Product leaders typically get away with somewhat lower reliability. As customers have fewer alternatives, they are typically willing to wait for the product leaders' products. Operational excellence players work with minimal margins, so they need to work with minimal inventories as well. They may primarily choose to reduce the product portfolio, but for slow-moving products they may increase the lead time and work MTO, or they may guarantee only lower availability. Think back to the examples we gave of the stunt promos at the hard discounters. They don't want to have leftovers, so they buy a limited amount and 'everything sold' means 'job well done'.

A third crucial parameter in defining responsiveness is 'volume flexibility'. The most difficult is unpredictable volume flexibility. Think about the example from Barco. If we are launching a new product for meeting collaboration or we are venturing into corporate projectors, the forecast is 100 but we are aware the actual sales could equally be 10 or 1,000. How are we going to organize for flexibility instead of efficiency? Or think about the example of the other company where operations had doubled its production in a three-month timeframe. If I'm a product leader I should not be surprised. As a product leader this is structural to my business and key to my success. So, as we mentioned earlier, think through how you will create that volume flexibility. Define scenarios on what is the impact on cost and capital employed if we need to double in three, six or 12 months' time. What are we willing to invest in strategic inventories? Are we willing to sacrifice margin to speed up from a six- to a three-month timeframe? If this is crucial to your business, then you have done this before. So, don't say you can't say what it will cost. You can even say what it costs if you go in unprepared!

The milder form is the 'planned' volume flexibility, such as significant seasonality. Here we typically face a 'level' or 'chase' decision. In a 'level' production strategy we level the seasonal peak and are willing to pre-build inventory. That may be more efficient from a production point of view but it will come at extra working capital. In a 'chase' production strategy, we build peak capacity and will decide to meet the demand as it occurs. Most companies decide to 'level' but with weak assumptions. If you have a high 'portfolio complexity' and 'mix variability' it can be hard to decide which inventories to pre-build. It is common to have 'high stocks' in the season but 'of the wrong products'. That is bad for the service level, bad for the cost (last minute changeovers) and bad for the inventory (cash). It doesn't really balance the supply chain triangle. The lean movement would tell us to invest in extra capacity. That allows us to decide later what to produce. It avoids waste or 'muda'. So, don't be naïve if you go for the levelling option: take a conservative assumption, assume you will make mistakes and they negatively impact the balance in your triangle. Maybe levelling is more efficient for production, but it is not necessarily more efficient for the supply chain! Again, if this is crucial to your business, you can't say you don't know. You have been there before. Be brave and be bold.

The fourth parameter in designing your desired responsiveness is the mix flexibility. We have defined it in Figure 6.2 as the capability to serve a portfolio of *y* SKUs, with a demand variability of *x* per cent on SKU level, within a given lead time and OTIF reliability. As we mentioned at the start of this chapter, people underestimate the impact of mix complexity. Think of the example where the business was doing the same sales as five years ago but with 50 per cent more SKUs and a shorter lead time. If you haven't designed your products for a kind of postponement, that certainly is going to create more inventory! You may try to think in scenarios: what if we halve the number of packaging variants, what if we double the number of packaging variants. You may assume a 20 per cent loss or a 20 per cent gain in sales volume. What do you expect this will do to your cost and your inventory? Cross-check what is the 'bang-for-the-buck'. Out of the three scenarios – 20 per cent less, equal or 20 per cent more – what scenario gives the best bang-for-the-buck or the best margin over inventory? Are customers willing to pay a premium for our broader offering? Can we reach the same distribution levels for the extra SKUs? Do we need to adjust our prices if we offer a broader product range? Do we need a cost-down on our products to improve margins? Reflect on your strategic positioning. Where do you want to be when it comes to product portfolio: at par, differentiate or dominate? This will indicate the desired response.

The fifth and last parameter in designing our desired responsiveness is innovation flexibility. We define it as the capability to serve a given number of product updates, a given number of new product launches, a given number of phase-outs. Think back to the example of the branded goods manufacturer versus the private label player. As a branded goods manufacturer I can expect I will have more frequent product updates, innovations in the formula, innovations in the packaging, new tastes, new formats... innovations to stay ahead in quality and brand equity. Think through what this is going to cost. Don't say that you don't know. If this is key to your business you know what to expect as an impact on the original equipment efficiency (OEE) and how that OEE translates into a cost per unit. Think through what will be the impact on inventory. Phase-ins and phase-outs typically require some temporary double stocking. Phase-outs may leave you with obsolete components or raw materials that you'll need to write off. If you are a manufacturer of equipment, think through the impact on the aftermarket servicing of the product. Will you discontinue servicing old versions of the product, and as of which point in time? What is your desired strategic position? Do you want to play at par, differentiate or dominate? Are customers willing to pay a premium for that? A lot of the aftermarket costs come only later in time so are often ignored when making promises to the early customers. Don't let that happen. If this is key to your business you have been there before. Overpromising may be how you drive sales but it is not how you drive value. That should not be accepted – it is unprofessional.

EXERCISE 6.3

Defining your desired response

Reverting to Figure 6.3, for each of the response drivers, think through your strategic positioning. You can't be all things to all people, so you need to make a choice. Where do you want to be at par, where do you want to differentiate and where do you want to dominate? For each of the response drivers, think through the impact on cost and on capital employed. Thinking in scenarios may help to get the conversation going. Don't say that you don't know or it can't be done. If it is structural to your business, you have done it before and you even know the cost and the impact on capital employed if you go in unprepared!

When defining scenarios, take a broad perspective from the supply chain. What is the impact on key suppliers? What is the impact on your own production plants? What is the impact on your distribution? What is the impact on your key processes? What is the impact on your people? On your IT systems? On your metrics?

CASE STUDY
Dreamland

WITH ANDRÉ CERON, DIRECTOR OF LOGISTICS

As introduced earlier, the challenge at Dreamland was threefold: high volume variability, with 55 per cent of the annual sales in a 10-week period, leading to sales of a factor four to five during the peak periods compared to the off-peak periods; a high mix variability, with 60,000 items over the combined offline and online business; and a high product portfolio variability, with around 30 per cent of the items new every year.

As you can expect, scoring high on the each of the variabilities leads to a high cost and high capital employed situation. In principle, if the consumer would be willing to pay a triple premium for that, it wouldn't be a problem. Dreamland has struggled to get to grips with this. The competition from online players like Bol.com and Amazon is putting huge pressure on prices.

For a long time, Dreamland didn't only want to be an innovator that was close to its customers; it also wanted to be the cheapest and guarantee the lowest price. That's not a surprise if you're part of the Colruyt Group, where Colruyt Lowest Prices is the dominant retail brand, and that still defines lowest price as the company DNA. However, there is an apparent conflict in being the most complex and aiming to be the cheapest.

That (now) apparent conflict resulted in different departments going in different directions. As an example, to get to the lowest price, purchasing was buying in the Far East, which was good for cost, but came with long lead times and high minimum order quantities, obviously not very good for the inventory, and given the important mix variability and product portfolio variability, that was ultimately leading to important write-offs.

A first breakthrough was to clarify the strategy, which Dreamland did by using the models described in this book: Treacy and Wiersema, and Crawford and Mathews. Dreamland decided it wanted to differentiate with customer intimacy and it has let go of the lowest price objective. Being part of a group with operational excellence in the DNA, this was not an obvious choice. When thinking in the model of Crawford and Mathews, Dreamland wants to play at par on price, so not differentiate or dominate; that is for companies like Action. Dreamland wants to dominate on access. In the bricks-and-mortar world they have the highest density of shops in their market; in the online world, they can leverage the network of the Colruyt Group to create a dense network of pick-up points. Next to physical access, they want to 'deliver a promise on which customers can rely'; this is an aspect of service.

Clarifying the strategy doesn't magically solve the problem, however. It doesn't kill the fierce online competition. Players like Bol.com, part of Ahold-Delhaize, works with the Amazon model and has a large non-food assortment, and it allows others to use its platform to distribute their products. As mentioned, these online platforms are putting a huge pressure on prices.

Clarifying the strategy also doesn't simplify the supply chain challenges. Delivering 55 per cent of your sales in a 10-week timeframe means many of your assets are practically idle in the off-peak periods. There are no magical ways to organize that. Offering 60,000 items with a renewal rate of 30 per cent requires powerful planning processes and tools, to manage the balance between availability, costs and inventories. But even with powerful tools and processes, you will need to carry significant inventories, and you will have misses leading to slow-moving and obsolete inventories that you eventually need to write off.

Efficiency – effectiveness – responsiveness

As we mentioned when discussing supply chain design fails, in our experience supply chains are often designed for lowest cost and highest efficiency. That may be a good fit with operational excellence as a strategy, but it is a misfit with customer intimacy, with product leadership, or basically any other strategy. As we captured in Figure 6.4, supply chains are on a continuum from being 'more efficient' towards 'being more responsive', where a 'more responsive' supply chain has a higher cost and a higher capital employed. To bring nuance to the supply chain debate, we introduced the idea of the 'effective' supply chain. The 'effective' supply chain could be more efficient or more responsive; it is the one that is aligned with our market, our strategy and our desired (strategic) response. In their book on supply chain management, Chopra and Meindl introduce the idea of efficient versus responsive.[4] They are less clear on how to define what is the effective supply chain. We've tried to answer that question in more detail in the text above.

Figure 6.4 and the concept of 'efficient' versus 'responsive' also brings us to the old debate about whether we need to be 'lean' or do we need to be 'agile', where it is popular to say we need to be both: we need to be 'leagile'. In our first book, *Supply Chain Strategy and Financial Metrics*, we spent quite some time defining the 'efficiency frontier'. That 'efficiency frontier' states that at a given point in time there is a limit to how much complexity and variability we can deal with at a given level of cost and capital employed. If I have applied all the best practices and done the proper investments in people, processes, tools and analytics, I reach a boundary on what I can do for a given level of cost and

FIGURE 6.4 Strategy-driven supply chain design: efficiency, effectiveness, responsiveness

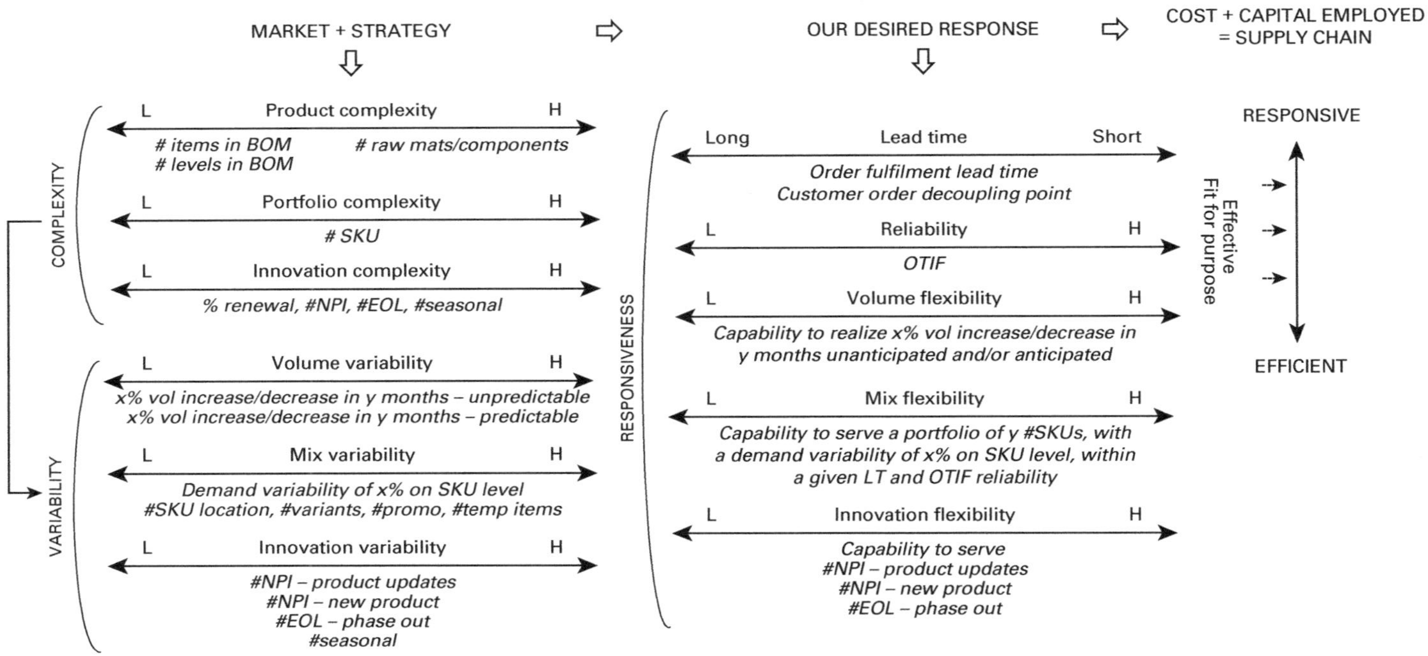

capital employed. At this point I need to make a choice: do I want to be more efficient, and am I willing to reduce my responsiveness, or do I want to be more responsive, and am I willing to increase my cost and capital employed? Agility, for me personally, is about the pursuit of shifting that 'efficiency frontier'. It is about the pursuit of finding new ways to become more responsive at a lower cost and capital employed all at the same time. If this is agility, I agree that we need to become more agile. Increasing agility increases the capability of what we can deliver and at which level of cost and capital employed. I'm also a big believer in breakthrough technologies like artificial intelligence (AI) or robotics. These will help us to shift the 'efficiency frontier' and to become more agile. However, agility should not be the excuse for not making strategic choices. Agility should not be the hammer with which we hit the supply chain. Remember that a lack of strategic choices blurs your image in the market and leaves your resources unfocused. That is not something agility should make up for. Make sure you are a focused company first, and then agility will help you to further improve the performance in the chosen focus!

Comparison with the SCOR model

In our first book we indicated that the supply chain operations reference model (SCOR) lacks notions of 'complexity'. The SCOR 'performance attributes' and 'level 1' metrics are listed below. The SCOR v12.0 quick reference guide is a good starting point for a quick overview.[5]

- Reliability
  - RL.1.1 Perfect order fulfilment
- Responsiveness
  - RS.1.1 Order fulfilment cycle time
- Agility
  - AG.1.1 Upside supply chain adaptability
  - AG.1.2 Downside supply chain adaptability
  - AG.1.3 Overall value at risk
- Cost
  - CO.1.1 Total supply chain management costs
  - CO.1.2 Cost of goods sold
- Asset management efficiency
  - AM.1.1 Cash to cash cycle time

- AM.1.2 Return on supply chain fixed assets
- AM.1.3 Return on working capital

In Figure 6.5 we have mapped the SCOR level 1 metrics to our complexity, variability and responsiveness drivers. You can see that SCOR is missing out on the complexity and variability drivers. These are essential in understanding how strategy translates into the supply chain. It is also missing out on the mix flexibility and innovation flexibility, which are key in responding to customer intimacy and product leadership. In that sense, we dare to state that SCOR is leading to a disconnect between the strategy and the supply chain, where the supply chain is almost automatically skewed towards efficiency and cost.

As discussed in our first book, when it comes to cost and asset management efficiency, we prefer to stick to metrics that are common in the financial world. It doesn't help to talk about 'total supply chain management costs' or 'return on supply chain fixed assets'. This situates supply chain on an island instead of connecting it to the broader business objectives.

SCOR has done a great job in professionalizing supply chain as a discipline. We hope to see the level 1 metrics enriched to allow for a better connection to strategy and to allow supply chains to become more strategy-driven.

Summarizing strategy-driven supply chain design

Figure 6.6 summarizes our resulting strategy-driven supply chain design. It takes the strategy-driven supply chain principle from Figure 5.13 and matches it with our 'design wheels' initially introduced in Figure 6.1 and shown in more detail in Figure 6.4.

So, in contrast to traditional business strategy, which often puts a blunt stretch on financial metrics, which in turn results in a blunt stretch on the supply chain triangle, a strategy-driven supply chain starts from a strategic value proposition that contains well-thought-through strategic choices, 'where to play and how to win', to quote another recent strategy book from A G Lafley, a former CEO of P&G.[6] Clear strategic choices will translate into a clear view of complexity and variability, and a clear view of the desired responsiveness, which in its turn will lead to a clear view of what is the corresponding supply chain, with a good balance of efficiency and responsiveness, making the supply chain effective and fit for purpose.

It doesn't feel like rocket science. But that is good. It feeds our hope it will help companies to avoid the strategy fails described in the previous chapter and the supply chain design fails we started with in this chapter.

FIGURE 6.5 Strategy-driven supply chain design: missing links in SCOR

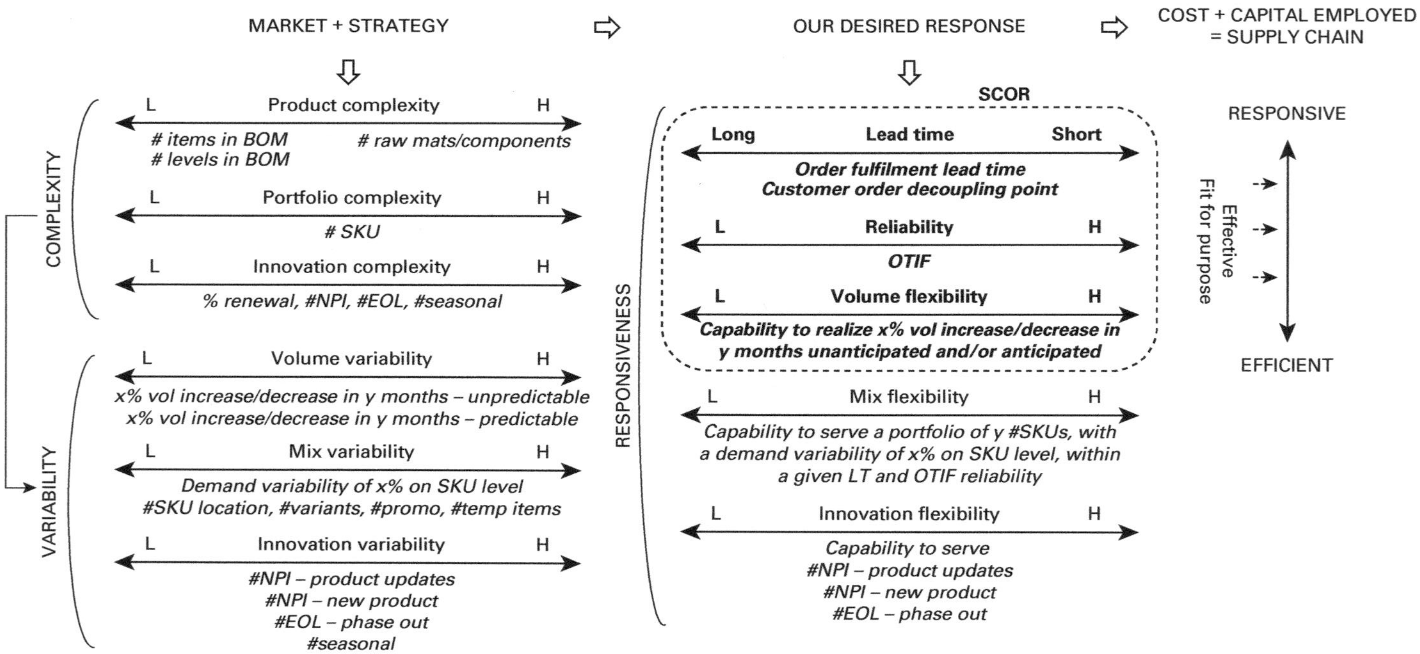

FIGURE 6.6 The resulting strategy-driven supply chain design

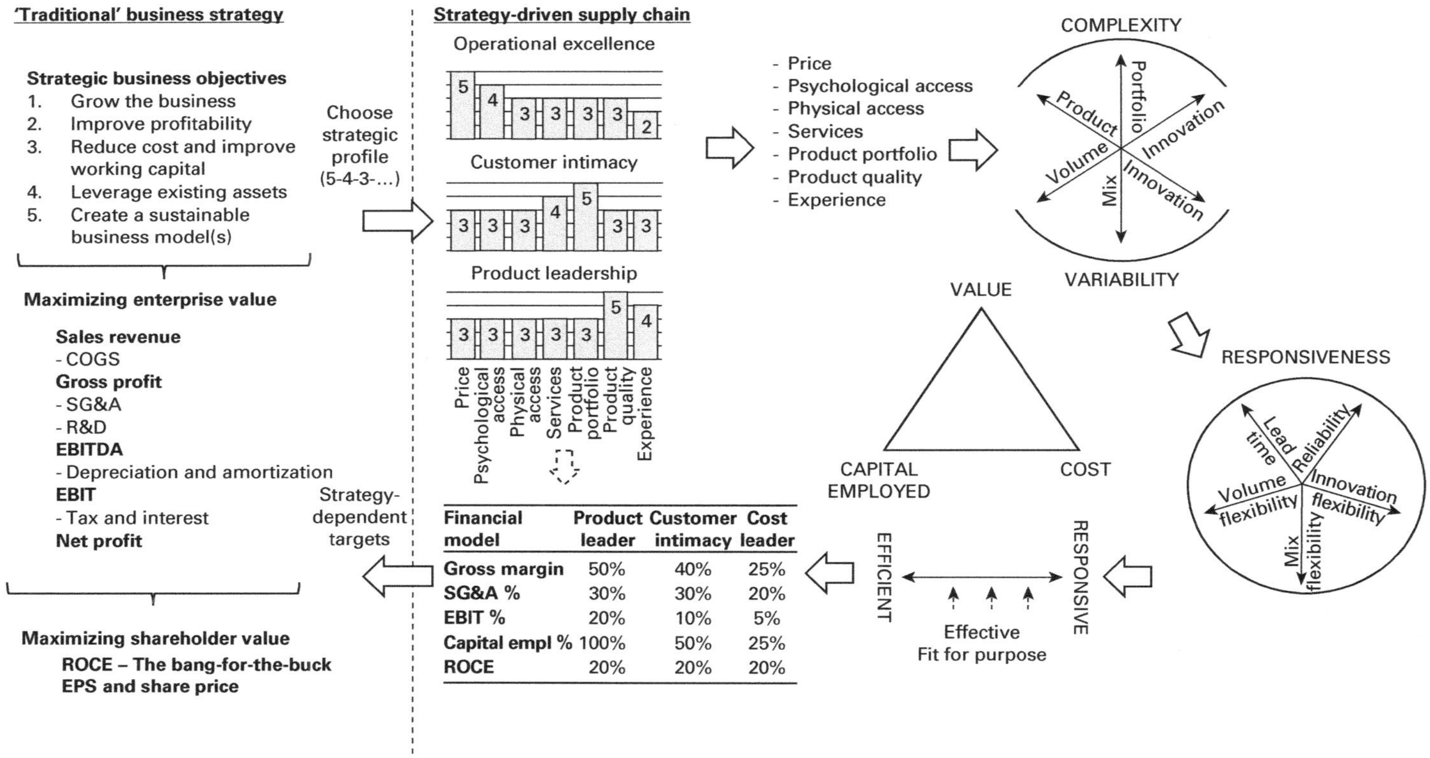

CASE STUDY

Colruyt Group: fresh bread

We will give a final illustration by freely translating the discussion on delivering 'fresh bread' into the different retail brands of the Colruyt Group. It is not an exact copy of the actual discussion; we use it to illustrate the subtlety of supply chain design.

Colruyt Lowest Prices is an operational excellence player. For an opex player, every addition to the assortment is scrutinized, as adding extra SKUs creates extra complexity, which increases costs and capital employed. Bread is a difficult product as it needs to be day fresh, where the traditional replenishment flows going to the central DCs take two to three days. Still, it was decided that fresh bread would be added, probably because they didn't want to fall 'below par' when it comes to assortment. To optimize costs, bread is delivered from a central bakery directly into the different stores, so skipping the central DC. The consideration here was lead time; we need to have the bread day fresh. The more cost optimal solution would certainly have been to distribute it from the central DC and piggyback on the existing transport volumes.

Then take a brand like Okay. As we've discussed in the previous chapter, Okay is operational excellence but with the psychological access first. We've seen experience features creeping in though as Okay wanted to be able to bake bread in its stores. Nothing beats the smell of fresh bread (= experience). To organize it as efficiently as possible, frozen dough is shipped from the central DC to the stores, where it is baked off in local ovens.

Bio-Planet started as a retail chain with a focus on 'truly good', which clearly goes more in the direction of product quality and product leadership. Locally baked bread is good, but the taste is even better if we could ship the dough at an ambient temperature rather than in frozen form. Shipping the dough at an ambient temperature increases costs from a quality assurance perspective. So yes, probably better from a product perspective, but coming at an extra cost.

And finally, in the Colruyt Group you have Cru. In the 2019 annual report Cru is described as a chain of 'multi-experience markets targeting people with a passion for delicious food, with experience and craftsmanship at the forefront'. The Cru shops have a fresh bakery, a fish market, a butcher, with craftspeople preparing in the shop. In this type of concept, obviously, you want to make your dough and bake the bread in the shop, rather than preparing the dough centrally. So here we will ship the ingredients and invest in local capabilities to make and raise the dough, and then bake the bread. You can't get it any fresher than that. Excellent from a product perspective, but most probably the most expensive and requiring the highest investment.

The different nuances almost seem a bit like gradually 'dreaming it up'. You can easily get carried away by enthusiasm. We believe that's a danger in real-life supply chains as well. Can we do this? Can we do that? People are proud. The answer will always be yes. The real question is at what cost and for what capital employed? What are the different options or scenarios? And, most importantly, is the chosen customer willing to pay the associated double premium for it? Though Colruyt Lowest Prices and Cru are part of the same group they have different customer segments, maybe serving the same people but for different occasions. Taking the example of Cru, people with a passion for delicious food may be willing to pay a premium for a premium product, but that is not on what Colruyt Lowest Prices wants to differentiate or dominate.

CASE STUDY

Sustainability in the supply chain triangle

WITH JOHAN HEYMAN, VP ORGANIZATIONAL EXCELLENCE, BARCO

Johan Heyman has been one of the early adopters of the supply chain triangle. He uses the triangle to stimulate a different debate across different departments. Over the last few years, Barco has made significant improvements in sustainability, so one of Johan's obvious questions was 'How does sustainability tie into the triangle?' We're not sure we have the answer, but this section summarizes the discussion Johan and I had on this topic.

Our strategy-driven supply chain design summarized in Figure 6.6 looks at strategy and financial metrics. As long as sustainability initiatives don't go against the strategy or the financial metrics, they are an easy sell. It becomes more difficult if sustainability goes against the strategy or against the financial metrics.

One of the discussions I had with Johan was about a modal shift. Can we shift transport volumes from airfreight to sea freight with a goal of reducing CO^2? While that is good for the sustainability, I advised against it, as for me it goes against the strategy. As a product leader, you want to keep lead times short to allow a short time to market for new products and product updates. If we park the strategic aspect for a second, within the triangle it becomes a question of balancing cost versus inventory. Shipping by boat will be cheaper, but because of the longer lead time the inventory will increase. As we explained in Chapter 4, Barco has been reducing inventories for over 10 years now. Instead of further reducing inventories, it has decided to keep its inventories stable and try to reduce CO^2 instead.

Coming back to the strategy aspect, in my discussions with Johan I suggested an alternative: more regional sourcing and production. That seems like the less attractive alternative. More regional sourcing and regional production might negatively affect the cost and require extra investment in fixed assets. It most probably goes against what we have been doing over the last 10 years. But it is reducing the lead times. And it might open opportunities to offer more local variants in a kind of regional 'assemble-to-order' process. For a product leader that reinforces the core positioning in the market. So the question becomes what we believe this could bring as extra sales or extra margin. Barco did not choose this option as it was too disruptive. But we mention it here as a reminder of the need to think through what the impact of sustainability on your strategy is. Look for ways to improve sustainability in a way that it improves the key levers of your chosen strategic positioning.

So, where will it go from here? Johan states that Barco is often asked questions on sustainability by big customers and shareholders. The least we can say is that global initiatives on sustainability, like the 17 Sustainable Development Goals of the United Nations, and global ratings for sustainability, like the one developed by Standards and Poor,[7] will add to the transparency and the pressure on companies. We can expect that governments will follow with legislation and will impose certain requirements on businesses. That will force the laggards to catch up, possibly at the expense of a short-term financial impact. Think about the trading in CO^2 emission rights. A bigger change would be to account for the societal costs directly in the P&L of companies. That would design sustainability straight into the heart of the financial system. We don't have a crystal ball, but we are enthusiastic about this evolution. We have only one planet, so we need to protect it for the future. Furthermore, we believe sustainability is a bit like lean and operational excellence as a management philosophy. When you start using it, you seem to focus on the extra cost of training people, the daily standups, etc. Once you're running it, it is more a way of life that doesn't come at an extra cost, but stimulates creativity to tackle things in a different and better way.

Conclusion

In this chapter we have outlined common 'fails' in supply chain design. We believe many supply chains are overly focused on cost, often resulting in conflicts with the strategic business requirements. Next we developed a methodology for a strategy-driven supply chain design, where we map the market and our strategic value proposition, to a given level of complexity and variability, and we explained how designing our desired response translates into a given level of cost and capital employed.

We continued by showing how the SCOR model is lacking the key dimensions of complexity and variability and how in that sense it may contribute to the cost bias when designing supply chains. We also discussed how sustainability is impacting our supply chain triangle and supply chain design. We shared some current experiences from Barco. We tried to peek into what the future might bring.

In the next chapter we will broaden the strategy-driven supply chain design to the wider question of strategic planning, and we will argue we need to better integrate strategic planning, financial planning and operational planning if we want to improve the balance in the triangle and drive more value. We call that the concept of strategy-driven integrated value planning and execution.

Notes

1 H L Lee, V Padmanabhan and S Whang, The bullwhip effect in supply chains, *Sloan Management Review*, 1997, 38, 93–102

2 Leading the aftermarket with over 95 per cent coverage for spark plugs, p 2, https://issuu.com/federalmogul/docs/fm_letstalk-automechanika-2014_en (archived at https://perma.cc/4RNT-Z5Q4)

3 E Feitzinger and H L Lee, Mass customization at Hewlett-Packard: The power of postponement, *Harvard Business Review*, 1997, 75, 116–23

4 S Chopra and P Meindl (2010) *Supply Chain Management: Strategy, planning and operation*, 4th edn, Pearson, London

5 APICS (2017) *SCOR: Supply chain operations reference model, Version 12.0 – quick reference guide*, www.apics.org/docs/default-source/scor-p-toolkits/apics-scc-scor-quick-reference-guide.pdf (archived at https://perma.cc/Z4JT-TDSE)

6 A G Lafley and R L Martin (2013) *Playing to Win: How strategy really works*, Harvard Business Press, Boston, MA

7 www.spglobal.com/ratings/en/products-benefits/products/esg-evaluation (archived at https://perma.cc/BNX2-TAEN)

07

Strategy-driven integrated value planning and execution

In this chapter we want to show how planning on different levels – strategic, financial and operational – are impacting the balance in the triangle. We also argue that a better integration of these planning processes is needed to have better strategy execution and value generation. We call that concept strategy-driven integrated value planning and execution (IVP&E), as illustrated in Figure 7.1. Underlying the process integration is a powerful financial modelling, for which we believe sales and operations planning (S&OP) models and tools are the perfect starting point. To come to that point, we will discuss each of the planning layers and discuss the opportunity and need for a better integration.

Strategy development

When talking about strategy development and strategic planning, we recommend the work of Kaplan and Norton and especially their book *The Execution Premium*.[1] It contains an excellent overview of different aspects of strategy development and strategic planning. While we have started from their work, we have complemented it in several important aspects.

The first is 'Start with defining your DNA'. Typical strategy work starts with mission, vision, values but we recommend starting with defining your DNA. Assume that you get a call from Treacy and Wiersema and their simple questions are 'Who do you want to be?' and 'What do you want to be known for?' Do you want to be a product leader, a customer intimacy player, or an operational excellence player? Think about the 'cult-like cultures' that

FIGURE 7.1 Strategy-driven integrated value planning and execution

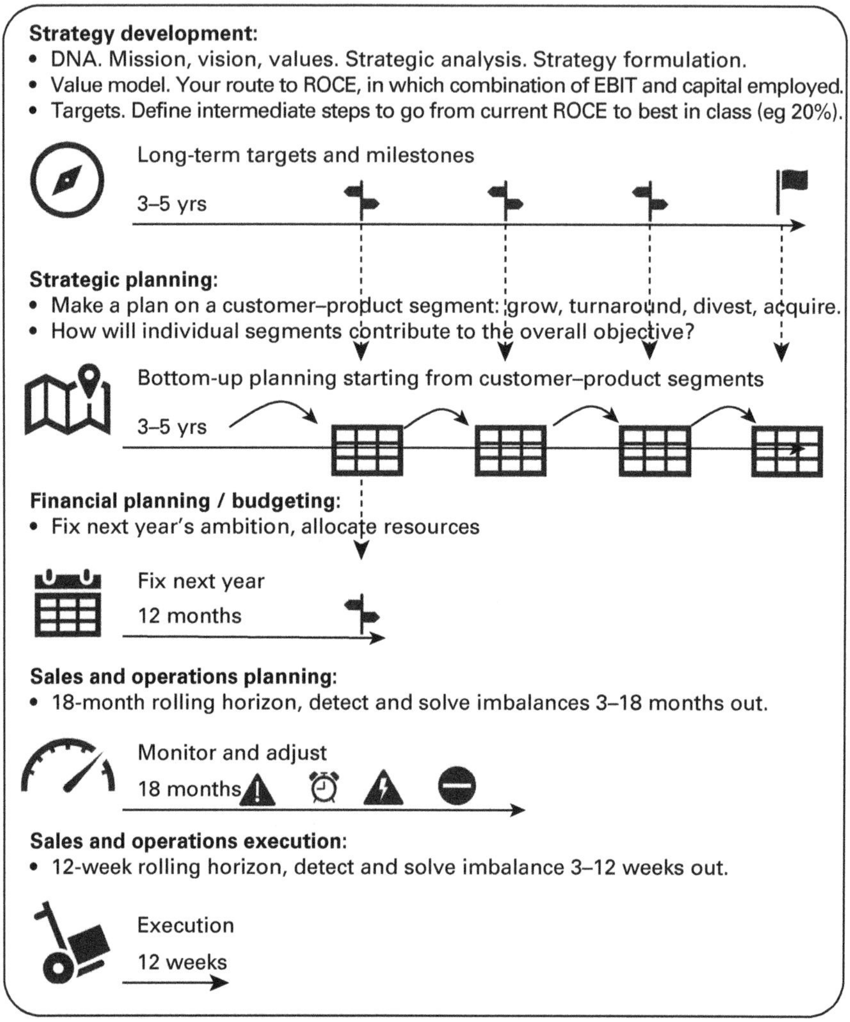

Jim Collins talks about in his book *Good to Great*.[2] Are you going to be Etihad, Lufthansa or Ryanair? Are you going to be Harrods, Kroger or Aldi? If you want to stand out, you must make a choice. That choice will influence your mission, your vision and your values.

Some companies don't seem to know. Think about the cases of Barco and Casio in Chapter 4, which have been changing or trying to change strategies. Think about the case of Bekaert in Chapter 5, where their ambitions were going in all possible directions. Defining your DNA is simple, though. Get back to your roots. You may need to travel all the way back to the foundation of the company. Your strategic DNA is embedded in the walls. If you haven't moved into new buildings you can probably just smell it. We believe that for Barco it is product leadership, for Casio it is operational excellence, for Bekaert it is also product leadership. We can understand that companies at times start hesitating, maybe because they are not successful in executing their strategy at a given point in time. We strongly believe, however, that changing strategies, though tempting and popular, is not the answer. We believe the answer is much simpler, but unfortunately also harder. If you are not successful in executing your strategy at a given point in time, then just try harder! You can use the exercises in Chapter 3 to reveal how well people are aligned on your current and your real DNA.

Once you have defined your DNA, as shown in Figure 7.1, clarify your mission, vision and values (MVV). The mission defines the organization's purpose. It should always survive. My mission is 'to turn supply chains into a competitive edge'. I may be working as a consultant, I may be working as a teacher, I may be working as a VP of supply chain, the mission is what always survives. The values are the internal compass that guides our actions. In addition to being a book author and an adjunct professor at the Vlerick Business School, I am the CEO of Solventure. Solventure helps companies to turn their supply chains into a competitive edge. At Solventure our values are engage, challenge, explore, share and achieve. They define how we work with each other, with our customers, our partners and our competitors. The vision is the aspiration for future results. Our vision is we want to be the McKinsey of supply chain. Your trusted advisor when it comes to turning your supply chain into a competitive edge. The McKinsey aspiration indicates we're not after the lowest cost but we're after the best quality. We want to be leading in supply chain thinking and in using supply chains to drive value. The DNA and the MVV establish guidelines for formulating and implementing the strategy.

Continuing in Figure 7.1, our next step is to perform a strategic analysis, in which we review our competitive and operating environment. We typically start with analysing the 'external environment' through a political, economic, social, technological, environmental and legal (PESTEL) analysis. How do global warming, growth of the world population, the rise of AI, global political instability and other trends affect our business? We also look at our 'internal environment'. What are our core capabilities and processes? What is the state of our human capital? What is the state of our digital capital? The 'environmental' analysis is typically summarized in a strengths, weaknesses, opportunities and threats (SWOT) table. What are the internal/external drivers, and are they helpful or harmful? The SWOT and the progress in the existing strategy define a strategic agenda that lists the need for key changes in the strategy.

The strategic analysis should help in deciding what business we want to be in. What is the market attractiveness (growth, technological evolution, etc)? What is the attractiveness for the company (competitive position, product profitability, etc)? A helpful analysis is shown in Figure 7.2. What is the growth potential of the market and what is our current ROCE? Markets without a lot of growth and high ROCE may be used as cash cows. Markets with a lot of growth either need a ROCE makeover or require investment in growth. Markets without a lot of growth and low ROCE you may consider quitting.

The strategic analysis brings us to the strategy formulation. Here we address the markets/niches in which we will compete. What are the customer value propositions that will differentiate us? Think about our treatment of Crawford and Mathews in Chapter 5. What are the key processes through which we will drive the differentiation? What is the impact on human capital and information capital? If you have a complex structure with different layers (corporate, divisional, business unit, categories) and multiple core competences, the book *Playing to Win* by A G Lafley, a former CEO of P&G, can be helpful in structuring and better formulating your strategy.[3]

As shown in Figure 7.1, what we'd like to add on top of the existing strategy models is the need to specify the value model. How are we going to drive value? In which combination of EBIT versus capital employed? What is our strategic value proposition? Which choices have we made? And what

FIGURE 7.2 Analysing ROCE and growth potential to decide on strategic investments

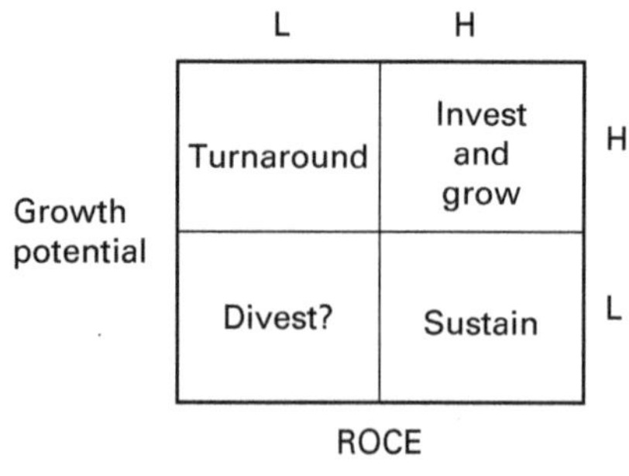

is the corresponding operating model? How are we going to deliver that value proposition? This is where the strategy-driven supply chain design from the previous chapter fits into the story.

We would also like companies to specify a ROCE roadmap. Think about the example of Hero Group in Chapters 2 and 3. What is your current ROCE (5 per cent)? What is a good target three to five years down the road (the 15 per cent of Nestlé)? What is a good target five to ten years down the road (the 35 per cent of Hershey)? And how are you going to drive this ROCE? As a true product leader? With premium quality products and premium brands (the Hershey direction)? Or more as a full-range total solution player (the Mondelez direction)?

Clarifying your value model and your ROCE roadmap will help in better judging your strategic projects by their (expected) value impact. It will also act as a better reference point for your budgets and your S&OP process. Are we on schedule for our value roadmap? As much as we like the work of Kaplan and Norton and their inclusion of non-financial dimensions like 'human capital' and 'organization capital' (culture), we like to strengthen the financial dimension of the strategic plan to come to better choices.

Charles Bouaziz was recently dismissed as CEO of Ontex, among other reasons for a lack of transparency on the Transform to Grow programme developed with McKinsey.[4] One of the shareholders, CIAM, asked for his removal and referred to the lack of a clear plan on how to drive value in the short and longer term. A clear plan starts with a clear ambition. We believe the Ontex story illustrates that this is not optional but mandatory!

Finally, we need to say that strategy development is never a greenfield exercise. We always build on historical strategy formulations. It is common for a company to reformulate its strategy every three to five years and have a yearly strategy update. We hope the above can be a checklist when you perform your next strategy update or more detailed review.

Strategic planning

Once we have 'developed' and 'formulated' our strategy, it is time to start making a strategic plan and start defining strategic projects. As is shown in Figure 7.1, we may zoom in on the individual markets (customer–product segments), understand which of them are contributing to the ROCE roadmap, which ones are problematic, and think about how we are going to turn

FIGURE 7.3 How strategic projects across different segments are driving the long-term ROCE roadmap

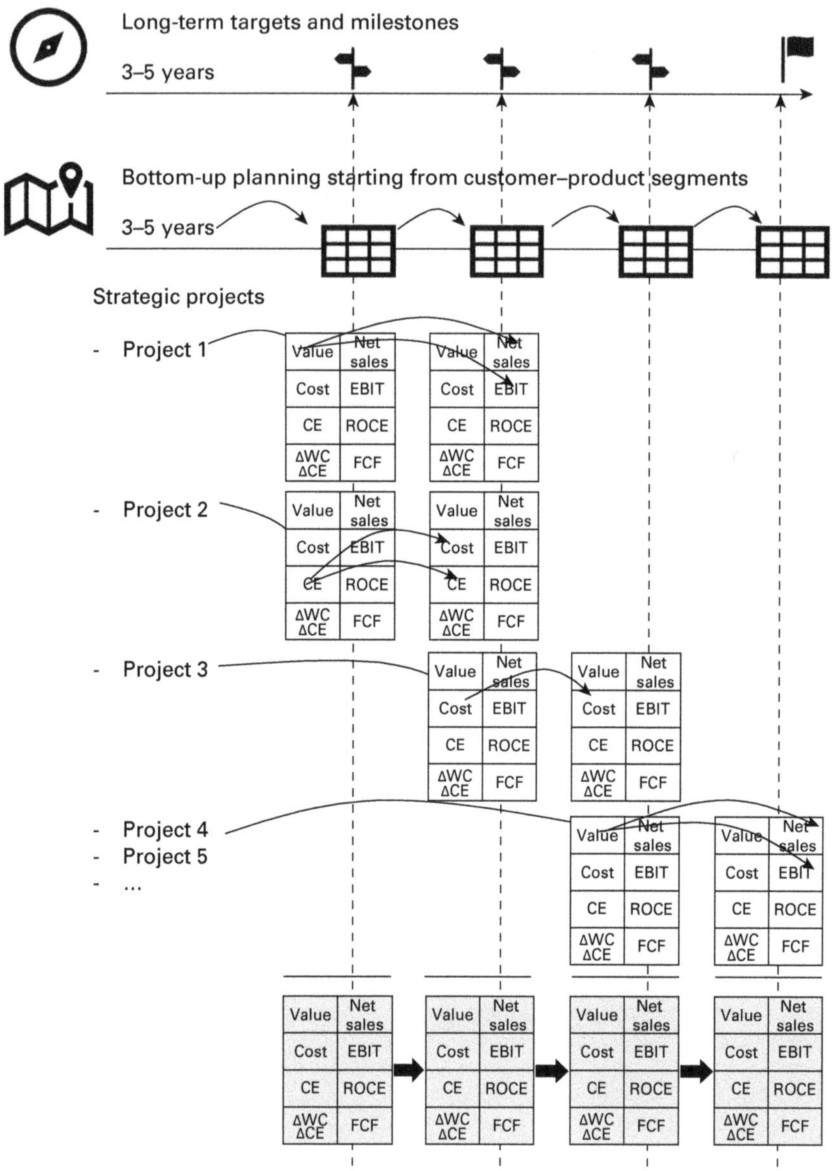

that around. Part of the analysis will already be done in the strategy formulation, like the analysis shown in Figure 7.2; part of the exercise will need to continue in the strategic planning.

We propose to visualize how individual projects contribute to our ROCE roadmap, as shown in Figure 7.1 and as shown in more detail in Figure 7.3. We are using our eight-cell strategy-driven scorecard introduced in Figure 3.19. On the first row are the value drivers, which contain our strategic value proposition, and show how we will be driving net sales or top line. The second row starts with the cost, the top line and the cost result into the bottom line, in this case shown as EBIT. On the third row, we start with capital employed, and EBIT over capital employed results in ROCE. On the fourth row, we look at the changes in capital employed and EBIT (actually NOPAT), and the changes in capital employed result in free cash flow. If we plan major investments, then analysing and showing free cash flow is key. It is our belief that if Ontex management had been able to structure their plans according to the format in Figure 7.3 there would have been a much better discussion with the board.

In their book *Strategy Maps*, Kaplan and Norton introduce strategy maps as a way of visually representing the intended outcome of strategic projects.[5] How do you want them to drive value? What will be the cross-functional effect, across sales, operations, R&D? What will be the impact on people and culture? In Figure 7.4 we have shown an adapted version. On the top right we have introduced the extended value drivers from Chapter 5, based on Crawford and Mathews. At the bottom we have added the physical supply chain, as that is key to understand investments in working capital and fixed assets. At the top we have introduced our supply chain triangle and ROCE as the balancing concept. At the top left we have introduced the value model. This adapted strategy map can be used to visualize the expected impact of individual strategic projects.

As we will discuss next, we believe that strategic planning, financial planning and S&OP planning should leverage a common financial modelling engine. The core of S&OP and the budgeting process is the same – it is the modelling of the cost of goods sold and gross margin. Those are the most complex. As we will argue, once you have these, expanding to a full P&L and balance sheet is relatively straightforward.

What we should do in strategic planning is leverage these capabilities to run scenarios and document assumptions. Through investment x in project y we want to reduce our direct labour cost with z in a two-year timeframe. What is the impact on ROCE and free cash flow? Planning tools have made an important evolution over the last 10 years and can support this type of analysis. It is more a matter of realizing that and having the courage to link the different planning layers in the organization.

FIGURE 7.4 Strategy map adapted to include supply chain triangle and value model

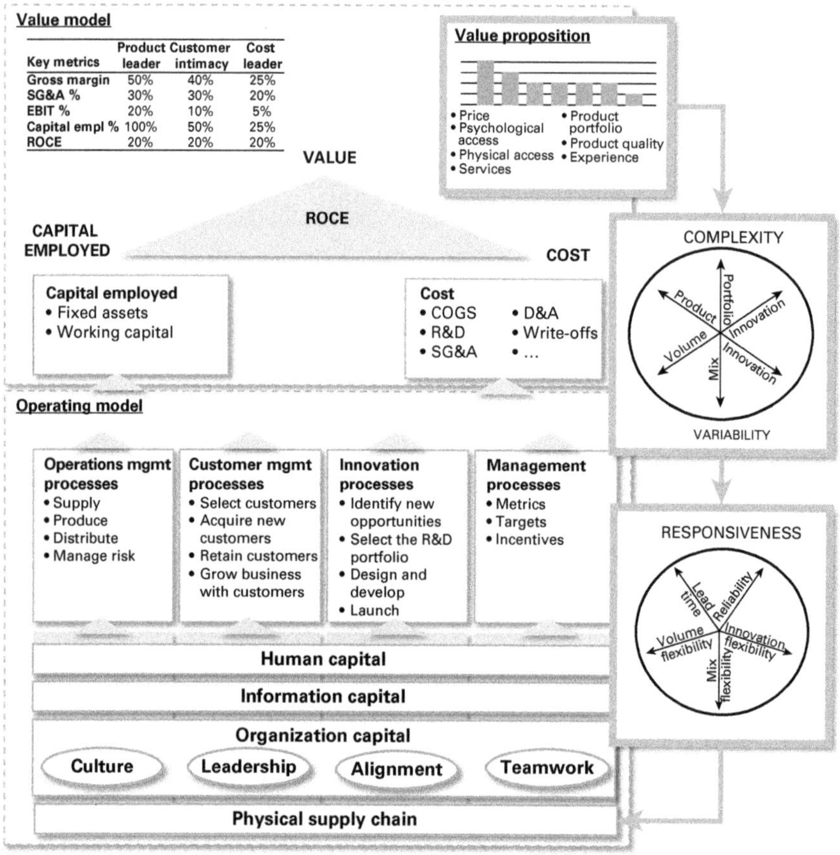

Financial planning and budgeting

In this section we want to take supply chain professionals in detail through how a budgeting process works. Because I came from a supply chain background, I had never been exposed to it in detail. If you have a finance background, you may decide to skip this section, or read it to validate we're close to the truth.

Just as many supply chain professionals lack a good understanding of how budgeting or financial planning and analysis (FP&A) works, I have noticed that many finance professionals have a weak understanding of how S&OP works. For that purpose, in the next section we also spend quite some time describing what S&OP is, based on the vision we have developed at Solventure. If you have a supply chain background, you may decide to skip that section, or likewise still read it, as a good summary, and check whether you agree with our statements.

If we want to bring both disciplines closer together, and leverage each other's tools and processes, creating an understanding of each other's worlds is key. So, you may want to bear with me through these sections. They don't immediately lead up to the conclusion of strategy-driven integrated value planning and execution, but I believe they are required from an education standpoint.

Out of the many finance books we have read, we have found *Accounting for Managers* especially useful when it comes to budgeting or financial planning and analysis. The book can be downloaded for free via https://2012books.lardbucket.org/, under a creative commons licence. It's a good introductory read. You may want to put it on your reading list if you want to know more about finance. Chapter 10 deals with 'How are operating budgets created?' It starts by spelling out the two primary goals of a budget: planning operations, and controlling operations. With respect to planning operations, it states that budgets are established in advance to help organizations communicate their plans to employees and to help employees coordinate activities across the entire organization. The authors give the example of Jerry's Ice Cream, which plans for 20 per cent growth and indicates production would never be able to plan for the necessary purchasing of raw materials, hiring of new people and potentially installing new capacity without the coordination of an operational budget. With respect to controlling operations, it states that by comparing the budget with actual results, companies can evaluate performance. They give the example of Jerry's Ice Cream again, where profits were less than expected despite the higher sales. The problem was not with efficiency in the use of materials or the efficiency of the personnel. It had to do with the higher raw material prices and the higher cost of labour.

From Figure 7.1 we can add that the budget fixes next year's ambition and allocates resources. As we will see, we budget certain operational expenses (OPEX) and capital expenditure (CAPEX). From an integrated planning perspective, it is important that the budget incorporates the key elements from the strategic planning. The budget should help navigate the business along the strategic course set out in the strategic plan.

Figure 7.5 shows the key elements and steps in making an operating budget. Compared to the book, we have added working capital as an element and included free cash flow as an important output of the budget, based on our discussions in Chapter 2.

FIGURE 7.5 Key elements and steps in the operating budget

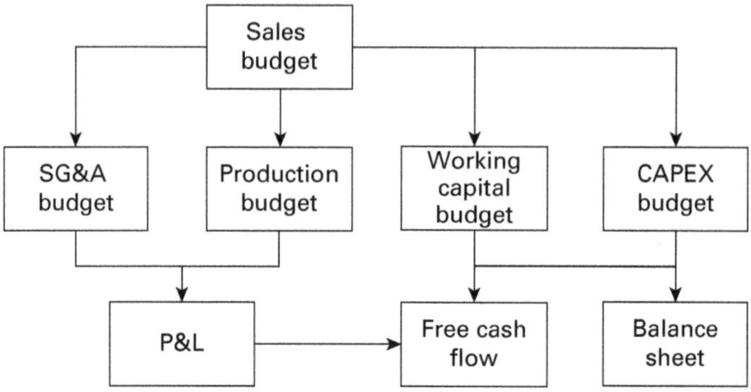

In what follows we will walk you step by step through how an operating budget is constructed.

Translating a sales budget into an operational cost and inventory budget

The first steps in a budgeting process are the making of a sales budget and the translation of that sales budget into an operational cost and inventory budget, as shown in Figure 7.6.

We start with the sales budget. We'll continue using the Jerry's Ice Cream example from the book where the sales manager, after careful consideration, forecasted the first quarter sales to be 40,000 units. The average price per unit last year was $6 (1 unit = 1 gallon), which he didn't expect to change. So, Figure 7.6 shows sales of 40,000 units x $6/unit or expected sales of $240,000 for the first quarter. The book has the details for quarters 2, 3 and 4.

Next step is to translate the sales budget into a production budget. Production is derived from sales using the following formula:

Production budget = required ending inventory +
sales budget – starting inventory

In supply chain terms, this is called a 'material balance'. It ensures no material 'gets lost'. The assumption made in the book is that the ending inventory is 10 per cent of next quarter's sales. Budgeted sales in Q2 is 48,000 units x 10 per cent = 4,800 units. The starting inventory for the first quarter is 4,000 units. This brings the production budget for Q1 to:

FIGURE 7.6 Translating the sales budget into an operational cost and inventory budget

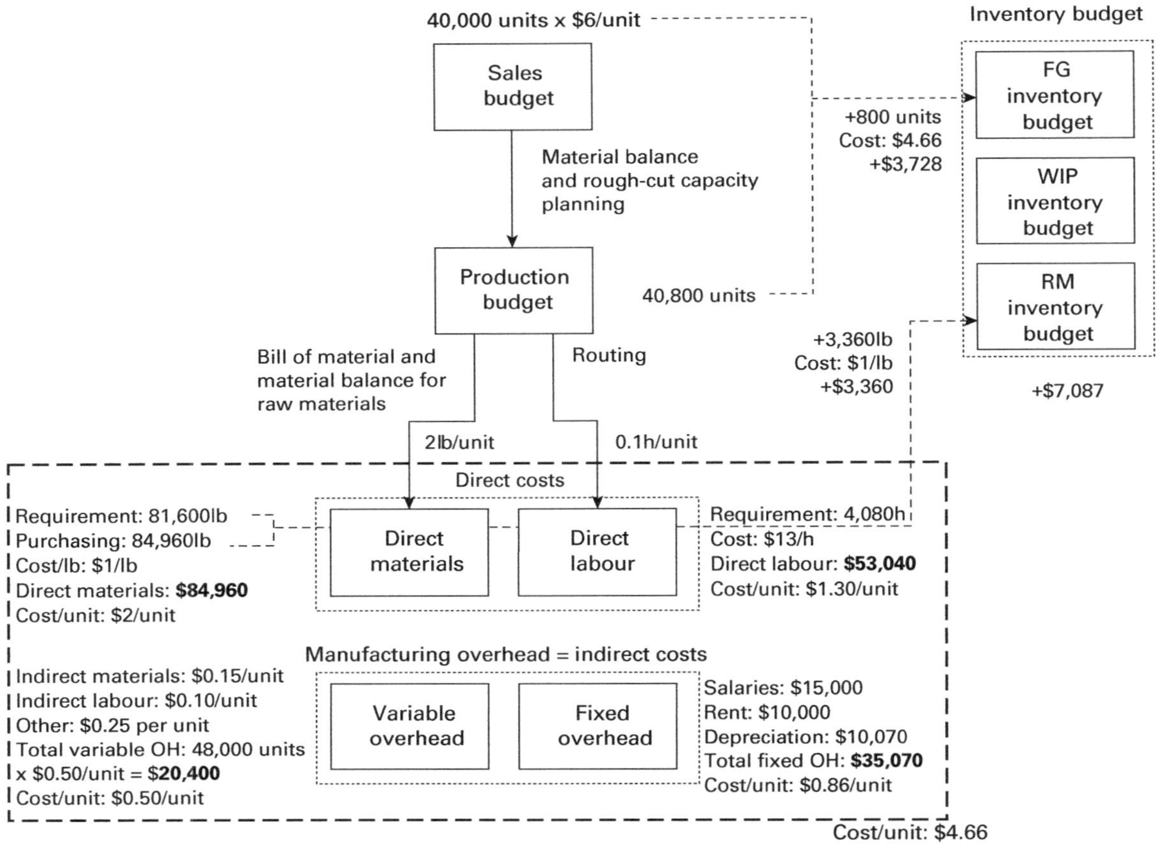

Production budget Q1 = 4,800 units + 40,000 units – 4,000 units
= 40,800 units

In Chapter 6 we talked about companies with seasonality and their decision to either 'chase' or 'level' the peak. Levelling the peak will require less fixed assets and will allow for a higher utilization of those assets, but it requires building a seasonal inventory. A significant inventory build-up will consume a significant amount of cash. So, in this case a correct modelling of the sales budget versus the production budget and the resulting inventory budget is important. In supply chain this is done through the rough cut capacity plan (RCCP) process. That process plans 3 to 18 months ahead, and in the case of a level strategy decides on the required stock build-up. As such, we mention in Figure 7.6 material balance and RCCP as the two elements that translate the sales budget into a production budget.

OK, so we've decided to produce 40,800 units, whereas we will sell only 40,000 units. This means the finished goods inventory will go up 800 units. Once we've calculated all costs, we'll understand the cost per unit is $4.66 so the finished goods inventory will increase in value by +$3,728. This is again shown in Figure 7.6.

Based on the production budget of 40,800 units, we can start calculating the total production cost. We make a difference between direct costs, being direct materials and direct labour, which can be allocated directly to the production of a specific product, and indirect costs, the so-called manufacturing overhead, which cannot be traced back to a specific product (think about the cost of planning or quality control). The manufacturing overhead is split into variable overhead, which changes with the quantity produced, and fixed overhead, like the depreciation of the machines, which is independent of the quantity produced.

Direct materials refers to the raw materials used in the production of the finished goods. For the ice cream example, one unit requires 2 pounds of raw material, let's say sugar, so for 40,800 units, we need 81,600 pounds (lb) of sugar. In supply chain, calculating the raw material requirement is part of the material requirements planning (MRP) process using the bill of material (BOM). What also follows from the MRP is that if the cost of the raw materials is $1/lb, the cost per unit of ice cream will be $2/unit.

The purchasing budget is calculated through a so-called material balance for the raw materials:

Purchasing budget = required ending inventory raw mats + raw materials required – starting inventory raw mats

The book takes 20 per cent of next quarter's production needs as the ending inventory for the raw materials, 20 per cent x 98,400 lb = 19,680 lb. We assume the starting inventory is 16,320 lb, leading to a purchasing budget of:

Purchasing budget = 19,680 lb + 81,600 lb – 16,320 lb = 84,960 lb

If the cost of sugar is $1/lb, the cost of the direct materials will be $84,960. If we buy 84,960 lb but use only 81,600 lb then the difference of 3,360 lb will be added to the raw materials inventory, which at a cost of $1/lb corresponds with a value of $3,360.

To calculate the direct labour cost, we need to know the amount of labour that goes into a unit of finished product. In supply chain this is found from the routing. The BOM defines the product structure of a manufactured end item, ie the materials going into the finished product. The routing defines all tasks required to manufacture an item, the work centres related to these tasks and the amount of direct labour required. Products may have alternative BOMs and routings that specify different ways to produce a product. For the given product we assume 0.1h/unit, leading to 4,080 direct labour hours, which at a cost of $13/h gives a direct labour cost of $53,040 or $1.30/unit.

For the variable manufacturing overhead, we start from estimates per unit. Total estimated cost per unit is $0.50 which for 40,800 units leads to a variable overhead of $20,400. The fixed overhead is, by definition, fixed. The estimated cost for Q1 is $35,070. It is independent of the amount of production. For a production of 40,800 units it corresponds with $0.86/unit.

Total manufacturing cost amounts to $4.66/unit, which we still need to translate our finished products inventory increase of 800 units into a value of $3,728. This means the total inventory, finished goods plus raw materials, is expected to increase by $7,087, assuming the work in process remains constant. This is important from a free cash flow perspective.

Combining a sales, SG&A and operations budget into a P&L budget

Figure 7.7 shows how we further extend our operations budget to come to a P&L budget. The top line will be the sales budget of 40,000 units x $6/unit = $240,000. If we sell 40,000 units, then 40,000 units x $4.66/unit = $186,382 are charged to the cost of goods sold while the remaining 800 units of production have been charged to the finished goods inventory. Net sales of $240,000 minus the cost of goods sold of $186,382 leads to a gross profit of $53,618.

Figure 7.7 also adds a selling, general and administrative (SG&A) budget. The accounting book talks about variable and fixed costs in SG&A.

FIGURE 7.7 Combining a sales, SG&A and operations budget into a P&L budget

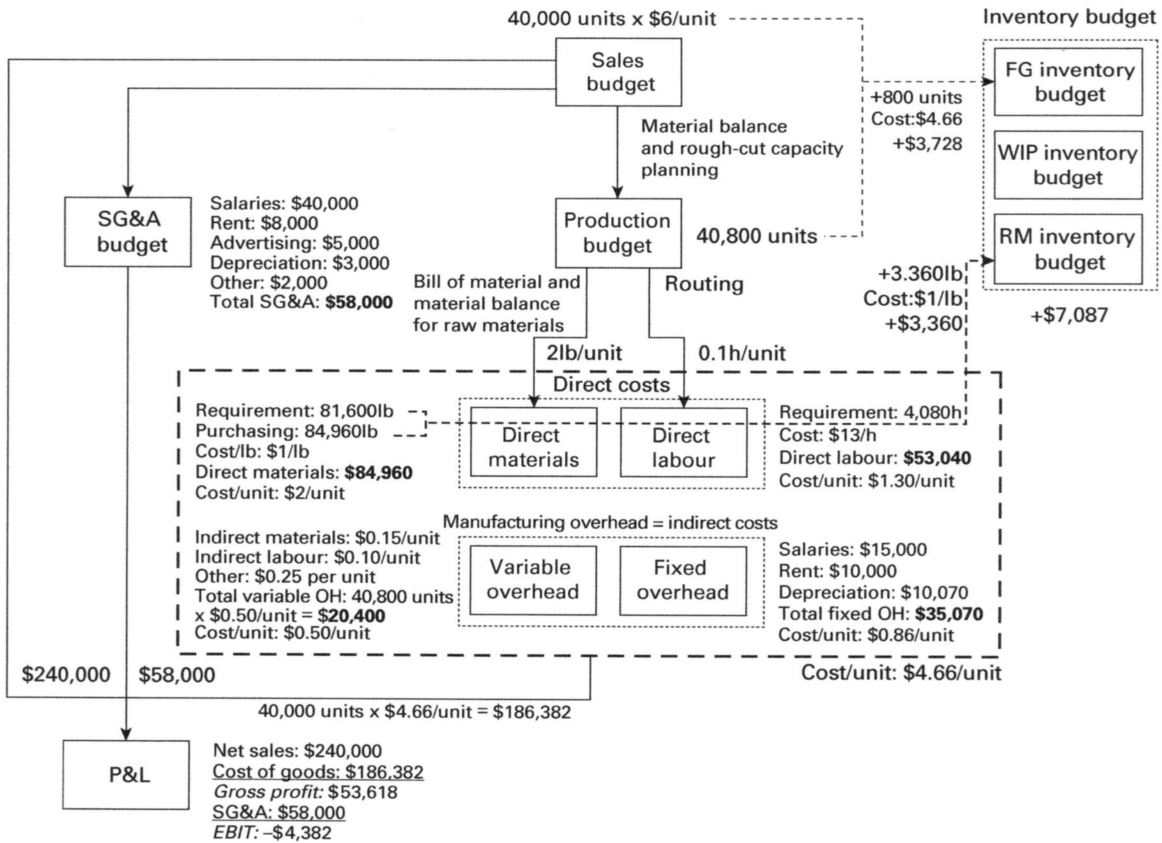

The Jerry's Ice Cream example talks about fixed costs only for a total of \$58,000 in Q1. The gross profit minus the SG&A leads to an operating income of –\$4,382 in Q1. So Q1 actually has a loss.

Adding the working capital and fixed assets budget

Figure 7.8 continues with adding a working capital and fixed assets budget. The sales budget defines the accounts receivable budget. The assumption for Jerry's Ice Cream is that 60 per cent of the sales is collected in Q1 and 40 per cent is collected in Q2. So the accounts receivable at the end of Q1 will consist of 40 per cent of the sales in Q1. The ending accounts receivable of Q4 consisted of 40 per cent of the sales in Q4. This allows us to calculate the change in accounts receivable.

A comparable approach can be followed for the accounts payable, which are derived from the direct materials cost. The assumption for Jerry's Ice Cream is that 70 per cent of the payables are paid during the quarter and 30 per cent are paid in the next quarter. Comparing the payables of end Q4 with those of end Q1 allows us to derive the changes in accounts payable.

All together this allows us to derive the changes in working capital as the changes in inventory plus the changes in receivables minus the changes in payables, as illustrated in Figure 7.8.

For free cash flow, we also want to know the D&A and CAPEX budget. D&A included in the manufacturing overhead is \$10,700. D&A included in SG&A is \$3,000, together making \$13,070. Our CAPEX budget should follow from our strategic projects' portfolio derived during our strategic planning. For Jerry's Ice Cream the planned CAPEX for Q1 is zero.

Completing the process with a budgeted free cash flow and balance sheet

Figure 7.9 continues our budgeting process by adding a budgeted free cash flow and balance sheet. In Chapter 2 we defined free cash flow as:

$$\text{Free cash flow} = \text{EBIT} \times (1 - \text{tax rate}) - \Delta\,\text{WC} + \text{D\&A} - \text{CAPEX}$$

So, as shown in Figure 7.9, the budgeted free cash flow follows from P&L and the changes in working capital and in fixed assets (D&A and CAPEX).

The changes in receivables, inventories and payables can also be applied to the corresponding entries in current assets (CA) and current liabilities (CL) in the balance sheet. D&A and CAPEX can be applied to the fixed

FIGURE 7.8 Adding a working capital and fixed assets budget

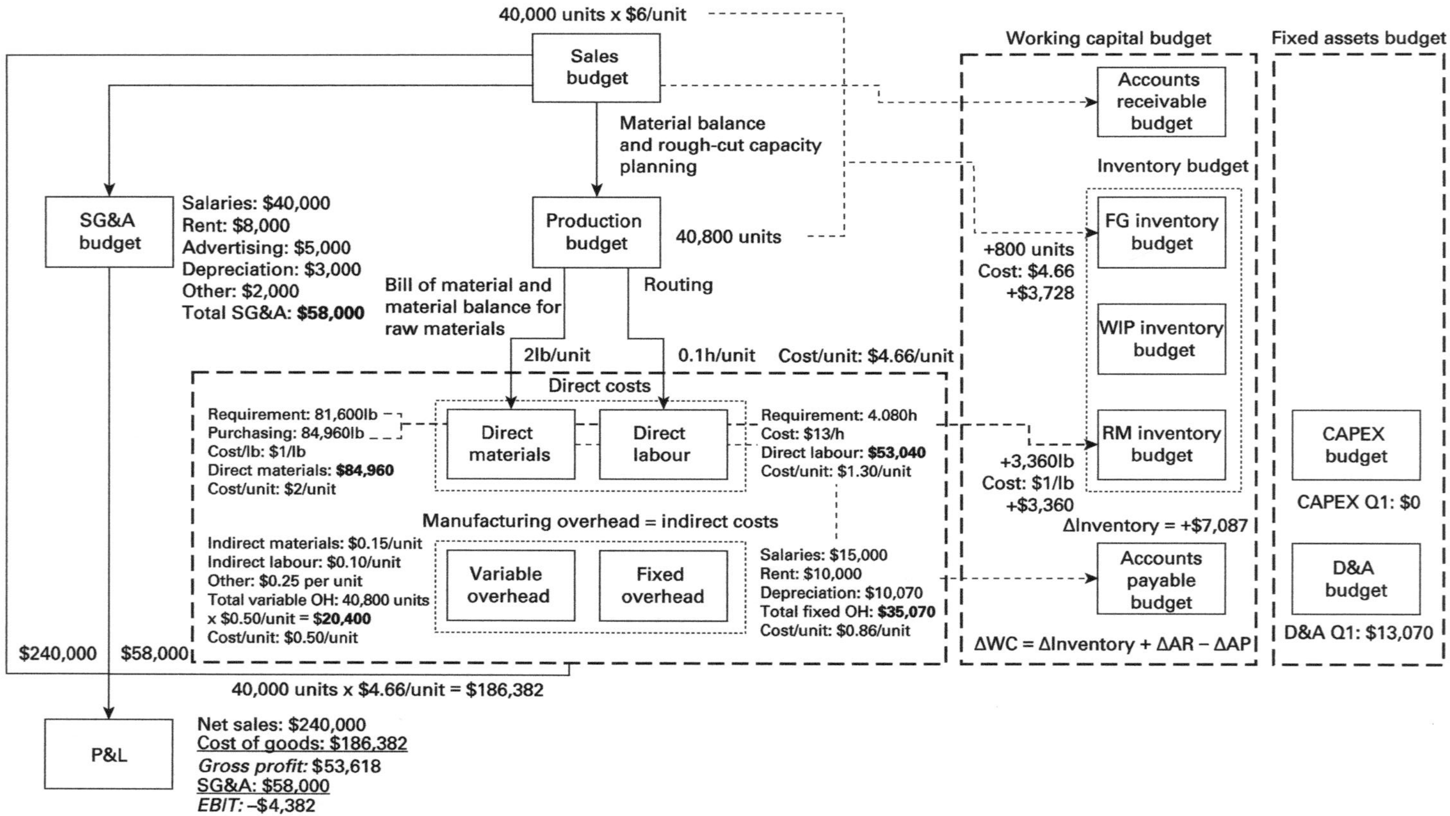

FIGURE 7.9 Completing the process with a budgeted free cash flow and balance sheet

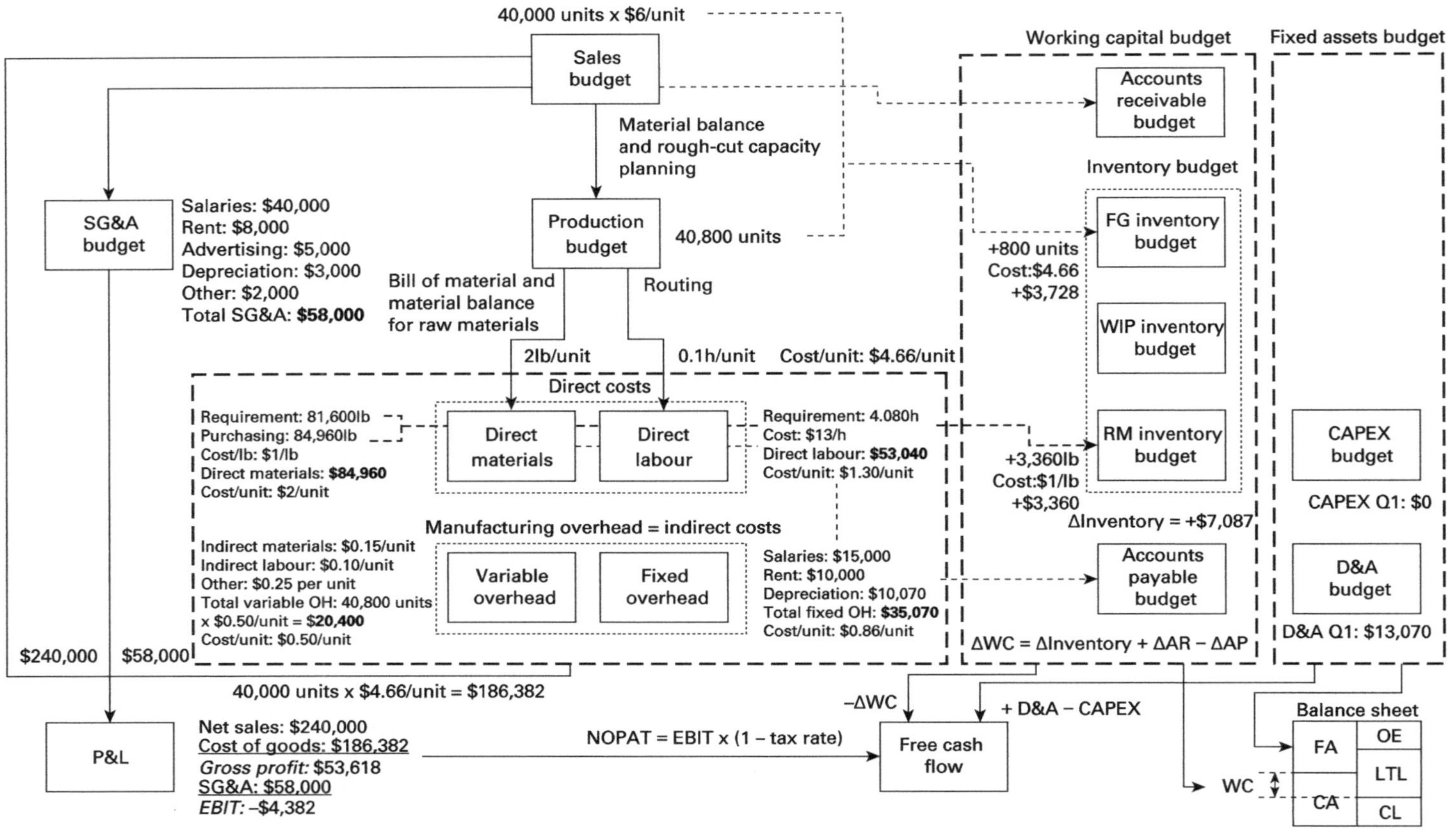

assets (FA) section in the balance sheet. Together they allow the budgeted balance sheet to be constructed, as shown in Figure 7.9.

The budgeted EBIT over the budgeted capital employed also gives us the budgeted ROCE, which is of primary interest to monitor if our budget helps us to progress along the ROCE roadmap defined in our strategic plan earlier.

Iterative process

The budgeting process is iterative. It could be started bottom-up, by asking different regions or business units to give their estimates on how next year will look like. If we add the ambitions of the individual regions and business units, we may end up with something that is not realistic. In that sense, top-down corrections are common and to be expected. Budgeting is also about setting expectations. We expect you to do better than last year on inventory turns, on labour efficiency, on sales prices. Tying that into the process requires multiple iterations.

Leveraging the sales and operations planning process and tooling

The reason we took some time to explain some details of the budgeting process was to be able to show the overlap with what happens in the S&OP process, which we tried to show in Figure 7.10. We notice that the budgeting process and the S&OP process in many companies are separate processes run with different tools, though the overlap between the two is obvious from Figure 7.10. As we will explain in the next section, S&OP starts from a forecast; it calculates target inventories, requirements for production, requirements for purchasing of raw materials, and all of that in a relatively sophisticated way.

We will discuss the concept of integrated business planning (IBP), which tries to 'monetize' the S&OP plan and compare it to the budget. We will argue that we should go a step further and combine this into one process and tooling capability of modelling the supply chain in a financial way, on the different levels from strategic to execution, which is our vision in strategy-driven integrated planning value planning and execution as shown in Figure 7.1.

Controlling and variance analysis

Figure 7.11 shows the annual budget for Jerry's Ice Cream. We refer to *Accounting for Managers* for the details. It shows what we 'expect' to happen. Figure 7.12 shows the actual result, which is obviously different.

FIGURE 7.10 Mapping the core capabilities of S&OP to the budgeting process

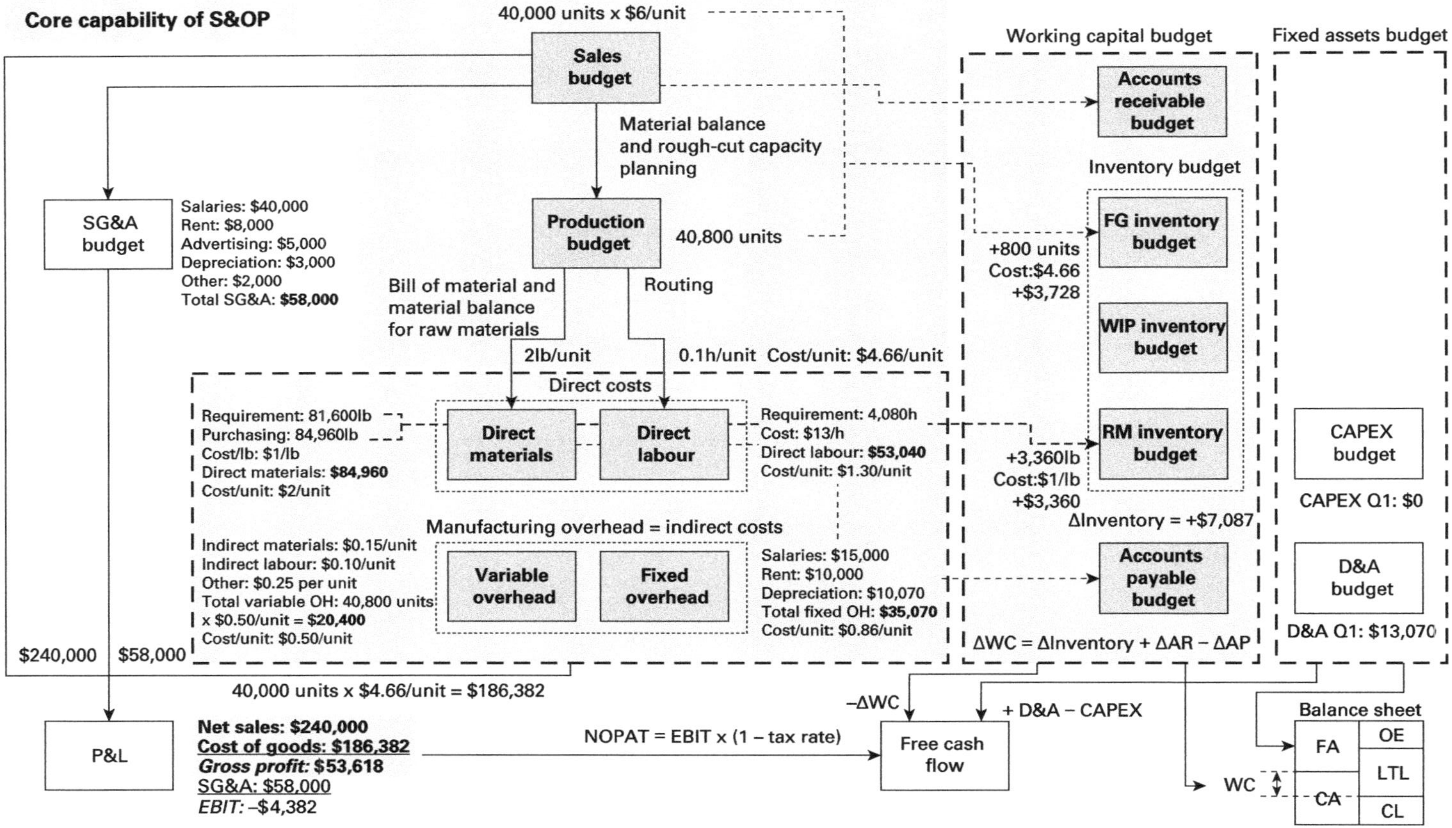

FIGURE 7.11 Annual budget for Jerry's Ice Cream

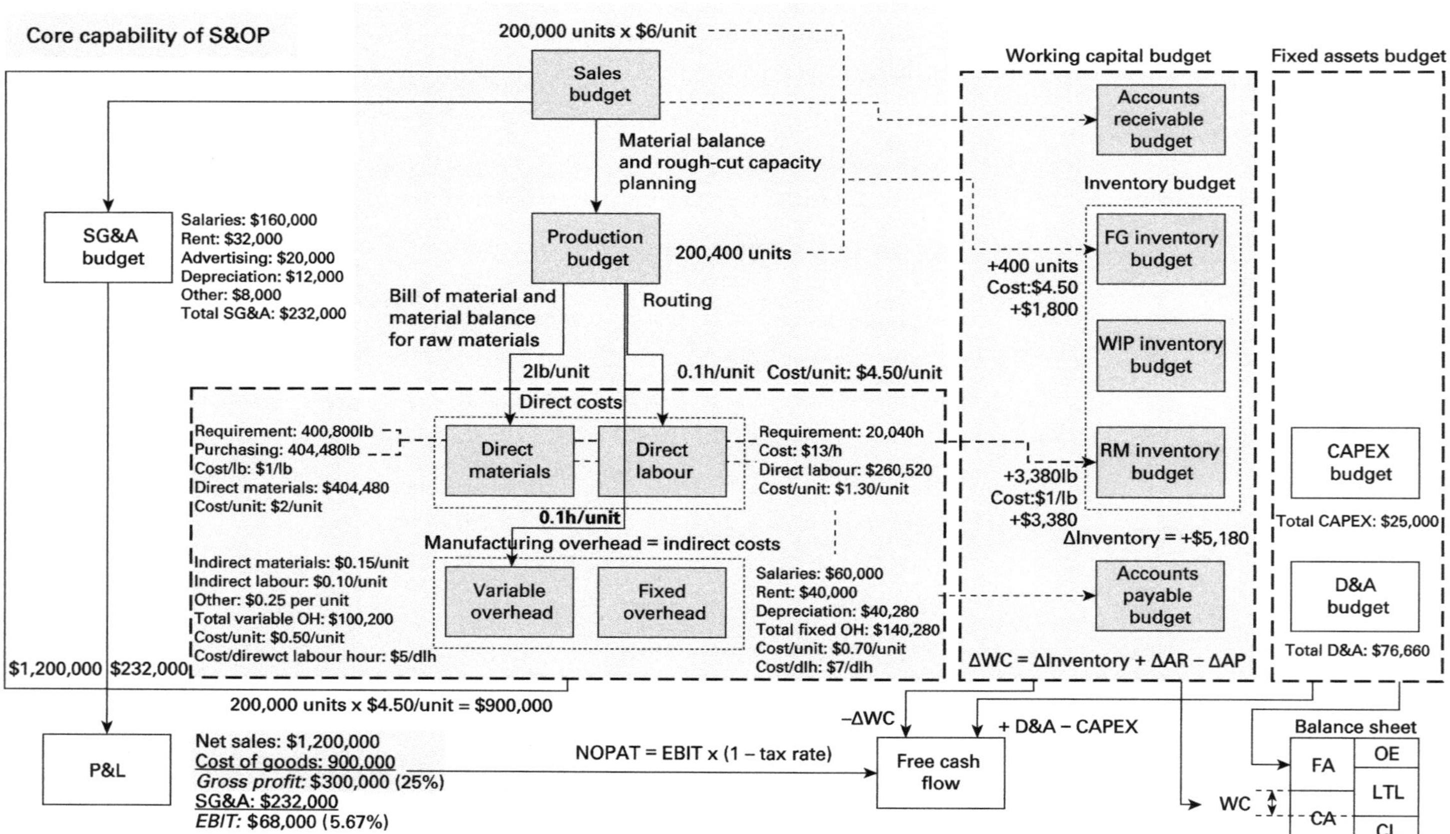

FIGURE 7.12 Actual result for Jerry's Ice Cream

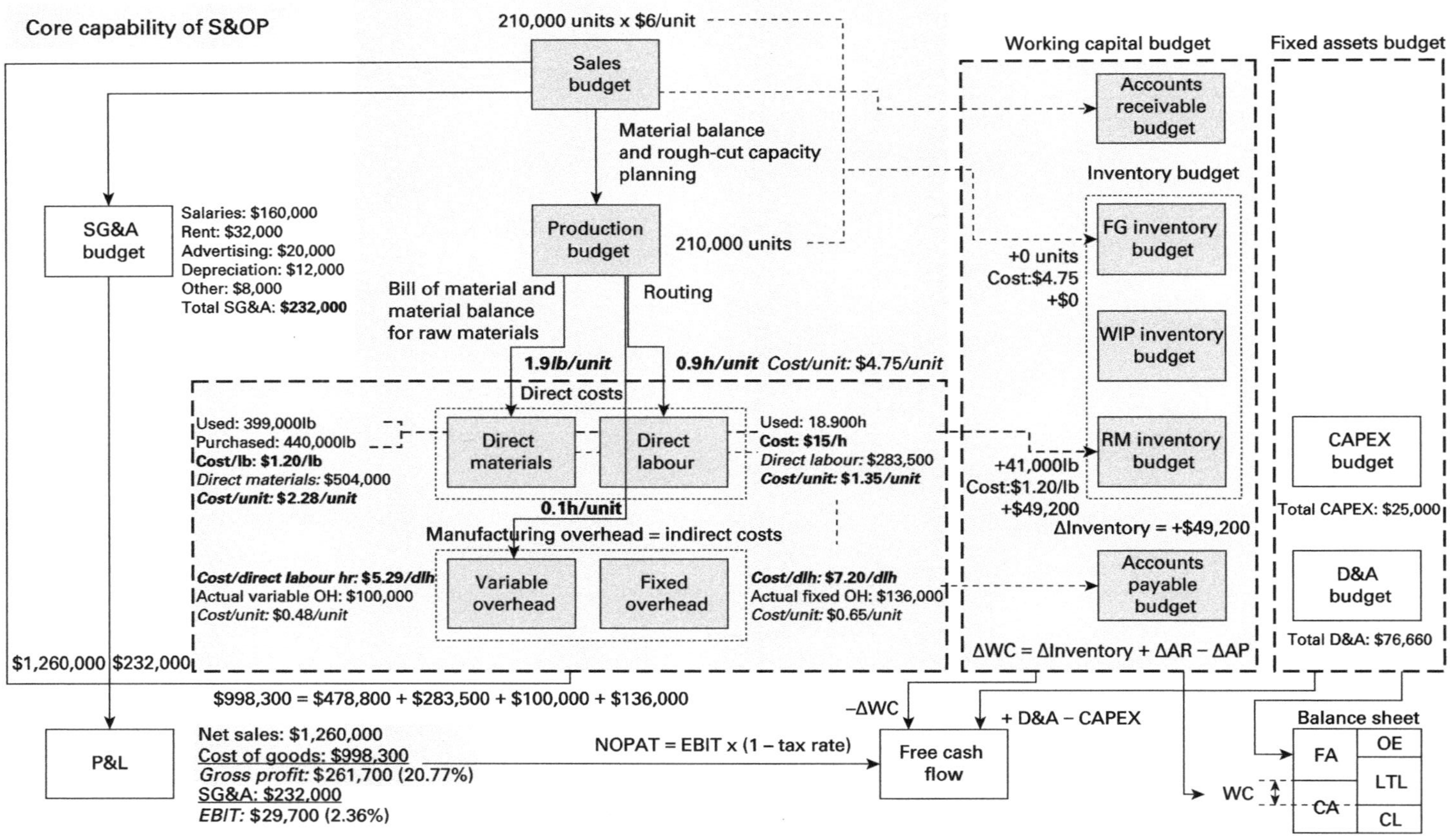

FIGURE 7.13 Flexible budget for 210,000 units

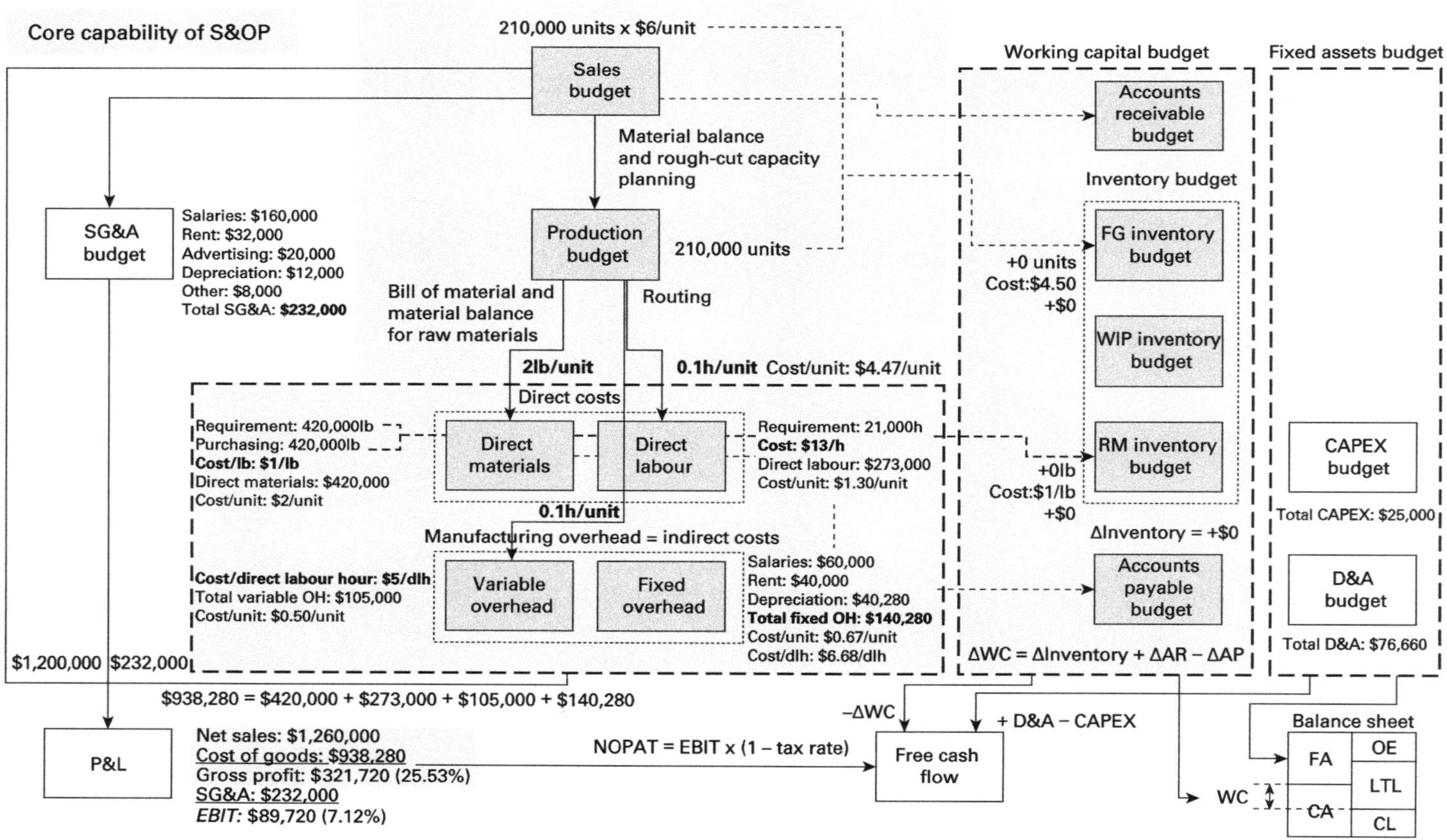

It starts with some good news. Instead of the budgeted 200,000 units, we sold 210,000 units, at the budgeted rate of $6. But that's about where the good news ends. Instead of the planned $300,000, our gross profit is only $261,000, which is a meagre 20.77 per cent instead of the planned 25 per cent. Despite higher sales, our EBIT is stuck at $29,700 (2.36 per cent) instead of the planned $68,000 (5.67 per cent). Explain that to your shareholders.

Variance analysis is used to analyse what the underlying drivers are and what is their relative importance. The variance analysis will compare the actual results with a so-called 'flexible budget'. The flexible budget is a budget for 210,000 units, assuming the same variable costs per unit as in the original budget. That flexible budget is shown in Figure 7.13.

Figure 7.14 compares the P&L for the budget, the flexible budget and the actuals. It shows that if we had stuck to the budgeted variable costs per unit, the extra volume would have further increased gross profit and EBIT as it would have allowed us to create extra leverage on the fixed overhead and SG&A costs. It makes the actuals look even worse.

In the Jerry's Ice Cream example, we have assumed that sales price and SG&A costs are constant, so when analysing the variance we can focus on the cost of goods sold. The actuals and the flexible budget are shown in Figure 7.15.

We start by analysing the difference in the direct materials, shown in Figure 7.16. The purpose of variance analysis is to split the 'volume' effect from the 'price/cost' effect. For producing the 210,000 units, we used 399,000 lb of sugar, where the budgeted volume was 420,000 lb of sugar, so we were clearly more efficient. So how does that influence the financial result? Well at the budgeted cost of $1/lb, the 'volume variance' is (399,000 lb – 420,000 lb) x $1/lb = –$21,000. Our cost of goods sold did not go down by $21,000, however, due to the higher price for the sugar. The real cost has been $1.20/lb instead of the budgeted $1/lb. What is the impact of that higher price? Well we used 399,000 lb so the price or cost variance is ($1.20/lb – $1/lb) x 399,000 lb = $79,800. So we used less raw materials,

FIGURE 7.14 P&L for the budget, the flexible budget and the actuals

BUDGET	FLEXIBLE BUDGET	ACTUALS
Net sales: $1,200,000	Net sales: $1,260,000	Net sales: $1,260,000
Cost of goods: $900,000	Cost of goods: $938,280	Cost of goods: $998,300
Gross profit: $300,000 (25%)	*Gross profit:* $321,720 (25.53%)	*Gross profit:* $261,700 (20.77%)
SG&A: $232,000	SG&A: $232,000	SG&A: $232,000
EBIT: $68,000 (5.67%)	*EBIT:* $89,720 (7.12%)	*EBIT:* $29,700 (2.36%)

but their price per pound was 20 per cent higher than planned. The combined effect is –$21,000 + $79,800 = + $58,800, which explains the increase in direct materials cost from $420,000 to $478,800.

The analysis for the difference in direct labour cost is comparable and shown in Figure 7.17. The actual direct labour hours used are 18,900, whereas the budgeted direct labour hours for 210,000 units was 21,000 hours. So we have clearly been more efficient than planned. The financial impact is calculated as (18,900 h – 21,000 h) x $13/h = –$27,300. It is the 'volume' side of the direct labour variance; we also talk about the direct labour efficiency variance. The total cost of direct labour, however, went up. This has to do with the higher cost per hour of $15/h instead of the budgeted $13/h. The impact of the cost or labour rate is ($15/h - $13/h) x 18,900 h = $37,800. That is the cost variance or the labour rate variance. The combined effect is –$27,300 + $37,800 = +$10,500. So we've been more efficient, but that efficiency is outweighed by the more expensive rate per hour. The +$10,500 explains the increase in direct labour cost from $273,000 to $283,500 shown in Figure 7.17.

Next we analyse the variance of the variable overhead. The variable overhead is typically allocated based on machine hours or based on direct labour hours (dlh). In the Jerry's Ice Cream example, we assume it is based on direct labour hours. Figure 7.18 shows a budgeted rate of $5 variable overhead per direct labour hour. The actual can be calculated as $5.29/dlh from the actual overhead of $100,000 and the actual labour hours of 18,900. Based on these inputs we can calculate the volume (efficiency) variance as (18,900 h – 21,000 h) x $5/h = –$10,500 and the cost (spending) variance as ($5.29/h – $5/h) x 18,900 h = + $5,500. Leading to a combined effect of –$5,000.

Finally, the fixed overhead variance is shown in Figure 7.19. We don't want to split this into a volume or cost variance as the fixed cost is fixed. We just show the fixed cost variance as the difference of the actual of $136,000 minus the budgeted fixed overhead of $140,280, being a favourable variance of –$4,280.

The overview of the cost variance analysis can be summarized in a waterfall chart, shown in Figure 7.20. We can also translate that COGS variance into a gross profit variance, as shown in Figure 7.21. The volume variance in direct materials has an impact of –$21,000 on the COGS and an impact of +$21,000 on the gross profit. The gross profit variance is a bit handier as it more clearly shows the impact on the gross profit. In the same fashion, we can also show the EBIT variance in a waterfall chart.

FIGURE 7.15 Cost of goods sold: actuals versus flexible budget

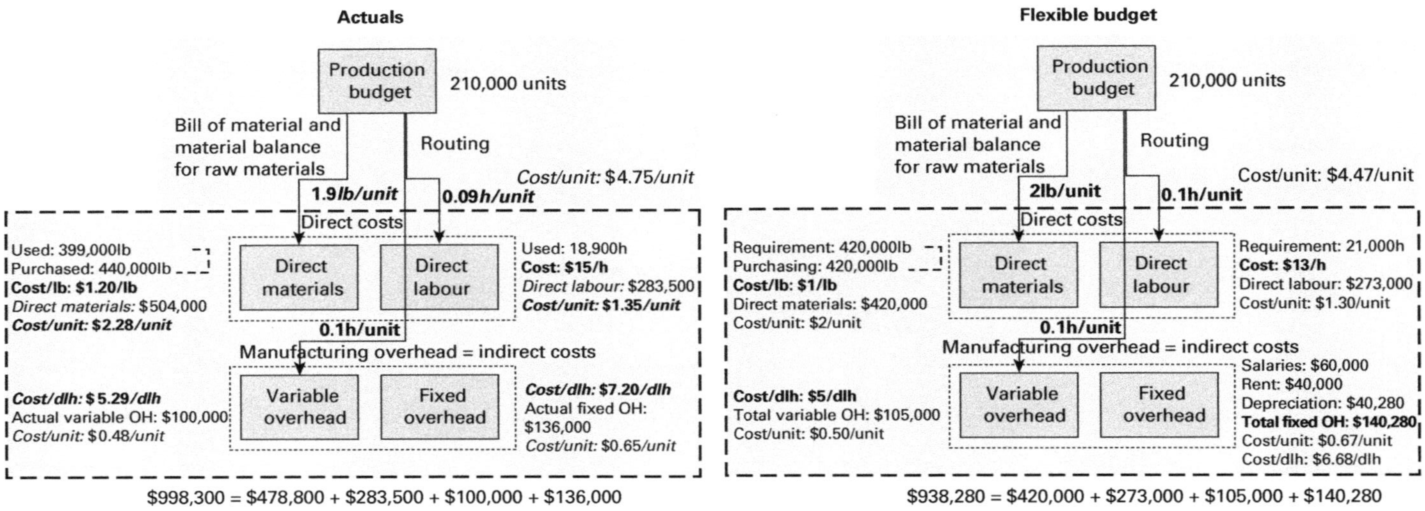

FIGURE 7.16 Direct materials variance analysis

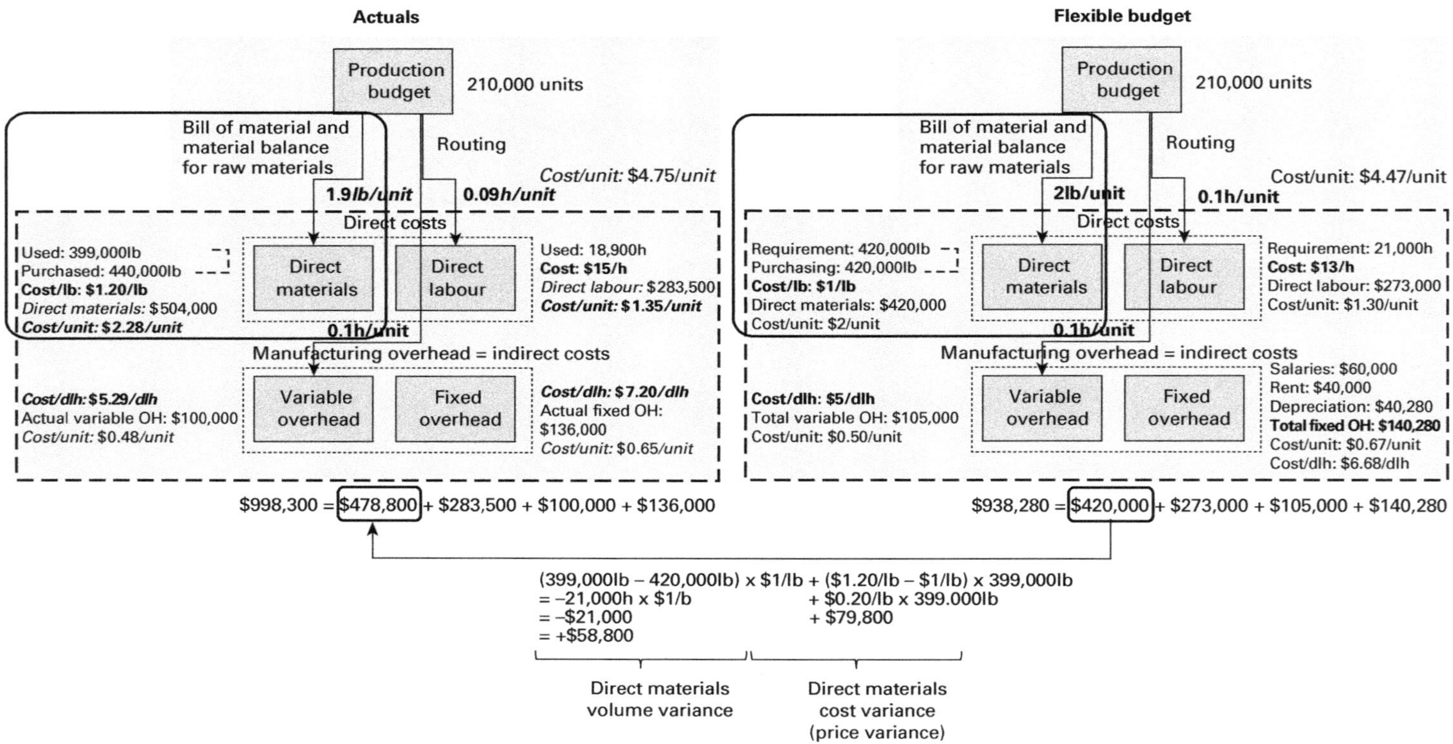

FIGURE 7.17 Direct labour variance analysis

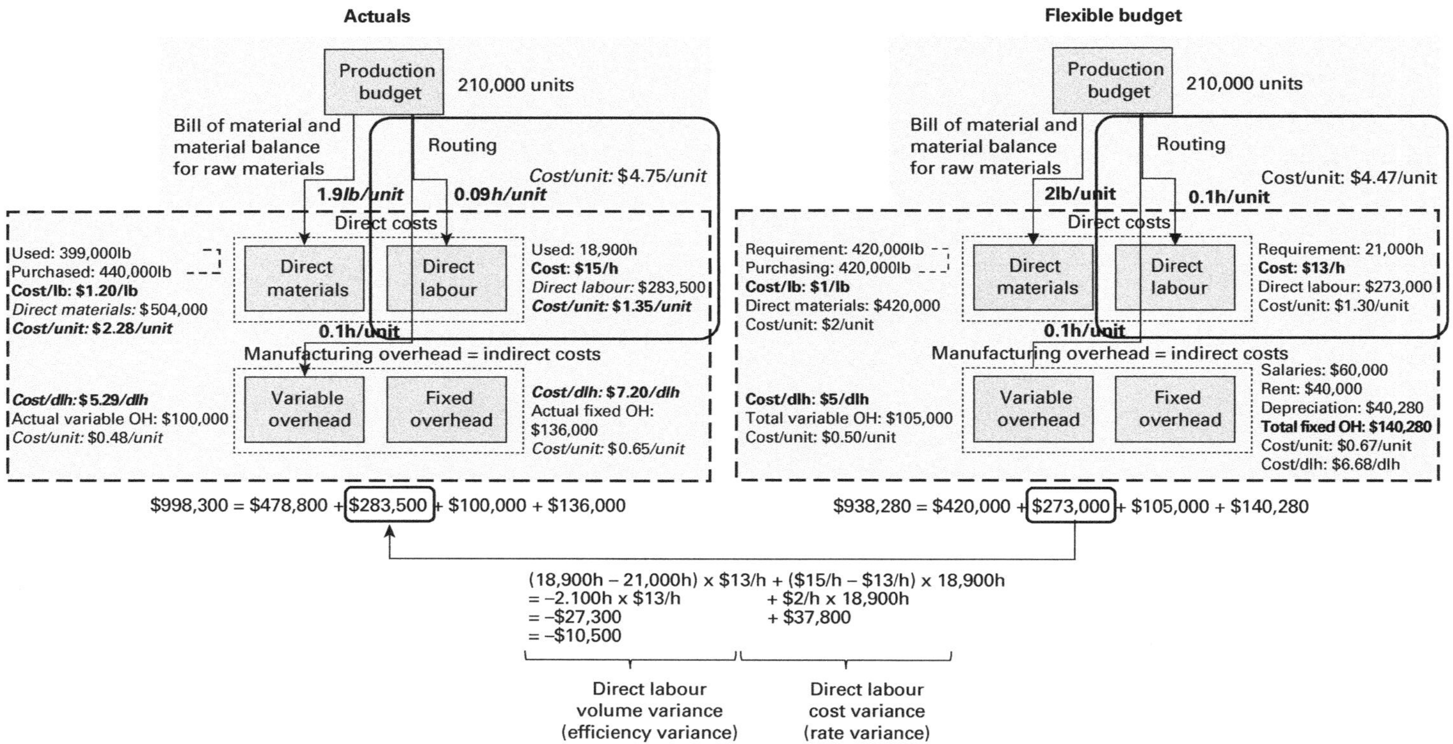

FIGURE 7.18 Variable overhead variance analysis

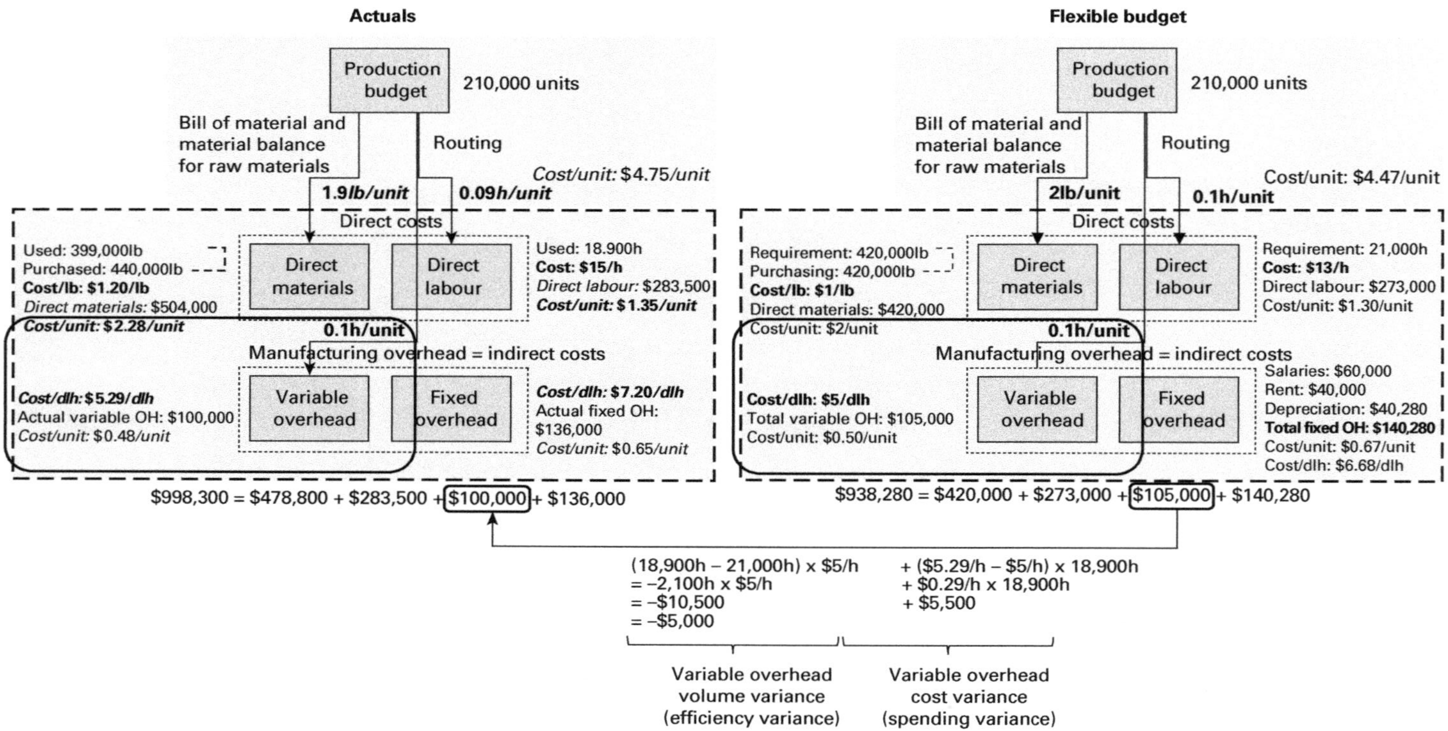

FIGURE 7.19 Fixed overhead variance analysis

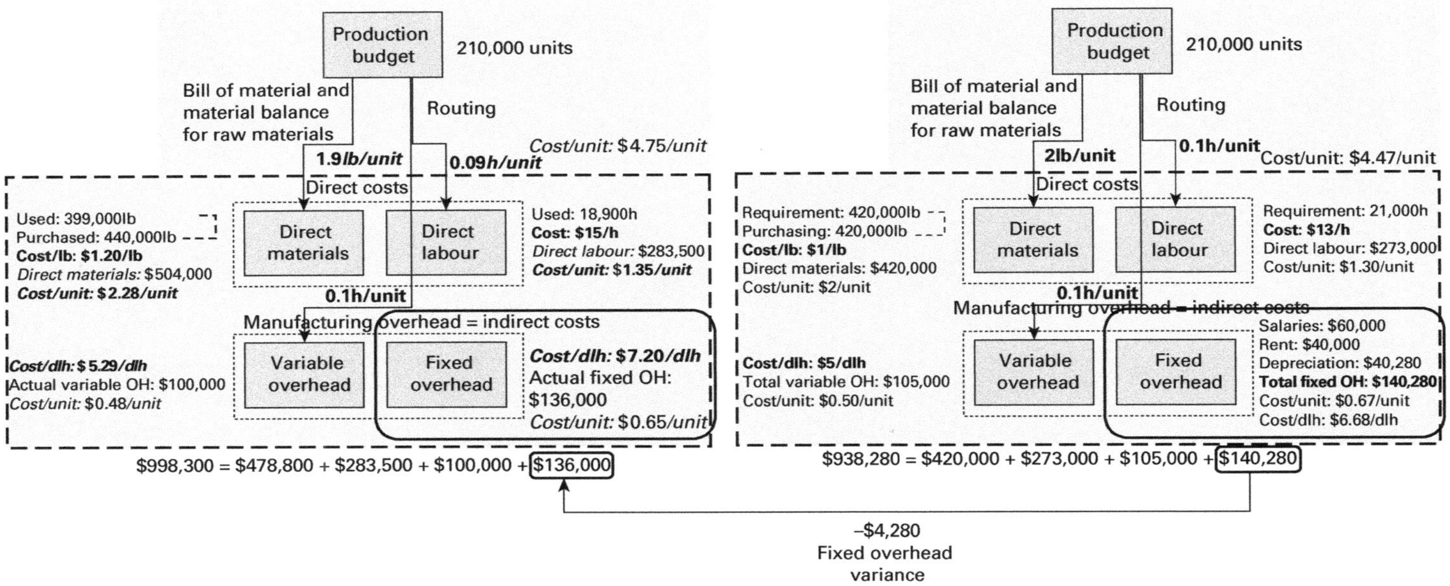

FIGURE 7.20 Cost of goods sold variance in a waterfall chart

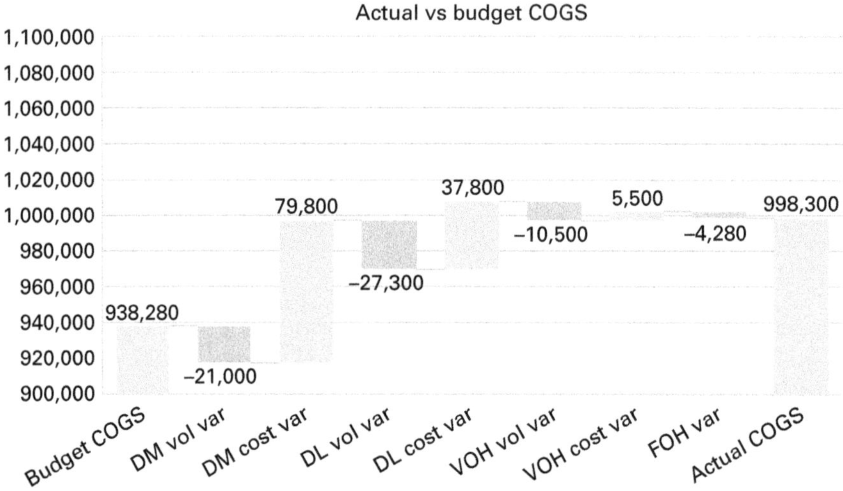

FIGURE 7.21 Gross profit variance in a waterfall chart

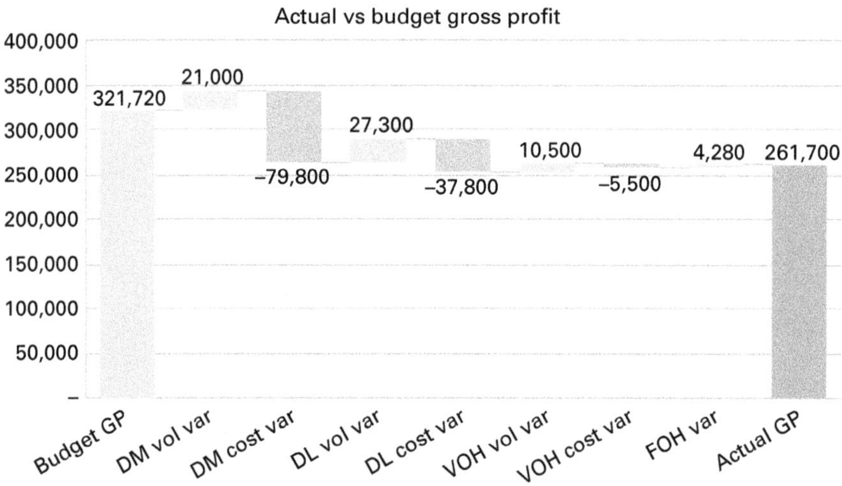

Integrating variance analysis in the S&OP process and tooling

The variance analysis we have just discussed should basically roll out of the S&OP tooling and should be included as a starter in the executive S&OP meeting. We can look back at the previous month or the previous quarter and try to understand variances going backward, to be able to project those variances going forward. If in the example of Jerry's Ice Cream the cost of sugar and the cost of labour are 20 per cent higher than planned, we don't want to wait for the next month or quarter to pass before we see that impact again. We want to be able to simulate what will be the projected impact of raw material and labour costs, and we want to devise strategies on how to mitigate the impact on gross profit.

In many companies we see double processes. We see 'business reviews' or 'finance reviews', which typically are backward-looking. We see 'S&OP meetings' that currently lack some of the financial aspects, and certainly the 'variance analysis' piece. We propose to integrate those meetings into one meeting where operational planning is reviewed from a financial perspective, with some time spent on reviewing the recent history, but with most of the time spent looking forward.

As mentioned earlier in the text, we took some time to explain budgeting and variance analysis in detail as we have found that many supply chain professionals do not know the processes. Equally, we will now spend some time explaining the sales and operations planning process in detail, as we notice that many finance professionals do not know the processes. If we want to bridge both worlds, we need to create a common understanding. We hope the common understanding will make it look as absurd to others as it looks to me to keep running these parallel worlds.

Sales and operations planning

Figure 7.22 shows the Solventure vision on S&OP. It builds on the basics explained by Thomas Wallace, the refinements brought in by Oliver Wight and our 15 years of consulting experience in this field.[6] We talk about sales and operations planning (S&OP) instead of integrated business planning (IBP). The terms S&OP and IBP are used interchangeably by many authors and practitioners.

Our vision of S&OP begins with 'segmentation'. It starts from the finding that many companies use the same service target for all customers and all products. Just making that statement makes you feel that it cannot be the right thing to do. No two customers are the same. They don't have the same volume, they don't have the same margins, they don't have the same willingness to innovate, or the same loyalty. Nor are two products the same. Some products more reflect the past whereas others reflect the future. Some products are easy for you to make, whereas others are a nightmare. We recommend segmenting both customers and products and differentiating

FIGURE 7.22 Sales and operations planning: our vision at Solventure

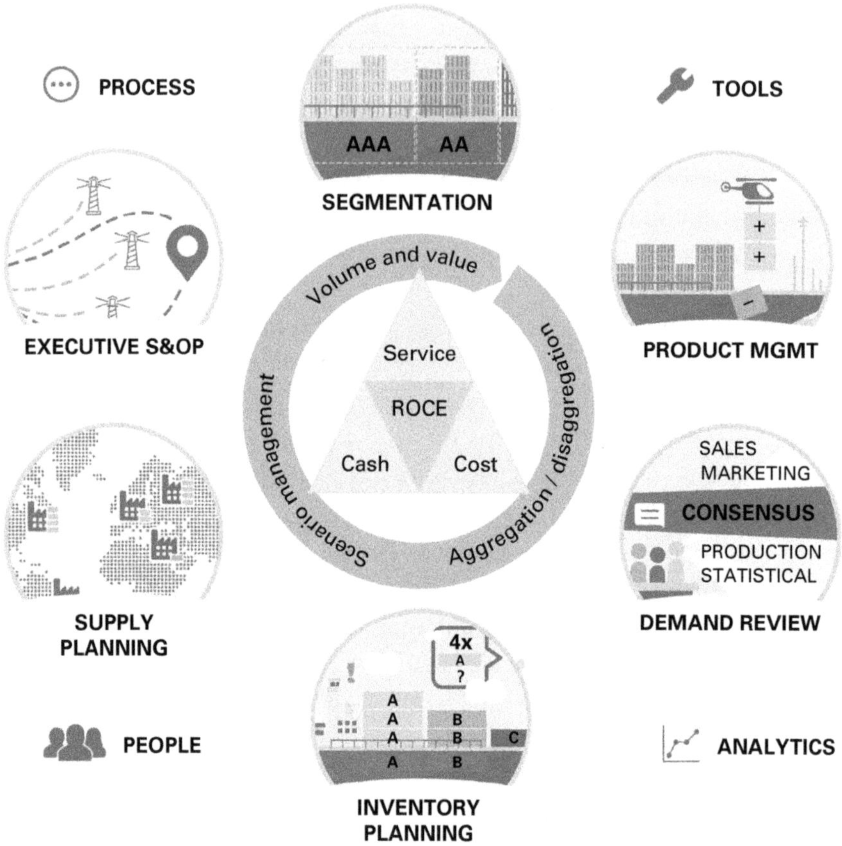

the service across those customer–product segments. We will give some examples on how to use the segmentation as we progress through the S&OP process steps. For more details on how to perform a segmentation, we refer to our vision paper on customer–product segmentation, which can be found on the book website at www.strategydrivensupplychain.com/resources/visionpapers/customer-product-segmentation

We continue with a product management review, which manages the new product introductions (NPI) process and the end-of-life process. We believe seven in ten NPIs are overstated. This typically leads to excess inventories. That also means that three in ten NPIs are understated. This leads to rush orders and extra costs, as of course we don't want to be short on a new successful product. So NPIs are notorious for knocking the triangle out of balance. By explicitly following them up in a monthly product management review, we can reduce the uncertainty and optimize the value. The second aspect is the end-of-life process. We often say that companies are very good at introducing new products, but very bad at taking old products out. Stopping SKUs runs into pushback from sales, who will say, 'We know those products are not profitable but you can't stop them as we are selling them to customers X and Y, and if we stop these products, we will lose these customers.' We already explained that if we can stop a product without impacting sales it is essentially a non-moving product and we are simply too late. We need to look at the margin that is generated over the inventory invested. That bang-for-the-buck typically declines near the end of the lifecycle. By stopping products in time, we keep our portfolio clean. It cuts the bad complexity out and keeps the good complexity in. This process is key at customer intimacy players given their broad product portfolio. Product portfolio complexity is like cholesterol. Some of it is good for the body but too much of it leads to a stroke! For more details on how to include product management in the S&OP cycle, we refer to our vision paper on product management which can be found on the book website at www.strategydrivensupplychain.com/resources/visionpapers/product-management

Many companies start their S&OP journey by starting a forecasting or demand planning project. A good forecast is the basis of a good plan. Over the last five years there has been a hype around demand-driven planning.[7] That movement states that forecasts are not needed and we should instead work using 'true demand signals'. In practice it means we only replenish an inventory buffer after there has been consumption. It is equal to the 'pull' principle recommended by the lean movement. The lean movement is less dogmatic than the demand-driven movement. Lean indicates a 'pull' is only possible if the demand is sufficiently stable. They even have a technique to stabilize demand called *heijunka*. The idea is that, instead of producing in batches, you mix different types (of cars) on the same production (assembly) line. That stabilizes the demand for the components on the production line instead of creating peaks. In short, if the conditions are right then pull principles do work. In practice, most of the organizations we visit lack the stability for the 'pull' to be sufficiently effective. If you have important seasonality, promotions, tenders… volume variability or mix variability (to use the terms of Chapter 6), then a good plan will start with a good forecast.

Making a good forecast starts with understanding your demand drivers. Think about what influences your demand. What are internal factors (eg promotions), what are external factors (eg macro-economic factors), which drivers do you control (eg timing of promotions), which ones don't you control (eg macro-economic context)? A good forecast starts with 'understanding your drivers', 'collecting data on your drivers', 'understanding how these drivers affected your demand in the past', to then 'predict the impact of these drivers into the future'. At Solventure we have done a lot of research on how to include these demand drivers into your forecast. You can find our vision on the book website at www.strategydrivensupplychain.com/resources/visionpapers/leading-indicator-forecasting

Don't fly blind, and don't rely on the traditional extrapolation techniques that just extrapolate recent history. At Solventure we improve the forecast accuracy by including external data. Take a look at the following link for an example indicator dashboard to be included in your demand and S&OP dashboards: www.strategydrivensupplychain.com/resources/macro-economic-dashboard

This 'mathematical' forecast is an input to a 'collaborative' process. This is a good place to tie in our customer segmentation. I often state that 'once we know who our A-customers are, we will stop guessing what these customers will buy from us, we will reach out and ask them'. For A-customers, our recommendation is to set up a collaborative forecasting process with the customer. Sales should reach out to these customers on a monthly basis and say 'Dear customer, Based on our latest estimates this is what we have forecasted for your demand. What do you think?' B-customers are still important from a volume and a margin perspective, but there are simply too many to ask sales to reach out to each of them individually. So, for B-customers we recommend that sales validate the forecast numbers and reach out to B-customers ad hoc. Finally, any company will have a long tail of C-customers. Here we propose relying on the mathematical forecast. We don't want to waste salespeople's time by managing all those details. To make the forecasting process efficient, you do need customer segmentation!

Finally, the only truth about the forecast is that it is wrong; the question is, how wrong is it? Make sure that you measure and report forecast accuracy. As we explained in Chapter 3 when introducing our strategy-driven dashboard, forecast accuracy is an important causal metric. If it deteriorates it has a negative impact on service, cost and cash. Be realistic in your targets. If you have important volume variability or mix variability, as introduced in Chapter 6, your forecast error will be higher than that of others. Your complexity is driven by your market and your strategy. So is your forecast error! For more details on demand planning we refer you to our vision paper, which can be found on the book website at www.strategydrivensupplychain.com/resources/visionpapers/demand-planning

Next we come to inventory planning. Many companies rely on relatively simplistic policies like the one described in the budgeting process at Jerry's Ice Cream. We aim for a buffer of 10 per cent of the sales. The problem with this type of simplistic policy is that 10 per cent will be far too much for some of the products (typically the fast movers) and not nearly enough for some of the others (typically the more variable products). There are statistical techniques to 'optimize' your inventory. These techniques account for lead times, lead time variability, demand variability or forecast error and allow you to define the targeted 'service level'. If you have a customer–product segmentation you can differentiate service for different customer–product segments. Applying these techniques typically allows you to lower inventory (on those products where you had too much) and improve service (by improving on those products where you did not have enough). It also lowers costs. If we are short on a product we will always try to close the gap by rushing orders through production and logistics. Supply chain people are good at this type of analytics. Instead of running separate processes on the finance side, finance should leverage the S&OP process, which contains more details and is more refined. This is the argument we illustrated in Figure 7.10. We also link this back to our discussion of on-time, in-full as a 'responsiveness' parameter in Chapter 6. Where do we want to be as a company? On par? Differentiate? Or dominate? We can also link it back to our discussion of the 'mix flexibility', which we defined as the 'capability to serve a portfolio of *y* #SKUs, with a demand variability of *x* per cent on an SKU level, within a given lead time and OTIF reliability'. You do want to run scenarios on this. Supply chain has the capabilities to do so. For more details on how to organize your inventory management, including more on inventory reporting and monitoring, we refer to our vision paper, which can be found on the book's website at www.strategydrivensupplychain.com/resources/visionpapers/inventory

The next step in the S&OP process is the supply planning step. Here we translate demand and inventory (target versus actual) into a production requirement. It essentially works as explained in the budgeting example for ice cream. A material balance ensures we produce a bit extra or a bit less in function of a stock build-up or build-off. The bill of material and the MRP translate the requirements of finished products into requirements for intermediates and raw materials. The routings allow us to map the production requirements to work centres. Work centres have a certain capacity that we may try to increase or decrease in function of the production requirements. On a 'tactical' horizon, three to eighteen months out, that process is called the rough cut capacity planning process. In the 'operational' horizon we talk about master planning or the master production schedule (MPS) and about detailed production scheduling. We will discuss those when we talk about the S&OE layer in Figure 7.1. In general terms, supply planning is all about trying to balance supply and demand. We can do that by increasing or decreasing inventories, by increasing or decreasing capacities or by sourcing from alternative locations. Different layers of supply planning (RCCP, MPS, detailed scheduling) do this at a different level of detail and on a different horizon. If you want to know more, we refer you to our vision paper on supply planning, which can be found on the book's website at www.strategydrivensupplychain.com/resources/visionpapers/supply-planning

Supply chain can build quite advanced models for supply planning. Optimization techniques like linear programming (LP) or variants called heuristics allow multiple and complex constraints to be specified. We may have a constraint on the capacity, we may have a limitation on the amount of raw materials, we may need to respect a certain sequence in production, we may have bottlenecks shifting upstream or downstream depending on the product mix, we may want to prioritize certain customers and products (linking back to our segmentation). Optimization tools allow you to find the best possible answer within all of these constraints. Supply chain people are good at this type of analytics. So, once more, instead of running separate processes on the finance side, we believe finance should leverage the S&OP process, as we argue in Figure 7.10.

The idea of S&OP is that it should roll up into the executive S&OP meeting. This has been a major challenge for many S&OP managers. We believe the key to a good executive S&OP is in the middle circle in Figure 7.22. First, we need an easy translation of volumes to values and vice versa. If we can't monetize the plan and only talk about volumes, then it is indeed more an operational and supply chain planning type of process rather than the business process we would like it to be. In that sense, whether we talk about S&OP or IBP, we believe not monetizing the plan is simply not an option. Second, we need easy aggregation and disaggregation. In supply chain planning the devil is in the detail. In the end, we need to make specific SKUs on specific machines and ship them to specific customers. But if we want to increase the relevance of S&OP as a management tool, we need to be able to aggregate and show the big lines. Where are we on schedule, where are we behind, what is the overall impact? Third, we need scenario management capabilities. If we are short on raw materials, what are the options? What is the impact on the top line and bottom line, and which customers will be impacted? Many companies start their S&OP with Excel, but this is where Excel breaks. You need powerful tools to run this type of process. The good news is that those tools are available, and investing in them can generate a lot of value.

That brings us to the four pillars shown in Figure 7.22. First, when implementing S&OP you need good process knowledge. Forecasting in FMCG is driven by promotions and requires a different approach from forecasting in a B2B environment. Second, you need professional tools. Stop wasting your time in trying to reconcile numbers from different sources. One set of numbers starts with having one integrated database. Don't settle for less than easy aggregation and disaggregation, easy volume to value conversions and swift scenario management capabilities. Without decent tools, the process will die. That has been tested and tried. Third, you need a consultant and analytics team that masters the analytical side of the S&OP process. Think about the mathematical forecasting, inventory optimization and optimization techniques used in supply planning. Analytics are like a turbo-charger. Once you have a good engine (process + tool), the right analytics easily get you to 30 per cent extra performance. But it is a matter of precision. If you plug in the turbo the wrong way, the motor will explode. Which, unfortunately, we have witnessed more than once. Last but not least, it is about the people. Though S&OP has been around for 30 years, it is still poorly understood. You will need to educate people on what S&OP is about and why it is needed. You will face believers and non-believers. In any case, we believe S&OP is an essential piece in managing the balance in the supply chain triangle. That is the reason that the triangle is positioned centrally in our S&OP vision shown in Figure 7.22. But, in the meantime, we have also learnt that S&OP is not enough. As we will conclude later in this chapter, we believe an integration of strategic, financial and operational planning is required. That is our concept of strategy-driven integrated value planning and execution (strategy-driven IVP&E).

Sales and operations execution

The final layer in Figure 7.1 is sales and operations execution (S&OE). The term was coined by Gartner to differentiate between the so-called 'tactical' planning layer and the 'operational' planning layer.

The S&OP process typically looks in monthly buckets and three to eighteen months ahead. As shown in Figure 7.23, it manages the so-called 'free period' where we expect the supply will meet the demand. If we see that one year from now our capacity is gradually getting full, that should trigger an investment request through the executive S&OP meeting. If we need more time to expand our capacity, then we should extend the horizon of the S&OP plan.

The master plan, or master production schedule, typically looks in weekly buckets and three to twelve weeks ahead. The master plan triggers the MRP run, which triggers the reordering of raw materials. If my key raw materials have a 24-week lead time, I will need to extend my master planning horizon to at least 24 weeks. Once we are in the master planning horizon, we can still decide to produce a bit more or less of SKU A or B, as long as we stay within the given raw material supply. That's why we say the master plan is managing the flexible period, as opposed to the free period for the RCCP. In the master planning horizon, raw materials have been ordered so the raw material supply becomes a constraint.

The detailed production schedule or the detailed production plan looks at the planning of different manufacturing steps. The MPS is typically on a finished product. If to make a finished product there are two or three distinct production steps, for instance an upstream step that performs blending, mixing, cooking or baking and a downstream step that does the filling and/or the packing, then the detailed production schedule will create shop floor orders for each of the relevant manufacturing steps. The horizon of the detailed production schedule is the total manufacturing lead time. If it takes five days from raw material to finished products, then the detailed production schedule will look at least five days ahead. If we are within the horizon of the detailed plan we talk about the 'frozen horizon' or the 'frozen period'. Once the manufacturing orders have been released to the shop floor, it is impossible to still change them. So that part of the plan is frozen.

Thomas Wallace was one of the first to talk about the difference between the 'volume' and the 'mix'. In S&OP and RCCP we try to get the 'volumes' right. We typically do the demand–supply balancing at an aggregated level here, a so-called 'S&OP family'. The MPS and detailed production schedule are all about the 'mix'. They ensure the right SKU is scheduled at the right machine at the right time, maximizing the service level, while minimizing the production cost and the inventory. If you have important volume variability, to use the terminology from Chapter 6, then you need a strong S&OP and RCCP process. If you have a lot of mix variability, you need a strong S&OE and MPS/detailed production scheduling process. The complexity and variability are driven by both the market and your strategy. So are your planning processes!

FIGURE 7.23 Planning horizons

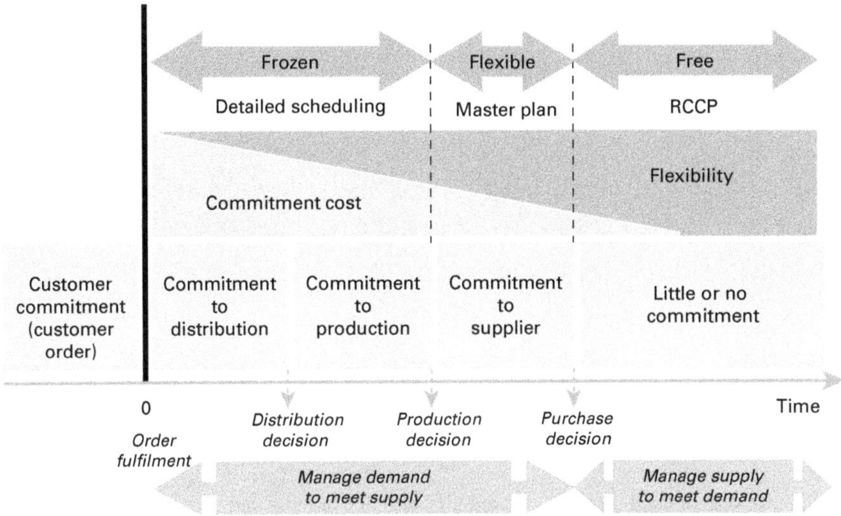

Conclusion

That brings us back to our main point of this chapter. We believe that if we want to create a better balance in the triangle, we need to better integrate the different levels of planning: strategic, financial and operational. We discussed at length in Chapters 3, 5 and 6 how strategy affects balance in the triangle. At the beginning of this chapter we outlined an approach for strategic planning that incorporates the need to make choices through defining your DNA. We have integrated our approach to strategy-driven benchmarking and target setting to ensure we have an ambition and a roadmap to drive value (ROCE) and have clarified how our strategic positioning affects the way we will drive ROCE (the value model). In many companies we see that the budgeting process and the S&OP process are somewhat disconnected from each other and from the strategic planning process. It is obvious that a stronger connection will lead to a better strategy execution and monitoring, and as a result will drive more value. We believe that S&OP and IBP have failed to deliver on that promise. If we want to come to grips with the triangle and with value generation, we need to take it one step further. That is our concept of strategy-driven IVP&E. Integrating the processes can be done by having a strong financial modelling at the core. We believe S&OP tools have those capabilities. There is no reason why these would not project a P&L, balance sheet and cash flow forecast 18 months out. There is no reason why companies would not adopt more rolling budgets that are reviewed and updated, for instance every quarter.

In the next chapter we provide insights on how to start your strategy-driven journey. We talk about a top-down and a bottom-up approach. We also look at how to make plans for strategy-driven value generation. We argue that we need to reshuffle the power balance in the executive team and redefine the role of supply chain if we truly want to drive more value.

Notes

1 R S Kaplan and D P Norton (2008) *The Execution Premium: Linking strategy to operations for competitive advantage*, Harvard Business Press, Boston, MA

2 J Collins (2001) *Good to Great*, Collins, Glasgow

3 A G Lafley and R L Martin (2013) *Playing to Win: How strategy really works*, Harvard Business Press, Boston, MA

4 www.tijd.be/ondernemen/consumentengoederen/ontex-ceo-bouaziz-moet-opstappen/10241813.html (archived at https://perma.cc/9F9D-ZA3R)

5 R S Kaplan, R E Kaplan, D P Norton, T H Davenport and D P Norton (2004) *Strategy Maps: Converting intangible assets into tangible outcomes*, Harvard Business Press, Boston, MA

6 T F Wallace (2004) *Sales and Operations Planning: The how-to handbook*, Steelwedge Software, Pleasanton, CA; G E Palmatier and C Crum (2002) *Enterprise Sales and Operations Planning: Synchronizing demand, supply and resources for peak performance*, J Ross Publishing, Fort Lauderdale, CA

7 C Ptak and C Smith (2016) *Demand Driven Material Requirements Planning*, Industrial Press, South Norwalk, CT

08

Your strategy-driven roadmap

Assuming we agree with the need to better balance the triangle, we understand the link with financial metrics like ROCE and free cash flow, we understand that different strategies lead to a different balance and are different ways to generate ROCE, we understand that different strategies lead to a different level of complexity and variability and our response to those results in different supply chains. Assuming we agree that better integrated planning processes will help in driving more value... where do we start? How do we put this into practice?

In this chapter we'll discuss two options. One is the more logical or chronological, top-down, from the strategy and the board down to the operations and the execution. The second is more bottom-up, starting from what supply chain currently has as its most important tool in balancing the triangle: the sales and operations planning process.

We'll continue with a seven-step approach that summarizes our experience on how to drive sustainable change and value. The approach was developed to implement S&OP, but can easily be extended to the implementation of strategy-driven Integrated Value Planning and Execution (IVP&E) and broader supply chain changes.

We conclude this chapter by analysing how really balancing the triangle requires a change in how we organize as an executive team. We will discuss the old 'conflict model' and the new strategy-driven value model. We believe it is time to redefine the role of supply chain as the guardian of value creation, centrally positioned in the triangle, with ROCE as the metric, and with strategy-driven IVP&E as the tool.

Defining your strategy-driven roadmap: top-down

What we have learnt from Chapters 3, 4, 5 and 6 is that it all starts with strategy, and that strategy is about making choices. If my strategy is not clear, or the trade-offs have not been clarified in detail, I get stuck in the design of my supply chain, how to prioritize in decision making, etc. In Chapter 4 we showed common 'strategy fails', illustrating that if strategy is about making choices, companies are bad at strategy. We hate to make choices, as we think choosing is losing, whereas the opposite is true. Choosing creates focus, and we need focus if we want to stand out and excel. So, as shown in Figure 8.1, if we can choose, we start our strategy-driven roadmap by defining our DNA. What is our strategic value proposition? Do we want to dominate on price, on product or on best total solution? How do we want to differentiate? How do we want to compete, and in which type of markets? We discussed this in Chapter 7, when discussing strategic planning. Defining your DNA is not a light choice. It is choosing to be either Etihad or Ryanair, to be either Harrods or Aldi. It is about defining, or rather discovering and (re)confirming your DNA. Often this brings you back to the founders of the company, to the principles they used to book the initial successes.

As shown in Figure 8.1, the strategic value proposition needs to be realized through a corresponding operating model. That operating model looks at the culture, capabilities, organization and metrics. And when it comes to the capabilities, we need to look at the people, the key processes, key systems and key assets. We start with culture; this is obvious. We referred earlier to the 'cult-like cultures' described by Jim Collins in *Good to Great*.[1] That goes hand in hand with metrics. Operational excellence will all be about cost whereas with product leaders it is about innovation and time to market. We will come back to the organizational part later in this chapter. Drilling down to the capabilities, the integrated value planning and execution introduced in Chapter 7 is a key process to control the balance in the triangle and generate more value, regardless of the strategy. Operational processes versus innovation processes versus customer management processes will be more or less dominant depending on the chosen strategy. Think about our improved strategy map we introduced in Figure 7.4. Powerful processes need to be powered by powerful systems. We also need to define the corresponding strategy-driven physical supply chain, as explained in Chapter 6. As we said in the previous chapter, earlier strategy models like the strategy map have often overlooked the importance of that physical supply chain.

It is essential, however, to define the level of capital employed and to define the level of cost, so key in defining how we will drive ROCE.

If we have defined our DNA and our corresponding operating model, it is important we bring them together and show our value model. How are we going to drive ROCE? In which combination of EBIT and capital employed. What is our ROCE roadmap? Where are we today? How do we compare to peers? How do different strategies lead to a different balance in our sector? What are realistic targets for me as a company, three to five years out? How do I back this up with financial modelling?

Clarifying your DNA, the corresponding operating model, the value model and the value targets creates the frame, the bones to which we can add the meat. Once we understand where this needs to go, we are in a better position to assess our current capabilities. What is the maturity of our

FIGURE 8.1 Defining your strategy-driven roadmap

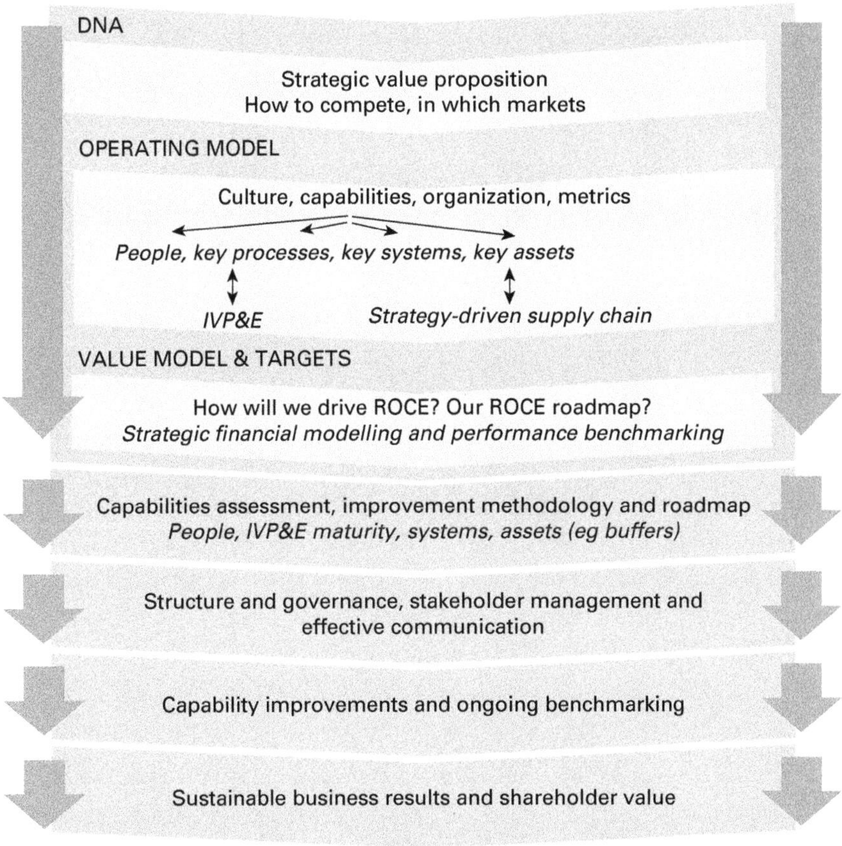

people, our processes and our systems? How aligned is our supply chain? What are the changes we need to make? What is the required supply chain redesign? Gartner Inc is well known for its maturity assessments and benchmarking in the space of sales and operations planning. It will be important to expand this type of benchmark into the integrated value planning and execution space, including strategic and financial planning, and expanding it into the assessment of capabilities, systems and the supply chains.

Once we understand where we are, where we need to go and what is our improvement roadmap, it is important to set up the right structure and governance, manage stakeholders and communicate effectively. As we improve our capabilities, we should be able to monitor business results and the impact on shareholder value. We believe this is where a more 'top-down' approach can meet a more 'bottom-up' approach explained in the next section.

Building your strategy-driven supply chain: step by step and bottom-up

The top-down approach can only be driven by CEOs and boards. We believe there is a huge lack of knowledge and understanding of how supply chain can drive value at that level. So, what do we do if our CEO is not convinced or has a different agenda? What do we do if our board keeps pushing conflicting messages and conflicting objectives? Well, if we can't build the strategy-driven supply chain top-down, we'll need to build it bottom-up.

The bottom-up approach is illustrated in Figure 8.2. Every company has the S&OE layer. Every company is doing detailed production planning and scheduling. Why? Because we simply must. If we don't tell production what to produce, obviously nothing will be produced. A first challenge for many companies is setting up a tactical planning layer, the S&OP layer. A lack of tactical planning often means you only notice significant demand–supply imbalances in the short-term planning horizon. That often leads to a huge pressure and a lot of operational firefighting. The awkward thing is that once companies are used to operational firefighting, especially if this has been going on for multiple years, and they have built a whole fire squad, it's not that easy to tell them your ambition is to prevent the fires from happening. You can expect pushback. People will think the tactical planning is way too abstract. They may also push back on the business case, as much of the firefighting costs are hidden or sunk. We will talk about business case building

FIGURE 8.2 Step-by-step approach to making your supply chain strategy-driven

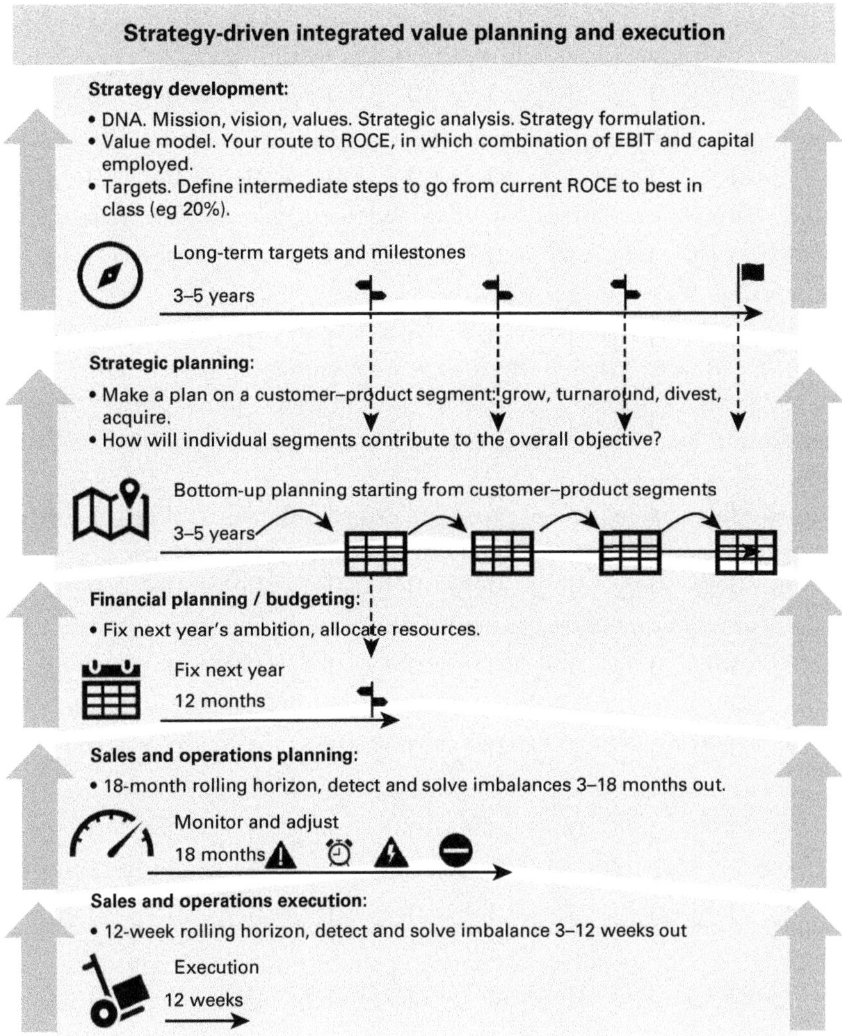

in the next section, but your best shot at it may be to talk about reducing the pressure. Organizations that are caught in short-term firefighting are often on the brink of burnouts. Tactical planning will reduce the risk for burnouts and increase efficiency. If the numbers don't work out, you may try that as an alternative. If you want to set up S&OP, we recommend our vision on S&OP as described in Chapter 7. We have also collected our vision papers on each of the steps on this book's website.

Once you have built the S&OP layer, you need to integrate it with the financial planning layer. As discussed in Chapter 7, the MRP calculation is at the heart of financial planning so expanding S&OP to tackle financial planning is both sound and logical. Avoid the variance analysis of last month or quarter to be discussed in business reviews or finance reviews, which are separate from the executive S&OP meeting. Integrate your capabilities into one process, one system, one mindset that is financially driven. Ensure your S&OP becomes the driver for your budgeting process. As discussed in Chapter 7, the traditional S&OP has all the elements to project a gross margin 18 months out and is precise in predicting changes in working capital. Extend it to include SG&A, CAPEX and D&A to be able to project P&L, the balance sheet and free cash flow 18 months out. This should focus the budgeting exercise on the real discussion: how will next year's budget support our strategic roadmap, rather than focusing on the Excel hell and gaming exercise it often is.

As our financial modelling capability grows and matures, this will enable better strategic planning. We should be able to translate strategic plans and transformation programmes into ROCE impacts, use the budgeting process to fix next year's ambition and use the S&OP process as the monthly cross-check on where we are. So, yes, by pushing on S&OP we have been doing the right thing from a supply chain perspective, but we should expand our ambition, and we should expand it significantly.

The seven-step approach to drive sustainable value and change

Important questions are 'How do we carve out manageable pieces?' and 'How do we put those manageable pieces on the rails?', especially if we take the 'bottom-up' approach. Figure 8.3 compiles our experience with implementing sales and operations planning in companies. We have expanded that approach into managing the broader implementation of a strategy-driven supply chain.

The approach consists of seven steps. It is built by experience. Skipping a step tends to lead to troubles down the road. It is tempting at times to cut corners, but we advise you to follow the trail. The seven steps may look heavy or sturdy. They shouldn't be in practice. You might feel more at ease if you see it as a checklist like you might have for travelling. You don't want to be at the airport and find you have forgotten a passport or visa. Same here.

It starts with 'awareness'. After one of my presentations on S&OP, somebody came to me and said that he wanted to do S&OP but he couldn't pull it off. When I started asking whether there were services issues, he said the service was fine; when talking about cost, the costs seemed to be under control. When I asked about inventory, he answered they were a family-owned company and the family didn't care about inventory. Cash was not an issue. So, I answered, 'Then maybe you don't need S&OP.' Which made him frown. S&OP, or by extension integrated value planning and execution, is a means to an end, it is not a goal in itself. Before talking about S&OP or IVP&E it is important to define the problem. We have good experiences with using the triangle as described in Chapter 1. If you gather a cross-functional group around the triangle, people automatically seem to converge on 'What is the issue?' We also have good experiences with doing a strategy mapping exercise as described in Chapter 3. Is our strategy clear? Have we made clear choices? All of this turns it into a business question rather than a supply chain question. It helps in engaging the broader organization. Once there is a common understanding of 'what is the problem' and an agreement that 'something needs to be done', that's the moment to start talking about S&OP or IVP&E as (part of) the solution. You'll have to explain what S&OP or IVP&E is about. How it works, what are the different steps, how they are connected. And remember that repetition is the mother of all learning, so you may need to explain it again, and again, and again. That is part of the change process.

Once people are ready for change, we'll need to refine 'where we need to go' and 'how we want to get there'. In Figure 8.3 we call that the 'envision' phase. Looking back at Figure 8.2, and based on the discussion in the previous section, where you want to go may depend on where you are as a start. If you are still stuck in operational firefighting, you may need to start by introducing tactical planning. If you have the basics of S&OP, you may need to work on the financial integration. If you have the financial integration and are running one process in one tool and with one team, then you may link in the strategic planning processes. So, after everybody is on board through the awareness phase, define your ambition. What is the next step? What is the longer-term roadmap? What is a high-level scope and timeline for building your capabilities (people, key processes, key systems)? What is the impact on the supply chain design? Extra assets? Consolidate assets? Increase buffers? What is the impact on your organization? Level of centralization? What are the high-level costs associated with that? How will this generate value? What is the high-level business case? These questions are part of the 'envision' step.

FIGURE 8.3 Seven steps to drive sustainable change and value through S&OP and IVP&E

Awareness

- Where are we in the supply chain triangle? Create a **common understanding**, a need for change, a **common ambition**. Where are we in our **strategy**? Is it **clear**? Clear **choices**?
- Identifying and explaining **strategy-driven integrated value planning and execution as (part of) the solution**. What is it? What are the steps? How are companies doing this?
- Create a **common language**. Focus on 'what is our ambition', instead of 'understanding'.

Envision

- What is our **ambition**? **Roadmap**? **Manageable next step** in building **capabilities**?
- High-level **scope** and **timeline**. Which competences? Processes? Systems? Advanced planning system vs enterprise resource planning. Which **supply chain design**? **Organization and metrics**? Where to start? How to continue?
- How will we generate **value**? Value **targets**? How will we **measure**? First **cost** estimate? High-level **business case**? What is a manageable step? How will we manage our **risks**?

Engage

- Impact on organization? How to **engage** key stakeholders? Sales? Finance? CEO? Board?
- Do we have the **right competences**? Hires? Shifts? How will we tackle **change management and communication**? How do we tackle our **data challenge**?
- What time is needed from which people? Free up **resources**? Do we need a backfill?
- What is our **refined ambition/roadmap/scope/timeline and business case**? Formal **GO**?

Design

- **High-level process/organization/metrics** design: inputs/outputs, roles and responsibilities, KPIs and targets.
- **High-level systems architecture**: inputs/outputs, what complexity/functionality in which process/module?
- **High-level supply chain design**: suppliers, plants, capacities, buffers, partners, etc.
- Training/shifting/hiring... **building competences**. Consider building a **centre of excellence**.

Implement

- **Detailed process/tooling design**: functional and technical analysis per process/module. Global template vs local intimacy. 20/80 Pareto. Value targets per process. KPIs? Targets?
- **Iterative** configuration/testing/training of key users, process owners and the broader organization. Integrate insights as they grow.
- **Detailed supply chain** design and **implementing** changes. Value targets?

Improve

- Spin up the process. Spin up the competences. Leverage the tooling and new supply chain.
- **Value and benefit tracking**. Targets put forward? Progress? Roadblocks?
- Harnessing the **power of analytics**. Start with the basics. Experiment, learn and adjust.
- **Continuous improvement**. Create a user community. Award the best idea. Gamification will bring the adoption to higher levels.

Sustain

- Sustain **value** generation: benefit tracking and monitoring.
- Sustain **knowledge and capabilities**: retrain where necessary. Think of career models.
- Continued updates. Inspiration.
- Envision a next step in your strategy-driven IVP&E **maturity**. Create awareness as needed. Engage for the next wave.

Once there is a common understanding of the problem/opportunity, a common ambition to do something about it, a high-level idea of where to go, how to get there, what are the associated costs and what it could bring as value, we'll need to engage the broader organization in the change we have ahead of us. So think about who will be impacted and who needs to be engaged. If you're at the start of the journey and want to implement S&OP, engaging sales into a forecasting process may be one of the key challenges. If you have an S&OP process but want to integrate with financial planning and budgeting, you will need to engage finance and the CFO. If you want to integrate with strategic planning you will need to engage the CEO and the board. As you engage key stakeholders, help them understand what's in it for them and how they will need to contribute. What are the resources you will need to drive the change? Do you have the right competences? Do you need to organize a backfill? Will you be introducing new roles? How will you tackle change management? Planning processes are all about data, and in 90 per cent of the companies data quality is an issue. So, think through upfront how you will tackle your data challenge. As you iterate, refine the ambition, refine the roadmap, the scope, the timeline, the costs, the benefits, the business case. Don't go for half work. It is far too important. Go for a clear and full 'Yes' from all stakeholders. This is the 'engage' step.

Once you have the formal 'go', you can start high-level design. You may have a rough idea that you want to start with demand planning, RCCP and MPS, but this is the time to further detail what this means, how these processes interact and how this influences the organization. Demand will be run in individual countries or may be consolidated per region or per category or brand by demand managers at the corresponding level. The data and the statistical forecasts may be driven by a centralized centre of excellence. RCCP may be a regional or a central responsibility. MPS may be a plant or regional responsibility. While some of that will have popped up during the envision and engage stage, in the design phase you take it one level deeper. Likewise, you come to a high-level architecture for your systems. What will I do in my ERP, what in my APS, and how will these interact? Will I need changes on the master data? Do I have a separate team and system to address that? Likewise, we may further design the impact on our supply chain. This may be about changing supplier contracts from cost-driven to include more volume flexibility. It may be about rationalizing the footprint to increase net PPE turns and cut costs or about creating extra buffers to stabilize planning and improve efficiency. Again, we may have ideas and directions from the earlier phases but we may need to refine them in this design phase. In parallel, we need to start building our competences through training, through hiring, through realizing the promised backfills. For organizations that have a history of local autonomy and decentralization, we strongly recommend building a supply chain centre of excellence that supports the implementation and the continuous improvement that follows. All of these are considerations in the 'design' step.

In the high-level process and systems design, the focus is on the interactions. What will we do on the RCCP level, what will we do on the MPS level and how will these interact? Or what will we do in the budgeting process versus the monthly S&OP and how do these interact? We clarify the interactions both on a process and a systems level. As we start implementing we will need a detailed design: a functional and technical specification per process and per module. Will the statistical forecast be leading or just shown as information? How will we report the forecast accuracy? Will we work with standard prices and costs going forward or adjust them based on an expected variance? When you get to the tooling, the rubber hits the ground. So, you'll need to think through how far you can standardize global processes into a single global template or how far you will need to adapt to local differences. Scrutinize specifications from a 20/80 Pareto perspective. People tend to start dreaming it up when after years of Excel they finally get a decent system supporting their job. As you start configuring your tool, do it in an iterative way. Implement, train, validate and integrate insights as they grow. Planning is complex. You only understand how it works when your data brings it alive. Implement any changes in the supply chain as decided upon earlier. All of these are considerations in the 'implement' step.

Before you pilot or go live, it is important to refine how you will measure and drive value. If you go live with RCCP you may expect to impact direct labour cost as there will be less last-minute overtime, and you may expect to impact seasonal inventories as you are able to plan them more efficiently. In the initial stages, the envision, the engage, and even the high-level design, you have expectations, but it is harder to quantify the expected impact. Once the data is in your systems and these are ready to go, the impact should be obvious from the system itself. It is important to make the planned improvements explicit, to define the KPIs, the targeted improvements, and to put the targets into the objectives of both the project team and the process owners who will be driving the process. Change should not be a free lunch. There is a lot of spending in the holy name of digitalization. Digitalization should not be a goal in itself. It is there to drive value. We need to hold ourselves accountable for driving that value. I also believe people are afraid to make it explicit, as that would lead to an explicit failure if we're not driving the value we planned. That is a lack of both courage and accountability. Let's stop sticking our heads in the ground. Failure should be an option, as long as we understand why and where we failed and how to correct it. Don't go for a half-hearted attempt.

In my history as an implementation consultant, I initially thought the go-live of the tool was where the project ended. That's also what customers have asked me to do. I have learnt the hard way that is not where it ends but where it starts, and my customers overestimate their own capabilities in driving the required change and improvements. It's like you first got your driver's licence. Yes, you studied the theory and passed a practical exam in a very controlled situation, but the day after, you are driving your car in the middle of Mumbai. Chances are, you're going to have an accident! It is irresponsible. Making the tool live is not where it ends but actually where it starts. The first iterations of your demand planning process or your adjusted and integrated financial S&OP meeting are typically a bit awkward, slow and looking for balance. Be prepared for that. Provide guidance to the newly born process owners from a project team or a centre of excellence. Take time and create focus on spinning up the new process and competences, on leveraging your new tools and supply chain. Ensure you do value tracking and monitoring. Are we getting to where we promised to be? What are the roadblocks? How can these be removed? Take time to harness the power of analytics. At the start, keep it simple and stupid – KISS. As you get to grips with the new way of working, start experimenting on how to leverage analytics. This could be statistical forecasting, optimization techniques, pricing optimization, transfer price optimization... Using analytics is not a linear process. Experiment, learn and adjust. Build the competence. Where a centre of excellence can do wonders in streamlining global processes and powering processes from a centralized expertise, don't forget the real innovation should be driven by the user communities. So, think about creating an internal user community. Think about how to drive continuous improvement based on the principles of lean thinking. Award the best idea. Organize competitions. Gamification works. All of this is part of the 'improve' step.

Finally, a key challenge in many organizations is to sustain a level of knowledge and capabilities. As people quit jobs or move around the organization you'll need to train and retrain. Think about career models that allow you to gradually develop a competence and retain it as people move through different levels of maturity. Provide inspiration to keep people challenged and up to date. And start thinking about what is your next step in your strategy-driven journey. How to create awareness. What is the problem and how it can be solved. Who are the key stakeholders and how to engage them. This is a journey, it is not a project. But the good news is, any step is touching the heart of value generation, the supply chain triangle of service, cost and capital employed. Companies that embrace strategy-driven thinking will simply drive more value by being more focused and more connected.

Defining a strategy-driven organization: the new role of supply chain

One of the elements of the operating model is the organization. Typical considerations are what functions and roles to centralize versus decentralize, or what to organize on a regional level and what to organize on a global level. Most global companies are run in matrix structures, with commercial functions organized in clusters or regions and with backend functions like purchasing and operations organized globally or per category. Customer intimacy players want to be close to their customers and typically are more decentralized. Operational excellence players want to create scale and efficiency. That typically aligns better with a centralized command-and-control type of structure.

What is often overlooked in these 'traditional' organization discussions is how the resulting organization impacts the balance in the triangle. Remember from Figures 1.6 and 1.7 how a traditional functional organization creates tension in the triangle. We have repeated them here as Figures 8.4 and 8.5. Though complex matrix structures make it less transparent, we believe that in many organizations there remains an inherent conflict between commercial functions, which are more service and top-line oriented, operations functions, which are more efficiency and cost oriented, and finance, which is more cash oriented. As we explained at the start of Chapter 2, balancing the triangle does matter, as balancing the triangle equals optimizing value, as measured by ROCE. That was first illustrated in Figure 2.3, which we have included here as Figure 8.6.

So how do we solve this inherent conflict? A common and popular approach has been shared KPIs. Let's take inventory as an example. Marketing and sales clearly have an impact, as they set expectations in the market with respect to the product portfolio, the required responsiveness and the like. Manufacturing clearly has an impact, as they define the batch sizes in production. Purchasing has an impact, as they define the minimum

FIGURE 8.4 A traditional organization and the corresponding KPIs

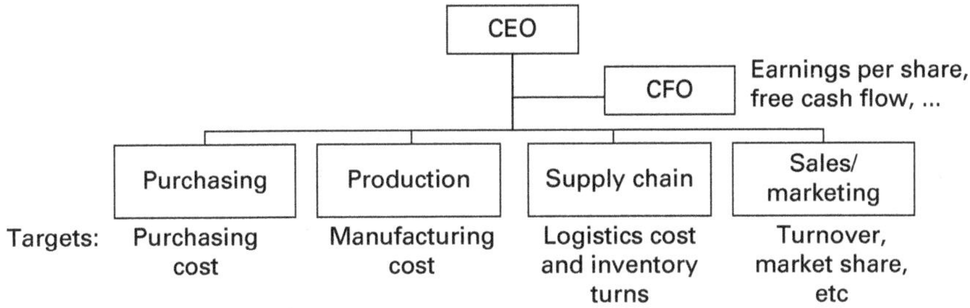

FIGURE 8.5 A traditional organization mapped to the supply chain triangle

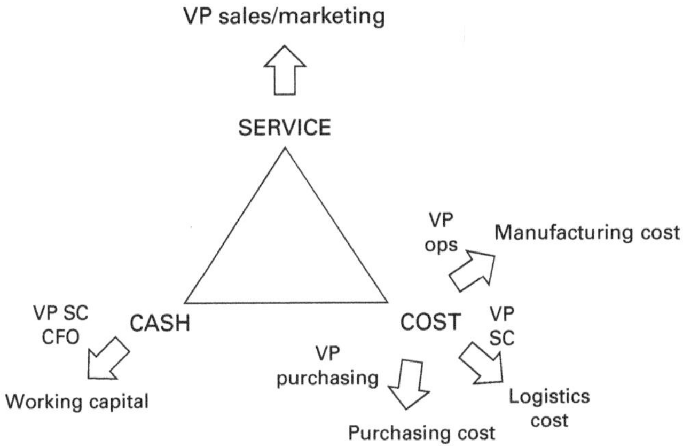

FIGURE 8.6 EBIT over capital employed gives a return metric like ROCE

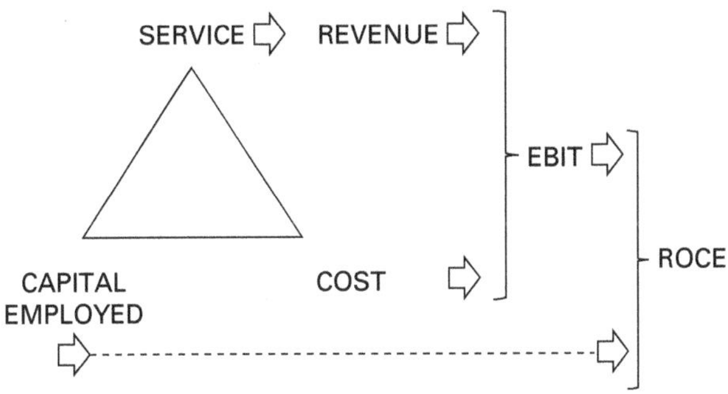

order quantities with suppliers. R&D has an impact, as they decide on the number of components in a product and how far these are shared across different products. Supply chain has an impact, as supply chain is responsible for defining the safety stocks in the distribution network. So, if everybody has an impact, then shouldn't we make everybody responsible? Though that seems logical, we don't believe it is the right approach. The problem we see is that if 'everybody is responsible', in our experience 'nobody is responsible'. I've seen organizations where part of the shared objectives was free cash flow, but the individual departments were not behaving accordingly. It was only after I suggested that inventory turns should be made part of the shared objectives that I understood it already was. Production was still producing way more than the forecast in the beginning of the year, with huge inventory build-ups as a result. Sales was behaving very opportunistically at year end, keeping the forecasts unrealistically high, with a huge risk on year-end inventories as a result. So, where is the logic? It seems that if 80 per cent of the objectives are functional, let's say top line for sales and cost or efficiency for production, and only 20 per cent are shared, let's say inventory turns, then people will focus on the 80 per cent functional, as that is what they feel they control, whereas they feel they have no impact, or maybe less direct impact, on the shared objectives.

So, what if we took this reasoning all the way, and made everybody responsible for ROCE as the single, dominant KPI? Well, I see a lot of hesitation on this in companies as well. If I make ROCE into the single KPI, how will I be sure that salespeople are still fighting for every order in the market? How will I rest assured that procurement is driving the lowest possible cost (for a given level of responsiveness) from my suppliers? ROCE is about balance, but I also need strength in the functions, and that is where functional KPIs can help. So, although I started my thought process years ago with creating shared KPIs, I'm no longer a believer. My current thinking is that I require strong functions, and functional KPIs will help me with that. I believe it's OK for my VP of sales to wake up with a focus on the top line, and it is OK for my VP of procurement to wake with a focus on spend or the VP of operations with a focus on efficiency, but I need to more explicitly balance that, and in the meantime we know that balancing doesn't happen by itself. So, our proposal is to make somebody responsible for that balancing act as an explicit task, with ROCE as a metric. And we believe that somebody should be supply chain. We believe that if we want balance in the triangle, we need to reshuffle the power balance in the executive team as shown in Figures 8.7 and 8.8. We will explain that in more detail below.

Figure 8.7 further maps the current and traditional organization of Figure 8.4 to the triangle. In our experience, in many companies, supply chain is still a semi-operational function, sometimes reporting to operations, sometimes to finance, sometimes into a commercial division, sometimes directly to the CEO or business unit president. Supply chain is often responsible for logistics, sometimes for customer service, increasingly for S&OP, and often for managing global inventories. We often say that finance doesn't understand inventory, as inventory is an operational thing, and the average finance professional lacks that operational experience. So, to ensure that inventories are under control, finance has sought and found a victim, being supply chain. As a VP of supply chain you can be flattered when you are asked to reduce the inventories by 20 per cent, but you should not accept this task lightly, as reducing inventories is about bringing balance in the triangle. Supply chain's best shot at balancing the triangle is an often poorly attended S&OP process. That's not only unfair, it is also highly ineffective.

As already introduced above, if we want to create balance in the triangle, and create more focus on value, we'll need to explicitly address it by making somebody responsible. Balancing doesn't happen automatically. We have proven that to ourselves over the last 20 years.

When it comes to balancing the triangle, we believe there are two logical candidates: supply chain and finance. While finance may have been the heir apparent, we believe supply chain is the better candidate. You can notice from

FIGURE 8.7 The old 'conflict' model and organization

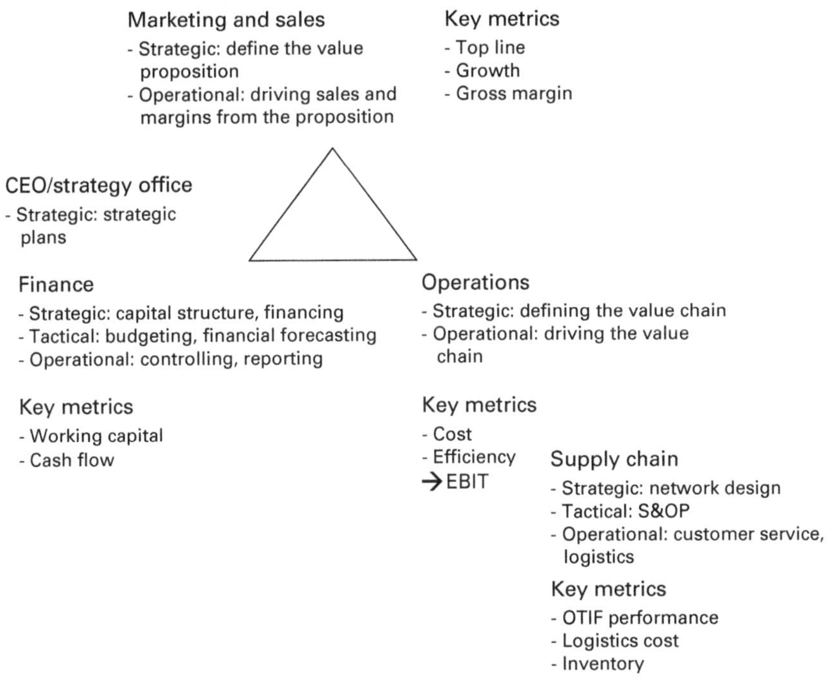

Figure 8.7 that supply chain is the only function that has a KPI on each of the corners of the triangle. Supply chain is responsible for the OTIF delivery performance, quite often for logistics cost, and increasingly for global inventories. That explains why supply chain feels the operational heartbeat in the triangle much better. I've had salespeople telling me 'If I need to choose, then I'd rather have supply chain.' When I asked why, they answered: 'If finance is to balance the triangle then the costs and the cash will be under control, but we will be left without customers.' That is anecdotal for the reality that in many companies finance is too distant from the operations to be able to balance the triangle well. Finance may have the ambition, though, as shown by their ambition 'to become a business partner'. The problem is that finance is not 'neutral' in the triangle. When explaining the importance of free cash flow in Chapter 2, we explained that focus on free cash flow is one of the reasons there is pressure on inventories, and the pressure on inventories is what is closing and creating pressure on the triangle. So I'm sorry, but you can't be the judge of your own case. We strongly believe the smarter move is to make supply chain responsible for managing the balance in the triangle.

To do so, we need to redefine the role of supply chain, as shown in Figure 8.8. First, supply chain should hand over operational responsibilities like logistics and customer service to operations and/or sales. If supply chain is to balance the triangle, it needs to be independent of the other functions and it should have no bias towards one of the corners in the triangle. Second, if we want supply chain to balance the triangle, we need to give it the proper means to do so; just S&OP will not do the job. So, we propose to make supply chain responsible for strategic planning. If we tell people that in conferences or to executive teams, we spontaneously see the sweat breaking out. Are you now telling us that supply chain is going to define the strategy? The answer is no. Supply chain is not going to define the strategy, as supply chain is not defining the forecast in the S&OP process. Supply chain is there to moderate the debate between sales, responsible for defining the strategic value proposition, and operations, responsible for defining the operational supply chain. It is up to supply chain to challenge sales and say, 'Do you really believe we will be able to achieve this level of prices and these types of volumes?', and to operations, 'What type of upward and downward flexibility do we have? Have we extended that into the contracts with our key suppliers?' It is up to supply chain to leave no stone unturned, just as it is challenging the sales forecast in the S&OP process. An active challenge, also in strategic planning, will simply lead to better decisions and more value generation.

Once we have agreed to put strategic planning in the hands of supply chain, and given that supply chain is already running the S&OP process, the next logical thing to do is to put financial planning and analysis in the hands of supply chain as well. As we discussed in Chapter 7, supply chain is already carrying out a huge planning effort in the S&OP process. What we are doing today is duplicate that planning effort into the finance department, and then tripling the effort, as we try to integrate these two planning processes. Of course, finance will never be in favour of anything that triples the effort. We have been chasing the dream of integrating operational planning and financial planning through so-called 'integrated business planning', but 20 years down the road we need to admit it has failed. The easiest way to ensure integration is to put both processes into one pair of hands, and we propose that should be with supply chain. So, basically, we propose to put supply chain at the centre of the triangle, with ROCE as the balancing metric, and with strategy-driven IVP&E as the tool. That is the essence of what is shown in Figure 8.8.

That leaves us with some important questions, like 'Where does that leave finance?' Well, maybe supply chain will do the financial planning but it will not start managing the investor relations. Managing the financial ecosystem of the company is clearly a finance responsibility. Nor should supply chain become responsible for accounting. We propose to focus finance on its historical strength, being accounting and control. And that creates a good synergy. Supply chain will be focused on planning the future, where finance will do the controlling and hold everybody accountable. From an auditing perspective, that type of split of responsibilities probably makes a lot of sense.

Getting supply chain into its new role also poses some important challenges. When I propose this to people the average VP of supply chain starts sweating as well. Is this really what I want? Am I up to this task? Well, the good news is, it doesn't really matter. If you don't want to give up on the operational aspects, you can still be the VP of logistics, but then you'll need to accept you will be reporting to the COO. If you want to move to the centre of the triangle, you'll need to work on your financial and strategic skills. We believe that defines the difference between the VP of supply chain and the chief supply chain officer (CSCO) shown at the centre of the triangle in Figure 8.8.

Switching from Figure 8.7 to Figure 8.8 is about shifting the power balance in the executive committee. That is a very sensitive topic. In Figure 8.7 the only person overseeing the three corners of the triangle is the CEO.

FIGURE 8.8 The new strategy-driven value model and organization: the new role of supply chain

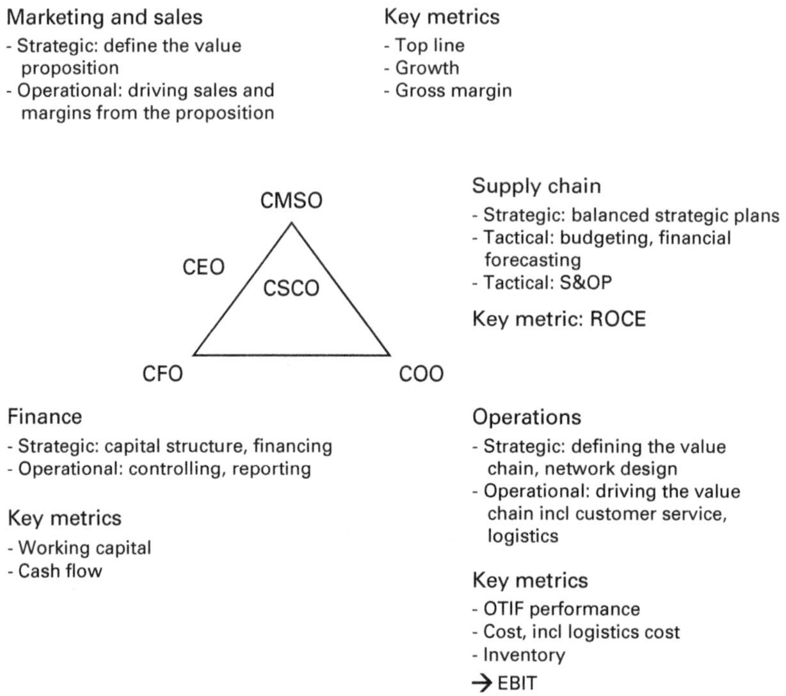

We came to call that the 'old school' or 'conflict' model. We still find CEOs who start the year or the budgeting process by defining conflicting objectives. They ask sales to grow the market by 10 per cent, ask production to reduce costs by 2 per cent and ask supply chain to reduce inventories by 20 per cent. What do you think you will get? Well you have two options. The first is chaos, as you find out six months down the road that the initiatives that the different departments have taken are frankly conflicting. The second option is that 'the strongest one wins'. If you are a sales-driven company then you know who is going to win. Though this traditional 'conflict' model is still quite common, it is nevertheless unprofessional. Creating a blunt stretch on the triangle is not how you create value. Owners and shareholders should simply not accept this. In comparison, Figure 8.8 is a new 'strategy-driven' or 'value-driven' way of organizing. We have strong functions, with functional KPIs at each of the corners, and we have a strong balancing function, being supply chain, with ROCE as a metric and strategy-driven IVP&E as the tool.

So how do we 'train' or 'grow' those new CSCOs? How do we prepare people for that role? As opposed to the 'functions', the chief marketing and sales officer (CMSO), the COO or the CFO, the CSCO will typically be light on staff. He or she will have a small though relatively senior staff. The CSCO will need to do the balancing job through influencing, as there is no hierarchical control of the peers in the executive committee. In that sense the CSCO ideally is a person who has earned credits earlier on in each of the functions. By understanding what drives the functions, showing comprehension but making the connection to the end result, the CSCO will need to enrich and improve the decision making of the peers in the executive committee. That means you are not born as a CSCO but you become one by rotating through senior functions at each of the corners. For many people this will sound a bit frightening, but we believe it can also be very rewarding. Instead of only the CEO overlooking the triangle, in the new situation the CSCO will basically become the wingman or woman. That makes the CSCO the logical candidate to follow up the CEO. At the same time, CEOs who came from a CSCO background will also be more balanced than many of the CEOs we encounter today. We believe that is good, and that it will result in more balanced thinking and acting, and in more value as a result.

CASE STUDY
The strategy compass

WITH MARTIJN LOFVERS, FOUNDER AND CHIEF TREND-WATCHER OF SUPPLY CHAIN MEDIA

Martijn Lofvers is the founder and chief trend-watcher of Supply Chain Media. Based in The Netherlands, he works to connect supply chain professionals by gathering, generating and sharing supply chain knowledge, both in The Netherlands and internationally. He organizes workshops with his extended European network of CSCOs on a broad set of supply chain topics. His Dutch *Supply Chain Magazine* and the international quarterly *Supply Chain Movement* are the de facto standard for supply chain interviews, management articles, vendor overviews (in subway maps) and news in Europe. In recent years, Martijn has performed research on differences in supply chain strategy and their drivers, which has resulted in what he has called the 'strategy compass'.

Martijn starts from the model of Treacy and Wiersema to indicate that there are different options to be leading in a market. He comes to six different supply chains around those three base strategies, as shown in Figure 8.9.

A first supply chain type is called 'long development, rapid deployment', and supports an R&D-dominant product leadership strategy, as opposed to the 'fast, continuous renewal', which supports a marketing-dominant product leadership strategy. Think about the difference between the medical devices business of Johnson and Johnson versus the fast fashion of Zara. Both are product leaders, but the first is more R&D dominant, whereas the second is marketing dominant.

The customer intimacy strategy is supported by a supply chain that is 'agile and flexible, focused on customer problems' or 'custom-configured'. Thinking in the 5–4–3–3–3 logic of Crawford and Mathews, we could think of putting 'product breadth' versus putting 'service' first. We tend to think of IBM as a player with a large catalogue, and being sales driven in trying to maximize the share of wallet in its bigger accounts, whereas something like the buildings business of Johnson Controls 'configures-to-order' and develops custom solutions to the heating and refrigeration problems in any complex building. We admit that differences are subtle and subject to discussion.

FIGURE 8.9 Six supply chain types around the three core strategies of Treacy and Wiersema

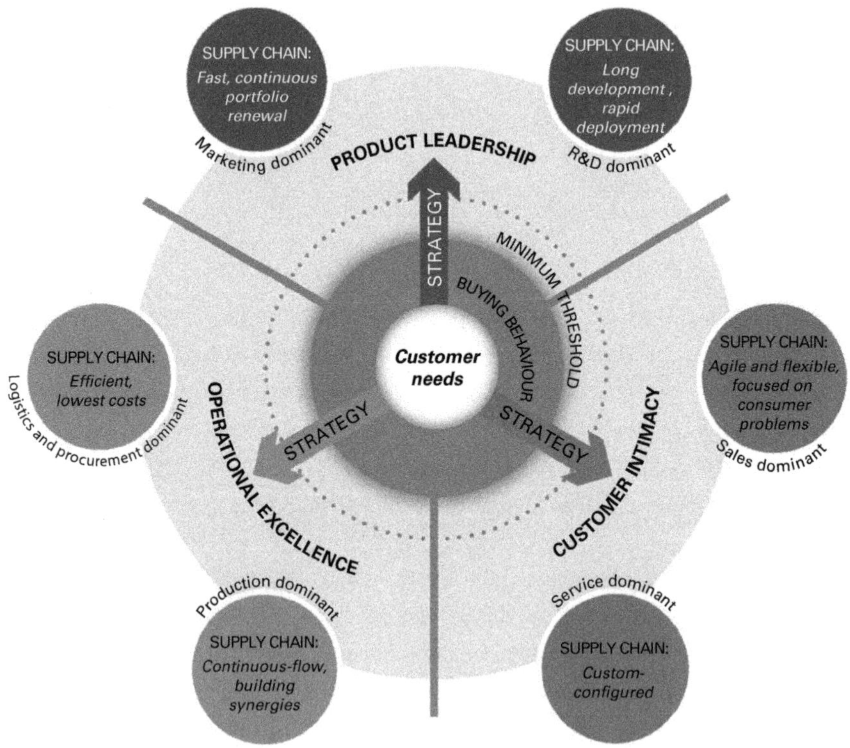

SOURCE © MARTIJN LOFVERS, 2017

FIGURE 8.10 The strategy compass of Martijn Lofvers: six supply chain types supporting three base strategies, supported by different operating models

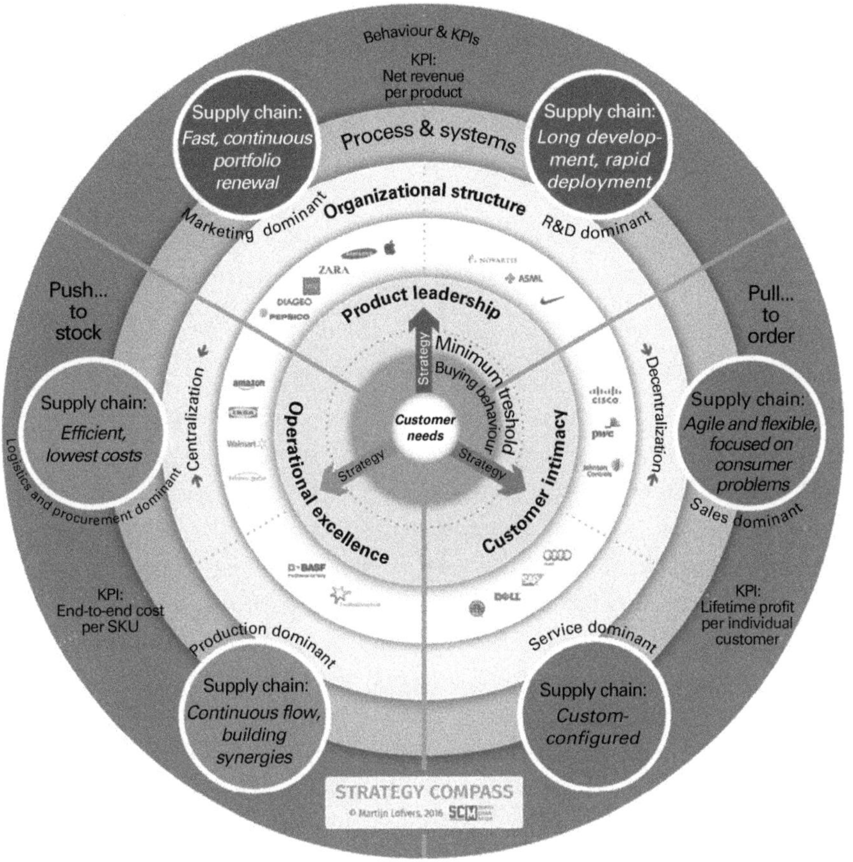

SOURCE © MARTIJN LOFVERS, 2017

Operational excellence, finally, is supported by 'continuous flow, building synergies' or 'efficient, lowest costs' supply chains, depending on whether the companies are production dominant (manufacturing) or logistics and procurement dominant (retail). In manufacturing, the low-cost advantage needs to come from stabilizing production and maximizing the turns on manufacturing assets. In retail, the focus is much more on minimizing purchasing cost and maximizing the turns on logistics assets. Private label manufacturers are typically following a low-cost strategy, as retailers want to differentiate on price using their private label products. As they're not branded, these companies, like McBride plc, active in private label household and personal care, are typically less familiar than their branded counterparts like Henkel and P&G. Walmart and Ikea are probably well-known examples on the retail side.

TABLE 8.1 Different product–market combinations may require different strategies and supply chains

Company	Category	Strategy	Supply chain
Disney	Movie DVD	Operational excellence	Efficient, lowest costs
	Infinity	Product leadership	Long development, rapid deployment
Starbucks	Fresh Coffee	Customer intimacy	Custom-configured
	Iced Coffee	Operational excellence	Continuous flow, building synergies
PepsiCo	Quaker	Product leadership	Fast, continuous renewal
	Lay's	Operational excellence	Efficient, lowest costs

SOURCE © MARTIJN LOFVERS, 2017

Figure 8.10 builds on this and adds that different strategies and supply chain types go with a different set of KPIs, a different organizational structure, such as a different level of centralization, and a different set of core processes and systems. Customer intimate companies tend to be decentralized to ensure customer proximity, where operational excellence companies are centralized to ensure control over the efficiency. This thinking aligns perfectly with the 'operating model' thinking of Treacy and Wiersema and Kaplan and Norton, introduced earlier in this chapter. Figure 8.10 also adds ample examples of the different supply chain types.

When asked how he applies this thinking with executive teams, Martijn comments: 'Within the same company, different customer segments, or product segments, or product–market combinations, may follow different strategies and as such have different supply chains.' Table 8.1 shows some examples of discussions he had with executive teams. 'Where PepsiCo follows a product leadership strategy for its Quaker oats, differentiating on product has become very difficult in potato chips, hence the operational excellence strategy for its Lay's chips.' Martijn also links this to the product lifecycle. 'A ground-breaking new product or product group typically requires a product leadership strategy, whereas a product near the end of its lifecycle may have commoditized and require an operational excellence strategy.'

When segmenting and differentiating the strategy and the supply chain, we need to remember Treacy and Wiersema's warning that different strategies come with different operating models, as illustrated by Martijn in the outer circles in Figure 8.10. There is a limit to what we can do with one 'organization'. If segmentation is required to be successful in different markets, we need to be aware that this comes with different supply chains and that different supply chains come with different KPIs, different organizations, and different processes and systems.

Martijn closes by saying, 'For years supply chain management professionals have been searching for how their discipline adds strategic value. It's similar to the quest for the Holy Grail in the film *Indiana Jones and the Last Crusade*.' He is thrilled that we are finally there. 'Just as the Holy Grail gives eternal life, the strategy compass will give the supply chain director a firm position on the board of directors. It makes supply chain management an integral part of the business, rather than merely a support function.' Let the supply chains indeed become strategy-driven!

Conclusion

We started this chapter by looking at how to implement the strategy-driven supply chain. We discussed the more logical top-down approach, starting from defining your DNA, your operating model, your value model, to then assess where you are today and what needs to be improved. Many supply chain executives may have to build it bottom-up, as they don't have the credibility yet to deliver this type of message, or their CEO and chair, do not yet relate to the messages we try to convey in this book. We believe S&OP is a good starting point, and we discussed how the vision of strategy-driven integrated value planning and execution can also be built bottom-up.

We summarized our seven-step model, which compiles our experiences of the last 15 years, on how to drive sustainable value through S&OP. We believe that approach can easily be adjusted to account for implementing strategy-driven IVP&E and for broader supply chain improvements.

We concluded this chapter by indicating the need to redefine the role of supply chain and reshuffle the power balance in the executive committee. If we really want balance in the triangle, we'll need to make it an explicit responsibility. We propose to make that into the new role of supply chain, by positioning the CSCO at the heart of the triangle, with ROCE as the balancing metric, and with strategy-driven IVP&E as the tool. Driving that change will not be easy and is not for the faint of heart. But we believe it is required and will help companies generate more value for their shareholders.

Note

1 J Collins (2001) *Good to Great*, Collins, Glasgow

INDEX

Italics denote a figure or table.

CPSIA information can be obtained
at www.ICGtesting.com
Printed in the USA
JSHW011152250421
13941JS00001B/2